THE FRONTIERSMEN
WHO COULDN'T SHOOT STRAIGHT

The Army vs. the Pioneers 1815–1845

Gregory Michno

Caxton Press

The Frontiersmen Who Couldn't Shoot Straight
ISBN #9780870046315
© 2020 by Gregory Michno

First Edition

LC record available
Library of Congress Control Number: 2020931114

Cover and book design by Jocelyn Robertson

Printed in the United States of America
CAXTON PRESS
Caldwell, Idaho

TABLE OF CONTENTS

THE FRONTIERSMEN
WHO COULDN'T SHOOT STRAIGHT

The Army vs. the Pioneers 1815–1845

Gregory Michno

INTRODUCTION

America is a nation built on myths. Some of the most seminal were the myth of the howling wilderness, the analogous myth of the virgin land, and a clashing myth of the garden. Inextricably interwoven with them all is the myth of the frontiersman, tied to both the wasteland and the pastoral utopia. The bucolic ideal was progenitor of the frontiersman, who was akin to the garden and akin to the wilderness, but offered as a sentimental pastoralist or an uncouth ruffian; he was paradoxically a hindrance to civilization while being the essence of civilization. One assurance—there was no live, flesh-and-bone, symbolic model of a frontiersman—there was only a ductile image shaped by Americans seeking to discover and define themselves. Perhaps because they lacked a history, or disliked their existing persona, or wished to withdraw from what they may have perceived as civilization's growing power and complexity, they grabbed on to an imagined, unspoiled, pastoral image. Perhaps because of the growing spirit of the Age of Romance, Americans propagated the heroic vision of an ancestor who never was. John Adams commented on our predisposition to don rose-colored glasses: "poets read history to collect flowers not fruits—they attend to fanciful images" and not to the crux of the matter. Most historians, on the other hand, realize that our nourishing poet-plucked roots produce only artificial flowers. Professor Leo Marx suggested that the process had a pathological nature, as if symptomatic of a collective neurosis, and part of modern man's predilection with "puerile fantasies." Left unchecked, "the result is a simple-minded wishfulness, a romantic perversion of thought and feeling."[1]

Romantic perversion might be one description of American history; or perhaps more aptly, our history can be explained as a ra-

---

[1]   John Adams, "Thoughts on Government," http://press-pubs.uchicago.edu/founders/documents/v1ch4s5.html; Leo Marx, *The Machine in the Garden: Technology and the Pastoral Ideal in America* (New York: Oxford University Press, 1964), 6, 9–10.

tionalized defense mechanism to sustain our narcissism—but more on that later. While historians may have seen behind Oz's curtain, the majority of Americans still cherish the smoke and mirrors. Indelibly linked with that mythical history is the frontiersman, defined as one living in the region between the settled and unsettled portions of a country. Historian James O. Robertson envisioned three American prototypes: backwoodsmen, frontiersmen, and pioneers. They represented the beginnings of a linear ascension from savagery to civilization, from dependency on guns and wits, to forest-clearer and soil-tiller, to husbandman, merchant, and town-builder. The partitions are tenuous and overlapping, however, for the backwoodsman could be synonymous with the frontiersman, the frontiersman kin to his cowboy cousin, and the pioneer tantamount with the settler or farmer.[2] Frontiersmen, pioneers, and settlers generally conjure sanguine images today, but not so in the past, when they were often scornfully called intruders, speculators, and squatters.

Contemporary authors still evince the dichotomy. For instance, one writes of the "white trash," the American underclass from colonial days to the present, arguing that we never were an egalitarian society, we never were a "city upon a hill," but more of a sinkhole, and that the portrait of America as an exceptional place was hogwash. We always had a colorful lexicon of pejorative labels for this class, such as "vermin," "scum," "squatters," and "crackers," who later became "rednecks" and "hillbillies." The term "white trash" first appeared in print in 1821, and within the next two decades that embodiment became a symbol of partisan politics, celebrated as the iconic Jacksonian common man. Another contemporary author writes glowingly of pioneers as heroic settlers, hard-working, honest, liberty-loving folks who brought American ideals to the wilderness. Beauty, it is said, apparently lies in the eye of the beholder.[3] Today, that populist "common man" is back, and

---

[2]   James O. Robertson, *American Myth, American Reality* (New York: Hill & Wang, 1980), 137–46.

[3]   Nancy Isenberg, *White Trash: The 400-Year Untold History of Class in America* (New York: Viking, 2016), 2, 3, 7, 109, 112, 135, 187; David McCullough, *The Pioneers: The Heroic Story of the Settlers Who Brought the American Ideal West* (New York: Simon & Schuster, 2019).

4

as hard to get rid of as the masked antagonist in a Hollywood slasher-horror film.

The case for the existence of a white trash underclass is persuasive, but we may need to expand the spectrum. We also have the frontiersman-pioneer-settler—alias intruder-speculator-squatter—who cuts across societal classes; although generally viewed as inhabiting the bottom rungs, people of this character and temperament could exist almost anywhere. A "frontiersman" could live along the Atlantic Coast, along the Ohio River, or from Florida to the Canadian border. You could take the frontiersmen out of the woods, but you could not take the woods out of the frontiersmen. Their contemporaries exposed them where they were and for who they were.

Words are artifacts. They have a past. They are part of our culture as much as potsherds and bones dug up by an archaeologist. Words are the true windows into our souls. In the ensuing pages you will read some bleak words about our frontier ancestors, viewed less through rose-colored glasses than through infrared goggles for night vision. Historians have revealed the darker side of the frontier people, but their efforts notwithstanding, the great majority of the American public still subscribes to the positive, heroic, storybook image. The frontiersmen with his trusty rifle, the yeoman farmer, and the merchant in the general store, conjure images of individualists, free, clean, and wholesome, hard-working folks who were the backbone of American exceptionalism. We have heard and seen that portrayal thousands of times in histories, novels, and films, but as the little boy in 1919 said to "Shoeless" Joe Jackson, baseball star of the Chicago Cubs after he and some teammates threw the 1919 World Series, "Say it ain't so, Joe." Heroes and icons were not supposed to behave in any other way than as described in the myth. But they did.

Much can be learned about the frontiersmen and their contemporaries from their conversations and writings. Some of them were scholarly and eloquent, but many were historically inarticulate. When listening to all of them, including the politicians, newspapers, and journals, the spirit of the Jacksonian era resonates.[4] Not that any of these venues would be one hundred percent accurate, but

---

[4]   Lawrence F. Kohl, *The Politics of Individualism: Parties and the American Character in the Jacksonian Era* (New York: Oxford University Press, 1989), 6.

perhaps more importantly, they provide insight into what the people were thinking and discussing. In the actual world of the frontiersmen, those who knew them best described them as avaricious, lawless, greedy, rapacious, frauds, cheats, liars, indolent, ignorant, illiterate, rude, corrupt, squalid, dirty, and dishonest. But these are just words. The illuminating power in word artifacts comes when placed in historical context, and then the truly egregious conduct and character of the frontiersmen has full impact.

It may appear we have only focused on the negative. A prime reason is because the contrary positive image is the one fully incorporated into the American myth. Thus, to swing the pendulum back toward the middle, the unflattering and scandalous need exposure. For debunking to have value, however, it needs to do more than replace one prejudice with another—it needs to drive out the fallacious beliefs.[5] Even if it cannot build a new paradigm, at least it should make it obvious that the old one is unsustainable. In this instance, debunking may help to unmask the myth of American exceptionalism, demonstrate that the army was not a legion of Indian-killers, show that American systems were grounded less on laissez-faire than on restraint and regulation, illuminate the broad role of the government in providing welfare to the needy, or provide insights about our sinister gun culture—exposures all worthwhile if leading to reappraisal.

This study focuses on the frontiersmen from 1815 to 1845, from the end of the War of 1812 to the onset of the Mexican War. It was when the army became professional, and when it learned that the frontiersmen, not the Indians, were the greater enemy. It was a time when the government expanded its role as regulator and welfare provider; when some frontier people became terrorists; when our gun culture blossomed; when our racism, bigotry, and xenophobia exploded; when our anti-intellectualism soared; when the populist "common man" seized the political scene; and when our conception of American exceptionalism took root, based on the creation of the heroic frontiersman icon. That fabrication was a long process, sometimes subconscious, but often a purposeful propaganda campaign to

---

[5] Stephen Jay Gould, *The Mismeasure of Man* (New York: W. W. Norton & Co., 1996), 352.

change the image of our forefathers from a distasteful reality into an enchanting fairy-tale. In the twenty-first century, nostalgic yearning for that old, worn storybook, with soiled cover and torn pages, with its violence, prejudice, and fear, grows increasingly toxic and harmful. It is badly in need of a reprint.

DEPREDATION FRAUD

No greater dishonesty than "defrauding the government"

America had declared its independence from England in 1776, ratified the Articles of Confederation in 1781, won its revolution in 1783, and created its constitution as the supreme law of the land in 1787. Now, after more than a decade of turbulence, the fledgling nation faced another set of daunting problems. England was at least temporarily out of the picture, but the Founding Fathers understood that successfully co-existing with the Native American tribes living generally west of the Appalachian Mountains was going to be the major issue for decades to come. The Founders realized the country was militarily exhausted, financially strained, and tired of war. They knew it was essential to establish and maintain diplomatic relations with the tribes, and that meant new territory must not be conquered by arms, but peaceably negotiated for and purchased. With past history and recent experience fresh in mind, the Founders unquestionably recognized this was going to be a great problem, because heretofore, the primary cause of Indian hostilities had been avaricious white men.

"Not a single Indian war has yet been produced by aggressions of the present federal government," wrote John Jay in 1787, but they had been started by the "improper conduct" of states unable or unwilling to restrain and punish their plundering citizens.[6] Thus, one of the most pressing issues was to codify rules to regulate the times and places the two sides could interact. These regulations were the various versions of the Trade and Intercourse Acts (TIA); the earliest, in 1790 and 1793, set standards for the Indian trade and provided for the punishment of non-Indians who committed crimes

---

[6]   Alexander Hamilton, James Madison, and John Jay, *The Federalist Papers* (Mineola, NY: Dover Publications, Inc., 2014), 13.

against Indians. Nevertheless, most whites ignored the prohibitions. Secretary of War Henry Knox was perpetually frustrated by "the extremely reprehensible conduct of some lawless white inhabitants of the frontiers." President George Washington, in his 1795 Annual Message to Congress, said, "We should not lose sight of an important truth which continually receives new confirmations, namely, that the provisions heretofore made with a view to the protection of the Indians from the violences of the lawless part of our frontier inhabitants are insufficient." It was obvious that "unless the murdering of Indians can be restrained" the fighting would never end.[7]

The third TIA, "An Act to Regulate Trade and Intercourse with the Indian Tribes and to Preserve Peace on the Frontiers," approved on May 19, 1796, was the strongest yet. It regulated white encroachment and said if any citizen committed a crime against the person or property of any Indian, he could be fined up to one hundred dollars and be imprisoned for up to one year. The offender also had to pay the Indian a sum of twice the value of the property. If the offender was financially unable to make the payment, the U. S. treasury would pay, provided that the Indian or the nation to which he belonged did not seek "private revenge."[8]

This hopefully addressed the problem of white violations, but the settlers also complained about Indian intrusion, so Section 14 of the 1796 Act gave the whites a gift. It said that if any Indians entered an American state or territory and stole property or committed murder, the citizen could apply to the Indian superintendent, provide proof of the crime, and apply to the guilty tribe for compensation. If the tribe did not make amends, "the United States guarantee to the party injured, an eventual indemnification," provided that the injured whites did not try to obtain private revenge. In addition, it was declared that the president could deduct a sum equal to the

---

[7] Larry C. Skogen, *Indian Depredation Claims, 1796–1920* (Norman, OK: University of Oklahoma Press, 1996), 24; Knox to Seagrove, October, 31, 1792, *American State Papers, Indian Affairs,* V. 1, 260 (hereinafter cited as ASPIA); Washington to Congress, December 8, 1795, http://gwpapers.virginia.edu/documents/washingtons-seventh-annual-message-to-congress/ (accessed 2-9-17).

[8] "An Act to Regulate Trade and Intercourse with the Indian Tribes and to Preserve Peace on the Frontiers," http://avalon.law.yale.edu/18th_century/na030.asp (accessed 9-29-14).

amount of property stolen or destroyed by Indians "out of the annual stipend, which the United States are bound to pay to the tribe."[9]

The articles appeared to be a just means to compensate both white and Indian, as well as a way to keep them from going to war. Unfortunately, deducting annuity money from a tribe because of one guilty individual amounted to punishment of the innocent. But, perhaps the biggest issue of all could be the problem of fraudulent claims. The act was debated in Congress, yet the problem of fraud was never seen as a potentially nullifying issue. Only Connecticut Representative Zephaniah Swift objected to the clause that stated white losses "shall be made good by the Government." He said that frontier settlers chose to live in a dangerous location, and by guaranteeing to compensate for their losses, *"a door would be opened to fraud"* [emphasis added], "as it would be impossible to ascertain with precision the amount of any damage done by the Indians." Swift had foreseen the upcoming problem precisely. Nevertheless, Congress neglected the warning and focused instead on how the fraud claims would be paid. When Section 14 was altered, Swift was satisfied that "the losses sustained by the frontier inhabitants could be deducted by the sum which government had stipulated to pay the Indians." Now he had "no objection to the measure."[10]

One might wonder how fraud would be prevented by subtracting indemnification dollars out of treaty funds instead of some other government funds. All Congress did was to put a cap on claims, limiting the payout to the amount held in the Indian annuity fund. In effect they had also denied sovereign immunity to the Indian nations, holding them liable for the acts of individuals. Washington's wish to provide justice for the Indians was severely compromised.[11]

Problems appeared almost immediately after the 1796 Act was passed. Winthrop Sargent, acting governor of the Northwest Territory, said that Shawnees had stolen white men's horses, and although proof "is not fully made," depositions alleged so, and Sargent was "inclined to favour such opinion." He hoped legal proofs

---

[9]   Ibid.

[10]   *Annals of the Congress of the United States 1789–1824.* Fourth Congress, 1st Session, Volume 5, December 7, 1795 to June 1, 1796 (Washington D. C., Gales and Seaton, 1834–1856), 894–905.

[11]   Skogen, *Indian Depredation Claims,* 25–26.

were not needed, "for they are almost impossible to be obtained," and if the accusing whites were not compensated, they would assume the "lex talionis" (retaliation in kind) and start another war.[12]

Resolution took years, so without clear evidence of guilt, Governor William H. Harrison was finally told to pay the claimants, and the money was deducted from Shawnee annuities. Indian agent Return J. Meigs believed it was impossible to apply the system equitably. If law and evidence were "strictly adhered to, the greatest part of those [claims] brought forward by citizens would be thrown out."[13]

The 1796 act was revised in 1802, with a final version in 1834. Claims would no longer be paid for all Indians guilty of depredating, but only those "belonging to any tribe in amity with the United States." In other words, money would not be taken from tribes at war with the United States, only those at peace; however, the standard rationalization was that peaceful tribes would not be depredating, and if they were, then they must be at war. This game was constantly played over the years by agents seeking to save government money.[14]

The claims were to be sent to the commissioner of Indian affairs, a new office created in 1832. Claims now had three-year time limits and the cap on funds was removed. If the Indian nation had no money, then the United States Treasury would pay. Also, a non-Indian could now file a claim if any Indian molested him while he was "lawfully within" Indian country—an addition framed in response to the growing westward movement of Americans whose "manifest destiny" was to spread their way of life from coast to coast. In addition, the 1834 Act allowed the military to enter Indian country to arrest Indians accused of committing crimes.[15]

---

[12]   Sargent to Pickering, May 25, 1797, TPUS, V. 3, Clarence Edwin Carter, ed., *The Territorial Papers of the United States, V. 3* (Washington: GPO, 1934), 468–69. (Hereinafter cited as TPUS.)

[13]   Francis Paul Prucha, *American Indian Policy in the Formative Years: The Indian Trade and Intercourse Acts, 1790–1834* (Lincoln, NE: University of Nebraska Press, 1970), 207–208.

[14]   Skogen, *Indian Depredation Claims,* 66.

[15]   Francis Paul Prucha, ed., *Documents of United States Indian Policy* (Lincoln, NE: University of Nebraska Press, 1990), 66–67.

The framers of the Trade and Intercourse Acts seemed oblivious to the possibility that the depredation claim system they constructed to keep the peace would be a Pandora's box, resulting in thousands of fraudulent claims. Accusing Indians of depredations usually meant the army had to investigate, leading to confrontations that greatly compounded the chance for war.[16]

A quotation attributed to Ben Franklin is apropos: "There is no kind of dishonesty into which otherwise good people more easily and frequently fall than that of defrauding the government." Four decades after Franklin's death, French visitor Alexis de Tocqueville commented that "stealing the public purse" was understood by every "wretch who comes along and who is able to hope that his turn will arrive to do the same." Americans continuously filed claims for nonexistent depredations, filed inflated claims, stole public and Indian lands, and cheated the government and the army in countless ways. Editor Hezekiah Niles saw an increase in speculation and corruption everywhere. The honest man appeared to be disappearing, and Niles implored, "Give me a pure heart on the dunghill, rather than a villain's in a palace."[17]

White deponents generally produced written affidavits, almost all of them being ex parte—without the participation or presence of the opposition. With Indians having no legal standing in court, it was white word against the Indian, and the Indian had little chance, especially when the plaintiff often got other white witnesses to support the allegation. Land Office Commissioner Josiah Meigs complained that the system sustained petitioners "on the evidence of one witness, and it is well known, that perjury the most bold and atrocious, has been very frequently resorted to for the purpose of substantiating claims." Secretary of State John C. Calhoun lament-

---

[16] The contention that false fraud claims led to war is made in Gregory Michno, *Depredation and Deceit: The Making of the Jicarilla-Ute Wars in New Mexico* (Norman, OK: University of Oklahoma Press, 2017).

[17] Benjamin Franklin, *The Life and Writings of Benjamin Franklin, vol. 2* (Philadelphia: McCarty and Davis, 1834), 460; Alexis de Tocqueville, *Democracy in America* and *Two Essays on America* (London: Penguin Books, 2003), 258; *Niles' Weekly Register,* July 29, 1820, V. 18, No. 22, 398. (Hereinafter cited as NWR.)

ed that "no care is taken to comply with the requisitions of the act."[18]

Fraud was rife, and it seemed that little could be done to prevent it. Georgia commissioners who signed a treaty with the Creeks in 1821 sent a complaint to Calhoun. The Indians were ceding five million acres of land for which the commissioners offered only nine cents per acre, or $450,000. They realized it was a paltry sum, but the Creeks would not even receive that much, for the citizens of the state made claims of $250,000 on them. After studying the claims, the commissioners said "...we cannot believe these claims, on a fair settlement, will exceed $100,000;" and if strictly adjudicated, would be worth considerably less. The situation was "extremely odious and objectionable" to them, as the Georgians' greed made them "considerably embarrassed."[19]

Claim inflation was the norm, but few took it to the extreme of trader George Johnson. Traveling with the Ohio Indians for years, Johnson always took his cut of claims out of the annuities paid to the Shawnees. While the tribe negotiated removal to the West, Johnson initially stated to Agent John McElvain that the Shawnees owed him $1,400, a seemingly reasonable amount. But before the final signing a Shawnee met James B. Gardiner, special agent of President Andrew Jackson appointed to supervise the removal of the Ohio Indians, about a matter of *great Importance.* The Shawnee had a paper from George Johnson that he had given to several chiefs to affix their marks, either not knowing what they were signing, or being in collusion with Johnson. The document, a "final settlement," acknowledged that the tribe owed him $20,510. Said Gardiner, "There was no difficulty in seeing into the gross fraud which Johnson was about to practice, if he could."[20]

Indian agents generally tried to be as fair as possible, but some, unknowingly or otherwise, forwarded questionable claims. In 1833, Commissioner of Indian Affairs Elbert Herring reviewed sev-

---

[18] Meigs to Morrow, February 28, 1815, TPUS, V. 15, 10; Calhoun to Governors and Agents, September 5, 1818, TPUS, V. 15, 431.

[19] Forney and Meriwether to Calhoun, January 9, 1821, ASPIA, V. 2, 254.

[20] Gardiner to Cass, December 12, 1831, *United States Congressional Serial Set,* 23rd Congress, Senate Doc. 512, "Correspondence on the Subject of the Emigration of Indians," 1831–1833, V. 2. 695–96. (Hereinafter cited as USCSS).

enteen depredation claims from Osage agent Paul L. Choteau, all flawed for various reasons: insufficient proof; the incident happened in Indian country; filing beyond the statute of limitations; uncertainty of the guilty tribe; suspicious witnesses; and contradictory loss estimates. Herring rejected them all. He knew the government was being conned. "There is no doubt that spurious claims for depredations are sometimes presented to the department," so a very strict examination was required. But while they rejected many claims, others "that are allowed ought to have been rejected; but having been proved by witnesses, and reported favorably by the Indian agents, the department has not the means of detecting the fraud."[21]

Americans found countless ways to cheat, and the army was an easy target. According to either Napoleon or Frederick the Great, an army marches on its stomach. Supplying an army on campaign has always been a challenge. Americans civilians showed how much they cared about the soldiers who defended them shortly after the war fever of 1775 had cooled. Between December 1777 and June 1778, about 2,500 men (almost one-quarter of the army) perished from exposure, illness, and starvation, caused in most part because civilians would not give them the food, supplies, and shelter they needed to survive—and what they did get was often overpriced, undercounted, shoddy, and rotten. It would never have happened if middle-class "patriots" had joined the army or actually cared for anything but their self-interest.[22]

The U. S. Army of the early republic relied on civilian contractors to do the job, but when the army needed reasonably priced, reliable food and supplies, and the contractors were there to make a profit, problems were inevitable. General Edmund P. Gaines was often at odds with contractors. He lamented about how the government always seemed to hire swindlers, cognizant of the fact that it often chose low bid over quality. Even then, the low-bid contractor

---

[21]   Herring to Choteau, June 20, 1833, USCSS, V. 3, 719–20; Herring to Ellsworth, December 17, 1832, USCSS, V. 2, 966 (quotations).

[22]   James Kirby Martin and Mark Edward Lender, *"A Respectable Army": The Military Origins of the Republic 1763–1789* (Chichester, UK: John Wiley & Sons, 2015), 104–105. See also E. Wayne Carp, *To Starve the Army at Pleasure: Continental Army Administration and American Political Culture, 1775–1783*, Chapel Hill, NC: University of North Carolina Press, 1984.

Edmund P. Gaines. *National Archives and Records Administration*
Gaines began his career not trusting contractors or Indians, but experience taught him that settlers were more trouble than Indians.

saw "before him the wretched alternative of selecting the cheapest, and consequently the worst provisions, or being involved in bankruptcy and ruin." Every command suffered as a result: the army got the "cheapest and coarsest provisions... which have, on many occasions, been so much damaged as to sicken and kill hundreds of our men." If the supplier sold the army damaged powder or flints he would be rebuked, but in selling rotten food that kills our men "the contractor is screened from military punishment," and then "abandons his contract whenever he finds it to be unproductive of gain."[23]

Gaines was not engaging in hyperbole. In 1809, Brig. Gen. James Wilkinson placed about two thousand soldiers in New Orleans to thwart a possible British incursion. Poor supplies, sickness, and the approaching summer dictated a move to a healthier location. Wilkinson sent them to Terre aux Boeufs, downriver from Natchez. The location proved to be worse, with heat, constant rain, mosquitoes, and a poor water supply. Then the supplies ran out. The men were in rags, living in tattered tents, and starving. The flour was said to be "mouldy, black, and full of worms," and the pork "old and stinking." Wilkinson may have colluded with the civilian contractor for a kickback on shoddy or non-delivered supplies. Half the army, nearly one thousand men, died or deserted.[24]

Wilkinson was also involved in another supply debacle at French Mills in upstate New York, where the U. S. Army retreat-

---

[23]   Gaines to Williams, December 16, 1816, NWR, January 11, 1817, V. 11, No. 20, 325.

[24]   Edward M. Coffman, *The Old Army: A Portrait of the American Army in Peacetime, 1784–1898* (New York: Oxford University Press, 1986), 27–28.

ed after its failed invasion of Canada. In November and December 1813, temperatures dropped and supplies ran out. Somewhere between 1,400 and 1,700 men were sick, freezing, and starving. Wilkinson intended to order 30,000 rations at the incredible price of one cent each. Contractors and officers colluded to steal the little remaining provisions and supplies. The British offered the Americans five months' pay if they would desert.[25]

Gaines's solution was to have an army commissariat superintend rations—a "*safer, a cheaper, and in every respect a better supply* than the present system of contract." Civilian contractors, who sought profit over all else, should be used only in emergencies.[26]

The TIA, set up to lessen chances of war by allowing aggrieved parties compensation for depredations, may have been a good idea on paper, but it had unforeseen consequences. The framers undoubtedly made naïve assumptions that were often erroneous: they presumed that frontier whites would file honest, accurate claims; they anticipated that whites would file claims only against the Indians; and they believed that whites overwhelmingly would be the aggrieved parties. They could not have imagined the tremendous number of dishonest people who were about to swindle and rob the Indians and the government, nor the genuine reality that in a majority of cases, it was the Indians who were the injured parties. The federal government quickly got an inkling of the approaching storm shortly after the end of the War of 1812.

---

[25]   John K. Mahon, *The War of 1812* (New York: Da Capo Press, 1972), 215; Donald E. Graves, *Field of Glory: The Battle of Chrysler's Farm, 1813* (Toronto: Robin Brass Studio, 1999), 289, 357.

[26]   Gaines to Williams, December 16, 1816, NWR, January 11, 1817, V. 11, No. 20, 324. The army began the office of Commissary General of Subsistence in 1818, a position held by George Gibson from then until 1861.

LAND FRAUD

"For sundry pretended sufferers by Earthquakes"

The great earthquakes that rocked the Mississippi Valley from November 1811 to April 1812 were perfect portents for the next three decades. Emanating near New Madrid in Missouri's boot heel were roughly two thousand tremors, some that would have measured from 7 to 8 on the Richter scale. They were felt as far away as Canada and Mexico, and they set bells ringing in churches hundreds of miles away. Towns were damaged and some were destroyed—New Madrid was inundated. The Mississippi River changed course, created new lakes, and actually ran backwards for a time. Since most of the area was very sparsely populated the death toll was not great, but the Christian folks of the day were certain God was angry, and religious revivals spiked, as thousands prayed that the Lord would spare them from His wrath. Preachers commented about the increase in church attendance. Unfortunately, when the danger passed, many of the "earthquake Christians" disappeared and returned to their old habits, presumably the ones that caused God's wrath in the first place.[27]

Disasters can bring out the good in people as they pull together to assist each other. They also have a way of exposing the worst in us. To help the people affected by the calamity, Congress, on February 17, 1815, passed "An Act for the Relief of the Inhabitants of the Late County of New Madrid in the Missouri Territory who Suffered by Earthquakes." It was the first federal disaster relief in our history. But to cite the adage that no good deed will go unpunished, the act itself proved to be a disaster. The United States quickly learned, if it had not already known, that its rapacious citizens would immediately find ways to defraud it. Thirty years later, on the

---

[27]   Jay Feldman, *When the Mississippi Ran Backwards: Empire, Intrigue, Murder, and the New Madrid Earthquakes* (New York: Free Press, 2005), 14–15, 233, 235.

eve of the Mexican War, Brig, Gen. William J. Worth, repelled by what American westward expansion had wrought, resigned himself to what had by then become commonplace: "Why mince matters now? Have not our Anglo Saxon race been land stealers from time immemorial and why shouldn't they? When their gaze is fixed on other lands the best way is to make out the deeds."[28]

Americans wanted land, and they would get it by fair means or foul. News of the act was slow to reach the New Madrid area, where only a few hundred people lived, with even fewer residing on lands made untillable or denuded of timber. The people of St. Louis heard, however, and speculators hurried to New Madrid, making the residents wonder why so many people suddenly wanted to buy their land. Of 516 redemption certificates issued, only 20 were held by the original landowners. General Land Office Commissioner Josiah Meigs knew right away there was going to be a problem, writing in June 1815 that "there has always been, and probably always will be, a steady and regular effort to deprive the U. States of their lands, under one plausible pretext or other—such as pre-emptions, earthquakes, Militia services, &c."[29]

The Act said that a claimant had to be a resident of the county during the time of the earthquakes, "whose lands have been materially injured," and was given the right to select a like quantity of public land, unless he had less than 160 acres, wherein he could claim up to 160 acres. No one could claim more than 640 acres, and none of the lands could include lead mines or salt springs.[30] With only two restrictions spelled out, the claimants assumed anything unnamed was fair game. In addition, since virtually none of the territory had been surveyed into its proper tiers and ranges, the "injured" claimants selected parcels everywhere, taking the best of timber or water resources, transportation routes, or sections to be

---

[28]   Scott to Meigs, January 27, 1817, TPUS, V. 15, 237; Worth to Lawson, November 1, 1845, cited in William B. Skelton, *An American Profession of Arms: The Army Officer Corps, 1784–1861* (Lawrence, KS, University Press of Kansas, 1992), 330.

[29]   Feldman, *Mississippi Ran Backwards*, 236; Meigs to Dallas, June 1, 1815, TPUS, V. 15, 59.

[30]   *Statutes at Large of the United States of America*, February 17, 1815, 13th Congress, 3rd Session, V. 3, 211–12.

reserved for schools. Complaints reached Meigs that "many disappointments, much mischief and difficulty" would be caused by people dividing 640-acre claims across multiple tracts in a variety of shapes and sizes.[31]

In no time the land recorders were swamped and confused, finding that multiple claimants had selected the same prime lands; one recorder, Frederick Bates, listed 234 cases amounting to 82,695 acres, averaging about 353 acres per person. He was certain that many claims were fraudulent, but he could do little. Only after a survey could the "many illicit practices" be brought to light. One of the schemes, Bates said, was for the "pretended actual settler" to collect false testimony that he owned lands destroyed by the quakes, select a new tract, print a notice in the newspaper, offer it at a good price, and "the fraudulent claimant sells his land, and is heard of no more." The surveyor goes to the tract and learns from neighbors that "such a man never was in their settlement—they perhaps never heard his name," he does not complete the survey, "and the innocent purchaser on official information loses his money."[32]

Territorial marshal and registrar of the St. Louis Land Office Alexander McNair spoke of the fundamental frauds: much of the land said to be damaged in New Madrid County was unaffected by the quakes, people who claimed their land was uninhabitable were still living on it, and speculators were buying up the undervalued, supposedly damaged lands to sell at great profit. In addition, relatives of deceased landowners applied for land, while the government explained that compensation was meant for actual sufferers, not relatives.[33]

Former Missouri representative John Scott pleaded that the government keep up efforts "to discountenance that spirit of encroachment and speculation, which Capitalists too often are disposed to indulge in, without regard to any principle, or to the rights of the weak and the feeble." Specifically, Scott wanted prohibitions

[31]   Rector to Meigs, August 9, 1820, TPUS, V. 15, 631; Hempstead to Meigs, September 10, 1815, TPUS, V. 15, 81 ("many disappointments" quotation).

[32]   Bates to Meigs, January 12, 1817, TPUS, V. 15, 229–30.

[33]   McNair to Meigs, January 13, 1817, TPUS, V. 15, 231; Matthews to Meigs, TPUS, V. 15, 293.

on "floating claims," which he described as lands chosen directly for speculative purposes, such as town lots, common lots, and school lots (section 16 in every township) meant to be reserved for the public good. What particularly irked him was that some people picked alluvial lands formed after the Mississippi changed course. These "lands," nothing more than sandbars in some cases, nevertheless intruded between St. Louis and the river's new course. If speculators were given title, "the town must inevitably be precluded from free access to the river, and the advantages that it would derive from being on the borders of a navigable stream will be evaded by individual Cupidity." Lastly, many people moved to the territory under preemption rights, but since no land office was opened to record those tracts, New Madrid disaster speculators swarmed in to claim parcels already being worked by pre-emptors. All of these schemes Scott declared to be shameful.[34]

The Committee on the Public Lands heard these complaints and studied the matter to find a remedy. It admitted that "in a few instances the ingenuity of speculation did elude the vigilance of the legislature," but Congress fine-tuned the rules, a process which they considered to have "annihilated the possibility of fraud." There was no further need for more regulations.[35]

While the committee studied, speculators found more ways to profit. Five million acres of public land were being surveyed and offered for sale in Kentucky, Illinois, and Missouri. Half of those acres were in Missouri and were Military Bounty Lands, to be drawn in a lottery and awarded to ex-soldiers. Offering free land to entice men to join the army was a good hook, but thousands had served their time and gone into other businesses or purchased land elsewhere. Many, when given land certificates, simply sold them for a fraction of their value to speculators, who then sold to other buyers at increased prices.[36]

The New Madrid claimants continued their schemes. The few hundred actual residents multiplied like rabbits. Many claimed that they owned lands with unregistered titles granted when under

---

[34]   Scott to Meigs, January 27, 1817, TPUS, V. 15, 237–38.
[35]   Robertson to House of Representatives, December 31, 1817, *American State Papers, Public Lands, V. 3, 264.* (Hereinafter cited as ASPPL.)
[36]   NWR, April 5, 1817, V. 6, No. 12, 82.

Spanish control. They petitioned Congress for land certificates, saying that they neglected to get proof earlier because they didn't know they needed to and it would have been troublesome, but since "the lots having become more valuable now," they wanted to cash in.[37] More aggressive claimants examined some of the best tracts in the towns of Boonville and Franklin, Missouri, where, the land registrar noted, "many respectable inhabitants on lotts [sic] well improved & titles derived from preemption claims" already had houses and tilled acreage. The New Madrid people, "all upon the alert," swept in and selected the best of them, which they planned to pre-empt from the pre-emptors at the next land sale.[38]

Land Office Commissioner Meigs attacked that scheme, stating that the preemption laws came earlier and were not to be arrogated by the Earthquake Act. "The nature & extent of a gift or grant is to be estimated and defined, not by him who *receives*, but by him who gives or grants."[39]

Land recorder Bates struggled with fraudsters for years, including those purporting to be agents "for sundry pretended sufferers by Earthquakes." Bates found the claims unverifiable or made by persons who did not reside in the county before the time of the quakes. Then a new scheme appeared: persons pretending to represent the landed interests of orphans of folks who once lived in the county but were now deceased. Without having letters of guardianship, Bates declined to issue them land certificates.[40]

William Rector, surveyor general of Missouri, Illinois, and Arkansas Territories, was inundated with the new land requests and was taxed to the limit trying to get the surveys done. After several years he was certain that "very little of the lands in that county are at all injured by earthquakes." He looked back on the congressional act as being "produced by a spirit of liberal humanity, but I have always believed it to be an unfortunate exercise of those admirable principals. But a very small proportion of the original claimants have been benefited by that law and many of them have I am convinced been

---

[37]   Petition to Congress by Inhabitants of New Madrid and Little Prairie, December 30, 1818, TPUS, V 15, 487.

[38]   Hammond to Meigs, December 27, 1818, TPUS, V. 15, 486–87.

[39]   Meigs to Crawford, March 12, 1819, TPUS, V. 15, 525.

[40]   Bates to Meigs, May 20, 1819, TPUS, V. 15, 540.

injured by it."[41]

By the time the Earthquake Act played out, 384 land certificates were held by residents of St. Louis alone, more than resided in New Madrid—with a few people holding as many as forty claims. Missouri Territory Governor William Clark, of Lewis and Clark fame, also joined the speculation, sending agents to purchase New Madrid lands to sell at higher prices. Soon, a "New Madrid claim" became synonymous with fraud. Litigation over the claims tied up the courts for decades, with the last case not being settled until 1862[42]—the year the Union army and navy battled Confederates at New Madrid for control of a river rearranged by earthquakes fifty years earlier, during a Civil War being fought in large part because of the same greed, malice toward all, and charity for none.

"It was all fudge"

Foreign visitors to America often commented upon the ingenuity and pragmatism of the people, often unfavorably, because American flimflam men and grifters were also as homegrown as blueberry pies. Land fraud occurred everywhere. "Another exceedingly convenient method has been adopted to fleece the people," reported the *Niles Weekly Register* in 1817. Frontier banks employed many engravers and paper-makers to produce banknotes, honored at other banks where the land business was booming. Cautiously given out and faithfully redeemed until the peoples' confidence was gained, the banks then flooded the market with numerous paper and easy loans. The farmer and mechanic "cheerfully gives his labor for them," then the banks, acting in collusion, depreciate the paper at seven to ten percent below value. "The difference is clear profit," said the *Register*, bemoaning that nothing could be done because they were "*legitimate* frauds." Why not, it suggested, do as some speculators do, and just print counterfeit notes? The operation was slightly different, but the effect was the same. People were cheated. What

---

[41] Rector to Meigs, August 9, 1820, TPUS, V. 15, 633 ("liberal humanity" quotation); Rector to Meigs, January 19, 1821 TPUS, V. 15, 700 ("injured by earthquakes" quotation).

[42] Feldman, *Mississippi Ran Backwards*, 236.

was the difference if the banker rode in his caparisoned coach, while the counterfeiter cut stone in a penitentiary? "Hundreds of men have been hung in England, whose aggregate depredations on the public have not equaled those of many individuals of our bank-directing speculators."[43]

John B. Hogan, a government agent investigating land fraud, encountered a man named Jones, who, although he knew Hogan's position, nevertheless asked him to join in the scheme. Jones explained that he could purchase all the claims in a section for a small sum, and with Hogan's assistance, "could make a fortune." Hogan played along. Jones said he could collect all the witnesses he needed for verifications, and buy even more land with Hogan's participation. Hogan said he had no money. No matter. Jones claimed to have $20,000 and if Hogan joined in, he could pay him $10,000 for only a few week's work. Hogan was shocked, but Jones declared they could make $100,000 because "he could get witnesses to swear anything." How? Because, Jones said, "it was all fudge," but it worked. Hogan persisted, wanting to know who the witnesses were, but Jones snickered, saying "they are such men as these, holding up the figure of a man cut out of paper." Jones said he had all the judges in the area "under his thumb" and could easily get them "to swear my paper men in."[44] Hogan feigned acquiescence, then went off to report his findings. Twenty years later, he was still engaged in the futile fight against fraud.

Michigan Territorial Governor Lewis Cass became aware of a scheme by whites who assumed Indian names and procured Indian children to claim Chippewa lands on a reservation near the Flint River. Cass directed the registrars to closely examine the claimants' identities, but if it was found "that they have attempted to practice a fraud on the Public," the only recourse the registrars had was to instead offer the questionable tracts for public sale.[45]

One of the most inane, yet characteristic, methods to attempt fraud was typified by Christians whose fear of God was palpable, but yet not enough to deter them from a good swindle. How could a

---

[43]   NWR, August 2, 1817, V. 12, No. 23, 358.

[44]   NWR, May 16, 1818, V. 14, No. 12, 205.

[45]   Biddle to McLean, November 14, 1822, TPUS, V. 11, 295, 390.

believer place his hand on a Bible and swear to a lie? Simple. Take pieces of paper with the words, "21 years" written on them, stick them in the shoes of your family members, including your children, let them swear to the registrar they are "over 21 years" and thus entitled to a land donation. Conscience soothed. Even their God might appreciate a good joke.[46]

The battle against unscrupulous whites was incessant. In a thoughtful 1826 missive that might have appeared incongruent for a secretary of war, James Barbour wrote that since the discovery of America, "one master passion, common to all mankind—that of acquiring land—has driven, in ceaseless succession, the white man on the Indian." The Europeans' only justification was "their own maxims, which recognized power as the only standard of right, and fraud and force as perfectly legitimate in the acquisition of territory. It has been done, and time has confirmed the act." Barbour argued that policy and necessity should not stifle justice and humanity. It would be the most solemn question America would ever answer: whether to continue on its present course, or to be an example to the world "of the triumph of liberal principles over that sordid selfishness which has been the fruitful spring of human calamity." The honor of a nation was as important as self-defense and freedom. "The responsibility to which I refer is what a nation owes to itself, to its future character in all time to come." Barbour contemplated universal ideals, but in the end, he knew Americans could not live up to the promise. As there would be some Indians who would accept civilization, some would not. Likewise, "The imprudent of our own people are equally beyond the reach of legislative protection."[47] Again, one could take Americans out of the frontier, but rarely take the frontier out of Americans.

Land hunger drove people west, and there was constant competition between the wealthy speculator and the common folk as to who would grab it fastest. The speculator first seemed to have the upper hand, as land companies secured thousands of acres in the newly opened Ohio region after the Northwest Ordinance of 1787. Settlers convinced the government that the poor man ought to have

---

[46]   Wharton to Graham, August 15, 1828, TPUS, V. 20, 731.
[47]   Barbour to Cocke, February 3, 1826, ASPIA, V. 2, 647–49.

a chance, and in 1800, the first Preemption Act was passed, allowing "squatters" to purchase public land that they had improved. It provided an easy credit system for 320 acres to be purchased at two dollars per acre, with a discount for cash purchases. One quarter of the purchase price was due in forty days, and the next three quarters during the next three years. Even with the liberal terms, many could not afford it, and those who settled on and improved un-surveyed land risked loss if they hadn't kept up their payments when speculators or claim jumpers moved in.[48]

A new Preemption Act was passed in 1830, pushed through Congress by the South and West, because the East and North feared that easy land access would drain their districts of laborers. This time the squatter could get up to 160 acres at $1.25 per acre. A major point was that the act effectually pardoned all who had settled illegally. Once the government had granted this concession, it was nearly impossible to refuse it later, and the absence of punishments encouraged more illegal settlement. The Act's second section also caused innumerable problems. If two or more settlers claimed the same quarter-section, it was to be divided in half, and both settlers could preempt an additional 80 acres elsewhere.[49]

It was another New Madrid. Gideon Fitz, a registrar in Mississippi, was inundated by bogus schemes. "They come like the locusts of Egypt," he said, "and darken the office with clouds of smoke and dust, and an uproar, occasioned by whiskey and avarice, that a register at least can never forget." He said that they brought children, slaves, and hired hands, and pretend to have cultivated a hill of "goober peas or one turnip" that no one could find if he searched every inch. Fitz claimed that they kept the land for a year, denuded it, cut the timber, and vacated when the payment is due. Or, they made an almost non-existent improvement that a legitimate purchaser could never notice. He might buy the land, build a house and grow crops, and then the preemptor would arrive, assert he had an earlier existing claim, and get the improvements made by inno-

---

[48]   Roy M. Robbins, *Our Landed Heritage: The Public Domain 1776–1936* (New York: Peter Smith, 1950), 18–19, 30.
[49]   Robbins, *Our Landed Heritage, 50;* Jackson to Congress, May 29, 1830, ASPPL, V. 8, 635.

cent purchasers. According to Fitz, preemptors said that one of the most lucrative schemes was to find a partner to claim the same land, which allowed them to apply for new entitlements on better lands, and then repeat the process, or sell some of these "floating claims" to speculators. They said a man "would be a great fool to buy land, because those who purchase land and reside on it, can have no such privileges." Fitz was disheartened that cheating had "become so widespread, among old and young, that there is no harm in defrauding the public; that it is fair game," and that "people are no longer bound in honor to observe those great moral rules that bind a people together by equal burdens, and equal rights." He lamented that when persons "of tender age... learn to get valuable property by hard swearing, they will in the next generation" escalate from cheating the government to victimizing individuals. Fitz said these odious schemes would lead to "heart-burning litigation and bloodshed, if not something like a civil war."[50]

Fitz saw fraud close-up from his office in Mount Salus, Mississippi. Barbour saw unprincipled, uncivilized Americans stealing Indian lands "from New York to Arkansas." Both were concerned about the future of a nation idealistically espousing high moral principles, but when the gilded surface was scratched, a malicious, naked capitalism at the core was exposed.

In Alabama, public land sales were often attended by "a very extensive combination of individuals" who colluded to keep the prices down—by beatings and killings if necessary. One whistle-blower, Edward Harper, reported that men actually wrote resolutions to obtain public land "at the minimum price by putting down competition by the force of arms." They elected a man in each township to bid, while the rest "pledged to be at the register's office at the sale armed, and shoot any man that may bid against them." Harper said the lands would sell at from four to seven dollars per acre on open market, but these gangs wanted the land at less than $1.25 per acre or they would "sacrifice their lives" in the attempt. Those who dis-

---

[50] Fitz to Hayward, March 20, 1831, ASPPL, V. 8, 631 ("goober peas" and "heart-burning" quotations); Fitz to Hayward, May 8, 1831, ASPPL, V. 8, 632 ("locusts," "great fool," "fair game," "bound in honor," and "tender age" quotations).

regarded their warnings and built houses were visited at night by companies of thirty or more men, beaten, and driven away. Harper believed that "these men will murder any man or set of men who bid for this land against their body."[51]

Frauds in Arkansas Territory prompted George Graham, commissioner of the General Land Office, to tell the district attorney that the culprits must be prosecuted. The attorney was Sam Roane, who, during the conflict around Cantonment Towson several years earlier, was hostile toward the army and reluctant to prosecute whites for cheating or killing Indians. Graham said that many land claims were "founded on papers that were not genuine," and he had personally seen affidavits by claimants, grantees, and judges all "signed in the same handwriting." If Roane could not find anyone competent enough to aid in the investigation, Graham would "procure a person" for him. The Judiciary Committee, frustrated that the "government was greatly abused by claimants," suggested prohibiting further land entries and revoking all previous ones until they could be fully investigated.[52]

Fraud was rampant. In 1823, Congress passed "An Act for the punishment of frauds committed on the government of the United States." It said that anyone falsely making, altering, forging, or counterfeiting any deed, power of attorney, order, or certificate for the purpose of obtaining money, accounts, or claims from the United States, would be guilty of a felony and imprisoned at hard labor from one to ten years, or imprisoned five years and fined one thousand dollars.[53]

Paper laws, however, never stopped Americans. The battle between cheating civilians and the government inevitably involved the army. At Fort Smith, Capt. John Stuart of the 7th Infantry wrote to the secretary of war about "one of the most audacious frauds upon the... United States, that ever was committed on it." John

---

[51]   NWR, July 22, 1820, V. 18, No. 21, 365; Harper to Graham, April 22, 1830, ASPPL, V 6, 188.

[52]   Graham to Roane, April 30, 1829, ASPPL, V. 6, 41; Judiciary Committee to House of Representatives, January 14, 1830, ASPPL, V. 6, 38.

[53]   *Statutes at Large*, March 3, 1823, 17th Congress, 2nd Session, V. 3, 771–72.

Rogers, who owned 640 acres adjoining the fort, was using every means to persuade the government into buying it for military purposes at forty dollars per acre, when the land was not worth "one twentieth part of that sum." The land was unfit for cultivation and the timber was gone. Rogers colluded with other owners to raise the prices, and attempted to sway the legislators to convince the government to buy it. His men roamed the area, purchasing signatures and adding signatures of children and non-existent persons, until he had a five-hundred-name petition for the legislature at Little Rock. The petition asserted that the Indians were depredating in the area, which, said Stuart, "is evidently the most erroneous, and libelous accusation, that was ever made," because the Indians in the country were "perfectly quiet, and are on the most perfect terms of friendship." It was the "depraved portion of the whites" who committed "lawless outrages on the Indians, by killing and stealing their property and often by molesting their person." Stuart insisted that it was not fear of Indians, but pecuniary interest alone that drove the locals to demand more troops and more forts. Rogers and others wanted to sell land, corn, and supplies to the army, and would use any means to defraud the government. Stuart apologized for appealing to Secretary Cass, but he said that every officer knew what was happening, and he felt a strict sense of public duty not to remain silent.[54]

Chicanery was a national pastime. Benjamin F. Linton, district attorney in Louisiana, said that "Governments, like corporations, are considered without souls, and according to the code of some people's morality, should be swindled and cheated on every occasion."[55] In 1836, General Land Office Commissioner Ethan A. Brown discussed corrective options with the secretary of treasury, and in frustration said that there were "many tens of thousands" of preemption cases to be examined, the number of bone fide claims were few, and they were never likely to examine them all. The "floating claims" brought the most complaints, and entire families living together alleged to live in separate dwellings so they could "divide a quarter-section and obtain a float for each half." Brown categorized another "reprehensible" type as those who pretended to be settlers,

---

[54] Stuart to Cass, October 21, 1833, TPUS, V. 21, 803–805.
[55] Linton to Jackson, August 25, 1835, ASPPL V. 8, 444.

but were merchants, craftsmen, or speculators who lived in towns, obtained lands, and by "planting a few turnips or onions," claimed to have met the preemption requirements. Brown complained that government benevolence allowed adventurers to appropriate the choicest lands and town locations, and then intimidate legitimate purchasers and prevent vast sums of money from reaching the treasury. He believed the system was not worth the cost of running it, and the settlers did not deserve the government's generosity. Evasion, prevarication, and perjury were too common among "many of weaker morality." Brown concluded that a munificent government may have fostered in the settlers an "erroneous persuasion that they have acquired rights not given by law." Dishonest settlers threatened every honest man with a "system of terror."[56]

Settlers wanting free or cheap land and preemption rights were not always the wholesome backbone of the nation as depicted in frontier myth. Individually, they were prone to violence in taking what they believed to be theirs, and collectively, they joined in claim associations allegedly to protect themselves from speculators, but which were essentially, according to one historian, "formed in order to violate the law." Any rules that interfered with what squatters believed was owed to them "were unjust and of non-effect."[57] The Eastern/Whig attitude, per Senator John Davis of Massachusetts, was that squatters were scofflaws who had banded together to maintain their claims against all opposition and "to set at defiance the title of the United States to their own property." The Western/ Democrat attitude, per Senator Lucius Lyon of Michigan, was that the squatters were the true pioneers who opened the country. They only violated unreasonable laws "which do injustice to every poor man... and which are opposed to the moral sense of the people." Try to impose the laws against them, said Lyon, and "it would require a standing army of one hundred thousand men," and even then, "you never *can* enforce" them.[58]

---

[56]   Brown to Woodbury, January 28, 1836, ASPPL, V. 8, 441–43.

[57]   George M. Stephenson, *A Political History of the Public Lands from 1840 to 1862, from Pre-emption to Homestead* (Boston, MS: Richard G. Badger, 1917), 21.

[58]   Stephenson, *Political History of the Public Lands,* 22 (Davis quotation); *Congressional Globe,* January 29, 1838, 25th Congress, 2nd Session, 138 (Lyon quotations).

"Stealing is the order of the day"

O ne of the largest frauds ever perpetrated came as a result of the Creek Treaty of Washington, sometimes called the Treaty of Cusseta, on March 24, 1832, wherein the Creeks agreed to cede all of their lands east of the Mississippi River, about 5.2 million acres, for comparable lands in the West. Ostensibly, this was not a removal treaty, for the Creek chiefs were given the option to keep one section of 640 acres each, while the heads of every family would get 320 acres, accounting for about half of the total ceded land. The rest would be open to white settlement. After five years, the remaining Creeks could opt to keep their allotments, receive fee simple owner- ship, and become citizens. Or, the Creeks might choose to sell their allotments. And therein lies "the rub." Speculators quickly shaped it into a market-based removal of epic proportions.[59]

Article Five of the treaty said all intruders in the ceded por- tion would be removed until the land was surveyed, when they could buy the land legally—unless the intruders had already made im- provements, and then they could remain until their crops were gath- ered.[60] Suddenly hundreds, if not thousands, of whites in Alabama and Georgia swarmed in to claim they had improved the land, often occupying tracts already worked by the Creeks. Perhaps the Jack- son administration realized what would happen when it freed more than two million acres from control of tribal government: aggressive whites would grab it from comparatively unsophisticated Creeks for a pittance, leaving the Indians landless. They would now theoretical- ly have money to emigrate, but other whites would not allow them to leave without stripping them of their last dollar. Intended to benefit

---

[59]   Charles J. Kappler, ed., *Indian Treaties 1778–1883* (Mattituck, NY: Amereon House, 1972), 341–43; John T. Ellisor, *The Second Creek War: Interethnic Conflict and Collusion on a Collapsing Frontier* (Lincoln, NE: University of Nebraska Press, 2010), 47–48; William W. Winn, *The Triumph of the Ecunnau-Nuxulgee: Land Speculators, George Troup, State Rights, and Removal of the Creek Indians from Georgia and Alabama, 1825–38* (Macon, GA: Mercer University Press, 2015), 301–302; Mary Elizabeth Young, *Redskins, Ruffleshirts, and Rednecks: Indian Allotments in Ala- bama and Mississippi, 1830–1860* (Norman, OK: University of Oklahoma Press, 1961), 73–74.
[60]   Kappler, *Indian Treaties, 341.*

white farmers, the treaty ultimately was a boon for the speculators, who filed claims against Creeks for alleged depredations and debts. They stymied federal removal agents until they could bleed the Creeks dry, and when the Indians were dispossessed and penniless, the speculators took charge of the government removal contracts to grab additional profits.[61]

The center of corruption was in Columbus, Georgia. The town was being built by businessmen, planters, and lawyers at the falls of the Chattahoochee on the Georgia-Alabama border. On April 5, 1832, only twelve days after the treaty was signed, twenty speculators contributed funds to form the Columbus Land Company, so as many "extensive purchases shall be made as possible of lands in the Creek Territory from Indian chiefs and heads of families." The company sent out agents with supplies and liquor to get the Creeks to buy from them on credit and get them into debt, which the moneyless Creeks would have to pay off in land. The company sent Indians or slaves to hunt the Creek landowners down "like malefactors or wild beasts," to harass them until they agreed to sell.[62]

It took time to survey five million acres and determine that there were 23,566 Creeks, 90 chiefs, and 6,557 heads of families, meaning that 2.1 million acres were to be allotted and thus up for grabs by the whites who moved the fastest. With the surveying done in January 1834, the cheating went into high gear.[63] A major scheme of the speculators was called "personation," wherein whites hired Indians to impersonate heads of families, appear before the agents, and swear that they were the rightful owners. Paid witnesses corroborated, sales were made, and the whites ushered in others to repeat the process. For a few dollars or a jug of whiskey, whites obtained title to thousands of acres while the actual owners did not even realize their lands had been "sold."[64]

---

[61]   Young, *Redskins, Ruffleshirts*, 74; *Ellisor, Second Creek War*, 48–49.

[62]   Young, *Redskins, Ruffleshirts*, 75.

[63]   George D. Harmon, *Sixty Years of Indian Affairs: Political, Economic, and Diplomatic 1789–1850* (Chapel Hill, NC: University of North Carolina Press, 1941), 204–205.

[64]   Harmon, *Sixty Years of Indian Affairs*, 205; Cass to Tarrant, April 28, 1835, *American State Papers, Military Affairs*, V. 6, 594–95. (Hereinafter cited as ASPMA.)

Some whites entered the swindle before the surveying was complete. Accused of fraud, Eli S. Shorter, one of the heads of the Columbus Land Company, indignantly wrote to Secretary Cass demanding to know his accusers and wanting an investigation. He said he had been purchasing Indian reservations legally, at "an average of something over ten dollars each," and the sellers were fully satisfied, a fact he was certain would be validated "by any *honest and unprejudiced* agent of the Government." Shorter insisted that fraud allegations could only be supported by the perjuries and forgeries of men "who stab in the dark," and only out of jealousy because they tried and failed to buy the same lands. Certainly he would make enormous profits, but it had "nothing to do with the question of *legal right*." He was just using the system to his advantage, and asserted that if any government agent determined one of his deals to be fraudulent, no one "will be more willing or prompt in rejecting it than myself."[65]

Shorter referenced honest, unprejudiced agents, but some of those agents were also in the speculators' pockets. The Committee on Public Lands investigated the deluge of fraud allegations and found that many speculators themselves held high public office, did their best "to render this investigation odious among the people," influenced witnesses, and altered testimony. They hired stooges to threaten the commissioners with personal violence, intimidated buyers, and took the best lands for themselves. But the most successful means of cheating was "to corrupt the land officers, by a secret understanding between the parties that they are to receive a certain proportion of the profits," by which the operation went smoothly "without the hazard of detection."[66]

The Jackson administration appointed four certifying agents to approve the Creek land sales. John W. A. Sanford, Leonard Tarrant, James Bright, and Dr. Robert W. McHenry were to investigate the contracts before forwarding them to Jackson for final approval. They insisted they were loyal and honest, but acknowledged that chicanery was rampant. McHenry, for instance, said, "I have never seen corruption carried on to such perfection in all of my life before.

---

[65]   Shorter to Cass, July 11, 1833, USCSS, V. 4, 465–66.

[66]   Committee on Public Lands to Senate, March 3, 1835, ASPPL, V. 7, 732–35.

A number of land purchasers think it rather an honor than a dishonor to defraud an Indian out of his land."[67]

The "Great Creek Land Grab" was in full operation. Eli Shorter, who had once insisted all of his deals were legal, soon dropped all pretenses. He wrote to other company officers that he had been to McHenry's where sales, pay-backs, and impersonations were going full-tilt, with four hundred Indians hiding behind the hill to be paraded through his office, which would keep him "certifying the whole of next week." Shorter urged his confederates to action. "Now, if we are to do anything, you must *instantly* upon reading this letter, lay all other business aside, and gather up as many Indians who can be depended upon as possible," get them to the agency, and camp them "*out of sight of the road.*" "Stealing is the order of the day—and out of the host of Indians at the agency, I don't think there were ten *true* holders of land." Shorter said that they might think this was impossible, "but *I* say it is not only *possible*, but *certain.*" When he saw other men successfully scheming to get so much land so cheaply, he fumed, "I can almost tear my hair from my head." He worried, "The stream is getting wider, deeper, and stronger every day," but he believed the scheme would be over in one month so they had to work fast. Shorter's partner, Benjamin P. Tarver, wrote, "There is nothing going on at this time but stealing land, with about fifty Indians. Pay them ten or five dollars when certified, and get all the balance back, and get four hundred or five hundred contracts certified with fifty Indians is all the game." "Now is the time or never! Hurrah, boys! Here goes it! Let's steal all we can. I shall go for it, or get no lands. Now or never."[68]

---

[67] Winn, *Triumph of the Ecunnau-Nuxulgee*, 372; McHenry to Herring, March 25, 1835, ASPMA, V. 6, 648.

[68] Shorter to Scott, Corley, and Craven, March 1, 1835, Tarver to Craven, March 1, 1835, "Alleged Frauds on Creek Indians," Message of the President of the United States, July 3, 1838, 25th Congress, 2nd Session, Doc. No. 452, 93–95.

The Government Fights Back

John B. Hogan, former 4th Infantry major and member of the Alabama Senate, was appointed superintendent of Creek emigration in March 1835, but as reports came pouring in, he also got the job of investigating the frauds. He was overwhelmed. "The fact is that there are so many rascals at work to defeat the government that it is a most perplexing duty and makes me almost regret that I accepted the appointment."[69]

Despite his misgivings, Hogan believed he would have three to four thousand Creeks ready to emigrate by the summer, which proved far too sanguine an outlook. Speculators set up numerous roadblocks. The firm of Weir, Billingsly & Co., by lending Creek Chief Opothleyaholo money, had gotten him into their debt and talked him into buying land in Texas with the Creek annuity money. Hogan insisted they would not receive their annuities until they removed to Arkansas, but the company would not let them go until their debts were paid. Hogan saw it as a scheme to get ownership of the Texas purchase as well as the Creek homeland in Alabama. Whenever annuities were distributed, he said, "It flew like wildfire among the whites, for nearly every second man on the ground had his pockets filled with accounts against the Indians; and these scamps are the very men who retard the emigration, although they make great professions in favor of their removal." Charlatans, including "two jack-legged lawyers," spread lies about the worthlessness of the country they were to move to, and threatened to sue if the Indians did not pay all the claims against them.[70]

James Bright had been at work only a few months and was ready to give up. He wrote that he would be thrilled to have "any plan to put a stop to or even diminish those frauds; but I think it is beyond the art of human invention to put an entire stop to them, for as soon as one plan is adopted and put into execution another is invented to evade it." Robert McHenry believed he was making progress at detecting fraud. In the last five towns he collected 164

---

[69]   Hogan to Gibson, June 8, 1835, ASPMA, V. 6, 727.
[70]   Hogan to Gibson, May 9, 1835, ASPMA, V. 6, 724; Hogan to Gibson, June 18, 1835, ASPMA, V. 6, 729 (quotations).

claims, in which he found 142 were fraudulent; there may have been more, but he hadn't examined the remaining twenty-two as yet. He found the Creek complaints were proper, and the chiefs said they would punish the pretenders who illegally sold lands. McHenry heard complaints of fraud in John Sanford's district also. He directed the Creeks to go to him, but Sanford lived in Columbus, Georgia, and "They state that they are afraid to go there; that the white people tell them they will put them in jail there." Sanford, however, believed that the contracts he approved were legitimate and would get presidential sanction.[71]

The Creek chiefs tried to protest to President Jackson about Sanford, but land company agents attempted to divert "them to Columbus in order to arrest some of them for old debts, and enroll and send the balance to Arkansas." They asked Sanford to meet them on the Alabama side of the river, but he refused. When various companies got word that Hogan had called for a halt to contract approval during the investigation, they remonstrated to War Secretary Cass. The protest, signed by Eli Shorter and 22 individuals and land company representatives, insisted that they were not in collusion with Sanford and they had not, "by force, fraud, and menace, prevented the Indians from crossing the bridge" to see the agent. The Columbus Land Company disputed Hogan's authority to investigate the contracts, especially when he proposed to allow Indians to testify. Shorter said that each case was entitled to a jury trial, which, by law, forbade Indian jurists, witnesses, and testimony.[72]

There was no unanimous position on removal. Perhaps as many whites wanted to keep the Indians around as wanted to drive them out, and Shorter's desire to force the decision into the local court system was shared by many. Seminole agent Wiley Thompson discovered another angle. Whites wanted the Indians' black slaves, and they induced them, "by bribery or otherwise, to stir up hostilities among the Indians to the intended emigration, for the purpose of

---

[71]   Bright to Cass, June 24, 1835, ASPMA, V. 6, 661; McHenry to Cass, July 22, 1835, ASPMA, V. 6, 662; Sanford to Cass, August 18, 1835, ASPMA, V. 6, 662.

[72]   Creeks to President Jackson, August 25, 1835, Shorter, et al., to Cass, October 16, 1835, ASPMA, V. 6, 663, 668–69.

detaining the Negroes here… so as to enable fraudulent claimants to prosecute their claims in the territorial courts." If they could get the cases into court, they were almost assured of victory, for, as Hogan explained, the speculators could "have men hired to prove everything they wish." The courts should be involved, but only for prosecuting perjury, for "these fellows laugh at their villainy, and openly acknowledge they stole the land."[73]

When the government realized corruption also infected the land agents, it halted certifications and sales and the agents cooperated with Hogan to stop the frauds—at least marginally. Sanford was implicated in the fraud, and McHenry, although he pointed out schemes, was himself subject to scrutiny. It may be that both men realized they were fighting a losing battle and gave up trying to rectify the bad contracts. By January 1836, Secretary Cass told Hogan that "the services of Dr. McHenry have been dispensed with," and Hogan should get all his papers. Cass saw an amazing letter from McHenry admitting that nineteen out of twenty cases he certified were fraudulent. Shortly after, Hogan reversed 656 cases and told Cass that companies were now moving in to speculate on the reversed cases, and unless McHenry's successor was diligent, he too would be scammed.[74]

The situation became much more complicated after Seminoles attacked Maj. Francis Dade's command in Florida in December 1835, beginning the Second Seminole War. Suddenly, marauding Indians were seen in the shadows throughout Florida, Georgia, and Alabama. Panicked settlers began abandoning farms and heading for the towns. A Committee of Safety was appointed in Columbus, and governors called up volunteers to fight the bands of marauding Indians allegedly killing and burning throughout the countryside. John Hogan called it a sham: "the people of Columbus have resorted to their old tricks of getting up town meetings and calling for troops to save them from the Creek Indians. The farce is

---

[73]   Thompson to Herring, October 28, 1835, Hogan to Herring, November 2, 1835, ASPMA, V. 6, 64, 671.
[74]   Ellisor, *Second Creek War,* 112; Cass to Hogan, January 15, 1836, ASPMA, V. 6, 611 (quotation); Hogan to Cass, January 22, 1836, ASPMA, V. 6, 687.

too contemptible to excite any other feelings."[75]

It may have been a charade, but it worked. In late January, Georgians killed two Indians who were working in cotton fields for their white employers. About ten Indians crossed the river to recover their bodies, and word quickly spread that five hundred Indians were coming to loot and kill. John H. Watson took twenty-one men south of Columbus to investigate. Luckily for them, there were only a handful of Indians. Lt. John W. McCrabb, 4th Infantry, reported that the Creeks showed a white flag and made signs of peace, but Watson shot at them. The Indians returned fire and killed two volunteers while the rest ran away. McCrabb said, "The Georgians have thus set fire to the match." A larger force returned the next day and "carried the bodies subsequently to Columbus and exposed them in the courthouse," further fanning the fear. Hogan figured the Georgians "are determined on driving these people into hostilities," and were starting trouble simply "to put a stop to the investigation of the land cases." He hoped the "petty war" was at an end, but the episode was only the beginning of further strife.[76]

As Hogan struggled to rectify the fraudulent contracts, the Columbus Land Company brazenly propositioned him "to decline your present appointment under the government… and to accept an *interest* with us in the emigration of the Indians to their homes west of the Mississippi." They would form a new company, consisting of six of their cohorts, and title it "John B. Hogan & Co." Hogan tried to answer courteously and focused only on the debit-credit considerations, wondering how they hoped to make a profit by removing Indians at twenty dollars per head. Once the enormous number of Indians were assembled, the prices of food and supplies would skyrocket and the company had "no hope of realizing one dollar" from the enterprise. Hogan declined: "Under such circumstances I should be more than mad to enter a business concern with such prospects." He forwarded the correspondence to Secretary Cass, stating that he

---

[75]   Hogan to Gibson, January 23, 1836, ASPMA, V. 6, 748.

[76]   Winn, *Triumph of the Ecunnau-Nuxulgee*, 410–11; McCrabb to Jones, January 27, 1836, ASPMA, V. 6, 580 ("set fire" quotation); Hogan to Gibson, January 30, 1836, ASPMA, V. 6, 748 ("driving these people" quotation); Hogan to Cass, February 1, 1836, ASPMA, V. 6, 613 ("carried the bodies," "land cases," "petty war" quotations).

wanted "to place before you the facts should they attempt to do me an injury."[77]

Scorned, the Company lashed out at Hogan and blamed him for slowing the Creek removal and the increased Indian hostilities. John Sanford said that Hogan was dragging out his investigation far too long and it would be best to end it or forget about removing the Indians. The contractors and people did all they can to get the Indians out, he claimed, but "Colonel Hogan, backed by the War Department, works for the opposite points."[78]

Hogan and a few government agents, a number of army officers, and some scrupulous local officials were at complete odds with the majority of white settlers and wealthy speculators. The increased acrimony led the House of Representatives, in July 1836, to request another investigation. President Jackson appointed a commission led by T. H. Crawford and Alfred Balch, who studied the case for two years, and amply proved the existence of corruption and fraud, stating that "the land stealers" got almost every acre the Indians had, and at times it looked as if they only stole "in sport." There were also many attempts by the speculators to buy off those who expressed indignation at the blatant thievery. Completed in 1838, the report did little but close the proverbial barn door after the horses had escaped. By then, most of the Indians were removed and whites rejoiced in the millions of acres they had stolen.[79]

In the spring of 1836, however, the years of cheating and stealing from the Indians had reached a crisis. In early May, Creek warriors actually did begin raiding and killing on both sides of the Alabama-Georgia border. Hundreds of whites fled the Chattahoochee Valley to seek refuge in the towns, while others forted up in isolated cabins. As usual, the Columbus Land Company blamed John Hogan for the outbreak. Alabama governor William Schley said it was useless to treat with "such savages." There would never be peace until the Creeks, their "troublesome, murdering neighbors," were driven out. Schley shared the mindset of many fearful, intol-

---

[77] Walker to Hogan, April 14, 1836, Hogan to Walker, April 16, 1836, Hogan to Cass, April 24, 1836, ASPMA, V. 6, 708–709.

[78] Sanford to Gibson, April 22, 1836, ASPMA, V. 6, 763.

[79] Harmon, *Sixty Years of Indian Affairs*, 216.

crant people. It disgusted him that "whilst the sickly sympathies of some of the fanatics of the nation are excited in behalf of the *'poor Indian*,' it would be well if a portion of their commiseration could be drawn forth for their murdered fellow-citizens, men women, and children."[80]

The Creeks were in a no-win situation. As they lost their land, domestic violence and suicides increased. They were torn between whites who wanted them out and those who refused to let them depart until they paid their debts. They were starving and many returned to the hunt, but competition from whites led to a scarcity of game, and even that was denied them when Alabama passed a law that forbade Indians from hunting within state limits. Many were forced to beg or steal. Some asked permission to dig up whatever vegetables the whites left in their fields after harvest. Some whites tried to help, but most were shackled with the belief that "God helps those who help themselves," and charity would only encourage them to linger. Exploitation by avaricious whites and starvation were the chief causes of the Second Creek War.[81]

As for John Hogan's concern about how the land companies could hope to remove the Indians at only twenty dollars per head, the answer was simply to practice what had been done for years—lie, cheat, and steal.

There were a number of substantial voices crying in the wilderness for justice—mostly Whigs. Kentucky Senator Henry Clay condemned the white intimidation, threats, violence, and land fraud. "If reckless and unprincipled men" continued to defraud the government, honest men had no chance, and "corruption and venality must and will become the order of the day."[82]

---

80   Winn, *Triumph of the Ecunnau-Nuxulgee*, 437–38; Schley to Cass, May 12, 1836, ASPMA, V. 6, 712.

81   Ellisor, *Second Creek War*, 138–39.

82   NNR, February 2, 1838, V. 3, No. 23, 360.

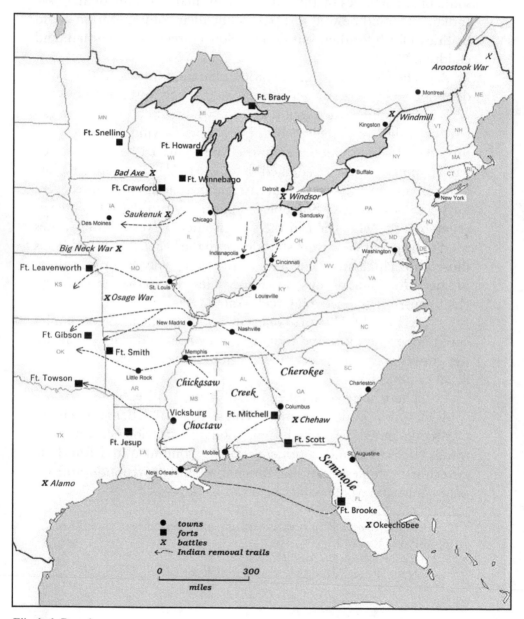

Aroostook War

Montreal   ME

Kingston   *X* *Windmill*
                VT   NH

Ft. Brady

Ft. Snelling   MN   MI

Ft. Howard   WI   Buffalo   NY   MA   CT   RI

Bad Axe **X**   MI   Detroit   New York
Ft. Winnebago
Ft. Crawford   **X** *Windsor*   PA

IA   *Saukenuk* **X**   Chicago   Sandusky

Des Moines   IN   OH   MD   Washington

Big Neck War **X**   IL   Indianapolis   Cincinnati   WV   VA

Ft. Leavenworth   MO   St. Louis   KY
KS   Louisville

X *Osage War*   NC

                New Madrid   Nashville

Ft. Gibson   TN
OK   Ft. Smith   Memphis   SC   Charleston

Ft. Towson   Little Rock   *Chickasaw*   AL
            AR   *Creek*   GA

TX   Vicksburg   *Choctaw*   Columbus   *Cherokee*
    Ft. Jesup   Ft. Mitchell   **X** *Chehaw*
            Mobile   Ft. Scott   St. Augustine
X *Alamo*   New Orleans   *Seminole*

            FL
        Ft. Brooke
        X *Okeechobee*

● **towns**
■ **forts**
X **battles**
◄--- **Indian removal trails**

0   300
    miles

Elizabeth Rosenberg

REMOVAL FRAUD: SOUTH

"The most unprincipled of the human family"

The idea of removing Indians from the settled portions of the East was a relatively new concept in the young American republic. Absorption, adoption, and amalgamation were usually seen as more reasonable options, for although a large number of folks would just as soon put extermination on the list of possibilities, the British and American governments would never officially sanction that final solution. Thomas Jefferson is "credited" with the idea of removal, mainly because in 1803, the Louisiana Purchase suddenly opened 827,000 square miles of "wilderness"—never mind that it was already the home of other tribes that did not want new immigrants. Washington, Knox, Jefferson, and others realized that most Indian wars were originated by trespassing, depredating whites. The several Trade and Intercourse Acts were passed to regulate white encroachment, and the army's task of enforcement would be much simpler if the antagonists were separated. In theory, Indian wars would cease.[83]

Prior to the War of 1812, the Chickasaws, Choctaws, and Cherokees were all approached with propositions to colonize in the West, but none came to fruition. After the war there was further incentive to disconnect the tribes from the influence of Great Britain; plus, with the partly mitigated threat of British and Indians lurking in the forests, white intruders rushed into the vacuum, forcing state governments to bend to their demands of Indian removal. The First Seminole War in 1817–18 contributed to the removal push, and a series of treaties inexorably stripped away Indian lands, shrinking

---

[83]   Annie Heloise Abel, "The History of Events Resulting in Indian Consolidation West of the Mississippi," *Annual Report of the American Historical Association for the Year 1906, 2 vols.* (Washington, DC: American Historical Association, 1908, V. 2), 243–45.

enclaves and edging the antagonists closer together.[84]

Some Indian leaders sought to capitalize on the turmoil. William McIntosh, a Creek chief who had helped General Jackson in the War of 1812 and the First Seminole War, was also a prosperous businessman. Believing resistance to white expansion was futile, he saw there was money to be made in removal, albeit dishonestly. He took a large bribe and then signed the Second Treaty of Indian Springs in 1825, ceding all the Creek lands in Georgia to the United States. Unfortunately, the Creek National Council had mandated the death penalty to any Creek who sold any more Creek lands. Creek police, called "Lawmenders," set McIntosh's house on fire, and when he emerged, shot and stabbed him to death. The action split the Creeks into nearly irreconcilable factions, and many of them, under William's son, Chilly, began to move west.[85]

They didn't get far before experiencing the bewildering behavior of whites who wanted them gone, and yet wished to hold them there to be exploited. Chilly McIntosh moved a contingent of about 740 Creeks through central Alabama. Stopping for a few weeks at Harpersville so stragglers could catch up, they were "harassed with attachments on our property, and thrown into confusion with false accounts." When they tried to get away, Chilly said, "We were still disturbed by persons laying claims to our property." They tried to march peaceably, but were "troubled by constables every five miles, with false papers." McIntosh got his band to the Tennessee River, choosing a water route to Arkansas Territory to avoid the white land pirates. The *Arkansas Gazette* disingenuously decried the treatment the Indians received back east. Arkansans, they believed, were more magnanimous and would make efforts to civilize them, unlike the people of Alabama and Georgia. Just what was official policy, the *Gazette* inquired? "If we are resolved to exterminate them, let us no longer add hypocrisy to the cruel intention.... Better let

---

[84] Abel, "History of Events Resulting in Indian Consolidation," 252–53, 260, 276, 322–23; Grant Foreman, *Indian Removal: The Emigration of the Five Civilized Tribes of Indians* (Norman, University of Oklahoma Press, 1953), 19–20. Between 1803 and 1830 there were twenty-three treaties made with the Cherokee, Creek, Choctaw, Chickasaw, and Seminole.
[85] David S. Heidler and Jeanne T. Heidler, *Indian Removal* (New York: W. W. Norton & Company, 2007), 20–21.

them have plenty of rum, 'rivers of whiskey'—they will then steal our property, and per chance, kill some of our people; and then we can find good reason for killing off those whom intemperance, the great destroyer, shall spare."[86]

The *Gazette*, however, soon learned that its Arkansans did not comprehend irony—or civilization. When some of the migrating Choctaws reached Arkansas Post, only about twenty miles west of the Mississippi River, the enlightened locals discovered them. Camped on the opposite side of the Arkansas River from the Post, the Choctaws apparently bought some liquor and became "troublesome" to Francis Lafargue who was camped nearby. Lafargue crossed the river to get help, but if there were any other Choctaws in the vicinity, only two remained when the armed whites confronted them. One of the Indians was said to have attacked Richmond Peeler with his knife, and Peeler shot and killed him. The other Indian was caught and hogtied. Regardless, fearing retaliation, the whites took the captured Choctaw across the river. Next morning, as the *Gazette* reported, the Indian "was found dead—with his hands tied, and his head shockingly cut with an axe or hatchet—to all appearances most inhumanely murdered." Peeler and Lafargue were arrested, but released on a writ of habeas corpus. The *Gazette* said that the "principal instigators of these disturbances" were the white liquor sellers. Then again, it reasoned that the disturbance, "we hope, will have the effect of causing the removal of all the numerous strolling parties of Indians, who are constantly prowling through the territory, killing up the game, and committing petty depredations on the property of our citizens."[87]

The people of Arkansas, Alabama, and Georgia were not the only culprits. Governor William Carroll of Tennessee, a friend of President Jackson, did all he could to get the Indians out of his state while the Indian Removal Bill was being debated. Carroll found that by "assailing the avarice of the chiefs and principal men... I think I

---

[86]   McIntosh to *Tuscumbia Patriot*, November 30, 1827, NWR, December 29, 1827, V. 9, No. 18, 276; *Arkansas Gazette*, April 17, 1827, in NWR, June 2, 1827, V. 8, No. 14, 227–28.

[87]   *Arkansas Gazette*, June 11, 1828, in NWR, July 19, 1828, V. 10, No. 21, 333–34.

can move among the Cherokees and Creeks without exciting their suspicion." He told Jackson his "avowed object" was to distract them with other issues, while "in a delicate way," he could bribe them into giving up their land. "These, and the employment of other means which may present themselves, I trust, will enable me to succeed."[88]

The Indian Removal Act, passed May 28, 1830, made it official policy to "provide for an exchange of lands with the Indians residing in any of the states and territories, and for removal west of the Mississippi River." It had been hotly deliberated for years, but finally passed in the Senate, 28 to 19, and narrowly in the House, 102 to 97.[89] The argument was often acrimonious, a precursor of the slavery debates that were to explode in the near future. The rationalizations presented in favor of removal became validations after passage. Secretary of War John H. Eaton gave the official version: no matter what people might argue, it was undeniable that getting the Indians away from the whites was the only hope to save them. If they moved, owned their new lands in severalty, farmed, and turned to industry and domestic pursuits they would prosper. If they stayed, "their utter and entire extinction as a people" would be the consequence. Many of the Indians, however, in particular the southeastern tribes, were already farmers and businessmen who embraced capitalism. Eaton also promised that the president had "the power to keep the white people from intruding upon them and settling on their lands, and this he will not fail to regard," but, on the other hand, "he has no authority to forbid a State to regulate her own internal policy." Eaton wanted the agents to explain that to the Indians so there would be "no misunderstanding."[90]

Caught in the squeeze, the tribes slowly bowed to the inevitable and began moving west in fits and starts, while the whites along the potential routes devised new swindles. Captain John B. Clark, 3rd Infantry, was ordered to escort some of the emigrating Indians to Little Rock. Beef cattle prices soared "from a belief that the United States will be compelled to purchase at *any price*." Corn

---

[88]   Carroll to Jackson, June 29, 1829, USCSS, V. 2, 76–77.
[89]   Heidler, *Indian Removal, 208.*
[90]   Eaton to Gilmer, June 1, 1830, USCSS, V. 2, 1 ("entire extinction" quotation): Eaton to Crowell, June 4, 1830, USCSS, V. 2, 6–7 (quotations).

went up to one dollar a bushel. At places along the route the people colluded to raise prices to exorbitant amounts and if the prices were not met, they refused to sell. Clark did not last long. The logistics were a nightmare and the cupidity of the people ground him down. He wrote that if he had anticipated the difficulties awaiting him he would have declined the job.[91]

Lieutenant James R. Stephenson, 7th Infantry, advertised government contracts at Cantonment Towson in Indian Territory, but he believed the bids were too high: beef at $0.39 per pound, corn at $1.67 per bushel, and salt at $2.00 per bushel. He wrote to Clark that the bidders had combined to raise prices. Only a few would supply the Indians with provisions, and they only "with the belief that they can monopolize the whole business." The man who got the salt contract had bribed the owner of another salt works to stand idle for a season, in order to keep the price high. The intention of the bidders, Stephenson said, "is very evident."[92]

Although there were exceptions, military men were often more scrupulous than the civilians. Captain John Page, 4th Infantry, had been involved with the Choctaws, Creeks, and Seminoles for twelve years, was versed in their languages, knew their character, and sought the job of assistant quartermaster to help remove them. Page saw that the government was turning more often to the army "to perform that duty, instead of giving it to citizens, as has been the custom heretofore. I have no doubt there will be thousands of dollars saved to the Government by adopting this plan." Civilians were untrustworthy when money was involved. In 1833, when Page was actively engaged in removing the Choctaws, he was even firmer in his opinion. Every time they opened bids, "we found there was a combination, and that every man calculated to make a fortune out of the contract." Page decided to purchase everything himself. He said the Indians were satisfied until they arrived in Arkansas, where they had to accept a contract, resulting in "a constant complaint about their weight and measure, and frequently [the Indians] could

91   Clark to Gibson, July 23, 1831, USCSS, V. 1, 439 (quotation); Clark to Gibson, August 9, 1831, USCSS, V. 1, 565.

92   Stephenson to Clark, September 20, 1831, USCSS, V. 1, 857–58.

not get their rations when they were due."[93]

Commissioner of Indian Affairs, Elbert Herring, weighed in on the controversy about paying the Indians' annuities before departure or after arrival. "There are some of our own people," he said, "so entirely without honesty and good feeling, that they would despoil the Indians of all their means, utterly regardless of the sufferings...It is to protect them from the machinations of such men, that the Government prefers paying them after reaching their future residence."[94]

The federal government was often caught in the middle between civilians and state and territorial governments that maneuvered for a chance to cash in. Army officers fought civilian collusion while local officials found ways to reward friends, re-pay debts, or get kick-backs by obtaining contracts for their constituents. Arkansas Territorial delegate Ambrose H. Sevier argued to keep agents William S. Colquhoun, who had been cashiered from the army for dereliction of duty in 1829, and Wharton Rector, who had been persecuting and killing Indians in Arkansas in the 1820s. Sevier said both had given up "lucrative engagements" to work as agents, and he hoped the government could find them permanent employment. Sevier also said that two acquaintances, R. C. Byrd and L. Belding, should be awarded contracts to supply the emigrating Indians with corn, because they were businessmen of energy, and a contract "could not be entrusted to more faithful agents." Byrd's proposal, although he admitted that corn could be bought for fifty cents or seventy-five cents per bushel, argued that the transportation costs, bad roads, and chance of drought meant that no one could furnish it for less than the one dollar per bushel he wanted. Byrd and Belding got contracts, and Rector and Colquhoun remained agents.[95]

The Indians arriving in the west also needed beef. Most of

---

[93] Page to Jesup, November 14, 1831, USCSS, V. 1, 784 ("dollars saved" quotation); Page to Gibson, February 14, 1833, USCSS, V. 1, 795–96 ("constant complaint" quotation).

[94] Herring to Currey, October 26, 1831, USCSS, V. 2, 362.

[95] Sevier to Gibson, December 16, 1831, USCSS, V. 1, 859 ("faithful agents" quotation); Sevier to Gibson, March 27, 1832, USCSS, V. 1, 861 ("lucrative engagements" quotation); Byrd to Gibson, October 10, 1831, USCSS, V. 1, 421–22.

the tribes understood the hazards of driving their cattle west, from weather, lack of water or feed, and from human vultures. The government solution was to sell the cattle at home, get vouchers for them, and turn them in for money or new cattle upon arrival. John W. Byrn, agent for Choctaw cattle sales, explained that whites and Indians quickly found a new way to defraud the government. An Indian would drive his cattle to the valuation and sale site, sell them, and the buyer would give them back to the Indian, who "drives them to the next place, has them valued again, and so on." After a few rounds the valuation might be $5.00 per head, but sales were only at $1.50. The Indians who wished to have cattle supplied at their new homes had no certificates, so they were "in the hands of speculators and traders." Worse yet, there were hundreds of counterfeit certificates floating around, "which will be a great trouble to the government." Byrn proposed that when he fixed a value to the cattle, and before he sold them, they should be branded to prevent them being valued more than once.[96]

Agent Colquhoun complained that the Indians did not understand their rights under the Dancing Rabbit Treaty of 1830 and were looking for copies to study, but, he said, "it seems the land speculators have *hooked* every one they could find in the nation." Speculators rushed in to buy the Indian cattle for quick cash. The Indians spent the money on whiskey and were penniless and without cattle replacement certificates when they arrived in Arkansas. Colquhoun also described an instance where a white man fathered a mixed-blood child and then claimed the right to dispose of the mother's property, illegally selling her black slave and ninety head of cattle. Other whites were buying Indian farms with small down payments, but reneging on the balances.[97]

The Choctaws, some of the first Indians to be removed, were under the supervision of Capt. Jacob Brown, 6th Infantry. When they left Mississippi in the fall of 1831, the weather was warm and they were thinly clad. When nearly 2,500 of them converged near Little Rock in December, the temperature fell to zero and hovered

---

[96]   Byrn to Cass, December 18, 1831, USCSS, V. 1, 717.
[97]   Colquhoun to Gibson, April 20, 1832, USCSS, V. 1, 605 (quotation); Colquhoun to Gibson, July 1, 1832, USCSS, V. 1, 619.

in the teens many days. Winds blew and six inches of snow fell, prompting Brown to remark it was virtually Siberian, for such cold had never been experienced in that country before. "Our poor emigrants, many of them quite naked, and without much shelter, must suffer." They still had 350 miles to walk "in mid-winter, through a country little settled, and literally impassible to anything but wild beasts." Local whites pounced. A new, sturdy bridge over Little River in Arkansas was mysteriously destroyed and the ferryman, said Brown, overcharged them by $500. When the emigration backed up, the ferryboat "was designedly cut loose and destroyed." The whites swooped in to sell the stranded Indians beef and corn at exorbitant prices, with corn going for more than two dollars per bushel. The "good people of that vicinity," Brown said, were guilty of "the most bare-faced extortions." Also facing high water and destroyed bridges, Captain Clark said that it would be cheaper for the government to build new bridges than to be held up and pay the locals for supplies at extortionate prices.[98]

The swindlers were everywhere. One man, L. Blake, contracted with Joseph Cooper to supply the Creeks with beef during their migration in 1830. Cooper delivered, but Blake would not pay. Cooper wrote to Indian Commissioner Samuel S. Hamilton, who responded that Blake was not a disbursing agent and had no authority to give government contracts. The Choctaw, Mushulatubbe, tried to get his people out of Mississippi, but, he said, "A white man, by the name of Johnson, practiced a fraud upon me in obtaining a note for upwards of nine hundred dollars, and sued me for the same." The chief had to go to "the courts of the white people," where he surprisingly won. Americans were equal-opportunity con artists.[99]

Not all civilians approved of the swindling. In December 1831, at Lake Providence, Louisiana, Joseph Kerr interacted with some of the emigrants slogging through a swamp. The weather was

---

[98]   Brown to Gibson, December 15, 1831, USCSS, V. 1, 427 ("poor emigrants" and "wild beasts" quotations); Brown to Gibson, June 28, 1832, USCSS, V. 1, 454–55 ("cut loose" and "good people" quotations); Clark to Gibson, October 5, 1831, USCSS, V. 1, 583. Brown was killed during the Mexican War, and Fort Brown, Texas, was named after him.

[99]   Hamilton to Cooper, November 19, 1830, USCSS, V. 2, 44; Mushulatubbe to Secretary of War, May 16, 1832, USCSS, V. 1, 763.

the worst he had ever seen and the Indians were destitute. The women had no warm clothing and only the flimsiest "cotton under-dress." As they passed Kerr's house he saw them eyeing his pumpkin field. "They would not enter without leave," he said, "though starving." He bade them to take all they could find, saying, "Those they ate *raw* with the greatest avidity." Kerr learned that the treaty provided one blanket per family, which he found outrageous; every person needed a blanket, plus moccasins, leggings, and stockings. He heard that they had been defrauded of much of their cattle, and Kerr gave them all of his own that he could spare. He said that the whites in charge were some of "the most unprincipled of the human family." The sole object of the contractors was "to make money without the least feeling for the suffering of this unfortunate people." Kerr learned the name of the supplier was "a Mr. Beldon"—probably the Belding recommended by delegate Sevier. Kerr said, "There surely is something wrong, and I fear will continue to be until these people are extinct." He bet that not one in fifty Indians who were promised ten dollars each when they reached their new homes would see a dollar of it.[100]

Captain Brown was alarmed by the cheating, but one local agent, Wharton Rector, did not appear concerned. William Ball, one of Sevier's cronies, learned that the Choctaws "have preferred all kinds of charges against him [Rector], and pray his removal from office." Ball told Sevier he hoped that Rector would not be removed "on the representation of a set of rascally Indians." "He is better qualified to manage a certain class of Indians... than any men I know; a man of firmness is required."[101]

When the Indians finally arrived they had more concerns, like replacing the cattle they had sold and getting enough to eat. The United States had promised one year's subsistence to the Indians until they could get their crops in, but at Fort Smith, Lt. Gabriel J. Rains, 7th Infantry, found that the Indians refused to accept one hundred barrels of pork, "alleging it was spoiled, and had been condemned at Cantonment Gibson." Rains learned that the pork was

---

[100]   Kerr to Cass, June, 14, 1832, USCSS, V. 1, 719–20 (quotations); Kerr to Gibson, August 17, 1832, USCSS, V. 1, 721 ("extinct" quotation).

[101]   Ball to Sevier, April 22, 1832, USCSS, V. 1, 446–47.

old when shipped there by Agent Colquhoun, more than four years ago, before he was cashiered from the army. Rains thought the pork was old, but still edible, and he would try to re-issue it. His understanding was that the civilians had plenty of cattle to sell and had prejudiced the Indians against the pork. Rains lamented the need to rely on the locals, for he hardly knew of any contract taken in the country "that there has not been some combination or evident attempt of fraud upon Government among the bidders." Their dishonesty demanded "the utmost vigilance to prevent the unlettered Indian from being cheated."[102]

Brown continued to discover swindles. He was swamped with complaints and solicitations from citizens in south central Arkansas along the emigration routes, many of them asking for money for services they claimed to have provided. Some claimed to have transported the Choctaws with their own teams and wagons from Ecor de Fabre (present-day Camden) to the Kiamichi River. The trip was said to have taken forty days. Brown knew the routes and knew that a wagon team could have gone from Little Rock to the Kiamichi in half the time traveling almost half the charged miles. The cost would have been about $150 per team, not $250. Brown learned the contracts were given by Sevier's friend, Belding. He discovered that Belding engaged the teams for the government, then made private contracts with the team owners for a lesser amount, and added charges for corn at two dollars per bushel, which allowed him to pocket two thousand dollars. Brown didn't believe the agents in charge "had any suspicions of these insidious transactions at the time the teams were engaged." Brown also learned that Agent Rector was supposed to follow the Lake Providence route but had taken another, allegedly to relieve Brown of excessive transportation and subsistence costs. Nevertheless, the conductors still ran out of funds and told the contractors to send the invoices to Brown. His deferral went up the chain from Byrd and Belding to Sevier, to Commissary General Gibson. Sevier demanded satisfaction "respecting the refus-

---

[102]   Rains to Gibson, June 10, 1832, USCSS, V. 1, 831 ("spoiled" quotation); Rains to Gibson, April 5, 1833, USCSS, V. 1, 841 (quotations).

al of Captain Brown to pay the wagoners."[103] Brown had to pay, but Belding complained that "I expected $2 per bushel, Captain Brown gave $1.75, with which I had to be satisfied." "I am accused of speculation," Belding protested, but paradoxically queried, "Would any man suppose that I took advantage of the Government" just because he had bought up all the corn in the country during a severe winter when the roads were impassible?[104]

The government honored its contracts, even most of the questionable ones, if only because it would have cost too much to defend itself in court. As Agent Benjamin F. Currey explained, since only half the whites were honest, and many of them lived by plunder, "to prevent these abuses, a guard of honest men would have been required, whose pay and expenses would have far exceeded the value of that description of property."[105]

Agent Colquhoun also deviated from the prescribed emigration route and lost his job, despite protestations from Sevier. Traveling through Mississippi in November 1832, Colquhoun argued with Agent J. P. Simonton as to who was in charge, and the agent said Colquhoun "excited a feeling of dislike for me," which made the situation most unpleasant. Their dispute was settled in Colquhoun's favor by ex-army major Francis W. Armstrong, now the Western Choctaw agent. Simonton acquiesced when Colquhoun decided to change the route from Pearl River to Vicksburg, by traveling down the Yazoo toward the Mississippi. The Yazoo was navigable by steamship far upriver, per Colquhoun, and they could save money by taking a boat, plus the countryside had plentiful food supplies. Simonton was skeptical, but they changed course and eventually learned that the country "was without any resources whatever," and that "steamboats could not even pass the mouth of the Yazoo." They had to head to Vicksburg across country where cotton was the only item for sale.[106]

The situation deteriorated. Whites were stealing their horses and they met people fleeing from Vicksburg where cholera was

---

[103] Brown to Gibson, July 3, 1832, USCSS, V. 1, 459–60 ("insidious transactions" quotation); Sevier to Gibson, December 31, 1832, USCSS, V. 1, 874 ("pay the wagoners" quotation).
[104] Belding to Gibson, May 18, 1833, USCSS, V. 1, 511.
[105] Currey to Hook, September 29, 1832, USCSS, V. 1, 627.
[106] Simonton to Gibson, April 8, 1833, USCSS, V. 1, 884–85.

raging. They by-passed the city and reached the Mississippi, board-ed steamboats and headed downstream, hit snags and nearly sank, and then traveled up White River into Arkansas. Colquhoun found a new adversary, arguing with Armstrong about how best to conduct the operation. When Armstrong reproached Colquhoun for his in-terference, the latter got drunk and shot Armstrong. Colquhoun was removed from the boat and discharged.[107]

Rector was also having problems. After the Choctaws com-plained about him, Commissary General Gibson chastised him for shortages in his account books. Explanations, such as "expended this money in furnishing a party of Choctaw emigrants," said Gibson, will not "be deemed sufficient evidence at the Treasury." He must give details of who, what, and when. A year later in 1833, Rector was still plagued with "certain irregularities" in his accounts. Gibson told Brown, "That gentleman [Rector] has been required to show what has become of 500 lbs. of hard bread" which he supposedly gave to Byrd and Belding, since it was not in their receipts. Gibson directly asked Rector to explain why the accounts showed fifty Choctaw em-igrants received 662 pounds of bacon when they were only allotted 375 pounds. There were more discrepancies. Gibson said, "Unless you show how they were disposed of, you will be charged with them."[108]

Brown, too, came under suspicion, being accused by some contractors of accepting higher bids from others, allegedly to be re-paid in kickbacks. Brown adamantly denied it and wanted to know who his accusers were.[109] Even the conscientious agents found the job unrewarding and difficult—if you could find any. In Arkansas, Cap-tain Clark said, "I fear that the number of qualified agents that will be required could not be had in this country," and had he known of the complexities of the job, "I certainly would not voluntarily have undertaken it."[110]

---

[107] Foreman, *Indian Removal*, 89–90; Gibson to Brown, December 11, 1832, USCSS, V. 1, 195–96.

[108] Gibson to Rector, June 21, 1832, USCSS, V. 1, 99 ("sufficient evi-dence" quotation); Gibson to Brown, August 20, 1833, USCSS, V. 1, 296 ("ir-regularities" and "gentleman" quotations); Gibson to Rector, August 30, 1833, USCSS, V. 1, 297–98 ("charged with them" quotation).

[109] Brown to Gibson, October 16, 1833, USCSS, V., 1, 535.

[110] Clark to Gibson, July 30, 1831, USCSS, V. 1, 561–62.

"Driven like a parcel of pigs to market"

As the Choctaw emigration falteringly proceeded, officials shifted attention to the Creeks, Chickasaws, and Cherokees. Removing them would be difficult given the number of conflicting schemes. Agent Enoch Parsons said that since the Dancing Rabbit Treaty the Creek country was thickly settled by whites, many "with a view to the hundred thousand dollars to be applied to the payment of the debts of the nation." The idea was to bring in liquor and merchandise, sell to the Indians on credit, back-date the invoices, and rake in the money. If the Creeks tried to emigrate, "bail writs, under the laws of Alabama, will be served upon almost every head of a family…and the jails of Alabama will be full of Indians, or the Indians will have to surrender their reservations" to be freed from custody. Every extension of credit made it harder to remove them. Parsons correctly predicted that if this continued, the government would have to pay all their debts, legitimate or bogus, or "will be compelled to remove them, protected by an armed force."[111]

In the spring of 1833, Parsons and Lt. Col. John J. Abert were commissioned to make another treaty with the Creeks, negating the individual allotment sales set up at Dancing Rabbit, and allowing the Creeks to sell their land directly to the United States, thereby eliminating much of the opportunity for graft. The attempt was met by howls of protest. Eli Shorter of the Columbus Land Company, after purchasing many hundreds of acres, "determined at once to defeat the treaty if possible, and gave notice…of my intention." M. W. Perry & Company blasted Abert and Parsons, stating that they had purchased reserves from 147 Creeks, given them advance payments, and threatened that if the agents annulled the contracts "to the injury" of the company, "then it will become necessary for them to prevent" the removal of any Indians out of the state.[112]

Abert, frustrated and losing hope that the Indians would ever be treated fairly, came to believe that "emigration is the last and only hope of self-preservation left to these people." "They are brow-beat,

---

[111]   Parsons to Cass, October 12, 1832, USCSS, V. 3, 483–84.
[112]   Foreman, *Indian Removal*, 119; Shorter to Cass, July 11, 1833, USCSS, V. 4, 465; Perry & Co. to Abert and Parsons, June 19, 1833, USCSS, V. 4, 455.

and cowed, and imposed upon, and depressed with the feeling that they have no adequate protection in the United States." They lived in "fear of the laws of the whites." One consequence of their social and cultural disintegration as a people was the increasing murder rate, and, said Abert, "the whites will not bring the offender to justice, for he, like Iago, no matter which kills, sees in it his gain."[113]

Even the Creeks who wanted to escape did not want Alabamians or Georgians in control—a situation akin to the proverbial fox in charge of the henhouse. Some of the same men who plied them with liquor and cheated them now had contracts to transport them west. John Hogan was dubious, but one of his agents, W. Blue, verified it, writing that the Creeks refused to go with them, because "they are the very men who have cheated the Indians out of their lands, and they now want to cheat them out of what little they have left, and while on the march they will be driven like a parcel of pigs to market."[114]

The Indians trusted the army more than the civilians, and one Alabamian said that the Creeks would submit only if "an officer of the army would accompany each and every party to see that they did not suffer." Captain Page, a conscientious, humane disbursing officer, had trouble getting someone to move the Creeks from Fort Mitchell, Alabama, to Memphis, Tennessee. Page found that the contractor with the lowest bid was irresponsible and untrustworthy. The next lowest bidder had second thoughts when he figured there would not be enough Indians to make the prospect worthwhile, plus he declined to give bond. Page took the third choice, Alexander Roberson, who also had misgivings about the number of Indians emigrating and the high price of corn.[115]

It probably was no surprise when John Sanford, ex-government land agent, formed his own company and negotiated a contract with Commissary General Gibson. For payment of twenty dol-

---

[113]   Abert to Cass, June 2, 1833, USCSS, V. 4, 424. The attitudes regarding Indian-on-Indian crime might be compared to twenty-first century attitudes regarding black-on-black crime.
[114]   Foreman, *Indian Removal, 126; Blue to Hogan, July 13, 1835,* ASPMA, V. 6, 733.
[115]   Benton to Gibson, August 20, 1835, ASPMA, V. 6, 782 (quotation); Page to Gibson, December 4, 1834, ASPMA, V. 6, 765.

lars per head, Sanford promised rations of one pound of bread or three-quarters of a quart of corn, and one pound of beef or bacon, "issued daily, if practicable." There would be one wagon for every fifty to eighty people. Sick, aged, and children would ride in the wagons or on horseback. Army agents would accompany each party, along with a surgeon, and the Indians would be treated with humanity. Yet, anyone too sick or unable to travel "may be left on the route at some proper place," cared for at the expense of the government. Sanford planned to move five thousand Creeks the first year, which would earn him $100,000.[116] Gibson had second thoughts about the contract and placed the burden on Hogan, telling him to ensure that the contractors lived up to the bargain and treated the Indians fairly. Gibson suggested not to leave the sick on the road to be "put at the mercy of strangers." He knew what was likely to happen because of "the cupidity of the whites," and that frauds would be attempted "upon the Indian's negroes and other personal property." Hogan was to be eternally vigilant.[117]

The thought of leaving their sick and dead on the road was horrifying to the Creeks. Sampson Grayson, scheming to keep the Creeks in Alabama, spread tales of distress, and many who had signed up refused to go. Grayson gave horrid descriptions of Arkansas, said that the government had food for only half the trip, and they would either starve or have to pay one hundred dollars per adult and fifty dollars per child if they wanted food for the whole journey. They would be sold as slaves to sugar planters in Mississippi, and any who died along the way would be left unburied.[118]

Wiley Thompson had similar concerns getting his Seminoles to remove. In addition to mistrusting the whites, they believed the Creeks would also make claims on their "negro property." Thompson said that he and General Clinch shared the view that "the character of the population surrounding them" with the "corrupt views

---

[116] Articles of Agreement, September 17, 1835, ASPMA, V. 6, 782–83.
[117] Gibson to Hogan, September 21, 1835, ASPMA, V. 6, 778. (Sanford tried to renege on the contract when he found he could not get enough Creeks together at one time to make the trips cost effective. Gibson would not allow it.) Gibson to Sanford, November 12, 1835, ASPMA, V. 6, 756.
[118] Estell and Connor to Hogan, July 3, 1835, ASPMA, V. 6, 734.

and projects of the rapaciously avaricious," dictated that the Seminoles be moved all at once. Those left behind would fall prey to men who will hold them until "the negroes now in their possession can be wrested from them." Thompson also worried that once out of Florida, swindlers would try to evade the intercourse laws by seizing on technicalities of the laws of the states and territories they traversed. Thompson's solution: the Indians should be "removed by water," for it would be cheaper and much harder to cheat them than if they went by land.[119]

Florida territorial governor John Eaton believed it imperative they be shipped out from Tampa Bay. If they went by land they would disappear into the swamps. They might be afraid to go by boat, but they were also "afraid to go by land," Eaton said, because "Bad men will raise up false accounts, arrest and throw them in jail, whereby to enforce payment."[120] Perhaps they would be cheated less at sea, but when Seminole sub-agent Joseph Harris sought contracts with ship owners in New Orleans and Mobile, he found the deals too expensive or unavailable. Harris finally found owners of a few vessels willing to ferry the Indians. He thought the prices exorbitant, and the cheapest bidder, who wanted ten dollars a head, would only agree if he could put 300 Indians aboard a schooner that Harris thought capable of carrying 120. With a deadline approaching and possibilities dwindling, Harris said, "I gave him a contract."[121]

Using steamboats may have impeded some white swindlers, but the journey wasn't necessarily safer. On the Red River on May 19, 1833, the steamboat *Lioness* exploded, likely because of carelessly stowed gunpowder and the proximity of candles or lanterns. Disbursing agent Lt. Washington Seawell, lost $241 of the Indians' money. He asked for reimbursement, but the commissary general said, "No power short of Congress can give you relief on the score of your having sustained a loss." That was just tough for the *Lioness,* Seawell, and the Indians, but worse yet occurred on the night of October 31, 1837, when the steamer *Monmouth*, one week out of New Orleans and traveling in a part of the Mississippi River reserved for

---

[119]   Thompson to Cass, December 12, 1834, ASPMA, V. 6, 521.
[120]   Eaton to Cass, March 8, 1835, ASPMA, V. 6, 493.
[121]   Harris to Gibson, November, 13, 1835, ASPMA, V. 6, 556.

downstream vessels, collided with another boat. The *Monmouth*, said to have been condemned because of its old age, was packed with 611 Creeks crammed "in a state unfit for human beings." The ship broke in two and swiftly sank. Only two white men died, but about 311 Creeks drowned, including four of Chief Jim Boy's children. It was blamed on the "gross carelessness" of a certain class of men.[122]

There were hundreds of incidents along the many emigration routes, from the petty to the deadly. In Mississippi, a white man named Crawford took a twenty-dollar bill from a Creek to get it changed into silver coins, and never returned. According to the *Memphis Gazette*, Chickasaws going through that city in 1837 were well-behaved, finely dressed, and "not a drunken Indian" was seen. There was difficulty clearing them from the town, however, "owing to the interference of the designing persons." "Emubby, chief counselor to the Chickasaw King, was murdered by a white man named Jones," and although trouble was anticipated, the agents quickly got them across the Mississippi.[123]

French traveler Alexis de Tocqueville saw the Choctaws migrating through Memphis, trying to cross the river, where "they cherished the forlorn hope" of finding a new home. It was exceptionally cold, snow covered the ground, and ice floes drifted downstream. The Indian families consisted of "the wounded, the sick, newborn babies, and old men on the verge of death. They had neither tents nor wagons," but he heard not a sob or complaint. When they boarded a boat their dogs remained on the bank. "When these animals saw that they were being left behind forever, they raised all together a terrible howl and plunged into the icy Mississippi waters to swim after their masters." The spectacle, Tocqueville said, "will never be erased from my memory."[124]

Captain John Stuart, moving Creeks across Arkansas in the winter of 1836–37, said that thousands of them were without shoes,

---

[122] Gibson to Seawell, August 17, 1833, USCSS, V. 1, 291 ("No power" quotation); Foreman, *Indian Removal*, 187–88 ("human beings" quotation); *Army and Navy Chronicle, and Scientific Repository*, V. 5, No. 20 (November 16, 1837), 314 ("gross carelessness" quotation). (Hereinafter cited as ANC.)

[123] Foreman, *Indian Removal*, 88; ANC, V. 5, No. 5 (August 2, 1837), 75 (quotations).

[124] Tocqueville, *Democracy in America*, 380.

nearly naked, wading in cold mud or cutting their feet on frozen ground. Many were frost-bitten and fell behind "to await the ability or convenience of the contractors to assist them." When some die they "are thrown by the side of the road, and are covered over only with brush, etc—where they remain until devoured by the wolves." Those who fell behind received none of the food issued by the contractors—occasionally they had to kill a hog or take a bushel of corn. The whites raised a great clamor and prepared depredation claims amounting to thousands of dollars.[125] The government was losing patience with the abuse of the TIA, because every missing hog was no proof of a depredating Indian.[126]

War Secretary Eaton understood many frontiersmen committed depredations, but his successor, Lewis Cass, blamed the Indians. He addressed Creek concerns by telling them that President Jackson had warned about accepting a treaty that secured individual reservations, because Indians "with the power to sell, would be sacrificed by the improvidence of your own people, and by the anxiety of ours to possess them." As for liquor traffic, Cass said, "If the white people are wrong in selling, you are wrong in buying." The Creeks stated that if they moved, whites would take possession of their land, just as always. Cass pledged the promise made by Americans to Indians since the beginning: move west and you shall own "the land as long as you may occupy it," whites "will be excluded from that region," and you will "enjoy unmolested your own institutions."[127] If you could get there alive.

In light of all that had happened to the Indian emigrants, General Winfield Scott seemed oddly oblivious to their plight. He was certain that the Indians "will so conduct themselves as to win the esteem of our citizens" as they traversed the country, but he also believed that no military protection was needed for the Indians, because he was certain "that sympathy and kind offices will be very generally shown to the emigrants by the citizens."[128]

---

[125]   Foreman, *Indian Removal*, 177–78.

[126]   Abel, "History of Events Resulting in Indian Consolidation," 377.

[127]   Cass to Creek Chiefs, August 20, 1835, ASPMA, V. 6, 776–77.

[128]   ANC, V. 7, No. 18 (November 1, 1838), 283.

"Hostile to all who differ from them in complexion": Stealing Slaves

Ingenious Americans discovered many ways to rob the Indians. The array of "avaricious traders, whose object is gain," and who are "perfectly indifferent" to the means used to achieve it, were among the most despicable characters on the frontier, according to Superintendent of Indian Trade Thomas L. McKenney. "The Indian is first debauched, and then plundered," and if the trader offers payment at all, it is at such a low price as to be pure chicanery. Even worse, McKenney said, some traders paid them in counterfeit money. He proposed to ban all such "disaffected and designing men" from the business, and build more government trading houses, called "factories," wherein public employees would deal fairly with the Indians, keep the peace, "and serve the great object of humanity."[129] Ten years later, because of unending complaints of unfair competition, the factories were discontinued and the whiskey sellers emerged triumphant. McKenney called them "incendiaries among the Indians—these murderers of the Indian's health, and peace, and life—the law should...be armed with such frightful vengeance as to deter them from the exercise of their avarice."[130] The law was ineffective.

There were men who didn't bother getting the Indians drunk before robbing them—strong-arm tactics could be even more effective. Georgia militia commander Alexander Ware told Governor George Troup that citizens were blatantly "intruding and trespassing on the Indians, by taking and conveying off the corn and other property." Civilians also raided Indian lands on the Tallapoosa, and Ware wanted advice on how "to put a stop to these plundering whites, divested of every principle of right and justice."[131]

Indians increasingly went west, by choice or coercion, to escape the whites, yet when they arrived they discovered some things

---

[129]   McKenney, December 14, 1816, NWR, March 22, 1817, V. 12, No. 4, 55.

[130]   Thomas L. McKenney, *Memoirs, Official and Personal: Thomas L. McKenney* (Lincoln, NE: University of Nebraska Press, 1973), 92.

[131]   Ware to Troup, July 11, 1825, ASPIA, V. 2, 819.

Thomas L. McKenney. *Charles Loring Elliott, National Portrait Gallery*
As Indian Superintendent, McKenney soon learned that cheating traders and whiskey sellers were the greatest problem on the frontier.

would never change. Cherokees in Arkansas appealed to Secretary of War Calhoun to help them. They were in their new homes, yet here came the whites, "killing our game and destroying our range; making farms and planting orchards, as if it were their intention never to quit the country." They pleaded to have the intruders removed.[132]

In Florida Territory, Governor William P. DuVal told of increasing white aggression and had the agent move close to the Apalachicola Indians, "owing to a set of white men who reside near the Indians, whose lawless conduct has hitherto annoyed and injured them." It did not matter. "No legal proof could be procured of their stealing the horses, cattle and hogs of the Indians but I had no doubt of the fact."[133]

Whites stole Indians' lands, crops, and livestock all across the country, but in the South, blacks were also a target. Slaves had been escaping their white masters and fleeing to Florida for centuries. Anglo-centered histories generally cite 1619 as the year black slaves were first brought to Jamestown, however, free blacks came to Florida with Ponce de León in 1513, and the first black slaves arrived in 1526. There were blacks living in what would become America nearly a century before the first English colonists arrived. When Pedro Menéndez de Avilés established St. Augustine in 1565, he found persons of African descent already living there, and his slaves escaped to join them in the wilds. Florida gained a reputation as a refuge for runaways. In 1683 the Spanish government granted freedom to runaways from the encroaching English Colonies to the north.[134]

---

132   Cherokees to Calhoun, July 24, 1821, TPUS, V. 19, 305.

133   DuVal to McKenney, November 9, 1826, AGO, RG 94, M567.

134   Larry Eugene Rivers, *Slavery in Florida: Territorial Days to Emancipation* (Gainesville, FL: University Press of Florida, 2000), 3–4.

Some of the escaping slaves joined Creek migrants and refugees, and were often accepted into the amalgamation of tribes that came to be known as Seminoles. Some Seminoles held slaves, but these slaves often had a better life than with their white owners—no whips, no overseers, no families torn apart. Black families sometimes farmed their own land and paid their masters a small stipend of the crops they grew. There was even a small bonus in being owned by a Seminole, since a free black was a potential target of white slave raiders. Then again, black Seminole slaves could be targeted too, for few bothered to differentiate, and who would testify otherwise in a white man's court?

White Georgians, in their quest for land and plunder, invaded East Florida in 1812. The Patriots, as they called themselves, tried to expel the Spanish from St. Augustine, struck the Seminole villages in north-central Florida, destroyed hundreds of homes, and killed or stole thousands of cattle. The Seminoles helped Spain, and after one pitched battle it was the Patriots who had to retreat. Nevertheless, fearing reprisals, many of the Seminoles relocated farther south down the peninsula.[135]

White raids into Florida were curtailed during the War of 1812, but when the British armed the Creeks and Seminoles, white fears increased, subsiding only after the Treaty of Ghent in December 1814. The First Article clearly stated that the United States would restore all the Indians' territory and property, including slaves owned by all parties. The Ninth Article stated that all hostilities would cease, and all possessions, rights, and privileges would be restored. The Tenth actually said that "Traffic in slaves is irreconcilable with the principles of humanity," and America would make an effort "to promote its entire abolition."[136]

In March 1815, War Secretary James Monroe said that it was incumbent that the United States "execute every article of this Treaty with perfect good faith," but the country was certainly not yet ready to abolish slavery, and neither the government nor the local

---

[135] John and Mary Lou Missall, *The Seminole Wars: America's Longest Indian Conflict* (Gainesville, University Press of Florida, 2004), 11–12, 20; Rivers, Slavery in Florida, 7.

[136] Treaty of Ghent, December 24, 1814, https://www.ourdocuments.gov/doc.php?doc=20&page=transcript

civilians were willing to give up the territory and property they had stolen during the war. By early 1815, both sides accused the other of dishonor. British Maj. Edward Nichols insisted that the Georgians were now trespassers on Indian land that was supposed to revert back to the tribes. The Georgians accused Nichols of not abandoning Florida and instigating the Indians, saying that he "and his *banditti* should be instantly driven off at the point of a bayonet."[137]

Indian agent Benjamin Hawkins protested to Nichols about harboring slaves in violation of the treaty. Nichols replied that his orders directed him to take the former slaves and send them to British colonies where they would be given land as free settlers. Nichols referred to the Ninth Article and asked Hawkins why Americans had not ceased hostilities and had not vacated Indian lands. In fact, Seminole Chief Bowlegs had informed him that white raiders attacked one of his towns, killed a man, wounded another, stole cattle, and plundered his people. Hawkins countered that Nichols had no right to interfere with the Indians. The *Augusta Mirror* and *Georgia Journal* indicated that Indians wanted Americans off their land simply because they were being coaxed by Major Nichols. It seemed that the Americans did not care what the treaty said.[138]

It was commendable that the federal government abolished the African slave trade in 1807; however, slaves were still funneled into the United States, and one major entry point was Amelia Island, Florida. The *Savannah Republican* described a variation of the Underground Railroad that decades later would channel blacks to freedom—only this railroad carried them *into* slavery. Blacks were sent upriver by way of a regular chain of posts. "The woodsmen of the country, bordering on the river St. Mary's, ride, like so many Arabs, loaded with slaves, ready for market." The paper claimed that false Indian alarms were raised whenever a new shipment was ready, in order to empty the woods and make the caravans less detectable. These "emaciated wretches" were dragged across the country "to

---

137   Monroe to Commissioners, March 11, 1815, TPUS, V. 15, 14; NWR, June 10, 1815, V. 8, No. 15, 261.
138   Hawkins to Nichols, March 19, 1815, Nichols to Hawkins, April 28, 1815, NWR, June 10, 1815, V. 8, No. 15, 261–62; NWR, June 17, 1815, V. 8, No. 16, 271; NWR, June 24, 1815, V. 8, No. 17, 285.

satisfy the cupidity of unfeeling adventurers."[139]

Although the *Republican* may have protested the slave influx, many Georgians saw the situation in a different light. It seems these slaves were leaving the state, thereby depriving profits to the locals. In 1820, Georgia demanded that the Creeks "restore to us the property as well as the negroes taken or destroyed by your nation" since the Treaty of New York in 1790—although one might wonder what Georgia would do with a "destroyed" slave.[140]

Florida also wanted back its slaves. Middle Florida, between the Apalachicola and Suwanee Rivers, was becoming a small replica of the plantation system in other parts of the Deep South. Planters convinced Lower Creeks who had helped Andrew Jackson in the First Seminole War to launch a slave raid. In May and June of 1821, they attacked a black village along the Manatee River at present-day Bradenton, Florida, and captured about three hundred blacks, keeping some and selling the rest to the northern Florida planters. Those who escaped fled to Key West or to the Bahamas.[141]

But Indians were not supplying the planters with slaves fast enough, so whites often attempted to carry off supposed slave women and children on their own, and at times were arrested for it. In 1821, War Secretary Calhoun defended the Seminoles, saying that "unprincipled individuals are enabled to fleece these poor ignorant creatures," and it must stop. He naïvely expected that "slaves who have run away or been plundered from our Citizens or from Indian tribes within our limits will be given up peaceably." In 1822, Governor DuVal told the Seminoles that if the chiefs would have "all the slaves belonging to the white men who have run away" be brought to St. Marks, "I will see that you shall be paid for your time and trouble."[142]

---

[139]   NWR, May 2, 1818, Supplement to V. 2, No. 10, 176.

[140]   Georgia Commissioners to Creeks, December 29, 1820, ASPIA, V. 2, 253.

[141]   Rivers, *Slavery in Florida*, 8, 192.

[142]   Bell to Worthington, August 21, 1821, TPUS, V. 22, 179; Calhoun to Bell, September 28, 1821, TPUS, V. 22, 219–21; DuVal to Seminoles, July 25, 1822, TPUS, V. 22, 504.

The proposal failed, and slave owners clamored for armed forces to bring them in. Petitions went to DuVal and President Monroe, using a type of reverse discrimination argument, stating that "the Law furnishes to the Indians ample means of redress for the aggressions of Whitemen," but they had to "look on with patience" while the Indians benefitted from the labors of their property. They wanted Monroe to restore to the white men their "long deferred rights."[143]

DuVal wavered. He told Commissioner McKenney that "the difficulty and trouble which these claims produce is incalculable, I cannot consent to that sort of left handed justice which gives all that is demanded to our citizens, or which withholds justice from this cheated abused and persecuted race." Florida whites who had been the loudest complainers were "those who have cheated under false reports." The Indians surrender their slaves, but "their own Negroes that have been taken from them are held by white people who refuse to diliver [sic] them up—I have felt asshamed [sic]."[144]

Nevertheless, because DuVal sought foremost to establish a plantation society in Florida, he eventually allied with the whites. He inconsistently insisted the Indians were being cheated and the slaves were pawns, and at the same time asserted that the Indian slaves were a "Serious nusance [sic]" because "by their art and cunning" they entirely controlled their masters and bent them to their will. Whether the slaves were pawns or masters, DuVal said it was a misfortune that the Indians kept them, and in order to promote Indian happiness, whites should "advise them to sell their slaves as soon as they can," after which, "you would never hear of the planters complaining" of runaways again.[145]

The Seminoles believed it was a ridiculous suggestion for them to give up their slaves so the whites could have them. They insisted they had returned the contested slaves long ago. "We do not like the story that our people hide the runaways from their masters,"

---

[143] DuVal to Calhoun, September 23, 1823, TPUS, V. 22, 744; Petition to the President, October 4, 1823, TPUS, V. 22, 763.
[144] DuVal to McKenney, March 17, 1826, TPUS, V. 23, 473 ("left handed" quotation); DuVal to McKenney, March 20, 1826, TPUS, V. 23, 483 ("false reports" and "asshamed" quotations).
[145] DuVal to McKenney, March 2, 1826, TPUS, V. 23, 454.

they said. They hoped the Great Father would insure justice for all, but they had doubts, because the whites "are not always willing to do right when they can avoid it."[146]

Seminole agent Gad Humphreys was in a quandary. He knew the whites were "hostile to all who differ from them in complexion." He also knew the blacks were almost wholly independent, slaves in name only, worked only when it suited them, were their own judges, and exercised great influence over the Seminoles. The two peoples looked upon each other as "fellow sufferers and companions in misery," and no white coercion would be successful.[147]

Humphrey's view of the situation differed from Duval's, and as he served as agent from 1822 to 1830, by the end of his tenure, he and the governor were at loggerheads. Civilians and legislators accused Humphrey of stealing Indians' cattle and annuities, dealing in illicit slave traffic, hiding slaves, obstructing delivery of slaves to white claimants, and insubordination. The Indian Department resisted the call to starve the Seminoles until they delivered up all their slaves; nevertheless, the governor was tired of being censured because he could not control his agent and Humphreys was removed.[148]

John Phagan was the next agent, but he was involved in a number of dishonest schemes and received the censure of Florida Territorial Delegate Joseph M. White, who wanted Phagan out. White said that no nation could furnish a parallel "of the fraud, oppression and inhumanity to which the Florida Indians have been subjected." The Seminoles mistrusted Phagan so much that they even hired their own interpreter. The agent was eventually fired because he had altered government vouchers and pocketed the difference.[149]

Then came Wiley Thompson, who had been a Georgia congressional delegate for a decade. Taking his new job in 1834, he

---

[146]   Tuckasee Mothla, May 17, 1826, TPUS, V. 23, 549–50.
[147]   Humphreys to McCarty, September 6, 1827, TPUS, V. 23, 911.
[148]   Hamilton to DuVal, November 8, 1830, TPUS, V. 24, 452; McKenney to Porter, November 1, 1828, TPUS, V. 24, 94–97.
[149]   White to Cass, January 23, 1832, TPUS, V. 24, 637; Missall, *Seminole Wars*, 87.

immediately discovered slave theft was still a problem. Thompson learned that whites, acting with "impatient avarice," filed a claim asserting that old Chief Econchattamico had stolen their slaves. Not waiting for court action, the claimants sent an armed force to attack his town on the Chattahoochee River and take them. The chief asked Thompson if he could defend his property by force, but the agent warned that if any whites were killed it would be nearly impossible to defend himself in court. Alexander Robinson, along with eight other white men, attacked and stole fifteen of Econchattamico's slaves, worth about $6,550.[150]

Florida was being invaded. Two men named Douglas and Brown, said to have organized a company in Columbus, Georgia, operated in the same area. This group of "negro stealers" threatened to invade John Walker's farm and take his slaves. They also hired a man from Mobile whose business was using dogs to catch runaways. Walker asked the agent what to do. As in Econchattamico's case, he wanted to defend his property, but if he did, he knew there was "no *civil law* that will protect me." He wondered if all Indian property would be carried off "and sold to fill the pockets of these worse than 'land pirates?'"[151]

The situation deteriorated. Thompson knew the whites were determined to get the slaves any way possible, "by bribery or otherwise." They convinced a number of Seminoles to fight against removal "for the purpose of detaining the Negroes" long enough "to enable fraudulent claimants to prosecute their claims in the Territorial Courts." Thompson wanted a strong military presence to coerce both the refractory Indians and the whites who were tampering with them.[152]

Brigadier General Duncan L. Clinch also noted the increased resistance to removal, noting that the Indians' "minds have been so completely perverted, by a set of interested & designing men, that no argument" but force would convince them. If they had to be removed, Clinch said it would be best to send them all at once,

---

[150]   Thompson to DuVal, January 20, 1834, ASPMA, V. 6, 452; Superior Court, West Florida, March 1836, ASPMA, V. 6, 469.
[151]   Walker to Thompson, July 28, 1835, ASPMA, V. 6, 463.
[152]   Thompson to Herring, October 28, 1834, TPUS, V. 25, 60–61.

because if sent in detachments, the property of those remaining would be unguarded and "soon fall prey to the cupidity of the designing white man who is lying concealed with false titles to pounce on their negroes, and, with whiskey, to defraud them of their cattle."[153]

Thomas S. Jesup. *Public domain*
General Jesup, frustrated by the Florida war, came to believe the problems were caused more by slavery than by Indians.

As many surmised, the blacks did have quite an influence over the Seminoles. Acting as counselors, interpreters, and family members, their interests were often intricately tied together, and they definitely fought against being sold or returned to cruel white masters. Should the Indians be removed, the blacks would lose their protectors; should the blacks be given up, the Indians would lose their allies. Whites wanted them all out because of the land they could grab and because there would be no more slave refuges. The animosities developed over land, food, and slaves, but the latter was central. Seminoles were outraged at whites constantly stealing their slaves, and whites were outraged when not all of the slaves they claimed to own were apprehended and returned. This impasse convinced Floridians that Indian removal or war were the only options. An increasing number of blacks and Seminoles came to the same conclusion. Blacks with high standing among the Seminoles, such as Abraham, John Caesar, Harry, Cudjoe, and John Horse, argued for a tough stand against removal and even for armed resistance. They won their case, and in December 1835, blacks and Seminoles massacred Major Francis Dade's command and killed agent Wiley Thompson, beginning the Second

153   Clinch to Jones, January 22, 1835, AGO, RG 94, M567 ("completely perverted" quotation); Clinch to Jones, March 9, 1835, ASPMA, V. 6, 71 ("cupidity" quotation).

Seminole War. Often called an "Indian War," the conflict could also be seen as the largest slave rebellion in American history.[154]

The army certainly had advocates of that interpretation. As the years advanced, it increasingly abjured its role as slave-catcher. Colonel Brooke was tired of the false claims and allegations of Indian depredations. He told the agents not to deliver blacks to the white men without absolutely clear proofs of ownership. Using the regular army as slave-catchers was inherently destructive and could lead to war—which is just what transpired. One year after the war's start, army commander in Florida, Major General Thomas S. Jesup, frustrated by his inability to bring the fighting to a close, wrote: "This, you may be assured, is a negro, not an Indian war."[155]

---

[154]   Kevin D. Kokomoor, "Indian Agent Gad Humphreys and the Politics of Slave Claims on the Florida Frontier, 1822-1830," Master of Arts Thesis, University of South Florida, 2008, 10–12; Rivers, *Slavery in Florida*, 203.
[155]   Rivers, *Slavery in Florida*, 200; Jesup to Butler, December 9, 1836, ASP-MA, V. 7, 821.

REMOVAL FRAUD: NORTH

"Like the white man cleans his hog"

Southern whites did not have a monopoly on defrauding the government, as they did not have a corner on fear, hate, and prejudice towards blacks and Indians. Some of the most virulent intolerance was found beyond the Ohio River in the Old Northwest Territory. The Ordinance of 1787 never abolished slavery and the states carved out of the territory installed some of the meanest, most restrictive laws against blacks, banning them from voting, testifying, and even entering the states. One traveler found "a most unparalleled prejudice" among people of the Old Northwest. Slaves weren't wanted, and neither were free blacks. Tocqueville said that prejudice was "stronger in those states which have abolished slavery…and nowhere is it as intolerant as in those states where slavery has never been known." There was more mixing of whites with blacks and Indians in the South than in the North.[156]

The frontiersmen and settlers in the North and South found similar solutions to their Indian "problem." The Jeffersonian ideal of incorporation and assimilation, a leftover from the Age of Enlightenment that viewed the future with optimism, was fading away. When nature did not yield immediate results and acculturation took longer than the aggressive whites were willing to wait, the Indians' future turned grimmer. Philanthropists may have had good intentions, but their goals did not concern the Indian-hating, land-grabbing frontiersmen.[157]

The Indian must go. Genocide was never official policy, but

---

[156]   Eugene H. Berwanger, *The Frontier Against Slavery: Western Anti-Negro Prejudice and the Slavery Extension Controversy* (Urbana, IL: University of Illinois Press, 1967), 4, 5, 7, 20, 21, 23, 30 ("unparalleled prejudice" quotation); Tocqueville, *Democracy in America*, 402 ("never been known" quotation).

[157]   Bernard Sheehan, *Seeds of Extinction: Jeffersonian Philanthropy and the American Indian* (Chapel Hill, NC: University of North Carolina Press, 1973), 7, 9, 10.

capitalism was, with its idea that individual greed will somehow promote the good of society inherent in the system. If, as it has been said, European whites had more of an intrinsic tolerance to alcohol as compared to Indians, they also had been exposed to capitalism longer and better understood its eccentricities. As one historian argued, many societies have disintegrated when exposed to the world capitalist system, and throwing the Indians into the maw of the marketplace was criminal.[158]

The Northern tribes were bogged in the same mire. The 1795 Treaty of Greenville had granted the Wyandots, Delawares, Shawnees, Ottawas, Chippewas, Pottawatomies, Miamis, Kickapoos, and other tribes lands in the Ohio country. Although treaties constantly gave whites land, it was never enough. President Madison issued a proclamation in 1815, demanding that the unlawful trespassers get out, but to no avail. Whites were stealing and killing the Indians' hogs, cattle, and horses. The attacks increased during the decade of the 1820s and the agents were bombarded with depredation claims—by Senecas and Delawares against the whites.[159]

There were still some "New York Indians," including Seneca, Oneida, and Stockbridge, who accepted the inevitable and sought to buy their own lands in Wisconsin. The Winnebago and Menominee did not want them, but were forced to sell. The promised presents and money, however, had the propensity to gravitate to everyone except the Indians. Pierre Menard Jr., Menominee sub-agent, was incensed at the graft. Only with slight hyperbole, he said his Indians never received a dollar. "It is not for me to say by what means, or for what objects, these things, so evidently and palpably unjust, have been done. Honesty forever; and honesty will prevail in time. Never was there, since the creation of the world, such a bare-faced and malignant imposition practiced on a set of beings, already rendered miserable and unhappy by the incessant persecution of the white citizens."[160]

Ohio Indian agent John McElvain also confronted men

---

[158] Ellisor, *Second Creek War,* 16, 36, 48, 137.

[159] John P. Bowes, *Land too Good for Indians: Northern Indian Removal* (Norman, OK: University of Oklahoma Press, 2016), 119, 124–25.

[160] Menard to Clark, November 12, 1830, USCSS, V. 1, 192.

whose hypocrisy and cupidity was endless. Every move he made was "closely watched by certain men, and the worst of motives attributed thereto, and every exertion is used by them to raise and keep up an excitement among the people" to keep the Indians in place. These were "the very men who, but a few years ago, said that the only way to preserve the natives" was to get them out, and who now insist it is "cruel" to tell them they must remove. White men told his Delawares that the land assigned them in the West "is a barren waste; that they can neither raise corn nor find any game in it, and if they emigrated…they would all be murdered by wild Indians." Yet, if they remained the whites would take their annuities.[161]

While some whites conspired to hold them, others impelled them to leave. Sub-agent Henry C. Brish moved a band of Senecas from their village to Dayton, Ohio. The trip, in November 1831, was one of bad weather and extreme suffering. Some wanted to return, but that was hardly possible. Brish left the village in the hands of men he believed were honest, but they swept in the moment the Senecas left and "commenced the work of destruction, carrying off windows, doors, brick and stone from the chimneys, fruit trees, flooring, fencing, &c." Brish pleaded for enforcement authority to prevent further white depredations.[162]

It did not help matters that the agents in charge of removal were at loggerheads. James B. Gardiner was appointed by President Jackson as special agent to oversee removal of all Ohio Indians, McElvain was agent, and Brish was sub-agent. Much of the time they worked at cross-purposes. McElvain accused Brish of selfishly trying to injure his reputation and wanted to fire him. Gardiner loathed association with McElvain, "as he is an embarrassment rather than an auxiliary." Neither Brish nor McElvain could stand Gardiner.[163]

Outsiders tried to influence all of them to represent their special interests. Interpreter William Walker Jr. led a delegation of

---

[161]   McElvain to Hamilton, September 20, 1830, USCSS, V. 2, 120.

[162]   Brish to Hamilton, November 28, 1831, USCSS, V. 2, 692.

[163]   McElvain to Eaton, May 22, 1831, USCSS, V. 2, 460; Gardiner to Cass, August 17, 1831, USCSS, V. 2, 560 (quotation); Bowes, *Land too Good for Indians*, 127–28, 131–32.

Wyandots to explore the proposed western tract and returned with contradictory reports. To some he said the game was plentiful, the timber was sufficient, and the soil fertile, leading Gardiner to anticipate a smooth removal. Walker told others the Wyandots did not like the land at all, nor the slave-owning whites of western Missouri. Gardiner learned that the delegation actually avoided the selected tract and they "never saw the country which had been proffered to them," but went on a sports hunting excursion instead. He charged that the trip was a scheme meant only for "filching from the Government the money for such a tour," while intending to keep the tribe in a "false security and complete subservience" to the few whites who would gain by their continued residence in Ohio.[164]

Some Indians tried to move but could not. The Senecas needed their annuities before leaving because they allegedly owed money, and wished "not to have the finger of any white man pointed at us" and calling them scoundrels. The whites told these Senecas, "they will not let us go unless we pay them; that they will take our property and imprison us."[165] Regardless of the holdups, small parties of Indians emigrated, and, as in the South, sometimes in the worst weather. Six ill Senecas were left behind, whom Brish believed would "no doubt die in a short time." Measles struck the Seneca children. By the time they reached western Missouri, four adults and five children died. Brish blamed himself for driving them too hard. "I charge myself with cruelty," he stated. McElvain, on the other hand, blamed the Indians. "If this party have suffered it is their own fault as they could not be persuaded to remove by water."[166]

Gardiner was an enigma. To Commissary Gibson he vowed to use all his power to stop "the filching from them the last dollar for which they have sold their heritage." Then again, he accused the Senecas of using "their own imbecility" in believing the government would care for them. They feigned fright over steamboats, not wishing to "move by fire," or be scalded "like the white man cleans his hog," or take a chance on their children being drowned. Gardiner joked to Cass about "the capacity of the Indian stomach," how

---

[164]   Gardiner to Cass, January 28, 1832, USCSS, V. 3, 154–55.
[165]   Cornstick, et al., to Eaton, June 15, 1831, USCSS, V. 2, 473–74.
[166]   Bowes, *Land too Good for Indians,* 130–31.

they "will take all they can get, and some of them are like the 'horse leech,' they will never say 'it is enough.'"[167]

Military and civilian clashes were common. Disbursing agent, Lt. John F. Lane, 4th Artillery, advertised for bids and believed he made fair contracts with respectable businessmen to supply the Indians, but Gardiner objected. Lane wanted to move them immediately and hold their annuities so the local whites would not get them, for "fraudulent acknowledgments of large debts have been obtained in anticipation of the payments." He was also charged with vaccinating the emigrating Indians but wondered how he was to pay the expenses. A few days later, Lane wrote, "I will no longer be silent." He saw too many errors and intrigues that would reflect badly on his reputation. This business, he said, "will be made a profitable job, to the detriment of the Indians, and the discredit of the Government." He had to get the Indians out of the white man's clutches. "A thousand little rills of profit flow from them; their removal will cut off the supply." The locals continued to "hoodwink or intimidate the Government officers, and to mislead the Indians as to their true interests."[168]

Gardiner and Lane's relationship quickly deteriorated. Lane accused him of never making known the emigration routes, ordering him to furnish rations at a certain point, then directing the Indians to take a different road, or giving orders to assemble and furnish rations at a place miles away with one hour's notice. Lane remonstrated while Gardiner appeared overwhelmed, replying, "all is chaos: I know not where the Indians will be tomorrow night." With the Indians strung out eighty miles in five detachments, Lane was forced to purchase locally at high prices, while protesting throwing government money away "to humor the malice of any man." Gardiner, Lane said, "is unworthy and incapable." He concluded, "It is useless to dally any longer with this man."[169]

Gardiner apparently was inclined to stop off in taverns along

---

[167]   Gardiner to Cass, June 2, 1832, USCSS, V.1, 687–88; Gardiner to Gibson, June 20, 1832, USCSS, V. 1, 689–90.

[168]   Lane to Gibson, August 14, 1832, USCSS, V. 1, 726 ("fraudulent acknowledgments" quotation), Lane to Gibson, August 18, 1832, USCSS, V.1, 726–27, (quotations).

[169]   Lane to Gibson, September 23, 1832, USCSS, V. 1, 729–30.

the route and drown his worries. Lane called him duplicitous and brutal, saying, "His drunkenness and destitution of character place him below gentlemanly notice." He asked that either he or Gardiner be relieved of duty.[170]

Gardiner, in turn, accused Lane of giving the Indians too much food while constantly carping to him that he was short of funds. Gardiner believed Lane was in some sort of conspiracy, so he planned to purchase beef on the open market, "defeating a *settled plan of extortion connived at and encouraged by the disbursing agent among his family connections.*" Lane protested: "In his drunken folly he [Gardiner] has accused me of being leagued with the contractors, and has uttered against me the foulest abuse. Am I to enter the bar-rooms and dispute with this gentleman?" He asked Commissary Gibson if he could he take charge of the Indians as the officers were doing in the South.[171]

For all their disagreements, Gardiner and Lane were united in their opinion of the local whites. As they left Greenville, Ohio, Gardiner wrote, "I would to God I could say we were also away from those miserable and mean wretches, who, for a paltry gain, carry disorder, mutiny, and distraction into our ranks as we pass along the road." He hoped things would improve in Richmond, Indiana, because he believed it to be an enlightened community populated by the Society of Friends. Regardless, "wretches are found to way-lay the miserable Indians with a keg or a jug, prostrate him by the road side, or in the street, and filch away his last penny." Gardiner resolved to travel by land as being more congenial to the Indian habits and because cholera had appeared on steamboats on some rivers. Yet, land travel meant he would have to face cholera on the road ahead in St. Louis, and, because of the recent Black Hawk War, they would meet violent whites in Illinois, where "a strong feeling of hostility exists against *all* Indians."[172]

---

[170]   Lane to Gibson, September 25, 1832, USCSS, V. 1, 730.

[171]   Gardiner to Gibson, October 8, 1832, USCSS, V. 1, 705–06 ("extortion" quotation); Lane to Gibson, October 1, 1832, October 3, 1832, USCSS, V. 1, 732–33 ("bar-rooms" quotation).

[172]   Gardiner to Cass, October 1, 1832, USCSS, V. 3, 479 ("would to God" and "last penny" quotations); Gardiner to Cass, February 25, 1833, USCSS, V. 4, 112–16 ("hostility exists" quotation, 116).

John J. Abert of the Topographical Engineers investigated the imbroglio and came down hard on Gardiner. He called Gardiner "a very weak man; swelled like a toad with his appointment, he falls into all kinds of follies, obstructs and bothers Lane with the object of getting rid of him." He added, "Gardiner puffs and swells" and "his name is a jest upon the road." He had become so obnoxious to the Indians that "if he don't look out he'll be tumbled over." Regardless, Gardiner was Jackson's man and could not be dismissed. Instead, he took himself out of the picture on November 2, 1832, by going on an extended leave of absence, to the relief of many.[173]

Lane may have been free of Gardiner, but he could never get away from the grasping whites. In Indianapolis, he reported that two men, Sailor and Carmer, filed depredation claims that Indian horses had gone into their fields "and destroyed ten dollars' worth of corn." Commissary General Gibson was sick of it. The government would not be responsible for trivial trespasses. Perhaps these pettifogging citizens should sue the horses. If Gibson were to "acknowledge the justice of such claims there would be no end to the exactions of persons to whose carelessness alone their losses are most probably attributable."[174]

Abert and Lane got one contingent into central Missouri in November 1832, hoping all the arrangements were made at their new homes, or, said Abert, "they will starve this winter." He told Gibson how the locals treated them on the road: "doors are slammed in our faces; yet some are bold enough to peep at us through the windows. However, so long as they do not stop our progress we don't care; and yet some of these whites will continue to sell whiskey to our Indians. About twenty of our Ottaways were drunk as David's sow yesterday." Abert moved them along, hurrying to beat the first snows.[175]

One party of Senecas from Ohio reached Arkansas Territory in the spring of 1833. There, Lt. Jefferson Van Horne, 3rd Infantry, who had been working with the Choctaws, took over as disbursing

---

[173]   Abert to Gibson, October 12, 1832, USCSS, V. 1, 384 (quotations);
Abert to Gibson, November 2, 1832, USCSS, V. 1, 392.
[174]   Gibson to Lane, October 25, 1832, USCSS, V. 1, 181.
[175]   Abert to Gibson, November 17, 1832, USCSS, V. 1, 399.

agent. He quickly discovered contractor Mr. Douglass was consistently late with the supplies or delivered short rations. The Senecas joined the Shawnees for the food distribution on June 17, but Douglass was absent. Since there was no corn in the area and it would take weeks to find a new source, Van Horne could only wait. When the wagons rolled in on June 22, the teamsters' excuse was that they were held up "on account of the flies." A flabbergasted Van Horne said that the Indians suffered considerably, but patiently endured, at least until they pointed out that the portions were short. Van Horne inspected the bushels being used, and discovered they held only sixteen quarts, the amount the Indians said they had been getting for the past six months. When Douglass arrived, Van Horne directed him to give eight additional quarts for each bushel. Douglass protested that he was only giving the same amount as the previous contractor, Mr. Bailey, had given. Van Horne calculated that during the previous six months, the Indians were shorted five hundred bushels of corn, plus a corresponding quantity of salt. In addition, Douglass said he had seen Bailey make issuances without any regard for weight or measurement to 250 Indians, while receiving government pay for feeding 396 Indians, "and he boastingly told Mr. Douglass that he had done so." Douglass informed on Bailey, but then it was discovered that Douglass too, had been receiving pay for supplying 258 Indians when the actual roll call was only 211. Commissary General Gibson ordered Van Horne and Captain Brown to deduct the overcharges from any future payments due to Douglass.[176]

Van Horne later learned the contractors' rationale for over-counting: "Indians were issued to, who were at the time living in Ohio; and who did not, and have not yet emigrated to this country." When he discussed the issue with the Indians, Van Horne said, "They looked at each other and laughed, and assured me that the roll taken by Major Brish was altogether incorrect."[177]

And so it went for another decade. Some of the last holdouts

---

[176] Van Horne to Gibson, June 30, 1833, USCSS, V. 1, 923–25 ("the flies" quotation, 924, "boastingly told" quotation, 925); Gibson to Van Horne, October 2, 1833, USCSS, V. 1, 310–11.

[177] Van Horne to Gibson, November 1, 1833, USCSS, V. 1, 927 ("emigrated" quotation); Van Horne to Gibson, December 7, 1833, USCSS, V. 1, 928 ("laughed" quotation).

in Ohio, the Wyandots of Sandusky, were still hanging on in 1840, hunting the little game they could find. On December 8, two white men, John Anderson and James Lyons, entered the shelter of Chief Summondowat and his sister and brother-in-law. The Wyandots fed them, but late that night the whites murdered them while they slept and stole their property. A search party of whites and Indians soon found Lyons and Anderson with the goods in their possession. They were arrested, but somehow escaped jail. The authorities never tracked them down and few Ohioans seemed to care. The incident was a catalyst that convinced the Wyandots to get out with their lives. The last of them, more than six hundred, left in the summer of 1843 to march to Cincinnati. Methodist Minister James Wheeler was astonished at the rapacious liquor sellers who accosted them on the road and by the desire of the citizens to take advantage of them. When they camped at night, whites stole the horses that had pulled the wagons. In contrast, Indians did not molest the 1,000-person white emigration using the Oregon Trail that same summer. When the Wyandots reached Cincinnati, two steamboat captains charged them $4,500 to take them to St. Louis. One of the captains was happy to take the money, but cared little for the passengers. On the last night of the journey he made the Indians disembark and sleep on shore.[178]

The Indians of the Old Northwest Territory likely knew what was to be their fate. Decades earlier they felt as if they were being pressed from all sides. In 1824, Seneca Chief Tall Man wrote to President Monroe that their hearts were sick. The whites passing through told them "this land is too good for Indians," and they feared they would be driven out. Of course it came to pass.[179]

"To pillage the public domain": Stealing Timber

Beyond swindling the Indians, filing false depredation claims, or reneging on army contracts, Americans found brazen plundering to be very lucrative. Perhaps the most widespread example was

---

[178] Bowes, *Land too Good for Indians*, 143–44, 146–47; Heidler, *Indian Removal*, 32.

[179] Bowes, *Land too Good for Indians*. 124.

the flagrant timber theft from Indian and public lands. As soon as the War of 1812 ended, Americans, with less to fear from the British and Indians, were emboldened to take to the woods. Mississippi territorial governor David Holmes, learning that "large quantities of cedar have been plundered" from lands along the Alabama River, directed authorities to "commence prosecutions against all persons who may have been concerned in such illegal practices."[180]

In Illinois Territory, Thomas Sloo, registrar of the land office in Shawneetown, while on his way to the lead mines far in the northwest, noticed men cutting "a great deal of the most valuable timber in the neighborhood." He ordered them to cease, but when he returned he found that a Mr. Moreland had claimed the land. Sloo discovered that Moreland made the claim "for the express purpose of striping [sic] the timber off," and had forty men hard at work to cut everything they could before he had to pay another cent. Sloo said, "This is a species of stealing that will be practiced frequently on the United States unless an express law is passed to prevent it."[181]

In November 1816, Sloo tried to stipulate that future purchasers must sign a clause promising not to "waste or destroy the public property," but he was unsure if it would help, because there were already 750 settlers on the tracts who "feel themselves under no obligation to the government [and] they cut and destroy at pleasure." The next month Sloo asked for instructions as to how to prosecute persons "committing depredations on the United States timber," because the nearest U. S. attorney was in Cahokia, 180 miles away. Also, Sloo wondered what to do when a person made a valid purchase of land, but a squatter was already living there and "will not give the purchaser possession."[182]

In 1822, Florida suffered an invasion of timber cutters from other states. One thirty-man raid, led by Aaron Smith of Connecticut, sailed in a large schooner up the St. Johns River to cut cedar on public lands. Lieutenant Colonel Abram Eustis in St. Augustine learned that Congress just passed an act for the preservation of tim-

---

[180]   Holmes to Carson, July 18, 1815, TPUS, V. 15, 543.

[181]   Sloo to Meigs, August 11, 1816, TPUS, V. 17, 374–75.

[182]   Sloo to Meigs, November 17, 1816, Sloo to Meigs, December 14, 1816, TPUS, V. 17, 428–29, 451.

ber in Florida, and Eustis was to send a Treasury Department cutter to prevent depredations—but to proceed with caution to avoid lawsuits. Marshal James G. Forbes found Smith on Black Creek dragging the cedars to the landing before shipment to London. Forbes escorted the vessel to Amelia Island and placed it in custody of the revenue inspector. Treasury Secretary William H. Crawford directed "the timber to be landed & suffer the vessel to depart, as no legal procedure can be instituted against her." However, as Eustis had been warned, Smith filed suit and the United States Department of the Navy ordered Smith's property restored, "giving such discharge as you may deem sufficient against all claims for damages on account of the seizure or detention."[183]

East Florida was not the only place targeted. Samuel Myers, Deputy Collector in Pensacola, complained to the Secretary of State that the surrounding lands and rivers were being filled "by the description of persons called squatters" who were destroying all the timber. There were great swaths of live oak and cedar "of singular beauty & value... in danger of total destruction, & will prove a loss to the navy, perhaps irreparable."[184]

Six years later little had changed. Benjamin D. Wright, U. S. Attorney for West Florida, said that not only were squatters cutting timber on public lands, but the depredators who excavated a type of clay found around Pensacola Bay were even more harmful. Wright believed this rare earth was "the only clay" in America that could be used to make the finest fire bricks. To make matters worse, the clay thieves then unthinkingly cut the best timber to use in burning the bricks. It was the same story in 1833. The latest U. S. Attorney, George Walker, said that there were currently about forty sawmills cutting government pines. It had to be stopped, but because the people "have been suffered to commit waste upon the public domain, with impunity, they now think [it] their right, and the officer who

---

[183]   Eustis to Calhoun, February 12, 1822, TPUS, V. 22, 363; Nourse to Eustis, March 11, 1822, TPUS, V. 22, 378–79; Forbes to Worthington, March 16, 1822, TPUS, V. 22, 384; Crawford to Clark, May 22, 1822, TPUS, V. 22, 436 ("vessel to depart" quotation); Thompson to Crawford, June 7, 1822, TPUS, V. 22, 451–52 ("detention" quotation).
[184]   Myers to Adams, December 18, 1822, TPUS, V. 22, 583.

now interfear [*sic*], would not only bring upon himself their ill-will," but would be sued. Walker did not know of any successful proceedings to halt the depredations.[185]

When the government increased efforts to stop the invasion of public lands to get clay to make bricks, the locals found an easier way. Lieutenant Leonard O. Brooke at Fort Taylor reported that "citizens are daily committing depredations" by brazenly entering the fort to steal bricks right out of the battery magazine.[186]

Florida suffered through three Seminole Wars which cost dearly in blood and treasure. In the waning years of the second war, with the army and militia seemingly unable to impose a lasting resolution, Missouri Senator Thomas Hart Benton got the idea to bring in settlers to fight the Indians. The proposal seemed ludicrous from one angle, since settlers were usually depicted as defenseless and in need of protection. Benton argued that a force of daring, armed settlers, given the chance to get 160 acres of free land—provided they build a habitation and reside there for five years—would happily take the offer, plus provide a cordon of staunch defenders to fight Indians. Thus, the Florida Armed Occupation Act of 1842 was passed, illustrating the adage that no good deed will go unpunished. When the Third Seminole War played out from 1855–58, few, if any, of the Act's permit holders signed on as volunteers. Dade County, for instance, had thirty-nine land recipients, but not one served.[187]

What did many of Florida's faithful defenders do instead? According to former governor William P. DuVal, they moved in "under the pretense as settling in this country, & under the armed occupation law to take out permits for lands in order to cut and ship off the live oak, and other valuable ship timber, and then abandon the lands." When the erstwhile settlers protested the army's attempts to stop them, U. S. Attorney General John Nelson stated that the settlers had "no right to cut or sell any timber, except for the purpose of

---

185   Wright to Graham, October 14, 1828, TPUS, V. 24, 84–84; Walker to Maxey, October 14, 1833, TPUS, V. 24, 893.
186   Brooke to Parker, November 27, 1820, AGO, RG 94, M566, R0130.
187   Joe Knetsch, and Paul S. George, "A Problematical Law: The Armed Occupation Act of 1842 and Its Impact on Southeast Florida," *Tequesta 1* (1993): 64, 77.

clearing, cultivating, enclosing and occupying the land," and would not be allowed "to pillage the public domain, and having done so, by abandoning it, to defeat the leading purposes of the enactment."[188]

Laws be damned. Timber plunderers were common in almost every state and territory. Jonathan Kearsley, receiver of public monies in Michigan Territory, wrote to Governor Cass "that the most extensive & lawless trespasses and waste of timber" were being committed daily, especially in St. Clair County and on Grosse Ile, a large island in the Detroit River. Suits against the despoilers always failed, usually for technicalities like being unable to identify the exact vandalized land parcel. Kearsley believed that marshals or special agents needed to pursue, remove, and prosecute the culprits, and that the confiscated lumber should be sold to compensate for the expenses involved.[189]

A Michigan territorial grand jury reported that congressional prohibitions on cutting timber were "frequently and habitually violated with impunity." Michigan did not have extensive, productive agricultural acreage, and timber equaled value. Denuded forests meant lower valuations, and was a major reason Michigan had so much unsold land. It was the "lawless intruder lured by anticipated gain" who stripped the forests like a plague of locusts, and as more people built sawmills, the "waste and destruction" escalated. Congress needed to protect all public lands, not just those reserved for naval use.[190]

Americans moved west to the echoes of falling timber. By the 1840s, the problem had shifted to Wisconsin Territory, where the ongoing battle sounded much as it had in 1815. Governor Nathaniel P. Tallmadge wondered what to do with a number of Mormons who were depredating on Menominee lands along Black River. A Mr. Miller wanted to purchase from Chief Oshkosh the rights to build sawmills and cut timber on Indian land. Oshkosh did not sell—one reason being that the land in question belonged to the government. It mattered little, for Oshkosh claimed that nearly one hundred men

---

[188]   DuVal to Upshur, October 15, 1842, Nelson to Upshur, August 11, 1843, TPUS, V. 26, 558, 715.
[189]   Kearsley to Cass, December 3, 1825, TPUS, V. 11, 817.
[190]   Territorial Grand Jury, May 24, 1830, TPUS, V. 12, 172–74.

were already there "engaged in cutting timber." Tallmadge was ordered to stop the depredations as required by the Intercourse Act. If he needed help, he was to call on the army. But the army was abdicating its role under threat of lawsuits.[191]

The frontier line is usually depicted as a cutting edge of upright pioneers and settlers inexorably moving west in wagon trains, tilling the soil with oxen and plow, but this "line" more often may have consisted of a cadre of plunderers whose cutting edge was the ax they wielded to destroy the forests that sustained them.

---

[191]   Tallmadge to Crawford, November 25, 1844, Crawford to Tallmadge, December 20, 1844, TPUS, V. 28, 755, 761.

THE FRONTIERSMEN WHO CRIED WOLF

"Indian hostilities in this country is pretty much a story of moonshine"

Most people are familiar with Aesop's Fable, "The Boy who Cried Wolf," where a bored shepherd boy sat on the hillside watching the village sheep. To amuse himself he called out, "Wolf! Wolf! The wolf is chasing the sheep!" Of course, the villagers responded to his cries, but found no wolf. They warned the boy to cease, but he persisted. When a real wolf finally chased the sheep away, the boy cried out again, but no one came to help. The moral was: "Nobody believes a liar...even when he is telling the truth!"[192]

There are American frontier parallels—even twenty-first century presidential parallels—but all too often the lies were either believed or accepted with a nod and a wink. British subject Alexander Arbuthnot, merchant and diplomat who had traded with the Seminoles and Creeks in Florida for years, had on numerous occasions commented about the American proclivity for stirring up war fever through false accusations against the Indians. In 1817 he commented on how difficult it was to maintain the tentative peace established by the Treaty of Ghent that ended the War of 1812. The United States was to restore all Indian lands, but the local whites cared not a whit for the treaty. Arbuthnot said the Americans tried to entice him and his Indian affiliates to join their cause, but finding themselves rebuffed, they sought "a pretext to attack us… by spreading false reports of our murdering the Americans, stealing their cattle, and preparing for war against them, while, in fact, it is the Americans who murder our red brethren, steal our cattle by hundreds at a time, and are daily encroaching on our lands, and maintaining the settlers in their ill-gotten possessions by armed force." Charged by

---

[192] "The Boy Who Cried Wolf," https://www.storyarts.org/library/aesops/stories/boy.html

Great Britain to protect the Indians' interests, Arbuthnot also reported false newspaper accounts of Indians murdering innocent settlers. In truth, it was the "backwood Georgians" who entered a Seminole camp in June 1817, killed three men and a boy, and scalped the boy. Others killed one of Bowleg's head men on the St. Johns River in July.[193]

Regardless of protestations by Arbuthnot and his protégé, Robert C. Ambrister, General Jackson, certain that the Indians were the culprits, invaded Florida, captured both men in April 1818, charged them with aiding and abetting the enemy, and executed them. The United States did not want another war with Great Britain, but in the years from the War of 1812 into the mid-1820s, the army did not march in step with national policy. Its political and amateur generals had minds of their own, promoted regional and sectional interests, were antagonistic to foreigners, hated Indians, and were sympathetic toward the frontiersmen. It was not until West Point-bred officers infused the army with more professional, subordinate, responsive, and accountable attitudes that a one-time Indian-hating army came to embrace its role as peacekeeper and became more tolerant of the Indians' dilemma and less patient with the aggressive frontier whites.[194]

The learning curve was gradual, but visible. General Edmund P. Gaines, who began his army career on the frontier distrusting Indians and favoring the settlers, came to reassess his prejudices. By 1818 he still saw most Indians as untrustworthy barbarians, but was beginning to reevaluate the constant white alarms. It was very probable, he wrote to War Secretary Calhoun, "that apprehensions of danger might be excited by land speculators, where no danger really existed, in order to deter" the number of potential bidders. Calhoun responded that he too feared the "disgraceful motives" of the whites in exaggerating Indian danger. Still, if hostilities began, they should blame the Indians, "for the world ought to be satisfied that we are not activated by motives of aggrandizement in waging

---

[193]   Arbuthnot to Governor General, May 3, 1817, ASPMA, V. 1, 726; Arbuthnot to Nichols, August 26, 1817, ASPMA, V. 1, 725.

[194]   Robert V. Remini, *Andrew Jackson & His Indian Wars* (New York: Viking, 2001), 154; Watson, *Jackson's Sword*, ix, x.

or carrying on this war. That our object is not Florida, but protection."[195]

Rare was such a blatant admission that Americans planned to steal land under the guise of protecting settlers, and blame the Indians for any resultant war. President James Monroe was not so obvious, but he still knew where the problem originated. The Georgia-Florida borderlands were, he said, "the theatre of every species of lawless adventure." The scoundrels and fugitives from many countries were there, "misrepresenting the claims and titles of the Indians to land, and in practicing on their savage propensities," were the actual ones to blame for the Seminole War. The white rogues "deserve to be viewed in a worse light than the savages."[196]

The wolf cries were nearly constant. Seminole agent Gad Humphreys was tired of them, and said that Indian depredation reports were greatly exaggerated in proportion to the fear of those reporting. Certainly the Indians had stolen cattle and caused some alarm, "but they have the authority of example from the whites." Humphreys investigated one allegation, only to discover "no complaint from the inhabitants themselves, who were said to be the losers; and I venture to predict that...the loudest complaints will be found to have come from those who either have not suffered at all, or but slightly. Of the motive of the authors, I have nothing to say."[197]

Florida territorial governor William P. DuVal figured building a military post in the Alachua area was "as essential to the protection of the Indians, as of the Citizens, it would check in the bud any improper design formed by either party." As for the alarmists, he said "that many who complain loudly have sustained no loss," and he would demand legal proofs before submitting claims to the war department, a step by which he believed "all clamour against the Indians will be silenced."[198]

Since the Trade and Intercourse Acts provided no penalties

---

[195]   Gaines to Calhoun, September 18, 1818, AGO, RG 94, M566, R0106; Calhoun to Gaines, October 2, 1818, AGO, RG 94, M566, R0106.

[196]   Monroe, Message to Congress, November 16, 1818, American State Papers, Foreign Relations, V. 4, 214 (Hereinafter cited as ASPFR).

[197]   Humphreys to Walton, May 14, 1825, ASPIA, V. 2, 632.

[198]   DuVal to McKenney, January 23, 1826, TPUS, V. 23, 424.

for false reporting, threats or demands for proof were of little concern to alarmists and phony claimants, and the frontiers were likely home to more wolf-criers than wolves. Fort St. Anthony was at the cutting edge of the Minnesota wilderness in 1822. Colonel Josiah Snelling, 5th Infantry, spent much of his time responding to accounts of hostile Indians "of so vague and uncertain a character as to be entitled to no credit." Some warnings accused the Sauk, Fox, and Sioux of banding together to attack the whites and called for more troops and forts. Snelling knew the Sauk and Fox were mortal enemies of the Sioux and said that reports of them attacking whites were "idle and groundless." If the Indians ever did attack, he said, "I should deserve to forfeit my reputation."[199]

In Wisconsin (then Michigan Territory) there was a minor "uprising" of Winnebagoes in 1827, who were reacting to a slew of white lead miners entering their territory. There were several white deaths and it ended with the arrest of the guilty and large Indian land cessions. One consequence was that the whites now had another specter of murdering Indians stalking the woods. Richard H. Bell, the assistant superintendent of United Stated Lead Mines in 1829 and 1830, found no hostility among the surrounding tribes and, like Snelling, had little apprehension of them forming an alliance. Bell said that the constant rumors of Indian attacks stemmed from a number of causes. First, whites on an extended frontier were prone to magnify the dangers and were "always subject to extravagant exaggeration." Second, was "the rooted animosity at all times prevailing in the frontier settler towards the Indian, as well as a Cupidity always urging them on to depredate on Indian rights, that they may get their lands." Third, the settlers found it lucrative to be "enrolled & taken into pay by the United States" to obtain money and munitions. Thus, fear and greed had "a most preponderating influence to mislead the better judgment of the best of men." Bell did not wish to censure anyone in particular, but he believed all the frontier troubles could be "ascribed to the machinations of interested white persons."[200]

In 1832 the Pottawatomies in Indiana and Illinois ceded

---

[199]   Snelling to Atkinson, April 22, 1822, AGO, RG 94, M567, R0002.
[200]   Bell to Macomb, August 16, 1831, TPUS, V. 12, 333–34.

their territory to the United States, but were allowed to remain on the land to hunt and fish. Illinois settlers wanted them out, so they harassed and robbed them. Some Indians gave up and abandoned their homes. In central Illinois, inhabitants of the Spoon River settlement wanted them driven out because they had allegedly killed some hogs, and if they came to town, said John C. Owings, "there is whites that will kill some of them."[201] Trying to avoid trouble, the Pottawatomies asked friendly Sauk Chief Keokuk for help, and he relayed their concerns to the army. Keokuk explained that the Indians were not killing hogs, but that "the frontier people kill each other's hogs and charge them with the offence." It was an old ploy. Secretary of War John H. Eaton understood that missing hogs were no proof of Indian depredations, and remarked that whenever the "aggrieved" persons were frontiersmen, it was "just possible the Indians were not the aggressors."[202]

Federal officials were skeptical of tales of Indian theft and murder, while regular army officers almost universally viewed civilian wolf-criers and volunteers with contempt. Trustworthy, truthful militiamen were rare, but Major General Thomas S. Jesup found one. He described Lt. Col. David Cawlfield, commanding a battalion of Alabama volunteers, as entirely reliable, one of the best volunteers he had ever seen, and "a man of perfect truth." In the midst of the very real Second Seminole War, Cawlfield followed his orders to search for and fight the enemy, but he had a problem: the supposed hordes of hostile Indians were not to be found. His companies scoured the countryside, but Cawlfield said, "Indeed, to be candid, and use a vulgar phrase, my own opinion is that the whole matter of Indian hostilities in this country is pretty much a story of moonshine, the object of which I leave others to conjecture for the present." There might have been "a few miserably wretched Indians secreted somewhere," he said, but he did not believe any of them

---

[201]   Owings to Reynolds, January 29, 1833, AGO, RG 94, M567, R0078. Spoon River, said to be a fictional town written about by Edgar Lee Masters in his 1915, "Spoon River Anthology," was actually a settlement, and Owings and nine others wrote to the governor as "the inhabitants of Spoon river."
[202]   Keokuk to Macomb, February 17, 1833, AGO, RG 94, M567, R0078 ("each other's hogs" quotation); Abel, "History of Events Resulting in Indian Consolidation," 376–77 ("just possible" quotation).

were disposed to hostility "further than their own preservation is concerned."[203]

Cawlfield's was a lonely voice of reason. Most volunteers and many newspapers thrived on enhancing the fear that would make money and bring in troops and contracts. Some press, however, sought to quench the flames. The *New York Journal of Commerce* examined several letters from Florida and concluded, "You must not believe in the murders and accounts of excitement, &c, which you see, daily, published. Those reports are gotten up by interested individuals, who are anxious to bring in some of the Territorial Volunteers, who will rob the money of Uncle Sam, and eat the bread of idleness."[204]

Marine contingents also operated against the Seminoles and Creeks. Five companies camped near the Forsyth Plantation in Georgia, when the overseer, Abraham Collins, blamed the Indians and the Marines for "depredations committed on the plantation." The accusation elicited an investigation and response from Marine Col. Archibald Henderson, who found that absolutely no injury was done to the crops, while his marines provided security to Forsyth's slaves. The culprits actually were a company of Georgia Volunteers. Henderson reported that Collins admitted it was "Captain Love, with his lawless company, had ruined his cotton field, and that he had often threatened to shoot the horses they had turned in there." The complaint was groundless.[205] As was often the case, it was easier for a man to get money from the government than from his neighbor.

Still, accusations against the Indians never ceased. The *Little Rock Gazette* in 1838 said they were "hostile and insolent" and were murdering whites. Congress needed to authorize more forts and increase the size of the army. There were thousands of "blood-thirsty savages" forced west after despoiling Florida, waiting to "glut their vengeance on the unoffending and unprotected citizens of Arkansas."

---

[203]   Jesup to Jones, August 2, 1837, ASPMA, V. 7, 843 ("perfect truth" quotation); Cawlfield to Jesup, July 15, 1837, ASPMA, V. 7, 843–44 ("moonshine" and "wretched Indians" quotations).
[204]   ANC, V. 6, No. 21 (May 17, 1838), 332.
[205]   Lindsay to Henderson, Henderson to Jones, December 24, 1836, AGO, RG 94, M567, R0126.

Only a greater army presence would avert an imminent "bloody and desolating war."[206] From the *New Orleans Bee* came similar warnings. The United States had knowingly moved sixty-six thousand Indian warriors from the east to the west, all of them armed and angry. Accounts received daily showed that "the savages are on the point of taking up the hatchet, and rushing with all their hellish atrocities and cruelties upon the settlements of the whites." With most of the army fighting in Florida they needed thousands of militia to protect them. Two months later, the *Bee* changed its mind. They were happy to announce that all the war rumors "proved to be groundless."[207]

The Creek Opothleyaholo asserted that his people were not hostile and asked the agent to find out who was spreading the rumors, saying, "We cannot rest contented till we know who that person is," for such lies "are calculated to do us much injury." Cherokee John Ross called on the army to protect them from the whites, because "evil disposed persons are apt to fabricate false reports from sinister motives," and the tales needed to be investigated.[208]

In February 1838, Delawares living near Fort Leavenworth asked permission to tap nearby sugar maple trees. Given approval, they went about their work, but inadvertently crossed the line into Missouri, where whites howled about an "Indian invasion" and accused them of killing their hogs. Colonel Stephen W. Kearny investigated, found the Delawares had not killed any hogs, but learned one hundred "squatters" had formed a company to repel them. Kearny found that the savage hordes consisted of three men with a few women and children. He reported to Brig. Gen. Henry Atkinson and both agreed to take no action against the Indians.[209]

Atkinson had been headquartered in St. Louis and Jefferson Barracks for the past few years, safely distant from Indian danger. However, the *Louisville Journal* of October 4, announced, "ATTEMPT

---

[206]   ANC, V. 7, No. 4 (July 26, 1838), 58.

[207]   ANC, V. 7, No. 11 (September 13, 1838), 174; ANC, V. 7, No. 18, (November 1, 1838), 283.

[208]   ANC, V. 7, No. 15 (October 11, 1838), 237 ("much injury" quotation); Ross to Arbuckle, May 14, 1839, AGO, RG 94, M567, R0180 ("evil disposed" quotation).

[209]   Roger L. Nichols, *General Henry Atkinson A Western Military Career* (Norman, OK: University of Oklahoma Press, 1965), 208.

TO MURDER GEN. ATKINSON." Riding in his carriage on the road to Jefferson Barracks, the general and his family were attacked by "two ruffians," one of whom dashed in front of the horses while the other grabbed the reins. As more accomplices ran towards them, the quick-acting driver pulled a pistol and shot the man holding the reins, then whipped the horses and they raced away.[210] Atkinson may have been safer in Indian country.

Constant reports of missing hogs exasperated the army officers as well as a few honest volunteers. After citizen complaints in Lowndes County, Georgia, Lt. Nathan Norton of the Florida Mounted Volunteers scouted south from Fort Gilmer, Georgia, to the Okefenokee Swamp, and never found any indication that Indians had been in the area for months. "I have never heard of any cattle or hogs being missed by any of the inhabitants" that he questioned, Norton wrote, and he believed the citizen complaints of depredations "to be greatly exaggerated if not entirely destitute of truth."[211]

Norton's superior, Captain J. Bird, also scouted the area and talked to the locals, but found no Indians. Lieutenant Rains investigated, forced the locals to take him where the Indians were and where the stock was allegedly stolen or killed. The whites "failed completely to show any sign," and Rains believed "their reports to have been mere fabrications."[212]

Commanding Fort Moniac in East Florida, Captain Ephraim K. Barnum, 2nd Infantry, assessed the situation and concluded that "many if not all of these alarms originate in persons who create them from interested motives." A local woman, exasperated with the lazy locals, said that if only they "would go to work and make their crops there would not be so much talk of Indians." Barnum said, "The men prefer to receive pay and subsistence from the government for the performance of very little service, to cultivating their farms, and so long as volunteers are received into the service...so

---

[210] ANC, V. 7, No. 16 (October 18, 1838), 252.

[211] Norton to Barnum, March 15, 1840, AGO, RG 94, M567, R0218.

[212] Bird to Barnum, March 22, 1840, Barnum to Twiggs, April 5, 1840, AGO, RG 94, M567, R0218 (quotation).

long will the excitement in this part of the country be kept up."[213]

The civilians protested when the army dismissed their wolf-cries. When an alleged murder occurred, mail contractor William C. Taylor was "convinced that no one else is to blame" except the disbelieving Colonel Zachary Taylor. The contractor insisted that the colonel placed no value on white lives, because where he stationed his men to guard the mail "is of no more use or service than ten pine stumps would be." Colonel Taylor defended his actions, saying the civilian howling was entirely without foundation, made "with the sole purpose of having mounted troops mustered in…not for service but for pay, [and] must be resisted as one of the means to be adopted for putting an end to this disastrous war."[214]

With the end of the Second Seminole War in August 1842, the wolf-criers lost their usual suspects, but this did not change old habits. The following year inhabitants of northern Florida still wailed about murderous Indians. Brigadier General William J. Worth denounced a "miserable sheet published at Jacksonville" currently making the rounds of the press, announcing numerous Indian outrages in the area. An attempted murder of a woman in Newnansville "in the midst of a thick population and at noon day was clearly…not the work of Indians." Since the war ended a year before, "not an outrage or offensive act has been committed by Indians."[215]

War or no war, apparently nothing would prevent whites from spreading false alarms. From 1815 to the very end of our time frame in 1845, and from Florida to Wisconsin Territory, white settlers' behavior had not changed. Governor Henry Dodge wanted the army to move the Winnebagoes out of the territory because of petitioners accusing the Indians of depredations. Lieutenant Ferdinand S. Mumford, 1st Infantry, in command at Fort Winnebago, replied that removal would need the sanction of the war department, and added that he had traveled for sixty miles in all directions

---

213   Barnum to Twiggs, March 23, 1840, AGO, RG 94, M567, R0218.
214   W. Taylor to Poinsett, March 25, 1840, AGO, RG 94, M567, R0218 ("to blame" and "pine stumps" quotations); Z. Taylor to Poinsett, April 14, 1840, AGO, RG 94, M567, R0218 ("disastrous war" quotation).
215   Worth to Jones, TPUS, June 19, 1843, V. 26, 665–66.

around the fort "and never have met a single individual who was in any way aggrieved by an Indian, all the old settlers represent the Indians as peaceable and well disposed." The new settlers arriving from the East were edgy, "and the sight of an Indian fills them with apprehension."[216]

On July 15, settlers at Fox Lake petitioned Mumford that fifty to one hundred Indians "fired rifles at a house and were committing every species of depredations," and they expected an attack at any minute. Mumford took thirty-six men, made a forced march of twenty-eight miles in one day, and the next morning found the Indians. There were two of them quietly paddling a canoe near a beaver dam on Fox Lake. A perturbed Mumford "expressed to the citizens my dissatisfaction at their exaggerated statement and unwarrantable call for protection." A Mr. Cruden had been selling liquor to a several Indian men and women. When one woman wanted more, an argument ensued, and "Cruden knocked her down with a club." A drunken row took place between Cruden and his companions and the Indians. Fearful of retaliation, Cruden and his friends embellished the story and cried for the army to save them.[217] Lieutenant Mumford learned what George Washington knew six decades earlier: lawless, aggressive, greedy whites caused most of conflicts with the Indians.

---

[216]   Dodge to Crawford, July 7, 1845, TPUS, V. 28, 854–55; Mumford to Dodge, July 20, 1845, TPUS, V. 28, 863 (quotations).
[217]   Mumford to Dodge, July 20, 1845, TPUS, V. 28, 863–64.

THE FRONTIERSMEN WHO
CRIED FOR WELFARE

"Put His Lancet in and Bleed the Treasury"

Americans have an image of themselves as rugged individualists, utilitarian, practical people who pulled themselves up by
their own bootstraps and succeeded in the world through their own
initiative, intelligence, and drive. Nearly everyone, from the educated capitalists to the untutored backwoodsmen, allegedly had a
laissez-faire belief that governments must abstain from interfering
in the workings of the free market. Certainly many of the patri-
cians accepted the metaphor in Scottish economist and philosopher
Adam Smith's 1776 book, *Wealth of Nations*, that an "invisible hand"
guided self-interested individuals through a system of mutual inter-
dependence to promote the general benefit of society. Ben Franklin
apparently agreed, exposing his darker side in 1780 when he argued
that nature should run its course. Society was divided by two types
of people, he claimed, those who "live comfortably in Good Houses" and those who "are poor and dirty and ragged and vicious and
live in miserable Cabins and garrets." The idle must simply "go without or
starve."[218]

That face of Franklin is usually not found in schoolbooks,
and, thankfully, that attitude was not how the government initially
viewed its role in preserving peace and tranquility. The laissez-faire
model ran concurrently with the traditional Christian principle that
man was his brother's keeper. It took some decades for the incorporation of America to replace concepts of the nourishing garden with
the callous machine, and the rationalization that greed, after all, had
its advantages. While almost all the later business leaders denied the
Darwin-Spencer concepts of evolution, they did accept the related
substantiating notion that only the fittest would survive. The idea
that Americans were Americans because of their perseverance and

---

[218]   Franklin to Bache, September 25, 1780, in Isenberg, *White Trash*, 76.

hard work was part of a cherished myth.

Of course, the economy and the people occasionally needed a generous helping hand from the government, but many relegated those circumstances to aberrant times such as the Great Depression of the twentieth century. The true history of relief assistance, however, was explained by President Franklin Roosevelt's New Deal spokesman, Harry Hopkins, while lobbying for the Social Security Act in 1937. Hopkins showed that welfare was nothing new in America. Federal money was always available "to relieve the distress of individuals," and there were more than one hundred acts of Congress, dating back to 1803, to "provide special subsidies or concessions to help groups of citizens recover from disaster or other circumstances." This was not official generosity, but policies "to promote the general welfare in accordance with the Constitution."[219] It turns out that the government was a safety net and welfare provider since the early years of the republic, and its rugged individualist populace were frequent beneficiaries of its largesse.

The War of 1812 was a close-run affair, with the fledgling United States hovering on the brink of bankruptcy and defeat, yet on the eve of the conflict, America sent $50,000 to aid sufferers from an earthquake in Venezuela. Three years later it provided "indefinite" funding to assist the victims of the New Madrid earthquake, wherein many "sufferers" promptly found ways to steal from the hand that helped them.[220]

During the War of 1812, Congress allowed, in addition to the soldiers' monthly pay, a stipend of forty cents per day for officers, and twenty-five cents per day for others who used their own horses. The act provided compensation for horses killed in battle, but not if lost from accident, over-work, starvation, or theft. The war was not yet over when men of Andrew Jackson's Creek expedition and William H. Harrison's Canadian invasion sent claims to the government for loss of their horses. In the latter, the troops left their horses near Lake Erie in a large enclosed wood, figuring they could fend for

---

[219]   Michelle Landis Dauber, *The Sympathetic State: Disaster Relief and the Origins of the American Welfare State* (Chicago: University of Chicago Press, 2013), 9, 46, 86. In 1803 and 1804, Congress granted funds for "sufferers by fire" in Portsmouth, New Hampshire, and Norfolk, Virginia.

[220]   Dauber, *Sympathetic State*, 46.

themselves. They were gone for five weeks, however, and returned to find the horses injured or dead. The U. S. was not liable for the men's neglect.[221] It was an early example of calling on the government for relief, as well as another attempt to defraud it. The con was ongoing. During the Second Seminole conflict, War Secretary Joel Poinsett complained that volunteers colluded to affirm that their horses were appraised "at the exorbitant price of three hundred dollars," while none were even worth half that amount.[222]

When the War of 1812 ended there was a rush of claims for government assistance and compensation for alleged losses. For example, in 1815, Judge Harry Toulmin wanted assistance for militia that had left their homes to go to war—they had already been paid for their service, but he said they needed more. "It is true," Toulmin admitted, "that the losses of some may have been over rated," and "impositions may have been practiced," but abuses shouldn't negate the principle of compensation. Five Mississippi counties wanted $128,000 for alleged Indian depredations, and Toulmin believed it was "wonderful" that it was not three times that amount, and that the settlers' losses should not be dismissed as the fortunes of war, for such a taciturn attempt to sooth adversity "falls far short of what might be expected from the American or the Christian character."[223]

Toulmin subsequently begged another point. He understood that the law prohibited illegal intruders on public lands, but the government had "no conception of the distress which numberless poor families will endure." They were "broken down" after traveling through the wilderness, and it would be "a merciless stroke upon them" to drive them out. "It is true the law literally prohibited such settlements," the judge conceded, but he argued that the spirit and intent of the law was really meant "to strengthen these settlements."[224] Toulmin's rationalization that a law explicitly prohibiting illegal settlers really invited illegal settlers apparently was a notion shared by many.

---

[221]   Yancey to House of Representatives, December 5, 1814, *American State Papers, Claims*, V. 1, 443–44. (Hereinafter cited as ASPC.)

[222]   Poinsett to Jesup, December 2, 1837, ASPMA, V. 7, 855.

[223]   Toulmin to Lattimore, December 1815, TPUS, V. 6, 586–90.

[224]   Toulmin to Lattimore, December 28, 1815, TPUS, V. 6, 631.

The begging was unashamed when the Missouri Territorial assembly petitioned Congress in 1816. The people claimed to have lost much in the war, and even had to defend themselves from the "savage host" with their own money and supplies. As for specifics, it was "too painful to your memorialists to recapitulate," but, take their word, it really happened. "They do not ask the General Government to make the sufferers rich," but perhaps "a quarter section of land to each sufferer would not be thought an unreasonable compensation."[225]

One might question the patriotism of Americans who would not defend themselves without being paid. On the other hand, some states zealously raised militia and billed the government. Virginia, Delaware, New Hampshire, New York, and Massachusetts were investigated for raising more men than required, raising men when there was no emergency, raising men without authority, and asking for additional pay.[226] Two states raised troops, but would not let them fight, hoping to appear neutral to the British for their own protection. "It really is a fact—" editorialized the *Niles Weekly Register*, "strange as it may appear, that the states of Massachusetts and Connecticut are seriously engaged to prosecute certain claims against the United States for *the services of their militia in the late war!* We were not prepared for this—to use a sheer Yankee phrase, 'it bangs every thing'—first, to disobey the orders of the general government, and then claim an indemnity for the cost of the act of disobedience!"[227]

Not only the states tried to bilk the government—the citizens were often the most boisterous and demanding. The idea that Americans had a right to petition the United States for compensation for famine, flood, disaster, and war caught on early and was the beginning of what has come to be known as the Welfare State. Most Americans assume compensation is a comparatively recent phenomenon. For example, the Victim Compensation Fund (VCF) organized in the wake of the September 11, 2001, terrorist attacks, soon came under fire as being "unprecedented" in American history, since the standard belief was that direct payments from the feder-

---

[225]   Caldwell et al., to Congress, January 25, 1816, TPUS, V. 15, 196.

[226]   Crawford to Clay, March 7, 1816, ASPMA, V. 1, 639.

[227]   NWR, January 18, 1817, V. 11, No. 21, 337–38.

al treasury to relieve "sufferers" from calamities was immoral in a country saturated by a contrary myth of rugged individualism. Actually, since the early republic, Federalists, Whigs, Democrats, and Republicans viewed federal relief for blameless victims as constitutionally unproblematic. Law Professor Michelle Dauber concluded that the 2001 VCF was "strikingly similar" to the commission established for the relief of the victims of the War of 1812.[228]

That commission was created primarily as a result of the British destruction of Buffalo, New York, in December 1813 and January 1814. The *Buffalo Gazette* cried out that the people "will burn with indignation, not to be quenched, until that government...shall amply remunerate their losses, by a prompt and honorable liquidation of their claims."[229] The newspaper clamored for action, not because there was no vehicle for redress, but because the government was not making payments fast enough. The commission was sanctioned by "An Act to Authorize the Payment for Property Lost, Captured, or Destroyed by the Enemy, While in the Military Service of the United States, and for Other Purposes." Passed on April 9, 1816, and headed by Richard Bland Lee of Virginia, it approved compensation for various property lost, including horses, wagons, and houses. The houses, however, had to be destroyed by the enemy "while the same was occupied as a military deposit, under the authority of an officer or agent of the United States."[230]

Lee and his commissioners collected testimony and paid claims. Operating with a loose interpretation of the Act, Lee figured it was his job to make as many liberal payments as quickly as possible, and with little regard for questionable testimony. Between July and December 1816, Lee made 850 decisions and awarded more than $229,000, the majority of the claims being minor ones for animals and personal property. The section that posed the biggest problem was the one dealing with compensation for houses damaged or destroyed while occupied pursuant to officers' orders; these claims were much more expensive, often exceeding $10,000 each. The Brit-

---

[228] Michelle L. Dauber, *The War of 1812, September 11th and the Politics of Compensation*, V. 53, DePaul Law Revue (2013), 289, 293–94, 340.

[229] *Buffalo Gazette*, January 28, 1817, in Dauber, *Politics of Compensation*, 289.

[230] Dauber, *Politics of Compensation*, 296–97.

ish had burned entire towns in New York and Maryland, unoccupied and containing no military caches. How could the claimants recover their losses? They merely produced proof that was nonexistent for the most part, and Lee helped them by allowing them to make a simple oath in lieu of evidence.[231]

Dishonesty is stronger than an oath. When payments skyrocketed, President Madison and War Secretary William Crawford quickly sought to rein in Lee, criticizing him for being much too generous in his interpretation of the Act, for example, paying for claims for partial injuries to oxen or horses, or $175 to one man for trampled crops.[232] Particularly suspect were the hundreds of claims flowing in from Buffalo, where there were not enough officers, soldiers, and supply deposits to occupy a fraction of the houses claimed to have been damaged. Lee, however, let the claimants' oaths suffice, although he admitted neighbors could "magnify each others' losses" to boost their rewards. A second problem was that Lee discovered that New York had already paid out $50,000 in relief funds, giving the Niagara sufferers "a two-fold compensation...for the same injury." When he forecast a payoff of nearly half a million dollars by the end of 1816, the president and the treasury department rebelled.[233]

By December, the Committee of Claims criticized Lee and his "erroneous decisions," recommended a repeal of some of the act's provisions, and transferred settlement decisions to the war department.[234] While the edifice crumbled, Buffalo claimants insisted the rules of the Act were too narrow, and they deserved even more payments. To avoid a "disgraceful squabble," they believed they should be compensated based on "sacred principles of union and equality." Unwittingly, they had exposed Lee and their own dishonesty. Their homes were never occupied and Lee had "accepted perjured testimony based on some vague principles of sympathy and the social contract."[235]

---

[231]   Dauber, *Politics of Compensation*, 306–308.

[232]   NWR, January 11, 1817, V. 11, No. 20, 329; Dauber, *Politics of Compensation*, 319.

[233]   Dauber, *Politics of Compensation*, 312–14.

[234]   Yancey to House of Representatives, December 17, 1816, ASPC, V. 1, 486–87.

[235]   Dauber, *Politics of Compensation*, 323.

Some were not ready to admit public welfare was part of the social contract. John Randolph of Virginia argued in Congress that the United States had been "most shamefully and scandalously plundered, under pretense of equitable claims, to the amount of some forty, fifty, or sixty thousand dollars," and every other person was being "allowed to put his lancet in and bleed the Treasury. If the public veins contained more blood than Leviathan himself," Randolph said, "it would not satisfy them all."[236] Special agents were appointed to look for fraud, but it was so extensive and woven into the fabric of the claims it could not be ferreted out. In 1818, the Committee of Claims castigated the Buffalo claimants, concluding they had perpetrated a massive "system of fraud, forgery, and perhaps perjury."[237]

The situation was not resolved until 1825, when another bill allowed resubmission of claims and capped compensation at $250,000, divided among all the claimants, leaving few fully satisfied. Comparing the 1816 and 2001 situations, Professor Dauber argued that a moral trajectory is inherent in the nature of compensation: after a time "claimants are transformed from virtuous to grasping, from deserving of charity to worthy of suspicion." In public estimation, blameless victims can quickly become greedy swindlers.[238] Although many indeed lost property in the War of 1812, a great proportion of them used the opportunity to defraud the government in a process not unlike current home and auto insurance fraud. It seemed that opposition to remunerations stemmed less from philosophical principles of laissez-faire, than from resentment that the pie was not large enough for everyone to get a piece. The idea that one could get money by falsely accusing Indians of depredations, with little demand for proof and no penalty for lying, was a seed planted with the TIA. The 1815 Earthquake Act and the 1816 Property Loss Act were the fertilizer. Their germination consumed the dogma shared by men such as Paine, Jefferson, Jackson, and Thoreau, that the government is best which governs least.

---

[236]   *Annals of Congress,* 14th Congress, 2nd Session, December 1816, 387–88.

[237]   Dauber, *Politics of Compensation,* 335.

[238]   Dauber, *Politics of Compensation,* 335–36, 348.

Salus Populi

T he belief that the antebellum United States was a land of anti-government individuals, relying on the invisible hand in a free
market, with few regulations, was simply another myth of American
exceptionalism—and a late comer. Early America was a well-regulated society, combining tradition, public spirit, local self-govern-
ment, and adherence to law. Private interest was subservient to the
public welfare. It was distilled in the phrase, *salus populi suprema lex est*
(the welfare of the people is the supreme law). The government existed to protect the people; laws were tools of regulation; regulation
was a tool for social order; the social order and the people's welfare
were the primary objects of governance.[239]

For every person who echoed Franklin's words that the idle
must "go without or starve," there were many others with a more
compassionate approach. Early on, the government realized it was
beneficial to feed the hungry, although it soon learned that such programs could become a quagmire. In March 1815, a deputation of
inhabitants from River Raisin visited Judge Augustus B. Woodward
of Detroit, pleading for help. The sympathetic jurist agreed that the
area was desolated since the war, the people had no homes and were
"obliged to resort to chopp'd hay, boiled, for subsistence." He requested provisions and seeds be sent immediately. President Madison
was supportive and authorized a fund of $1,500 worth of provisions
and other necessities.[240] The money was not nearly enough, and in
September, Governor Lewis Cass received approval "to issue to the
indigent and distressed people of the Territory" provisions from the
public stores. Requests for relief were to be made to commanding
army officers, who would investigate eligibility and issue certificates
countersigned by Catholic priests or Justices of the Peace. Three
classes of people were eligible: aged, infirm, and invalids; widows or
other women with families; and laboring men without employment

---

[239] William J. Novak, *The People's Welfare: Law and Regulation in Nineteenth
Century America* (Chapel Hill, NC: University of North Carolina Press, 1996), 7, 9,
34, 42.
[240] Woodward to Dalles, March 5, 1815, TPUS, V. 10, 513–14; Dalles to
Cass, May 25, 1815, TPUS, V. 10, 542.

or with jobs that did not pay enough to subsist a family.[241]

The categories and the intent are remarkable as they presage nearly identical classifications for assistance distributed for much of the twentieth century: Food Stamps (now SNAP); Social Security Disability; AFDC (Aid to Families with Dependent Children—now TANF—Temporary Assistance for Needy Families); and AFDCU (Aid to Families with Dependent Children/Unemployed Parent). The argument continues over whether these programs are an entitlement or a temporary help for families to achieve self-sufficiency, just as it did after the War of 1812. By May of 1816, War Secretary Crawford told Governor Cass that enough time had elapsed, and since "things must have now returned to their regular channels," it was time to stop issuing provisions.[242]

Easier said than done. Governor Cass complied, but asked Crawford to explain to the president "the extreme distress, which must result from now withdrawing the bounty of the Government." The problem, in Cass's estimation, was that there were too many Canadians! Their "moral character" was in question because they were descendants of fur traders and Voyageurs who never properly learned to work farms, were now unemployed, and spent much of their time in "indolence and amusement." The few established farms "shew the extreme defect of agricultural knowledge. The spinning wheel and the loom are unknown in the Country." The people threw away sheep wool, did not care to learn how to make soap, and did not even know what to do with their manure. "I could go on," Cass wrote, "pointing out to you their ignorance of the most common acts of domestic life," but he believed Crawford would think he was rude and exaggerating. His solution was to dilute this "indigent and helpless people" by a migration of morally and physically strong Americans from the states. As it was, with a low tax base and few resources, Cass could "not maintain one person in ten...who must depend upon publick [sic] charity for support." He immediately needed "two hundred rations per day of meat, bread and Salt" to

---

[241]   Regulations for Administration of Relief, September 23, 1815, TPUS, V. 10, 645–46.
[242]   Crawford to Cass, May 7, 1816, TPUS, V. 10, 633.

Lewis Cass. *Library of Congress*
Cass could be hardline with regard to feeding the Indians, but
he did want welfare assistance
for indigent whites.

prevent a state of wretchedness among them.[243]

Crawford declared that provisions could no longer be supplied; continuing to distribute food would only protract "the helpless state" of the people. "If we supply all their wants gratuitously there is but little probability that they will make the necessary exertions to help themselves."[244]

Americans accepted the idea of a social contract, but were already hesitating to include "foreigners" and their own "indolent" citizens. Some said the social contract was only an opportunity to milk the State, a view that appeared sustained when claims of depredations, damages, and pleas for compensation flowed in from all corners of the land. Hearing that money was being paid to folks on the Niagara frontier, Michiganders from River Raisin to the St. Clair River affirmed that they were also victims of "distresses and sufferings, the remembrance of which can never be obliterated from their minds." Certainly the British and Indians caused death and destruction, but these citizens wanted remuneration for damages caused by the United States troops who turned their houses into barracks or stables, cut down their fences, stripped their orchards, and seized their grain. When their claims were first rejected, the petitioners changed tactics. They insisted they were not seeking "the

---

[243]   Cass to Crawford, May 31, 1816, TPUS, V. 10, 642–44. For comparison, in 2016, Michigan had about 39,000 TANF recipients out of a population of about ten million, or .39%. In 1816, Detroit's population was only about 850. Cass said he would need two hundred rations per day, meaning 23% of the people were on assistance. Cass also speculated "that the evil is to increase" because the drought and cold ruined the crops. 1816 was called "the year without a summer" because of the extreme weather conditions in many parts of Europe and North America, the result of the Tambora volcano eruption in 1815.
[244]   Crawford to Cass, July 2, 1816, TPUS, V. 10, 658.

bounty or the charity of their Country,—no—they ask, as American Citizens… nothing but their rights.—Rights founded in the Social Contract,—on the broad principles of political justice, and express-ly guaranteed to them by the constitution of their Country." Peter Hagner, a treasury department auditor appointed in the wake of Lee's excesses, denied their claims; their appeal to a social contract may have been philosophically edifying, but it was not spelled out in the act's provisions.[245]

The idea that government welfare was a right had taken root, and it ran as a parallel riptide under the weaker surface current of laissez-faire. All across the frontier people wanted in on the deal. Citizens of Missouri Territory argued that since they were on the border during the war, they experienced great hardship and suffer-ing. There was so much danger that they spent much of the war en-sconced in forts and were "debarred the advantages enjoyed by their fellow-citizens elsewhere, of cultivating the soil for their necessary subsistence." Missourians were aware of the situation elsewhere, be-lieved "the bounty of Congress has not been extended to all who merit it," and in compensation, they asked that all the people who bore arms in the war should have the right of one free quarter-sec-tion of land.[246] The paradoxical statements that people who hid be-hind fort walls also shouldered arms to fight the enemy apparently were not challenged.

Pleas to the federal government for assistance were sundry and incessant: the states and territories wanted public buildings, roads, canals, lighthouses; they wanted swamps drained, rivers bridged, harbors dredged, surveys, railroads, mail routes, more forts, more protection, free land, widows and orphans pensions, and plen-ty of compensation for any perceived injuries or affronts. In 1817, Congress passed an act to pay the widows and children of soldiers, militia, and volunteers half of their prior pay for five years.[247] In

---

[245]   Michigan Citizens to Congress, February 7, 1820, TPUS, V. 11, 7–9; Hagner to Crawford, February 29, 1820, TPUS, V. 11, 12. The Michigan Legis-lature again petitioned Congress for compensation in 1826 and in 1834.

[246]   Missouri Citizens to Congress, March 14, 1820, TPUS, V. 15, 595.

[247]   *Statutes at Large*, March 3, 1817, 14th Congress, 2nd Session, V. 3, 394–95.

1822, Congress passed an act to reimburse soldiers, militia, and volunteers who fought in the Seminole War for the loss of any guns, horses, or equipment.[248] In 1832, Congress passed an act to raise volunteers to fight in the Black Hawk War, promising to compensate them for wounds or disabilities, and the following year passed an act to reimburse all of them for the loss of horses, guns, or equipment.[249] There were scores of similar acts passed to reimburse losses, compensate for suffering, pay for alleged depredations, feed the hungry, or rebuild after fires or other disasters, including funds for "sufferers by fire" at Alexandria, Virginia, in 1827; and even an 1820 act to aid "Distressed American seamen in foreign countries."[250]

In 1826, petitioners in East Florida jumped on the bandwagon and argued that back in 1812, they too had "suffered greatly by the invasion and occupation" of marauding Georgians. Incredibly, they prayed that Congress would ascertain how much they had lost and "provide for the speedy payment." The Committee of Foreign Relations responded that the memorialists provided no evidence, nor should they bother, for they had no claim against the United States and acceded that their judgment would be unfavorable before any investigation could begin.[251]

By 1828, it was apparent that Americans were comfortable with soliciting "the Humanity of Congress for support." The people of Wayne County, Michigan Territory, said that there were too many unproductive invalids, paupers, widows, orphans, and ex-soldiers and sailors in the neighborhood. Worse yet, "two thirds of the paupers" were emigrants, "and a great share of the other third are foreigners." The petitioners said that all frontier people "may well

---

[248]   *Statutes at Large,* May 4, 1822, 17th Congress, 1st Session, V. 3, 676.

[249]   *Statutes at Large,* June 15, 1832, 22nd Congress, 1st Session, V. 4, 533; *Statutes at Large,* February 19, 1833, *22*nd Congress, 2nd Session, V. 4, 613.

[250]   Dauber, *Sympathetic State,* 4–5, 46, 60. In 1931, Wisconsin Senator Robert M. La Follette, Jr., tried to convince President Hoover to aid the suffering people, citing (incorrectly) the appropriations for victims of the 1827 Alexandria fire as the first instance of Federal disaster relief. Refusing to aid victims of the 1930s Depression, said La Follette, would be the true "violation of traditional American policy."

[251]   Forsyth to House of Representatives, March 10, 1826, ASPFR, V. 5, 829.

imagine the heavy Burthen a horde of Paupers must be to such a Community." Apparently churches and charitable donors were insufficient. Wayne County needed a poorhouse but the citizens would not build one at their own expense. "Therefore to relieve the distressed, to lighten that oppressive tax and to make an Asylum for the poor Soldier, Sailor, or Emigrant," they asked Congress to give them the land and the money.[252]

When, in 1832, the good people of Michigan heard "the cry for succor" echoing from Illinois, they felt it was also their duty to fight the Indian hordes of Black Hawk. G. Mott Williams, representing the militia, explained that every patriotic tradesman, mechanic, and farmer left home to pick up a rifle. "The waste & harvestless fields... amply attest to the public spirit of the Citizens of Michigan." These hardy souls, said Williams, endured suffering without military equipment and stores, and performed forced marches over impassable roads while "personal interest & convenience were forgotten." They were motivated solely by helping people in distress, and it was not their fault that the war ended before they arrived. Although they mustered out only twelve days after they mustered in, apparently they faced so many hardships that Williams demanded that these poor men receive adequate recompense from the nation's "overflowing coffers." Twelve day's pay would hardly cover the cost of a blanket, so "this pittance will be rejected with contempt. Nothing less than a month's pay would be worth accepting." The department would not grant the request.[253]

Two more applications surfaced in Arkansas Territory in 1830. Squatters, it was said, had no means of defense from "fearless and vindictive savages." Additional preemption rights supposedly would remedy this by giving them a reason to defend themselves; apparently if they had homes, the "bold and the fearless" would rear "a hardy race of sons" and secure the wilderness. After all, "Other countries have made donations to her settlers," the pe-

---

[252]   Michigan Citizens to Congress, November 29, 1828, TPUS, V. 11, 1218.

[253]   Williams to Cass, December 8, 1832, TPUS, V. 12, 554–55. In February 1833, Congress did pass another reimbursement act for property lost in service, but not for time off from work.

titioners argued, so why not us?[254] Another plea surfaced only a few weeks later, with the usual call for protection from savages who were "appeased only by human blood," but this time preemption would not be enough: "nothing but a dense population will secure to us peace and safety." This bizarre argument suggested that because Indians killed settlers, the remedy would be to place more settlers in proximity to the Indians. Every man who settled within twenty-four miles of the frontier was to be given one-quarter section of free land; thus, "A barrier of bold and hardy pioneers will be established."[255]

Arkansas submitted another compensation application in 1832. This time the memorialists complained that "relentless Cherokees, who, fond of wreaking their vengeance upon the white man," had driven squatters from their homes. Although the episode allegedly occurred fifteen years earlier, they wanted compensation now. The Committee on Public Lands was incredulous: "Congress is now asked to indemnify men, not named or numbered, for improvements, not valued or known, made upon the public lands against [the] law."[256] Apparently there were few schemes bold enough that hardy pioneers would not try in order to collect a government handout.

Mississippi Territory Representative F. E. Plummer well understood that the Trade and Intercourse Acts forbade intruders from squatting on Indian lands, but he also used the poor-whites-deserve-a-break argument. The illegals had spent "their *little all* in getting there," and they could not feed their wives and children without first harvesting their crops and making "a manly resistance." Plummer said it was true that the federal government was the legitimate landlord "and she has the right to remove all intruders," but states' rights should take precedence in all land disputes. Let the Indians, Plummer demanded, redress their grievances in the state courts.[257] The chance of an Indian winning a court decision was slim—the chances of an Indian ever appearing in court was slim. The Cherokees

---

[254] Arkansas to Congress, January 11, 1830, ASPPL, V. 6, 33.

[255] Arkansas to Congress, February 1, 1830, ASPPL, V. 6, 136.

[256] Wickliffe to House of Representatives, February 21, 1832, ASPPL, V. 6, 389.

[257] Plummer to Cass, May 22, 1832, USCSS, V. 3, 363.

explained it precisely. Their white neighbors stole their cattle and the Cherokees gave chase, "but all that they can effect is to see their cattle snugly kept in the lots of these robbers." The whites had no regard for the laws of humanity, but reaped "a plentiful harvest" through the law of the state, "which declares that no Indian shall be a party in any court created by the laws or constitution of that state."[258] They felt abused, and doubly so when the states refused the legal right of redress. If they could not work through the courts, the only other recourse was

Winfield Scott. *Public domain*
General Scott angered Floridians when he disparaged them for seeing "an Indian in every bush."

filing through the TIA, but that process could take years, as it was overloaded with false or exaggerated claims against Indians. White Americans could take succor from a generous government; people of color would have to wait a little longer.

"A disease in the public mind"

The question about the limits of government responsibility continued in Florida. Within weeks of the start of the Second Seminole War in December 1835, hundreds of pioneer families had fled their homes. General Scott viewed the evacuation as unnecessary: "The panics which have recently possessed the good people of several large districts of this Territory are infinitely humiliating." Scott said that the people saw "an Indian in every bush, and therefore continued to fly." He protested that "no General, even with extensive means, can cure a disease in the public mind, so general and so degrading, without some little effort on the part of the people themselves." Scott's derisive Order No. 48, issued May 17, 1836, mocked and shocked the Florida settlers enough that the government felt

---

258   NWR, June 27, 1829, V. 12, No. 18, 287.

it necessary to issue a rebuke.[259] Army officers may have harbored similar opinions for years, but they were not supposed to make their feelings public.

Hundreds, perhaps thousands, of dislocated families presented the army with additional problems of how to feed and shelter them. Individual charity never had been a viable solution to large-scale adversity. As early as February 1, 1836, Congress passed a resolution that authorized "rations to be delivered from the public stores to the unfortunate sufferers, who are unable to provide for themselves, and who have been driven from their homes by Indian depredations in Florida."[260] Each "white person" over age fourteen would get a full army ration, which then consisted of 1 ¼ pounds of beef or ¾ pound of pork, eighteen ounces of bread, four pounds of coffee and eight pounds of sugar per one hundred, four quarts of vinegar per one hundred, and two quarts of salt per one hundred. Whites under age fourteen got a half ration. "Colored persons" over age fourteen got only a ration of meat, bread, and salt, while those under age fourteen got a half ration. All claimants had to go to the post officer and prove they were "unfortunate sufferers" who had been driven from their homes by Indians. The officer was to keep a record of their "names, ages, sex, color, and condition," and could stop issuance if he thought the "provisions would be wasted, or improperly applied." Sufferers had to apply at the post nearest to where they resided "in order to prevent persons from drawing double rations."[261]

It did not take long before the abuse began. War Secretary Cass learned that people of "means, either in cash, in slaves, in land, or in other species of property" were drawing on government stores. Florida Territory governor Richard K. Call believed the women and children should be moved to distant locations and provided with food and shelter; only then would the men "more willingly engage

---

[259]   ANC, V. 2, No. 24 (June 16, 1836), 377.

[260]   *Statutes at Large,* February 1, 1836, 24th Congress, 1st Session, V. 5, 131.

[261]   "U.S. Army Ration 1830s," http://regimentalrogue.tripod.com/blog/index.blog/2355705/us-army-ration-1830s/; ANC, V. 2, No. 6 (February 11, 1836), 95–96.

in the service" to fight the Indians.[262]

Men shirked service while families "double-dipped" for free provisions. By August 1837, the food was running out as the government tried to assist legitimate sufferers while weeding out the cheaters. The object of Congress was "to succor the immediate wants of a people," said War Secretary Poinsett, but "not to continue during the whole war to maintain them gratuitously" so they would have no motivation to go back to their farms. He declared that by October 1, 1837, provision distribution must cease.[263]

The government learned again that once it has provided a service to the people it is very hard to take it away. One month before the program's end date, a new commission evaluated the situation and added new restrictions: food would only be given to those who could prove they were unable to return to their farms; owners and employees of liquor or gambling establishments could no longer collect; all able-bodied men who refused the work offered were refused rations, except for their families with "children under fourteen years of age, and negroes under ten years." Most of the food recipients in the towns were removed from the rolls—fifty families from St. Augustine alone—the reasoning being that their condition was not rendered worse by the war, but the war had actually benefited them.[264]

The struggle was endless. In 1839, Poinsett harangued General Taylor to do something about the cheaters. He heard perpetual complaints that people with sufficient means were nevertheless "drawing rations for themselves, families and negroes." He told Taylor to scour the rolls, strike out the swindlers, inform the agents to guard their supplies, and use "constant vigilance to prevent a recurrence of similar frauds."[265]

Government efforts notwithstanding, there were those who managed to obtain aid until the end of the Seminole War in 1842. With the conflict winding down, petitioners were still crying for

---

[262]   Cass to White, April 15, 1836, TPUS, V. 25, 275; Call to Cass, April 28, 1836, TPUS, V. 25, 281.

[263]   Poinsett to Jesup, August 3, 1837, TPUS, V. 25, 411.

[264]   ANC, V. 5, No. 17 (October 26, 1837), 269.

[265]   Poinsett to Taylor, May 30, 1839, TPUS, V. 25, 613.

compensation. East Florida planters claimed their lands were ruined by the "unrelenting savage" who reduced them from wealth "to their present unhappy and impoverished condition." They asked that Congress create a commission to ascertain the amount of losses they sustained from the Indians as well as the army, losses they estimated to be about $2.5 million. The petitioners also wanted the Treasury to immediately issue scrip to them as a means of liquidating the claims—the scrip to draw interest of six percent from the date of the alleged property destruction. As collateral, the government could have all the public land in Florida it needed—which it already owned.[266]

Another land giveaway occurred in Florida in 1842. The Second Seminole War had been ongoing for more than six years and scores of schemes and solutions to end it had been unsuccessful. One stratagem was to allow the Indians to live unmolested south of a line drawn from Tampa Bay east to New Smyrna, and encourage hundreds of armed and determined settlers to occupy land to the north, creating a buffer zone. The idea had already been suggested in several states and territories. Missouri Senator Thomas Hart Benton was a proponent of settler expansion and believed yeoman farmers would protect the area from Indians, but Northern legislators believed that small farmers would not go to Florida—instead, the act would only attract big planters and spread slavery. They also believed that continued government giveaways might create a nation of dependents. If you gave away three million acres in Florida it would set a precedent for giving land away everywhere.[267]

One of Benton's allies, Surgeon General Thomas Lawton, believed Florida's climate was not as unhealthy as detractors said, and it had plenty of arable land. He said that the establishment of "Military Colonies" would end the war. Instead of the army searching the swamps for the Seminoles, they would emerge "and attack the whites within their lines of defense, and where the skill and intelligence of the civilized man can have its influence." Lawton be-

---

[266]   Planters to Congress, March 1, 1842, TPUS, V. 26, 454–56.

[267]   John K. Mahon, *History of the Second Seminole War 1835–1842* (Gainesville, FL: University of Florida Press, 1967), 313–14; *Congressional Globe*, Appendix, 25th Congress, 3rd Session, February 26, 1839, V. 7, No. 13, 202.

lieved that was how the West "was won from the Savages." Hardy pioneers "pitched their camps and built their Block Houses thro [*sic*] the Country, and there fought a little, and worked a little, until the Indians finding that they could not dislodge the white man, pulled up stakes and retired beyond the Mississippi."[268] While some officials propagated the Western myth, the army did not see the process as benign and held a more jaundiced view of the settlers' martial prowess.

Some Floridians on the other hand, said the armed occupation proposal gave them the "most fearful apprehensions." They argued that the Indians would never stay south of the line, but would murder and plunder as they always had. The only solution was to completely remove them from the territory, and to do that they needed at least ten thousand more volunteers.[269]

Government agent for the preservation of timber on public lands, Capt. Hezekiah L. Thistle, also had misgivings, but for different reasons: it was not the Indians who would cause mayhem, but the whites. The proposed act would never work because the land was a swamp, and it would only lure men who had no intention of farming, but would take all the best timber and in five years "there would not be a stick of Live-oak or cedar fit to put into a Sloop-of-war upon the whole Peninsula of Florida." Instead of giving the land away, Thistle said it should be removed from sale and saved as a naval reserve. As for removing the Indians, Thistle's plan, which he admitted "might probably be considered unpopular to the north," was to simply place "a bounty on each Indian's head." Thistle wanted Congress to pay $500 "for each Indian or Indian-negro taken prisoner & nothing for those accidentally killed," plus an award of 320 acres of good land after the Indians were gone. In addition, he believed that if Congress designated a certain number of men, furnished them with rations, arms, and ammunition for one year, "there would not be an Indian left in Florida." Apparently not wanting to sound too iniquitous, Thistle again said his method would not be popular, but it was more charitable than the proposed act which

---

268   Lawton to Benton, December 30, 1838, TPUS, V. 25, 556.

269   Citizens of St. Johns County to Congress, February 16, 1841, TPUS, V. 26, 265–66.

would be a license to kill, for if "the settlers have no inducement to save an Indian's life or take a prisoner, they would shoot them down as the wolves in the forest, & then let them lay."[270]

Thistle's plan was ultimately unacceptable, and pouring volunteers into the conflict for six years had not solved anything. Benton and his advocates won out. "An Act to provide for the armed occupation and settlement of the unsettled part of the peninsula of East Florida" was passed on August 4, 1842. For one year from that date, any man over eighteen years old capable of bearing arms could get 160 acres provided that he resided on the land for five years, built a house, and cleared five acres. The government thereby hoped to give title to up to 200,000 acres.[271]

The Act may have been a case of closing the barn door after the horses escaped, for ten days after it passed, General Worth declared the war over. Regardless, more than 1,300 permits were issued, adding about 6,500 people, or about one-tenth of Florida's entire population.[272] Thistle's concerns were borne out. Settlers moved in and ignored the Act's stipulations. They killed Indians, stole timber, provoked a major confrontation with Thistle, and caused problems for General Worth. The Act prohibited settlers from moving within two miles of a military reservation. Worth did all he could to drive off "all intruders and other persons obnoxious to the good order and discipline of the troops," but they thumbed their noses at the law. There was little recourse, short of killing them, but that was generally frowned upon.[273]

Americans swindled and begged. As Cherokee agent Return J. Meigs observed back in 1809, frontier intruders were shrewd and desperate characters who would take whatever they want and then plead it as their right, "making a merit of their crimes."[274] By the 1820s and 1830s, although a significant number of Americans had

---

[270]   Thistle to Tyler, July 8, 1842, TPUS, V. 26, 505–08.

[271]   *Statutes at Large*, August 4, 1842, 27th Congress, 2nd Session, V. 5, 502–503.

[272]   Mahon, *History of the Second Seminole War, 314*. Mahon suggested this act was the model for the Homestead Act of 1862.

[273]   Worth to Jones, May 22, 1843, TPUS, V. 26, 652.

[274]   Meigs to Eustis, October 26 and November 16, 1809, in Prucha, *American Indian Policy*, 160.

become comfortable with theft of public lands, tens of thousands of more ethical men preempted lands and actually made payments. In fact, settlers or speculators bought so much land that the United States had a problem it seldom had to contend with ever since: what to do with the excess money. While Democrats generally wanted relaxed preemption laws and Whigs wanted higher tariffs, the money flowed in from both sources. Whig Henry Clay's solution was to distribute the surplus from the land sales directly back to the states for internal improvements. There would be no need for taxes. Although the strict constructionists conjured constitutional issues of "degrading sovereign states into pensioners of the Federal government," there was something to be said for all the free welfare—as long as you labeled it otherwise.[275]

Hypocrisy was manifest in taking handouts, pretending you had not, and then cloaking it behind a façade of suffering and impoverishment. When thieving Americans got in a bind, they cried for relief. By the early National period, they were getting quite used to being aided and abetted. The storied land of rugged individuals who shunned government aid and regulation was a fairy tale. The people were fed, reimbursed, given relief, and licensed. For example, a sample of Michigan statutes in the 1830s included regulated highways, bridges, ferries, trade, sales, weights and measures, burials, public health, travel, taverns, illegitimate children, paupers, timber, water, banking, dueling, cheating, firearms, and even gunpowder. The question of gunpowder regulation was pervasive in the nineteenth century, for as production grew, so did problems of storage and usage. After many explosions and fires burnt down cities, stricter rules were needed for the manufacture, storage, and sale of gunpowder. Regulations permeated antebellum society.[276]

Americans also wanted the government to subsidize their private pursuits. Between 1789 and 1850 there were more than three hundred internal improvement acts, including 112 to construct public roads and turnpikes; 45 to build or improve harbors, dams, rivers, breakwaters, and canals; 14 to construct public buildings; 12 for railroads; 10 for bridges; and 62 for lighthouses, buoys, and beacons. In

275   Stephenson, *Political History of the Public Lands,* 28–31.

276   Novak, *People's Welfare,* 15–16, 59, 62.

1847, Congress even passed an act to provide relief for those suffering because of the Potato Famine in Ireland. One historian reported that by mid-century, it had passed about fifty relief bills for various issues from grasshoppers, to floods, to Indian wars.[277]

There were many more. Congress passed about 1,960 laws, statutes, and acts, both public and private, to aid the suffering and needy, as well as those perhaps not so deserving, including 389 pre-emptions and land grants, 187 issues of bounty lands for veterans, 369 military pensions, 117 pensions for widows and orphans, 156 invalid pensions, 265 acts to remunerate for horses and property lost, fifteen fire relief acts, three earthquake relief acts, and eight poor relief acts. The scope of payments was remarkable. There was money for citizens who lost property due to the Whiskey Rebellion in Pennsylvania, relief for insolvent debtors, payment of funeral expenses to widows, relief for the family of Oliver Hazard Perry, payment to ex-Indian captives, bounties to U. S. citizens who lived in Canada and sided with the U. S. during the War of 1812, land grants to illegal settlers to remove them from Indian land, pensions to executors of deceased pensioners, relief for Canadian refugees, land grants for Polish exiles, food for sufferers from Indian attacks, relief for paupers and the insane, relief to sufferers in Santo Domingo during the Haitian Revolution, ransoms for captives of Algerian pirates, relief for workmen for tools lost in a fire, payment for use of a house as a hospital, damages for the erection of a dam, payment for destroyed tobacco, and payment for a drowned horse. None of this includes the additional money paid out in depredation claims filed under the TIA. Americans were very compensated by their government.[278]

As historian William Novak noted, people of the nineteenth century had a vision of a well-regulated society far into the postbellum years, but that past has been nearly erased. Many conservatives today still posit a young nation of minimal government, low taxes, individual freedoms, self-interested entrepreneurs, and laissez-faire economics, but "such a world never existed."[279]

These were myths to help us transform the frontiersman-pi-

---

[277]   Dauber, *Sympathetic State*, 19, 30.
[278]   *Statutes at Large*, passim.
[279]   Novak, *People's Welfare*, ix, 2, 3.

oneer from something he was not, into the more formidable icon of heroic exceptionalism. There is widespread dissonance in need of rationalization when multitudes insist they do not want the government to give away free pie—unless, of course, they too can get a big slice with whipped cream on it. An open secret of many Americans is how they pretend to despise government handouts while soaking up its largesse in farm subsidies, dams, flood control, mineral rights, water rights, timber, oil, gas, coal, and even free grazing on public lands. They continue to engage in the behavior the myth repudiates. Of course, back in the good old days, handouts were much more acceptable when the recipients were overwhelmingly white men of European stock, and assistance had not yet become the pejorative "welfare" that it became once non-whites and non-European immigrants were enfolded into the assistance package.[280]

---

[280]   Ian Haney Lopez, *Dog Whistle Politics: How Coded Racism Appeals Have Reinvented Racism & Wrecked the Middle Class* (New York: Oxford University Press, 2014), 7, 31, 72.

THE FRONTIERSMEN WHO COULDN'T SHOOT STRAIGHT

"A sword in the hands of a madman":
The First Militia

Americans today have a romantic attachment to the citizen militia who fought in our colonial wars, the Revolution and the War of 1812. We often view them as homespun heroes who left their farms to take up muskets and fight the enemy, although they have been caustically described by a contemporary as "awkward boobies [who] have been taken from the ploughtail."[281] Paradoxically, they also have been styled as expert marksmen veritably born with rifles in their hands. Certainly there were small numbers of proficient gunmen, namely the famed Roger's Rangers of the French and Indian War, or Morgan's Riflemen and Francis Marion's men of the Revolution. But regardless of the exploits of Roger's Rangers, and British General Jeffrey Amherst's belief that Americans were a "nation of riflemen," he soon learned to his dismay that they had only a rudimentary knowledge of how firearms worked, how to care for them, and how to shoot.[282]

The actual record of our citizen-soldiers of two centuries ago was often less than flattering. George Washington's problems with militia were unremitting. In 1775, when the Rhode Island and Massachusetts militia threatened to leave because they would only get twelve paychecks per year instead of the thirteen on a lunar cal-

---

[281]   Robert Coram, 1791, cited in James B. Whisker, *The Rise and Decline of the American Militia System* (Selinsgrove, PA: Susquehanna University Press, 1999), 75.

[282]   Ibid., 111. The dearth or glut of firearms in America is contested by historians. For example, Michael A. Bellesiles, *Arming America: The Origins of a National Gun Culture* (New York, Vintage Books, 2000), argued that firearms were rare in early America (albeit with questionable source usage), while Clayton E. Cramer, *Armed America: The Remarkable Story of How and Why Guns Became as American as Apple Pie* (Nashville, TN: Nelson Current, 2006), argued, as a direct counter to Bellesiles, that firearms were universal.

endar, Washington could not believe their petty avarice and their "egregious want of publick [*sic*] spirit."[283] In 1776, independence was declared, but the *rage militaire* of the previous year was already over. Washington knew that a bounty was needed to spur enlistments, because the citizens who actually signed up were "no more than a drop in the Ocean." They were not "influenced by any other principles than those of Interest."[284] It was especially trying to keep them from running away from every battlefield. And they couldn't shoot. In June 1776, a frustrated Washington ordered the militia to "load for their first fire with one musket ball and four or eight buckshot," because by using their weapons like shotguns they were more likely to hit the side of a barn. He called them loose and idle, with a "dearth of public spirit and want of virtue," and said that they were so troublesome that, "Could I have foreseen what I have, and am likely to experience, no consideration upon earth should have induced me to accept this command."[285]

The militia rarely improved with experience. In 1780, after their poor showing in the Carolina campaigns, which Washington called "the late disaster," he again lamented "the fatal consequences of relying on militia." The following year, Washington said he might have defeated Britain years sooner with a regular army, instead of being brought "to the verge of ruin by temporary enlistments and a reliance on militia," which did nothing but waste money, stores, arms, ammunition, provisions, and clothing, all for benefits "which are no more than mushrooms" of short duration leaving the country forever in debt.[286]

The militia exasperated Washington to the extent that he almost quit, and very likely never would have become president. How the colonists succeeded in defeating Britain is less attributable to stalwart, sharp shooting citizen-soldiers than to the facts that they had home field advantage and outnumbered the British by about

---

[283]   Robert G. Parkinson, *The Common Cause: Creating Race and Nation in the American Revolution* (Chapel Hill, NC: University of North Carolina Press, 2016), 165.

[284]   Martin and Lender, *"A Respectable Army,"* 77.

[285]   Whisker, *Rise and Decline of the American Militia*, 295 ("buckshot" quotation), 297 ("dearth" and "no consideration" quotations).

[286]   ANC, V. 2, No. 8 (February 23, 1836), 117.

ten to one. About 396,000 men served in the Revolution, with about 164,000 being militia. Britain never had more than 42,000 soldiers stationed in the Colonies.[287] Ten men with fly-swatters could defeat one British Grenadier with a Brown Bess. What is most surprising is how Britain fought on for eight years.

The tremendous gulf between today's legend and yesterday's reality was no better conveyed than by Lt. Col. Ebenezer Huntington. "I despise my countrymen," he wrote in 1780. "I wish I could say I was not born in America...The insults and neglects which the army have met with from the country beggars all description." Huntington censured his "cowardly countrymen" clutching "their purse-strings as though they would damn the world rather than part with a dollar for their army."[288]

The self-styled citizen militia of today who ritually dress up in camouflage and shoot their guns in the woods in some sort of paean to a mythological past might reconsider if they understood the widespread eighteenth- and nineteenth-century assessment that the militia were dangerous mobs when they had their prey outnumbered, and laughingstocks otherwise. The current idea that militia need advanced weaponry to protect themselves from government is divorced from history and reality. George Washington understood that the state was much more in jeopardy from white men with guns than conversely. In 1786, disgruntled farmers in western Massachusetts, after failing to pay their taxes, took up arms against the government in "Shay's Rebellion." An extremely distressed Washington wrote to Henry Knox: "I feel...infinitely more than I can express to you, for the disorders which have arisen in these states. Good God! Who besides a tory could have foreseen...or did they judge of us from the corruption, and depravity of their own hearts? The latter I am persuaded was the case, and that notwithstanding the boasted virtue of America, we are far gone in every thing ignoble & bad." "When this spirit first dawned, probably it might easily have been checked; but it is scarcely within the reach of human ken, at this moment, to say when—where—or how it will end."[289]

---

[287]   Ibid., 292.
[288]   Martin and Lender, *"A Respectable Army,"* 152.
[289]   Washington to Knox, December 26, 1786, https://founders.archives. gov/documents/Washington/04-04-02-0409 (accessed February 26, 2018).

Washington was afraid of fanatical white men with guns, and the Founders knew the only reason to employ them was because America did not yet have a professional standing army—something else they were afraid of. We often believe we had more freedoms and rights back in "the good old days." Economist and college president Thomas Cooper argued during the Constitutional debates that government was not merely theoretical and abstract, but "guided by past experience. We are not required to shut our eyes to notorious facts. The great object of all laws is the general welfare—public utility." Men had rights, but they had to be restricted for the benefit of all. "If we know that a lunatic, or a man given to habitual intoxication, cannot be safely trusted with the management of his property, we appoint guardians and trustees for this purpose. If a man cannot be safely trusted with liquor or with arms, he has no right to them," any more than "a sword in the hands of a madman."[290]

Gunpowder and guns were viewed as dangerous, and although at times their use was necessary, so were restrictions. This contradiction constantly taints analyses. A regular soldier had to obey even when ordered to kill women and children; militia and volunteers did not have to obey when ordered *not* to kill women and children. Who had the moral compass? Familiarity with guns and marksmanship may never have been pervasive on the American frontier, and attempts to "play soldier" were often lampooned, but there was no doubt that Americans could be merciless killers. British General James Wolfe called them "the dirtiest, most contemptible cowardly dogs you can conceive," while General Amherst bemoaned their unwillingness to fight professional French soldiers. "If left to themselves," he said, "[they] would eat fried pork and lay in their tents all day long." At the same time, Wolfe understood the frontiersmen's propensity for the "skulking" way of war, and "the barbarity which seems so natural" to them when they were unleashed to kill and intimidate noncombatants.[291]

Since Americans had no professional army for 175 years,

[290]   Thomas Cooper, *Two Essays: On the Foundation of Civil Government; On the Constitution of the United States* (New York: Da Capo Press, 1970), 15–16.
[291]   John Grenier, *The First Way of War: American War Making on the Frontier, 1607–1814* (New York, Cambridge University Press, 2005), 130 ("cowardly dogs" and "fried pork" quotations), 139 ("barbarity" quotation).

they had always engaged in *petite guerre* (small war), destroying economies, burning, looting, assassinating, and killing and capturing noncombatants. Unprofessional as they were, they could certainly be motivated by the opportunity to make a profit. Paying bounties for Indian heads, scalps, or captives was a part of the American way of war since the early 1600s. No professional army was needed in 1637 for colonists to slaughter about five hundred Pequots and burn their town. Even the women could get into the act. When Abenakis captured Hannah Dustin and her child in 1697, she reversed the usual plot and methodically tomahawked and scalped her captors, and then turned in the scalps to Massachusetts for a £50 reward. Since the government could not afford large-scale war, they privatized it. Issuing letters of marque and reprisal, rewarding privateering, and tendering the possibilities of land, captives, and plunder were great inducements for civilians to fight. By the mid-eighteenth century, some Americans had become, in the words of one historian, *"entrepreneurs de guerre,"* for when daily wages were only two shillings, payment of £10, £20, or even £100 per scalp were economic windfalls. Commercialized war became legitimate, and many Americans embraced it.[292]

"Plunder and devastation ever march in the train of irregulars," wrote Alexander Hamilton, and their fighting was "desultory and predatory." While willing to wage private wars on their own terms, they were reluctant to be under colonial or state control, yet frequent conflict compelled them to do so. Hamilton said the Revolution was a narrowly-won affair, and he hoped he would never see the likes of it again. The militia scheme was a "system of imbecility," and although depicted as the nation's "natural bulwark," that doctrine "had like to have lost us our independence." It wasted millions of dollars, brought us to the brink of ruin, and, he warned, Americans should not "be the dupes of such a suggestion" again.[293]

Regardless of Hamilton's misgivings, there were a number of acts to establish and organize a militia. The first plan was formulated by War Secretary Henry Knox and presented by President Washington to Congress in 1790. Knox knew that militia had poor

---

[292]   Ibid., 4, 5, 10, 41–42.

[293]   Hamilton, *Federalist Papers*, 33, 114, 118.

discipline and habits, but the nation's new leaders expressed concerns with a standing army, given their history in Europe and the recent encounters with Great Britain. As a result, Knox stated that "An energetic national militia is to be regarded as the *capital security* of a free republic, and not a standing army." America would only need an army if its people were vice-ridden and corrupt, only "when public spirit is despised, and avarice, indolence, and effeminacy of manners predominate," would the minds of our youth stray from the paths of virtue and honor and necessitate a standing army.[294] Knox did not realize that time had already arrived.

The first Militia Act of 1792 was passed as a response to the disastrous defeat of Arthur St. Clair by the Northwest Indians in 1791. States were authorized to call out able-bodied males between ages eighteen and forty-five to counter any foreign or domestic threats. Having a force readily available to check actual Indian incursions was one thing, but it seemed the states had their own ideas of what posed a threat. Militia abuses began almost immediately. In 1793 in Georgia, for example, about two hundred mounted militia raised for defense crossed the Oconee River to search for Creeks. Indian agent James Seagrove did not know why they went, but said it could be for no good purpose. If they did not stop initiating mischief, he could not negotiate a treaty. Georgians were belligerent, but "if they studied the good of the country, they would not wish to make a war." They wanted to fight Indians without the assistance of Congress, but "I fear, they will have a hard task to subdue them."[295]

The New Year of 1794 began with the news that South Carolina militia had killed two Cherokees and abducted one of their women as they were peacefully trading in a border settlement. Captain Richard B. Roberts, commanding at Fort Fidius, Georgia, learned that on December 28, Georgia state militia, after camping and supping with a small party of peaceful Creeks, committed "the most perfidious and wanton murder" of two of them. The Creeks asked the army for help. When militia attacked the Indians near Milledgeville, Georgia, Captain Roberts said the natives "flew to this garrison for protection." He shielded and hid them for a time, then

---

[294]   Washington to Congress, January 21, 1790, ASPMA, V. 1, 6–7.
[295]   Bernard to Seagrove, October 17, 1793 (quotation), Seagrove to Knox, October 21, 1793, ASPIA, V. 1, 415.

The Nation's Bulwark. A Well Disciplined Militia. 1829. *Library of Congress* Sarcastic cartoons depicting the militia as buffoons were commonplace during the first half of the nineteenth century.

"got them off safe" across the river, but he feared the militia would find and kill them.[296]

The militia could rarely be trusted and often caused more problems than they were worth. By the War of 1812, most army officers were fed up with them, one stating that they were "little better than organized bandits who wasted public property, insulted private citizens, and freely engaged in desertion, robbery, [and] disorderly and mutinous conduct."[297]

In 1813, Edmund P. Gaines, then lieutenant colonel of the 24th Infantry, admitted he did not know how to discipline the militia, and said they would never be disciplined without a radical change in the laws. The current system, said Gaines, "has long been the hobby horse of our country," with the militia "caressed and dandled in the lap of its indulgent mother," and like the spoiled child was still not formidable or respectable. They believed they were slaves if they were given orders, they evaded every duty, and their constant allusion to liberty meant no more than "disobedience, perjury, and ruin to the vital interest of my country." The present system produced

---

[296]   McKee to Blount, November 18, 1793, ASPIA, V. 1, 474; Roberts to Mathews, January 2, 1794, ASPIA, V. 1, 474 ("most perfidious" quotation); Roberts to Knox, May 10, 1794, ASPIA, V. 1, 483 ("flew" and "safe" quotations).
[297]   Dauber, *Politics of Compensation*, 301.

men who read a book on tactics, marched on a muster field for a dozen days a year, who never saw an enemy, or ran away when they did, who defied every order, and who deserted their posts, yet were still depicted as brave heroes in the newspapers. As it stood, said Gaines, "militia" was just an empty name.[298]

The militia had performed abysmally during the War of 1812. Despite its record, Englishman Elias P. Fordham, visiting during the post-war years, noted the "prejudice" that Americans would not give up: the belief that they "are the best soldiers in the world."[299] Actually it was a wonder that the British, who succeeded in burning the White House in Washington, did not conquer the nation. The militia system might have been on its way out sooner, were it not for the January 8, 1815, Battle of New Orleans, fought after the War of 1812 was technically over. There, General Andrew Jackson, with about 4,500 regulars, militia, volunteers, and pirates, faced British General Sir Edward Packenham's 5,300 soldiers. Packenham lost because he had poor intelligence, moved too slowly, lacked the element of surprise, and attacked across an open field against a fortified position liberally covered by artillery. It was the proverbial case of "shooting fish in a barrel." Despite the reality, the popular assessment was that the skilled backwoods marksmen with their rifles could annihilate any foe. The militia concept dragged on for another half century.[300]

"Twenty-four feet of Bologna sausage": The Post-War Militia

With the war over and all the instances of a failed militia system fresh in mind, War Secretary James Monroe still believed it was the best solution. The only recourse would be a standing army, but, "A policy so fraught with mischief, and so absurd, ought not

---

[298]   Gaines to Cushing, January 20, 1813, AGO, RG 94, M566, R0023.

[299]   Elias Pym Fordham, *Personal Narrative of Travels in Virginia, Maryland, Pennsylvania, Ohio, Indiana, Kentucky; and of a Residence in the Illinois Territory: 1817–1818* (Leopold Classical Library, nd. Originally published Cleveland, OH: Arthur H. Clark Co., 1906), 128–29.

[300]   Whisker, *Rise and Decline of the American Militia*, 327–28.

Grand Fantastical Parade. New York, 1833. *Library of Congress*
The New York "Invincibles" dressed with pumpkins, codfish, goatskins, beards, and false noses.

to be imputed to a free people in this enlightened age."[301] The *Niles Weekly Register* shared the fear of a standing army, but argued that "as a government gains power the people must suffer restraint." The militia knew nothing about survival, sanitation, cooking, shelter, or fighting. They had to learn from veterans, but by the time the lessons took effect many more recruits died of disease or accident than in battle. The constant turnover meant that fresh recruits would have to begin the process anew. The country needed to "retain a sufficient portion of those who have 'learnt the trade.'"[302]

It would take many more examples of egregious behavior before the militia concept would be purged from the body politic. Shortly after Monroe expressed confidence in the militia, Judge Toulmin of Mississippi Territory voiced his concerns. The Indians were bad enough during the recent war, but then their "protectors" arrived and "the soldier succeeded the savage" like locusts following the hail. The militia, Toulmin complained, had a strange notion that it was "their right to press, as they termed it—your corn—your cattle—your horses—in short everything." Toulmin's neighbor's cotton gin house was "pressed" by militia who turned it into firewood

---

[301]   Monroe to Giles, February 11, 1815, ASPMA, V. 1, 605–606.
[302]   NWR, December 20, 1817, Supplement to V. 1, No. 17, 273–74.

simply because it was easier than cutting trees. They scavenged the countryside, stealing everything not nailed down. Heaven forbid, Toulmin even knew of "families with from 50 to 80 negroes who have not a dollar to buy one single article for family use." With peace came privation.[303]

Colonel William Russell, 7th Infantry, said that he was frustrated trying to "grattify [sic] the whims of the people" on the frontier while being burdened with "useless rafts of Militia."[304] In Florida, 4th Infantry Lt. Col. George M. Brooke needed officers, and requested West Point cadets, since he was "well convinced, that they make infinitely the best officers," while two out of three citizen officers were "good for nothing, and a disgrace to the army."[305] Disparagement of citizen officers continued throughout this period. When the 1st Dragoons were organized in 1833, regulars grumbled about how many civilians were appointed, and when the 2nd Dragoons were established in 1836, thirty out of thirty-four of the officers were chosen from civilian ranks, mainly southerners and westerners. Lieutenant Colonel Kearny, 1st Dragoons, said his regiment "is decidedly the worst officered one in the army," and changes had to be made to keep it from being disgraced. When in need of officers, "a selection should be made from the graduates from West Point in June, to fill all vacancies, which selection, if pursued each year, may in the course of time produce a change in its favor."[306]

There were plenty of militia defenders, but increasing numbers of civilians came to view them as clowns. A Pennsylvania newspaper reported that its militia were training again, using canes and cornstalks for rifles. It called the exercise ridiculous, serving only to drag men from work to try to teach them "eyes right" from "eyes left," set them loose to make "'charges' upon whiskey," and go home fatigued and drunk, simply to allow "a parcel of silly ones" to take a high-sounding title and strut about the fields.[307] Pennsylvania hoped to abolish its militia system as Delaware had done. It cost three mil-

---

303   Toulmin to Lattimore, November 12, 1815, TPUS, V. 6, 568.
304   Russell to Crawford, April 24, 1815, TPUS, V. 15, 48.
305   Brooke to Parker, June 17, 1820, AGO, RG 94, M566, R0130.
306   Skelton, *American Profession of Arms,* 143–44; Kearny to Jones, April 11, 1835, AGO, RG 94, M567, R0110.
307   NWR, June 27, 1829, V. 36, No. 928, 284.

lion dollars annually to "support the caricature of an army." No one, claimed the *Niles Weekly Register* in 1829, who has ever seen a militia muster would doubt that they are "a ridiculous burlesque— as schools of vice, deplorable." Youths saw it as an excuse to get drunk and the entire system fostered "insubordination, disorder, and debauchery."[308] Five years later, the *Register* had not seen any improvement. Militia laws were farcical, injurious, a waste of time, and people should "laugh them out of existence." The regulations of the "Buffalo corps of Fantastics" stated that "no person should be allowed to wear a cap more than twelve feet high—that no person should wear a sword more than fifteen feet in length—that no officer should be allowed more than two dozen red herring for an epaulette, or twenty-four feet of Bologna sausage for a sash."[309] Denunciations surfaced in many venues. South Carolina governor George McDuffie stated at a public dinner that the militia system was a mockery, and he "was astonished that respectable citizens could consent to make themselves the common, repeated laughing stocks of boys under ten years of age, in the parades, in the public streets."[310]

There were other jaundiced observations. In 1833, *The Military and Naval Magazine of the United States* called the militia system "radically bad." It may have served a purpose in decades past, but was currently ripe for ridicule. Participators mocked it. In Vermont, the "soldiers" turned out with various attires and accoutrements, stuck various colored feathers in their hats, and used broomsticks for muskets, while a band beat martial tunes. In New York, nearly four hundred men who called themselves "the Invincibles" were led by a man dressed as Napoleon, with statues of the emperor on his shoulders, wearing green spectacles, and wielding a sword four feet long and a foot wide. "Caps were of all shapes and colours: one wore a pumpkin with the long leaves of a carrot for a plume; another was distinguished by a chapeau five feet in length, and a cod-fish for a sword; wigs, beards, and false noses were common; and the coats were of bright scarlet, brown woolen, green baize, deer skin, and split cane." There was a "Satanic majesty with a pitch-fork and tail." One man dressed as a Highlander, one man carried four muskets,

---

308   NWR, September 5, 1829, V. 37, No. 938, 21.
309   NWR, November 1, 1834, V. 47, No. 206, 134.
310   NWR, June 13, 1835, V. 45, No. 238, 264.

Black Hawk. *Public domain*
Sauk Chief Black Hawk could have dealt with the honorable regulars, but was afraid of the unrestrained civilians.

and one wore a goat-skin like Robinson Crusoe. "Never before," said the observer, "was such an array witnessed."[311]

Nevertheless, there were militia defenders. The next issue of *The Military and Naval Magazine* carried a rebuttal by William H. Sumner, Adjutant General of the Massachusetts Militia. He deprecated attempts to ridicule the militia and said the men who joined the regular army were less intelligent and poor citizens. Sumner claimed, "The militia is what is left after society is purified by army enlistments."[312]

The militia may have been purified, but it was dysfunctional. In 1828, the newly-formed American Peace Society was opposed to war and saw no sense in maintaining a militia with all the "vice and drunkenness and idleness which attend them." Also emerging in the 1820s and 1830s, the Transcendentalists were opposed to war and military service. Organized labor argued that the burden of service fell most heavily on the laboring poor, who could ill afford to leave their farms and jobs to play soldier. As the militia faded away, the volunteer stepped in as a replacement. Volunteers were independent contractors, likely more skilled with firearms than the militia, but poor in discipline, and could be enlisted in times of emergency and disbanded when the crisis ended. In the words of one historian, "Independent, often only semicivilized, sometimes bitter and revenge-minded, the volunteers fought for a wide variety of personal, rather than patriotic or nationalistic, reasons."[313] The for-profit, scalp hunters were back.

---

[311] "Notes on the Army of the U. States of America," *Military and Naval Magazine of the United States*, V. 1, No. 2 (April 1833), 104–105.

[312] "Militia of the United States," Military and Naval Magazine of the United States, V. 1, No. 4, (June 1833), 237.

[313] Whisker, *Rise and Decline of the American Militia*, 330.

"Ten times more damage as the Indians":
The Black Hawk War

Volunteers showed their potential in the Black Hawk War of 1832. Its causes were similar to so many other frontier conflicts: whites, mainly from Illinois and Michigan Territory, encroached on Sauk and Fox land, took over their mines, moved into their villages, and abused and killed them. Whites severely beat Sauk Chief Black Hawk after accusing him of killing their hogs. The army tried to remove squatters from Sauk land, but they swarmed back in once the army left. Since it was impossible to remove the whites, General Gaines and his regulars arrived in June 1831 to remove the Indians, by negotiation or force. About 1,400 Illinois volunteers eagerly assembled, hoping for plunder. Black Hawk realized that Gaines would not harm him, but when he saw that civilians were riding with the army, he abandoned the town of Saukenuk at the junction of Rock River and the Mississippi and moved his people to the other shore. "I would have remained and been taken prisoner by the *regulars*," he said, "but was afraid of the multitude of *pale faces*, who were on horseback, as they were under no restraint of their chiefs."[314]

Black Hawk fled, and Gaines was pleased he avoided violence, but not so the volunteers. Illinois governor John Reynolds had called them out, but knew they were nearly uncontrollable. Even if the Indians had stayed and surrendered, he believed that they would have shot at them "with or without orders." Reynolds believed that Gaines slowed his approach purposely to give Black Hawk a chance to escape, and said, "I was glad of it." "The headstrong Americans being so many in the brigade that hated Indians, wanted *fun*," and there would have been a bloody tragedy if a fight had begun.[315]

To make up for missing a fight, the volunteers looted and burned Saukenuk, while some ghouls dug up nearly twenty Indian graves, and threw at least one corpse into the fires of the burning

---

[314]   Patrick J. Jung, *The Black Hawk War of 1832* (Norman, University of Oklahoma Press, 2007), 38, 52, 53, 63; Black Hawk, *Life of Black Hawk*, Milo Milton Quaife, ed. (New York: Dover Publications, Inc., 1994), 52.

[315]   Jung, *Black Hawk War*, 52, 53, 62–64; John Reynolds, *My Own Times: Embracing also the History of My Life* (Belleville, IL: B. H. Perryman and H. L. Davison, 1855), 338 (quotations).

lodges. Sauks later returned to rebury their dead, but the whites would not allow it, and Agent Felix St. Vrain had to accompany them so they could properly cover the graves. He reported that whites confronted one Indian, stole his horse, broke his gun, and whipped him, while other whites destroyed canoes and shot at Sauks crossing the river. The volunteers did not limit their destruction to the town. Local settler John W. Spencer said they swarmed onto his farm. "I had a field of twenty acres of corn and potatoes and the volunteers went for the fence. We tried to stop them from taking the rails, but could not." Reynolds and Gaines ordered them to desist, but when they left, more than four hundred men trashed the place. Spencer said, "I lost all my crop for one year, for which I never received a cent, the soldiers doing me ten times more damage as the Indians had ever done."[316]

General Gaines gave the Sauks corn to replace their destroyed crops. When the volunteers learned of the deal, they derisively labeled it the "Corn Treaty." They wanted blood. When Black Hawk brought his people back east of the Mississippi River the next year, the volunteers finally got their chance, but it didn't work out as they planned. Reynolds again called for volunteers and about 3,250 responded, far outnumbering Gen. Henry Atkinson's six hundred regulars. As they followed Black Hawk's retreating people up the Rock River, the volunteers were nearly uncontrollable. Editor, writer, and poet William Cullen Bryant was traveling through Illinois at the time. As he neared Dixon's Ferry, where the so-called "Army of the Frontier" was gathering, he passed their camps and saw their horses grazing on the prairies and how "their way was marked by trees barked or girdled" and the countryside beaten down. Bryant said they were a "hard-looking set of men, unkempt and unshaved," wearing calico shirts and long, hooded capotes. "Some of the settlers complained that they made war upon the pigs and chickens." Bryant talked to a young man in one volunteer company, and later learned

---

[316]   St. Vrain to Clark, July 23, 1831, in Ellen M. Whitney, ed., *The Black Hawk War, 1831–1832*: V. 2, Letters and Papers (Springfield, IL: Illinois State Historical Library, 1973), 112; *John W. Spencer, Reminiscences of Pioneer Life in the Mississippi Valley* (Davenport, IO: Griggs, Watson, & Day, 1872), 49 (quotations).

it was Abraham Lincoln.[317] Apparently Lincoln desired to fight so his men could "meet powder & lead." They found and accused an old Pottawatomie of being a spy, and wanted to kill him, but Lincoln intervened. Later, Lincoln joked that he had never seen an Indian, "but I had many bloody struggles with the musquetoes [*sic*]."[318]

The volunteers started the war. Isaiah Stillman led a two-hundred-man mounted battalion ahead of the army to locate Black Hawk. The Sauk chief tried to ally with the Pottawatomies, but they turned him down and he figured it would be best to make peace. On May 14, 1832, he sent three warriors with a white flag to meet the approaching whites and ask for a parley, while five more men stayed back to cover them. Stillman captured the first three and fired on the other five, killing two. Black Hawk quickly brought up forty more warriors and set up a firing line. Stillman's men rode right into it, received blasts of well-placed bullets, and disintegrated. The survivors ran back to Dixon's Ferry twenty-five miles away, defeated by a force less than one-fourth their number. Three Sauks and twelve whites died.[319] Sixth Infantry Lt. Philip St. George Cooke was with the approaching regulars. He wrote that the militia "(that prosopopoeia of weakness, waste, and confusion)," apparently believed they were on a frolic, murdered a few innocent Indians in cold blood, and then "retreated at speed in utter confusion." He said they ran for forty miles and reported that they had a battle with 1,500 warriors.[320]

Many of the volunteers were so humiliated that they went home, forcing Atkinson to ask Reynolds to call up another three thousand men. As they reorganized, Col. Hugh Brady, 2nd Infantry, said that they could not corner the Indians because of the "difficulties & disappointments which have been thrown in the way of General Atkinson, by the ridiculous conduct of the Militia." In one instance, on June 25, the men decided to test their guns by wildly firing into the sky. Lieutenant Cooke witnessed the roar and the flashes of

---

317   Jung, *Black Hawk War*, 65, 79; William Cullen Bryant, *The Prose Writings of William Cullen Bryant*, V. 2. Parke Godwin, ed. (New York: D. Appleton & Company, 1889), 20.

318   Jung, *Black Hawk War*, 79, 82.

319   Ibid., 88–89; Nichols, *Henry Atkinson*, 163.

320   Philip St. George Cooke, *Scenes and Adventures in the Army: Or, Romance of Military Life* (Santa Barbara, CA: The Narrative Press, 2004), 107.

firearms in the night, which lit up the river and stampeded one thousand horses. The regulars rushed across the river, believing "that the devil was certainly let loose amongst our militia friends." Entire battalions blasted away into the night air, while their commander climbed upon a stump and unsuccessfully tried to stop them. Said Cooke: "their General finally damned them to all posterity, and resigned his commission in violent disgust." The volunteers spent the next day trying to catch the horses.[321]

William Clark had been Superintendent of Indian Affairs since 1822, and knew well of the chronic prejudices of the people of Illinois and Missouri. As the "Army of the Frontier" regrouped in Illinois in May 1832, a delegation of Sauk and Fox parleyed with Clark in St. Louis. They were afraid of "the inveterate hostility of the Illinois militia" who crossed the Mississippi and threatened to attack them. Squatters on the Des Moines River were organizing to attack Taimah's (Fox) village, while Illinois militia menaced Keokuk's (Sauk) people. Said Clark, "[T]hey ask the protection of the U. States." Taimah told Clark the rumor that Americans planned to capture all their men, both old and young, "and deprive them of those parts which are said to be *essential* to courage; then a horde of negro men were to be brought from the South," who would forcefully mate with the Indian women to raise a new stock of slaves. Such tales were calculated to drive the Indians to war, whereupon they could be killed or removed, opening up more land for the whites.[322]

Atkinson spent the next few months chasing the elusive Indians through the tangled country and marshlands of southern Wisconsin, but now they were reinforced by a number of Pottawatomies who had joined because the Illinois volunteers could not refrain from "committing depredations upon the innocent and unoffending Pottawatomies, whom they met with on their march."[323] Newly appointed Col. Zachary Taylor said, "The more I see of the militia

[321] Jung, *Black Hawk War,* 127 ("ridiculous conduct" quotation); Cooke, *Scenes and Adventures,* 110 ("devil" and "violent disgust" quotations).

[322] Clark to Cass, May 30, 1832, in Whitney, ed., *Black Hawk War, 1831–1832,* 482 ("inveterate hostility" and "U. States" quotations); Jay H. Buckley, *William Clark Indian Diplomat* (Norman, OK: University of Oklahoma Press, 2008), 208 ("essential" quotation).

[323] Owen to the Public, June 5, 1832, in Whitney, ed., *Black Hawk War 1831–1832,* 528.

the less confidence I have in their effecting anything of importance; & therefore tremble not only for the safety of the frontiers, but for the reputation of those who command them, who have any reputation to lose."[324] Lieutenant Cooke tried to be objective, but sprinkled his narrative with barbed comments about the volunteers. In one camp a militia sentinel nervously shot a friend, which Cooke said was a common occurrence, as they are "generally more dangerous to their friends than to their enemies." The volunteers were "improvident and wasteful" with their supplies, and were far too timid to guard the wagons. One convoy was only about two miles from Cooke's camp when the

Henry Atkinson. *Public Domain* General Atkinson chased Black Hawk across Illinois and Wisconsin, hoping that his volunteers would not attack innocent Indians.

guards "imagined" they had seen an Indian, abandoned the wagons and ran away. Cooke read a Western senator's recent column in the *National Intelligencer*, that the army consisted of degraded men, the "sweepings of the cities," while the "frontier men-militia-rangers" were "infinitely superior," and could fight, subsist themselves, and travel fifty miles a day. The politician, Cooke said, "excels in humbug!"[325]

As the volunteers closed in they captured straggling Indians. A ten-man party under Dr. Addison Philleo, from Galena, Illinois, caught and shot a warrior. Philleo took the dying man's own knife and began scalping him. The Indian begged for mercy, but Philleo taunted him: "If you don't like being scalped with a dull knife, why didn't you keep a better one?"[326] Cooke heard of such incidents and sardonically chalked it up to the typical behavior of our "magnani-

---

[324] Taylor to Atkinson, June 2, 1832, in Whitney, ed., *Black Hawk War 1831–1832*, 503.
[325] Cooke, *Scenes and Adventures*, 112, 114.
[326] Jung, *Black Hawk War*, 130, 149–50, 162.

mous volunteers."[327]

About 750 volunteers caught a rearguard of 120 Sauks and their Kickapoo allies at Wisconsin Heights on July 21, 1832. In a tough fight, Black Hawk held them off until his people crossed the Wisconsin River, although he had lost forty or more warriors. Cooke heard the volunteers extolling their "intrepidity and coolness" in battle. He also heard that they cried out, "Come forward, boys, and draw your ponies!" as the lure of capturing Indian horses drew them on. When they began comparing "Wisconsin Heights" to "Tippecanoe," Cooke had enough. Despite their boasting, he said, Black Hawk got his women and children across a river "in the presence of three regiments of American volunteers! And they were now gone—the victors could not tell us wither."[328]

The worst calamity to befall the retreating Indians occurred on August 1–2, along the banks of the Mississippi River below the mouth of the Bad Axe. The harried Indians fled through the high grass and sloughs in the marshy bottoms along the river and tried to swim to two islands. Nearly 1,200 regulars and volunteers caught up to them and there was pandemonium. Only about 150 of the 500 Indians were warriors, and many women and children were shot or drowned in the melee. Perhaps 200 Indians made it across the river. After months of frustration, the pursuing whites, and some regulars, took out their anger with a vengeance. "Suffice it to say," wrote Capt. Henry Smith, 6th Infantry, "that quarters were in no instance asked or granted."[329]

Foul misdeeds tipped the affair from the battle to the massacre category. Perhaps regulars committed some of the atrocities, but many volunteers participated with a relish. Frightened, fleeing Indians, the majority being women and children, were the perfect prey. The volunteers scalped many of the dead and dying, and flayed the skin off the backs of some Indians to make razor strops. One of Henry Dodge's volunteers purposely shot a woman carrying a child on her back, killed her, and shattered the child's arm also. Doctor

[327] Cooke, *Scenes and Adventures,* 123.
[328] Ibid., 116–17.
[329] Jung, *Black Hawk War,* 171–72; Henry Smith, "Indian Campaign of 1832," *Military and Naval Magazine of the United States,* V. 1, No. 6 (August 1833), 331.

Philleo amputated it without any anesthetic. Another of Dodge's men said that they "killed everything that didn't surrender," including three naked "squaws." There were also hints of rape, but no outright accusations. A volunteer named John House relished shooting children, making a spectacle of calling his shots as he picked them off one by one as they tried to cling to pieces of driftwood in the river. Another man chastened him for his cruelty, but he replied, "Kill the nits, and you'll have no lice."[330]

Despite the ghastly acts, one volunteer denied them: "We have been accused of inhumanity to those Indians. It is false as hell, we never did it." Lieutenant Cooke, in his restrained style, stated that he hoped all the women and children fell by random, mistaken shots, "but it is certain that a frontiersman is not particular, when his blood is up, and a redskin is in his power."[331] Volunteer John A. Wakefield said that they killed non-combatants, but it was the victims' fault. "It was a great misfortune to those miserable squaws and children," but they should have surrendered in the morning when they had the chance. He said it was horrid to see the wounded and suffering children, nevertheless "they were of the savage enemy." Wakefield found justification in God. "[T]he Ruler of the Universe, He who takes vengeance on the guilty, did not design those guilty wretches to escape His vengeance for the horrid deeds they had done.... He here took just retribution for the many innocent lives those cruel savages had taken on our northern frontiers."[332]

"Half-horse, Half-alligator": The Boone-Crockett Enigma

After the Black Hawk War was over, Philip St. George Cooke pondered his experience. He believed frontiersmen had changed. "There was a time when our frontier's-men were the most formidable light-troops... that the sun ever shone upon. But what made

---

[330]   Jung, *Black Hawk War*, 173–74. The "nits" statement might be compared to a similar one said to be uttered by Col. John Chivington of the Colorado Volunteers before the Sand Creek Massacre in 1864.

[331]   Jung, *Black Hawk War*, 173; *Cooke*, Scenes and Adventures, 129.

[332]   John Wakefield, *Wakefield's History of the Black Hawk War*, Frank E. Stevens, ed. (Chicago, IL: The Caxton Club, 1908), 132–33.

Philip St. George Cooke. *National Archives and Records Administration* Lieutenant Cooke was troubled by the behavior of the volunteers and lamented that all the old formidable frontiersmen were gone.

them such?" He thought it was their constant exercise of arms, vigilance, and endurance resulting from cease-less warlike toil, when the times were filled with real danger. Cooke believed Daniel Boone and his ilk were the ultimate frontiersmen who had subdued the Indians of the For-est—Indians who Cooke claimed were much more formidable than the Prairie Indians. But now those men were gone. Infantry resting in frontier forts took their place, and the once formidable border men had become squirrel hunters and "the foes of timid deer." Cooke be-lieved that old "once well-founded, notions concerning this class, which naturally linger in the minds of a succeeding generation," contin-ued to influence Congress to prefer irregulars—a false notion that harmed the country's development. Frontiersmen had become "in-dividuals who have never acknowledged the common restraints of society; who confound insubordination with a boasted equality; who cannot endure the wholesome action of discipline, or even obedi-ence," and would never be the match of regular soldiers.[333]

There is a glitch in Cooke's assessment: the characteristics he attributed to the frontiersmen of the 1830s were the same as those ascribed by the Colonial and Revolutionary generations. Some rang-er companies of the eighteenth century may have caused concern among the Indians, but they were few and far between—and Daniel Boone was not one of them—he and his compatriots were more often than not described in pejorative terms. Yet, Cooke looked back on some imagined rosy past when frontiersmen were Ameri-ca's true heroes. Regrettably—or thankfully—that mythical nation of sharp-shooting frontier riflemen never existed—it was gone for

---

[333]   Cooke, *Scenes and Adventures,* 151, 152, 155.

Cooke in 1832, but it never existed in Jeffrey Amherst's world in 1759, either.

Americans, however, were building the myth. Major Benjamin Forsyth of the Regiment of Riflemen had captured a number of British in 1813. As the surely apocryphal story goes, a British officer admired Forsyth's marksmen and wondered if he could see a demonstration of their prowess. Forsyth, wary that any of his men were up to the task, "gave the wink to one of his officers then at hand, who departed" to locate two soldiers who might be able to pull off the stunt. Forsyth stepped out of his tent to call over two "random" men, who set up a knife in one tree fifty paces away, and an ace of clubs in another. The men fired, walked to the trees, and returned with a split ball, supposedly cut in two by the knife, and the card with the club shot out. The British officer was supposedly "confounded and amazed," and even more so when Forsyth told him that only weeks before, "those men were in the capacity of husbandmen."[334]

Tales of this sort appeared in the 1950s Disney yarns about Davy Crockett, who could split a musket ball on the edge of his ax, and even catch a ricocheting ball in his teeth. However, what children might actually swallow in the twentieth century was seen as a farce in the nineteenth. The images of frontiersmen of the Daniel Boone (1735–1820) and Davy Crockett (1786–1836) model, conjured in the minds of their contemporaries, were more problematic than they are today. As early as 1783, John Filson published a sketch of Boone that helped define the tradition of the Western hero. He was a simple woodsman and Indian fighter, a hunter and farmer, and a sensitive philosopher in Rousseau's "natural man" cast.[335] In 1813, Boone's nephew wrote a grandiose epic of his uncle as an architect of social progress, "chosen by the angelic Spirit of Enterprise to bring Civilization to the trans-Allegheny wilderness." Heaven itself required him to tread the grand road of empire. But by this time a growing number of people had soured on that old image; in their view Boone actually shunned civilization and preferred to hunt and

---

334   NWR, January 11, 1817, V. 11, No. 20, 332.
335   Kent Ladd Steckmesser, *The Western Hero in History and Legend* (Norman, OK: University of Oklahoma Press, 1965), 4–5.

live in the woods. He supposedly continued to move west to keep one step ahead of the settlements, but some of the more jaundiced newspaper editorials said he moved only because he failed at his get-rich-quick land schemes.[336]

The latter image may have been more accurate. Back then, the "settlers" were more often known as intruders and troublemakers who caused Indian wars. Anglican minister Charles Woodmason called the inhabitants of the Appalachian uplands "people of abandon'd Morals and Profligate principles, the lowest Pack of Wretches my eyes ever saw," living a "low, lazy, heathenish, hellish life." Richard Henderson, who knew and worked with Boone and was the force behind the founding of Boonesborough, nevertheless called the Boone-type characters who infested Kentucky "single, worthless fellows," intractable and seeking only adventure and easy wealth. Pioneers were often profiteers who speculated in land and defrauded both Indians and whites as much as did the rich landowners back east whom they claimed to despise.[337]

The Boone character and image developed concurrently with America's hunger for land. The vast wilderness of "virgin" territory was theirs for the taking, regardless of the Indian inhabitants who might have a different idea. Boone did spend much of his early years as a backwoods hunter, or, more accurately, a poacher, where he was caught in Kentucky with his accumulated skins and barely escaped execution. When Boone could not survive as a hunter, he sought government contracts, transitioned to agent for land speculators, worked for the Transylvania Company, was a land commissioner, a surveyor, and a land-finder for absent purchasers. He owned baronial tracts of land, but lost them because he lacked business acumen. One historian said, "Boone's land-hunting demonstrated the corruption of the homestead ethic." Boone defaulted on debts, was sued, and got death threats for his shady dealings. In 1798, Boone was under arrest for defrauding a land purchaser out of six thousand acres, but the sheriff could not find him—he had fled the

---

[336]   Henry Nash Smith, *Virgin Land: The American West as Symbol and Myth* (Cambridge, MS: Harvard University Press, 1970), 53–54.
[337]   Stephen Aron, *How the West was Lost: The Transformation of Kentucky from Daniel Boone to Henry Clay* (Baltimore, MD: Johns Hopkins University Press, 1996), 13, 32.

country.[338]

Boone disingenuously claimed that civilization molested him and forced him to flee from Kentucky to the wilderness of Missouri. There, manifesting the myth that grew around him, he allegedly was exceedingly offended because "a ____ Yankee had settled within fifty miles" of his abode.[339] Boone also inconsistently stated, "Nothing embitters my old age but the circulation of the absurd and ridiculous stories that I retire as civilization advances; that I shun the white man and seek the Indians.... You know all this is false. Poverty and enterprise excited me to quit my native state, and poverty and despair my native land."[340]

Daniel Boone. *Unfinished portrait by Chester Harding. 1820. Public domain* Boone never endorsed the heroic image created of him, and said that poverty and despair made him flee the United States.

The lone, sharp-shooting, honest backwoodsmen, self-sufficient and attuned to nature, may have been an image conjured by novelists and historians hoping to sell books, but that notion would have been ridiculed by many of those gentlemen's contemporaries.

Davy Crockett's legend was propagated after Boone's. Crockett was a long-hunter and hardscrabble farmer, a politician, a debtor, and died as the "martyr of the Alamo." He fought the Creeks with Andrew Jackson and participated in the slaughter at Horseshoe Bend in 1814. Even though his fellow backwoodsmen generally hated Indians, he changed his tune once in Congress, where, at least for a time, he advocated for Indian rights and against removal—but not at the expense of white squatters. His biggest push was for the poor

---

[338] Ibid., 18, 77 (quotation), 84–85; Richard Slotkin, *The Fatal Environment: The Myth of the Frontier in the Age of Industrialization 1800–1890* (New York: HarperPerennial, 1994), 66.

[339] NWR, November 1, 1834, V. 11, No. 9. 134.

[340] Lyman Draper Collection, Wisconsin State Historical Society, cited in Steckmesser, *Western Hero*, 5.

David Crockett. *Public domain*
Most people viewed Davy Crockett as an illiterate country bumpkin and wished he would go away.

pioneer whites, who, contrary to the image of Westerners as laissez-faire, independent, anti-government individualists, wanted as many "free" government handouts as they could get—like welfare, roads, canals, and land.[341]

Every one of Crockett's land bills was defeated in Congress. Part of his problem was his lack of formal education and his relishing of that fact. The unwashed, hard-drinking, cursing, good old boy who could shoot the eye out of a squirrel and grin down a b'ar, was a successful gimmick only so long. Although the anti-intellectual strain in America has not disappeared, even Jacksonians grew tired of it in their politicians. When enough of them viewed Crockett as a nearly illiterate, naïve, country bumpkin, they wished he would go away. Crockett admitted to lying while running for office, passing out booze to get votes, and his foul invective became so repulsive that one newspaper warned him that his slandering of rivals and reprehensible behavior was a new low, and hopefully would not be imitated by others.[342] Candidates engaged in lying, bullying, and name-calling in 1830s elections apparently found a tougher road to office than they do today.

Crockett was an Indian lover who killed Indians and slaveholder who hated slavery. He called himself the "savagest critter you ever did see," and swore he could "run like a fox, swim like an eel, yell like an Indian," and "swallow a nigger whole." His ability to speak "Cracker" fluently helped endear himself to his white-trash kin, but

---

[341]   James R. Boylston and Allen J. Weiner, *David Crockett in Congress: The Rise and Fall of the Poor Man's Friend* (Houston, TX: Bright Sky Press, 2009), 7–8, 34–35, 120.
[342]   Ibid., 21, 39, 61, 83.

that persona soon lost its novelty.[343] No matter how one might like to smooth his rough edges, he was a frontier American with all the baggage. He disliked cities and the corruption and temptation he believed they embodied. In a tour of the Northeast he decried a culture where certain people didn't know their place, and reportedly said that in the city there was too much "Black and white, white and black, all hug-em-snug together."[344]

Crockett was for banks that gave cheap credit, which only swelled the ranks of the debtors. He hated professionals and was against the Military Academy at West Point, voting in 1830 to try to abolish it. In Congress, he padded his mileage accounts and went on book tours while he was supposed to be at work. Like Boone, he sold warrants to land speculators, and had creditors chasing him. Crockett ended up hating Jackson and Martin Van Buren and changed party from Democrat to Whig, while they did all they could to discredit him and oust him from office. When Crockett, man of the people, was resoundingly defeated by those people in 1835, he told them "they might go to h-ll and I would go to Texas." Even so, Crockett hatched more schemes, wanting to get an Indian agency, a seat in the Texas convention, and said, "I am in hopes of making a fortune for myself." Most of his constituents were glad he was gone—and the Mexicans were not so welcoming either.[345]

While Crockett was still in Congress and fighting with Jackson and Van Buren, the debate about the value of a militia system was yet alive. The aforementioned 1833 New York militia parade, in which the observer noted the attendees wore pumpkins, codfish, giant hats, and false noses, made one more very telling observation of this "entirely burlesque" review: one participant was dressed as "half horse, half alligator."[346] The reference was certainly to Congressman David Crockett, who had arrived in Washington from Tennessee some years prior, and whose appearance, mannerisms, speech, and comportment, were novel and fresh—at least for a time.

---

343   Isenberg, *White Trash, 117.*
344   Slotkin, *Fatal Environment, 170.*
345   Boylston and Weiner, *Crockett in Congress* 77, 84, 121, 123, 286.
346   "Notes on the Army of the U. States of America," *Military and Naval Magazine of the United States,* V. 1, No. 2 (April 1833), 105.

On the stump, he often proclaimed that he could "whip his weight in wildcats, jump up higher, fall down lower, and drink more liquors than any man." Or, he was "a ring-tailed roarer, half-horse, half-alligator," an appellation that Crockett proudly proclaimed was exactly what people expected.[347]

But Crockett's novelty wore off, and he became an uncouth boor and a laughingstock. The semi-literate, bumpkin persona was no longer funny. His opponents lampooned him; one wrote that Crockett was so valiant "that thousands of wild cats and panthers did quake and tremble at his name."[348] The ridiculing of Crockett illustrates that many Americans in the 1820s and 1830s ascribed to a different mythology than was popular with the Walt Disney-influenced, baby-boomer crowd of the mid-twentieth century. The fringed buckskin shirts and coonskin caps worn proudly by the children of 1955 were worn by the militia of 1830 only in burlesque.

Boone's and Crockett's persona as empire builders or children of nature changed as America changed. Folklorist and ethnologist Richard M. Dorson studied the Boone-Crockett phenomenon and found "little trace of heroes in oral tradition." Boone or Kit Carson, for instance, lived on in books more than in folk tales. Crockett was different because he was the he-man, regional eccentric, and Munchausen figure rolled into one genuine folk hero—and folk heroes only survive in oral anecdotes because they are ridiculed and spoofed rather than exalted. These old American idols all rose from the ranks of the common man, with "manners of unwashed democracy, spitting, bragging, brawling, talking slangily, ridiculing the dandy, and naively trumpeting their own merits."[349]

The mocked Crockett abandoned his family and ran to Texas, where his death resuscitated his image and built his legend—succumbing to overwhelming odds in a last stand being an almost

---

[347] Boylston and Weiner, *Crockett in Congress*, 22–23 (quotations); David Crockett, *The Autobiography of David Crockett* (New York: Charles Scribner's Sons, 1923), 186.

[348] Crockett, *Autobiography*, 83.

[349] Richard M. Dorson, *American Folklore* (Chicago, IL: University of Chicago Press, 1959), 200–201.

sure-fire avenue to apotheosis.[350] Suddenly Davy was a hero—much more so than he ever was in life. Almost immediately, Crockett Almanacs appeared, with the usual weather prophesies, zodiac signs, planting tips, and now braced with the wit and wisdom of Davy Crockett. People whose only book might have been a bible bought Crockett Almanacs, and they loved them, loaded as they were with Jacksonian crudity, violence, anti-intellectualism, racism, and chauvinism, where Davy "butchers the varmints of the forest, sneers at book learning and educated Easterners, despises niggers, Injuns, and Mexicans, and arrogantly trumpets the supremacy of Uncle Sam in foreign lands." These were good old American traits, and Crockett exemplified them.[351]

Jacksonian Democrats were characterized as outsiders, accusatory, critical, unhappy, conspiratorial, anti-intellectual, obsessed with evil, believing themselves victims, and trying to halt modernization. Whigs were said to be more business-oriented, enterprising, optimistic, wanting government-regulated economic growth, tariffs, banks, internal improvements, and welfare for the needy. While it appeared that most people felt connected to a political party less on material consideration than on inscrutable psychological reasons,[352] Crockett's party flip-flop was pure political expediency. His true frontier traits offend twenty-first century sensibilities, so it is difficult to fathom their nearly universal acceptance without factoring in the propaganda that facilitated the makeover. That indoctrination was having its effect in the latter half of the nineteenth century, when Theodore Roosevelt and Henry Cabot Lodge founded the Boone and Crockett Club in 1887. An organization for "gentlemen hunters," it included prominent members such as Francis Parkman, George Bird Grinnell, Frederic Remington, Owen Wister, and Gifford Pinchot, and illustrated the growing fascination with frontiersmen.[353]

One could only hope that their veneration of these char-

---

[350]   Bruce A. Rosenberg, *Custer and the Epic of Defeat* (University Park, PA: Pennsylvania State University Press, 1974), 1, 115, 193.

[351]   Dorson, *American Folklore,* 206–207, 208.

[352]   Kohl, *Politics of Individualism,* 17, 21, 22, 63, 74, 225.

[353]   Richard Slotkin, *Gunfighter Nation: The Myth of the Frontier in Twentieth-Century America* (New York: HarperPerennial, 1993), 37.

acters had more benign motives, but the enchantment continued, and the disparity between myth and reality only seemed to grow. Charles Latrobe, who visited America in 1833, already discerned a disconnection between our talk and our walk. He said American writers had to "show an extreme predilection and fondness for their native country, its history, its institutions—to see the past enveloped in a mist of glory, and the future veiled in a golden dust of prophetic anticipation."[354] Americans had already donned their rose-colored glasses.

By mid-nineteenth century, depictions of pioneer settlers were changing like a chameleon from a no-good semi-savage to the prototypical, exemplary American. Thomas Jefferson cooed about his yeoman farmer who would spread American democracy across the continent, while Andrew Jackson invited his rowdy, drunken friends into the White House during the age of the common man. Westerners Tippecanoe Harrison and Tyler, with rum, plow, ax, and freshly-hewn log cabins were the trick to win elections from foppish, aristocratic, and educated Easterners. A real American needed practical, school-of-hard-knocks learning, not book learning.

Mercy Otis Warren's 1805 book about the American Revolution was an imaginative treatment more concerned with building an image of public virtue than with historical reality.[355] She may have been the precursor of the American folklorist-historians such as Francis Parkman; Hubert Howe Bancroft, imperialist supreme; James Fenimore Cooper (who modeled his Hawkeye on Daniel Boone); and Frederick Jackson Turner, who all glorified the settlers and pioneers in literature and history. The Boone and Crockett boosters were ascendant, and by the end of the century the divinely guided settlers were depicted as the backbone of a wholesome, rural land of American exceptionalism. It was one of the most successful propaganda plays in history.

By the 1950s, America was struck by a déjà vu regurgitation of the Crockett phenomenon. In December 1954, forty million Americans watched the first episode of *Davy Crockett, King of the*

---

[354]   Charles Joseph Latrobe, *The Rambler in North America 1832–1833* (London: R. B. Seeley & WE. Burnside, 1835), 83.

[355]   Martin and Lender, *"A Respectable Army,"* 211.

Wild Frontier, and they were hooked. Four more parts aired throughout 1955, and they were tremendous hits, especially with the baby boomers, who were flexing their consumer power even as children. In the first several months, more than $100 million in Crockett products were purchased. Director Steven Spielberg remembered that one day he went to school and everyone but he had a coonskin cap, powder horn, and an "Old Betsy" rifle. Without them, Spielberg was called Santa Anna. "And they chased me home from school until I got my parents to buy me a coonskin cap."[356]

It was more than a century since the initial Crockett spectacle, but the catalysts were similar. Said folklorist Dorson, both were engendered in "a cascade of manufactured publicity," only this time stimulated by cinema and television. "A juvenile audience," said Dorson, "relishes the moth-eaten conception of the frontier hero who fights Indians, kills b'ar, and dies gloriously."[357]

Perhaps Dorson's comment was a bit sarcastic; did he mean a juvenile audience or an audience of juveniles? The Boone-Crockett image was implanted in the adult American psyche too. Literally thousands of "Western" films had been made by the 1950s, and not only pre-teens loved the cinematic frontiersmen and cowboys. Even before Disney scored big with Crockett, in the 1952 presidential season Tennessean Estes Kefauver campaigned wearing a coonskin cap, understanding what his opponent did not. The log cabin, common man image was the one used by Harrison in 1840, and in the 1952 primaries it gained Kefauver millions more votes than his Democratic opponent, Adlai Stevenson. The political bosses were not so enamored, however, and chose Stevenson, who most Americans viewed as an intellectual "egghead." Eisenhower, a soldier, easily beat a man with "book learning."[358]

The juvenile, anti-intellectual, jingoistic strain was still plainly evident in the adults. For example, John Wayne's 1960 film, *The Alamo*, capitalized on the Crockett groundswell. Wayne played the

---

[356]   Landon Y. Jones, *Great Expectations: American and the Baby Boom Generation* (New York: Ballantine Books, 1980), 50–51.

[357]   Dorson, *American Folklore*, 203.

[358]   Michael Coyne, *The Crowded Prairie: American National Identity in the Hollywood Western* (New York: I. B. Taurus Publishers, 1997), 2.

hero, and his personal convictions—he considered intellectuals as "pseudo-sophisticates, the people who belittle honor, courage, cleanliness"—saturated the film. As Wayne would have guessed, those Eastern sophisticates savaged his art as polemical, chauvinistic, fatuous, self-important, and doctrinaire. Wayne's Crockett even had to get his Tennesseans to go to Texas by deceiving them with a false letter supposedly written by Santa Anna, impugning their manhood. The affront to red-blooded frontiersmen could not go unchallenged, and they agreed to fight the Mexicans. The film also addressed the conflict between a "professional" (Travis), and the irregulars (Bowie and Crockett). Although militia and volunteers proved ineffective one century earlier, in *The Alamo* they still reigned supreme. The politics of the Wayne-Crockett Alamo, per Richard Slotkin, therefore rested "on the legitimacy of falsification and manipulation to evade…a skeptical public scrutiny."[359]

Almost every baby boomer will remember the Disney image of Fess Parker as Davy Crockett, swinging "Old Betsy" in a hopeless last stand against the swarming Mexicans at the Alamo. It is an image that ought to enter the dust bin along with coonskin caps, saddle shoes, and Hula Hoops. Historian Henry Nash Smith said, "From the time of Daniel Boone, the popular imagination had constantly transformed the facts of the westward movement in accordance with the requirements of the myth." The current conceptions of frontiersmen and the West had less to do with verifiable facts than with what Americans wanted to believe was the essence of their national identity.[360] We want to believe our ancestors were something they were not, and our Declaration that alludes to the pursuit of happiness more often than not achieves that objective through the pursuit of a little whitewash. Perhaps Americans are exceptional, but what is sanguine in our eyes may be ugly to the rest of the world. Were the frontiersmen really the greedy, cheating, xenophobic, racists that the record often illustrates? If so, it could be argued that we are simply viewing the past through a modern lens, when it should be viewed and judged relative to its own times, not ours. Blame it on

---

[359]   Slotkin, *Gunfighter Nation,* 516–18.

[360]   Smith, *Virgin Land,* 102; David Lusted, *The Western* (London: Pearson Education Limited, 2003), 19.

the times. But remember, times don't make people—people make times.

"Shoot them so the women might get husbands of courage": The Second Seminole War

If, as John Wakefield said after the Black Hawk War, God worked through the hands of the volunteers, they wielded a bloody, indiscriminate sword. Volunteers played a prominent, often calamitous, role in the Second Seminole War. Before it even began, Florida territorial governor John Eaton knew the Seminoles would be removed, but he hoped they would go without coercion, for troops would only cause trouble. He hoped regulars would be sufficient; if not, "the militia will have to be called, which will end in the butchery of these miserable people." Whites wanted their land, and they meant to get it through fair means or foul. He reiterated, "Let not, by any means, the militia be appealed to; they will breed mischief."[361]

The war began in December 1835, and almost immediately recriminations flew between the regulars and volunteers. After the bungled Battle of the Withlacoochee on December 31, the two hundred regulars accused the five hundred mounted volunteers of dawdling at the river crossing and missing the fight. Their poor showing and "precipitate retreat" was attributed to their "determination to return immediately to their homes."[362] On the other hand, Richard K. Call, soon to be appointed Florida governor, led the volunteers and claimed that many of them crossed the river to save the army: "It was owing to their appearance in the field, and the gallant intrepidity with which they fought, that the regular troops were not entirely cut off." In fact, Call asserted the volunteers were the heroes because they "saved the regulars from havoc and slaughter."[363] He believed if he was in command of the army he would rapidly end the war. General Duncan Clinch, he said, was brave, but "too slow" to fight Indians. Call acknowledged that the volunteers mutinied

---

[361] Eaton to Cass, March 8, 1835, ASPMA, V. 6, 493.

[362] Harris to Gibson, January 3, 1836, ASPMA, V. 6, 562.

[363] Call to Eaton, January 8, 1836, ASPMA, V. 7, 220 ("cut off" quotation); ANC, V. 5, No. 9 (August 31, 1837), 139 ("slaughter" quotation).

Richard K. Call. *Public domain*
Florida governor Richard Call treasured his volunteers and believed they saved the army at the 1835 Battle of the Withlacoochee.

and deserted, but he said he could control them.[364] Clinch disagreed. If he only had a few hundred more regulars he could have "brought the war to a speedy close." Call's volunteers claimed their enlistments had expired, refused to cross the Withlacoochee, and exhibited "many symptoms of mutinous & insubordinate conduct." It was impossible to do anything with them and it was best to let them go home, Clinch said. "No military man would willingly risk his reputation" with such men.[365] Reproaches continued for two years. Clinch scoffed at Call's remarks, *"that HE, Achilles like, shielded and saved them* [the regulars] *from destruction."* Clinch's aide-de-camp. Maj. John S. Lytle, asserted that "Call was not in the battle."[366]

General Scott had similar problems trying to get the volunteers to follow instructions. He directed civilian Major Leigh Read to take his men up the Withlacoochee to select a site for a military post, but circumstances prevented him from doing so. Scott said his order had been strong and precise, but Read's failure was "disgraceful delinquency." Dealing with such officers and men, Scott said, "No man's honor is safe." He called Read's excuses and failure "an act of sheer cowardice." Although he knew that his language was risky because Read was a favorite of Governor Call, Scott, like Clinch, placed a premium on his reputation.[367]

Scott never let possible repercussions repress his vituperative disposition. Scott's Orders No. 48, issued May 17, 1836, condemned the humiliating conduct of the Florida settlers and volunteers. He

364   Call to Jackson, January 9, 1836, ASPMA, V. 7, 218.
365   Clinch to Cass, January 30, 1836, AGO, RG 94, M567, R0119.
366   ANC, V. 5, No. 25 (December 31, 1837), 385, 389.
367   Scott to Jones, May 11, 1836, ASPMA, V. 7, 281.

claimed five Indians had committed a murder in Middle Florida and instead of giving pursuit, "the inhabitants abandoned their plantations and fled to Tallahassee and Monticello." Similarly, when a few Indians appeared near Micanopy, a gang of white cow-stealers reported a horde of Indians approaching, and the "whole country from Micanopy to Black Creek instantly became wild with fear" and ran away. The army called the civilian alarms a "daring falsehood," sown so thieves would have easy access to the abandoned stock. Scott berated the settlers, "who fled without knowing whether they ran from squaws or warriors," and said that no general could cure such unwarranted public fear.[368]

As one might expect, Scott's comments were condemned by Floridians. In an understatement, he told Governor William Schley of Georgia that his letter had elicited "a strong prejudice against me."[369] It was not the first time. During the War of 1812, Scott had to plead with the citizen-soldiers to fight. "These vermin," he said, "who infest all republics, boastful enough at home, no sooner found themselves in sight of an enemy than they discovered" that they could not be constitutionally used for such purposes. Theirs was a pleasant doctrine for the "faint hearted."[370] Scott's crudeness had not deserted him. In a letter to Adjutant General Roger Jones, Scott lamented that he now had "the hostility of the whole body of the militia" against him. He said they were generally patriotic, had honor, intelligence, "and *individual* courage," at least while safe at their own firesides, "but in *masses*, but little of the latter quality." Scott tried to paint himself as the beleaguered whistleblower. There were many "unpalatable truths" about the volunteers, but who was to tell them, he asked. "Shall I do it?" The good of the country depended upon his fortitude and "it shall be done. My sacrifice will be inevitable." He then challenged that if anyone could convict him of making one serious blunder in his conduct of the war, then "let me be shot."[371]

---

368   Scott, Orders No. 48, May 17, 1836, ASPMA, V. 7, 294;
369   Scott to Schley, May 26, 1836, ASPMA, V. 7, 314.
370   Timothy D. Johnson, *Winfield Scott: The Quest for Military Glory* (Lawrence, KS: University Press of Kansas, 1998), 27.
371   Scott to Jones, May 20, 1836, ASPMA, V. 7, 298.

Scott was not shot, but the complaints guaranteed him a change in scenery. Territorial Representative Joseph M. White called for President Jackson to remove Scott from command. The citizens of Tallahassee burned him in effigy. White saw their point, given Scott's "degrading epithets and insults." If Scott could not defeat five Indians with five thousand regulars, how, White asked, would he do so after disbanding the militia? They would not take orders from Scott, and the situation "requires his immediate withdrawal."[372]

Representative White harbored an animosity towards Jackson too, and when the president did not act fast enough, White said that Jackson and Scott were one of a kind. White wrote in a letter that Jackson told him, "Let the damned cowards defend their country; that he [Jackson] could take fifty *women*, and whip every Indian that ever crossed the Suwanee, and that the people of Florida had done less to put down the war, or to defend themselves than any other people in the United States." Jackson said that if five Indians had gone to Tennessee, not one would have gotten out alive. "He said the men had better run off or let the Indians shoot them, that the women might get husbands of courage, and breed up men who would defend the country."[373] Jackson's defenders insisted he never uttered such words, but in any event, Scott was transferred to Georgia to campaign against the Creeks.

The army was not alone in its condemnation of the volunteers. Some local planters had great misgivings. One, from St. Mary's, Georgia, tried to travel to St. Augustine on business, but saw the people fleeing, telling tales of Indians destroying property, stealing Negroes, and bashing infants' brains out. He said that the militia had been called, but many of them would not muster, and "are hunted out by files of armed men and forced to march." The man concluded, "God knows how or when it will end—NOTHING BUT REGULAR TROOPS, and in CONSIDERABLE FORCE, too, can save East Florida—and they may be too late."[374]

The army battled with the frontiersmen and settlers, perhaps more than it fought the Indians. General Thomas Jesup reported

---

[372] White to Jackson, May 28, 1836, AGO, RG 94, M567, R0133.
[373] White to Knowles, February 15, 1837, TPUS, V. 25, 378.
[374] NWR, January 30, 1836, V. 13, No. 22, 369.

that Alabama volunteers "were utterly averse to be placed under the command of an officer of the army," and he had no desire to lead such men. Georgia and Alabama militia refused to serve in Florida. From his new headquarters in Columbus, Georgia, General Scott said all the militia in the state were against him, and he reopened an old wound by taking another shot at Richard Call when the Florida governor wrote, "A panic highly dishonorable to the whole country has spread over the land," giving Scott an opportunity for an, "I told you so."[375]

Governor Call was having a rough time with his volunteers, who made another poor showing in several fights along the Withlacoochee in October and November 1836. Jackson was disappointed that Call's large force was unable to cross the river and drive the Seminoles out, but retreated and exposed the settlements to more raids. Call was relieved from command and became estranged from his one-time friend. Something had to be done with these volunteers. During 1835 and 1836, more than 23,000 of them mustered into service, while the regular army totaled about 6,000 men, with only about 1,500 effectives serving in Florida. The nation would have to rely on volunteers to beat the Seminoles, which meant it would be a long and costly war.[376]

The army knew that citizen volunteers were unreliable in battle, costly, querulous, and covetous. In the South it also discovered they were lazy. General Jesup was frustrated. He could not get wagon-drivers, muleteers, or laborers. "The southern militia do not labor for themselves, and consequently cannot or will not labor for the public." He constantly had to use regulars for fatigue duty, building roads, or repairing bridges. When he asked a militia general to have his brigade repair a road, he was told "it would be impossible, as his men would not work." Jesup considered "southern volunteers inefficient for many purposes." He was pleased when the navy arrived in Tampa Bay and offered some sailors to help defend the de-

---

[375]   Cass to Scott, June 20, 1836, ASPMA, V. 7, 342; Jesup to Scott, June 20, 1836, AGO, RG 94, M567, R0131 ("utterly averse" quotation); Scott to Cass, June 21, 1836, ASPMA, V. 7, 297 ("panic" quotation).
[376]   Butler to Call, November 4, 1836, ASPMA, V. 6, 992; NWR, December 24, 1836, V. 1, No. 17, 262; Mahon, *History of the Second Seminole War*, 187–88.

pots. Jesup was greatly embarrassed by the difficulty of getting work-
ers. If the war continued any longer, he said, "I shall send to Cuba
for mule-drivers, and to New Jersey for artificers and laborers."[377]

Besides not wanting to work, the volunteers often did not
want to fight. When they signed up at all, it was often with so many
temporal or territorial restrictions that they were nearly useless. One
company, calling themselves the Whitesville Rangers, claimed it had
mustered in to protect Fort Heileman. The captain, who reluctantly
escorted wagons to Fort Drane, said he would not leave his territory
again. The Jacksonville Black Hawk Rangers signed up to protect
Jacksonville and would not leave the area. Moses Curry's company
signed up to protect the east bank of the St. Johns River, not the west
bank.[378]

The Seminole War caused disruptions all across the frontier
as men were called up and transferred to Florida. General Gaines
was on the Sabine River dealing with the turmoil created by the
Texas Revolution and requested dragoons from General Atkinson at
Jefferson Barracks, Missouri. Atkinson demurred. His frontier was
just as important, and if he sent the dragoons he would have no one
but volunteers, and relying on them "to preserve peace on the frontier is a dangerous experiment—particularly if composed of men
drawn from the border settlements, who…would upon the slightest
cause bring on a conflict that might produce a war upon our whole
line of northwestern frontier." If peace and tranquility were to be
achieved, "none but regular troops under discreet officers should occupy in times of peace our border posts."[379]

To meet manpower demands in Florida, Congress created
the 2nd Dragoons in May, 1836. Scott figured he could subdue the
Seminoles with 2,400 regular infantry and 600 mounted. He hoped
not to have to use volunteers, but Congress authorized ten thousand
of them to serve six or twelve months. The first of the dragoons
trickled down to Florida during the summer, but the entire first five
companies were not organized, equipped, and shipped south un-

---

[377]   Jesup to Butler, December 12, 1836, ASPMA, V. 7, 821 (quotations);
Jesup to Butler, December 23, 1836, ASPMA, V. 7, 823 ("Cuba" quotation).
[378]   Smith, Wahoman, Curry, January 17, 1837, ASPMA, V. 7, 836–37.
[379]   Atkinson to Jones, September 6, 1836, AGO, RG 94, M567, R0116.

til December, and the remainder, under Col. David E. Twiggs, did not arrive until October 1837. Florida raised a 1,400-man volunteer brigade, Tennessee sent 1,200, Alabama sent 950, Missouri contributed 600, plus there was a regiment of 1,200 friendly Creeks. When Georgia organized another 1,200 mounted riflemen, the government called a halt. Four-fifths of the volunteers were mounted, and although they furnished their own clothing, equipment, and horses, they were far too expensive. A private's pay was only five dollars per month, but a horse cost between $120 and $300. Since Florida was hell on horses, the exaggerated or completely bogus claims for stolen, starved, or dead horses would be astronomical. Authorities refused the services of the Georgia brigade.[380]

"Save us from our Friends"

Some Floridians probably wished the government had refused the services of the Alabamians. The *Florida Herald* reported their poor conduct as they marched across the Territory, under the headline, "Save us from our Friends," stating they had "committed almost every crime except murder, and have even threatened life, from wantonness, if from no worse principle." After camping west of St. Augustine, the volunteers visited the town, "paraded our streets, grossly insulted our females, and were otherwise extremely riotous in their conduct." After getting drunk they returned to camp by the bridge over the San Sebastian River, where they "overturned the sentry box into the river," threw in two guards, and threatened to kill them. One man hid in the reeds, but the Alabamians saw the other swimming to shore and pelted him with every missile they could find, until a few men called for the "fun" to end and let him escape. "Such conduct is deserving of condign punishment," the *Herald* exclaimed. They complained to General Jesup, but doubted if he could do anything with men who disrespected all authority. Still, the paper said, "the rights of our citizens are not to be outraged with impunity."[381]

---

[380] James A. Sawicki, *Cavalry Regiments of the US Army* (Dumfries, VA: Wyvern Publications, 1985), 28.
[381] *Florida Herald,* January 1, 1838, in ANC, V. 6, No. 4, (January 25, 1838), 56–57.

Regardless of the volunteers' shortcomings and expense, the paucity of regulars necessitated their use. In the 1837 Annual Report of the Secretary of War, Joel Poinsett reiterated that using volunteers for short periods rendered "their employment not only expensive but inefficient," and it only got worse when used for longer periods. Remuneration for their horses alone "amounted in six months to a sum nearly if not quite equal to their real value." The government had to pay a tremendous amount of money for the horses that died for lack of forage. Over all, the mounted volunteers were "by no means so efficient as one-half the number" of regulars.[382]

On Christmas Day in 1837, the volunteers failed again. At the Battle of Okeechobee, the Missouri Volunteers were given the honor of leading the advance. The Seminoles had a strong defensive position and there was no way to flank them. The first volley tore through the ranks, mortally wounding Col. Richard Gentry, and the Missourians broke and ran, while the 6th and 1st Infantry also took heavy casualties. Colonel Zachary Taylor criticized the Missourians' behavior, but Senator Thomas Hart Benton denied their cowardice and blamed it all on Taylor.[383] An officer, writing under the pseud- onym, "Sheer Justice," explained that the volunteers complained if they were placed in the rear, but when given "the post of honor" in front, they could not hold it "after their muskets had once been discharged." The officer said Taylor was in an impossible position, to tell the truth and be condemned by one side, or lie and be con- demned by the other. Benton blamed Taylor for expecting volunteers to have the same "steadiness and discipline of regulars." Taylor al- lowed for caution, but not for cowardice. Their behavior was legend: "ample proof in the united testimony of every general officer in the service, from the days of Washington to the present moment." "If these volunteers were not intended to fight," the officer asked, "why were they sent to Florida?" Did no one realize beforehand that they were "fathers of families, and sons of farmers?" It was no time to make this discovery during battle. The blame, said "Sheer Justice," was on those who constituted the army as to need the assistance of

---

[382] "Annual Report of the Secretary of War," December 2, 1837, in ASP-MA, V. 7, 572.
[383] Mahon, *History of the Second Seminole War,* 227–29.

militia in the first place.[384]

Complaints about the volunteers continued through the rest of the Seminole War. A critic signing as "Miles" acknowledged that the regulars held the volunteers in "contempt and dislike," simply because they "deserved it." A correspondent named "Quasi Major" declared that if the war were ever to be won, commanders could not rely on volunteers, but "take into action *men who can shoot*."[385] A man signing only as "L" said that facts are stubborn things, but "I fearlessly assert, that all volunteers have never stood their ground in any one instance of close contest." In 1839, an officer on the medical staff in Florida said that the only way to win was to increase the size of the regular army, because anyone who knew anything about volunteers and militia knew "that they are the most *useless, insubordinate, expensive*, and *inefficient* that we can have."[386]

Zachary Taylor. *Public domain*
Colonel Taylor complained that the Missouri volunteers broke and ran at the Battle of Okeechobee, while civilians said the army was deluded by notions of "cow-boy chivalry."

The *Army and Navy Chronicle* gave the officers and civilians an outlet to vent their frustrations, often by lampooning their adversaries. One contributor, calling himself "E-TIS-TE-NUG-GE-PUG-GE,"[387] asked the *Chronicle* to keep track of a band of self-appointed ambassadors from Florida who sought an audience with President Van Buren, hoping to tell him that the army was not wanted in Florida, and that the tactics of Scott, Jesup, and their ilk were "mere-

---

[384]   ANC, V. 6, No. 10 (March 8, 1838), 155.

[385]   ANC, V. 6, No. 16 (April 19, 1838), 250 ("deserved it" quotation); ANC, V. 7, No. 16 (October 18, 1838), 249 ("can shoot" quotation).

[386]   ANC, V. 8, No. 13 (March 28, 1839), 202 ("close contest" quotation); ANC, V. 9, No. 19 (November 7, 1839), 290 ("most useless" quotation).

[387]   Tustenuggee was a Creek-Seminole name for "warrior." The corruption used may have been a sarcastic attempt at "Fat Warrior."

ly cobwebs of the brain... inappropriate to Indian warfare. Their noddles, also, are filled with high ideas of 'cow-boy' chivalry." The regulars must go. They wanted "*paid* volunteers, to have their own way, and fight on their own hook, and be subject to control of the Government on *pay days* only." The correspondent hoped the government would not relinquish to them the field of honor, for it would certainly break the poor regulars' hearts, and only serve to embolden the fancy "that the 'cow-boys' are the *bulwark* of the Indian frontier."[388]

Although the *Chronicle* did acknowledge civilian concerns, its sympathies lay with the army. In an 1839 editorial, it was troubled that soldiers had been fighting for four years in Florida, "but they have been met in too many instances with taunts and reproaches instead of thanks, by the people of that Territory, a portion of whom imagined that, if left to themselves, they could have managed the war much better." Frontiersmen and settlers have always failed at dealing with the Indians, and they had to "begin at last to perceive that they are not as potent in the field, as their fancies had led them to conjecture they were."[389]

As the Second Seminole War wound down, almost all of those involved in U. S. government military operations knew that militia and volunteers were not worth the cost of the gunpowder to blow them to smithereens. Paymaster General Nathaniel Towson reported to War Secretary Poinsett that volunteers and militia were not wanted because they cost too much and they only "retard and embarrass" the army. It was never a good idea, he said, to take them away from their farms and businesses, because of "the loss the country sustains by diverting labor from its proper object, and turning producers into consumers." Poinsett, in turn, told then-speaker of the house, James K. Polk, that volunteers cost four times as much as regulars, not including "the wastage attending their ignorance of every administrative branch of the service."[390]

General Jesup was convinced that you got what you paid for. He believed regulars to be the most cost-effective and efficient. But

---

[388]   ANC, V. 9, No. 15 (October 10, 1839), 232.
[389]   ANC, V. 9, No. 20 (November 14, 1839), 313.
[390]   ANC, V. 6, No. 17 (April 26, 1838), 263, 264.

even if not, he said, "I have yet to learn that the blood of American citizens is to be estimated by dollars and cents."[391] Jesup was incorrect—American blood was always valued in dollars and cents.

The old militia system was dying. Delaware disbanded it in 1831, Massachusetts did so in 1840, Maine, Vermont, and Ohio ended compulsory enrollment in 1844, and by 1850, California, Michigan, Iowa, and New Jersey abandoned fines for non-enrollment. The volunteers were all the rage by the time of the Mexican War in 1846, when one hundred thousand recruits enrolled, and the regular army increased to nearly thirty thousand.[392] In 1843, President John Tyler said that the nation would hence look "mainly to the volunteer companies of the Union." In 1846, President James Polk extolled the volunteers and said we could "confidently rely" on them for all military needs. By 1848, he explained that America did not need militia, or drafts, or conscriptions. Volunteers could do it all. "Our citizen soldiers are unlike those of any other country... accustomed from their youth to handle and use firearms, and a large proportion...are expert marksmen." Polk slighted the regulars and praised the volunteers, as was the wont of the Jacksonian Democrats who were still afraid of a standing army. And, like the American folklorist-historians of the day, he completely subscribed to the putative fiction that frontier citizens could shoot a rifle.[393]

The Mexican War, besides proving that Americans would invade foreign soil to steal land, also had the harmful effect of infusing the armies with thousands of civilians. Polk, no admirer of West Point, believed most of the officers it produced were Whigs who were politically opposed to him. When he filled the ranks with civilians it actually did politicize the army and led to an increase of Indian-baiting, hatred, and fighting after the Mexican War—just what the more civilized, socialized Academy officers had tried to prevent during the previous two decades.[394]

---

[391]   Jesup to Cass, February 15, 1836, in ANC, V. 8, No. 13 (March 28, 1839), 201.

[392]   Whisker, *Rise and Decline of the American Militia*, 333–34.

[393]   Marcus Cunliffe, *Soldiers & Civilians: The Martial Spirit in America 1775–1865* (Boston, MS: Little, Brown and Company, 1968), 180, 203, 204.

[394]   Skelton, *American Profession of Arms*, 144–45.

This fear and hatred of a national academy for training regular army officers was integral to Jeffersonian and Jacksonian politics for decades, and proved to be an impediment to the civilization of the white frontier. The reliance on, and glorification of, the militia and volunteers was integral to the developing national myth, part of the "American exceptionalism" mantra, but it was in opposition to the facts, and was perhaps more harmful to our national psyche than Americans would ever deign to acknowledge.

THE FRONTIERSMEN VS. WEST POINT

"Namby pambys of buckram"

The army, such as it was, between the Revolution and the War of 1812, was rather dysfunctional, with politics and political generals dominating national interests, creating a blurred line between civilian and professional control. From 1810 to 1821 the army was still regional, sectional, antagonistic to foreigners and Indians, and sympathetic to the frontiersmen, possibly arising from the drubbing they took in the War of 1812. That war discredited the entire army, and the opprobrium attached to it convinced junior officers to support the belligerent civilian General Andrew Jackson in usurpation of constitutional authority and aggression towards Spanish Texas and Florida.[395]

The army was trimmed and reorganized in 1821, in an attempt to make it more professional, subordinate, responsible, and accountable. As the Military Academy at West Point began graduating more officers, a marked change occurred, as socialized, educated, apolitical "gentlemen" took over. This metamorphosing army of professionals took its job seriously; it was to keep the Indians in check when necessary, but it was also to be a peacekeeper, a constabulary agency enforcing the TIA, an arm for internal development, and a check against white aggression. Its experience with bellicose frontier whites greatly shaped army attitude—as it spent years countering white atrocities it came to sympathize more with the Indians and became increasingly antagonistic to the avarice, swindling, and violent behavior of civilian borderers.[396]

Many of the West Pointers arrived with an unsullied attitude, while even "old timer" frontier generals could change their views. Edmund P. Gaines, for one, a poor man from backcountry

---

[395]   Watson, *Jackson's Sword*, ix, x; Skelton, *American Profession of Arms*, xiv.
[396]   Watson, *Peacekeepers and Conquerors*, ix, x, xii, xv, 1, 3; Skelton, *American Profession of Arms*, xvi.

Virginia, began his career hating Indians, scorning education, disregarding rules, and forever getting into scrapes with his arrogance and abrasive personality.[397] He changed. In 1817, he said it would be delightful to bring "savage man" to civilization, but "The poisonous cup of barbarism cannot be taken from the lips of the savage by the mild voice of reason alone;" strong force had to be applied. In 1819, while still a Jackson advocate, he believed that while the frontiers had some lawless, abandoned characters, they were "for the most part, honest, orderly, patriotic citizens." Surely they were deficient in education and property, but that wasn't a crime. Gaines criticized Indian agent David B. Mitchell for changing his mind about the Indians, from guilty to innocent, but it was the same attitude adjustment that several more years on the frontier produced in Gaines.[398]

By 1825, Gaines had shifted his opinion of Indians and settlers nearly 180 degrees. His biographer stated that by the early 1820s, Gaines had "long since discovered that most Indian trouble could be traced to white influence." Instead of battling Indians, Gaines was nearly to the point of a shooting war with Georgia governor George M. Troup and his state militia. White men trespassing on Indian lands, Gaines said, were "certain to produce acts of violence upon the persons and property of unoffending Indians, whom we are bound to protect." He said that Troup's belligerence was exacerbated by reliance on rapacious state agents who had "greatly deceived" him. In fact, it was the Indians who were "as firm votaries of truth as any men I have ever known." Gaines said it was his duty to give the Indians protection and justice, and he would do so, even if it meant war between the army and the State of Georgia.[399]

Troup complained to President John Quincy Adams that Gaines was childish, insolent, insulting, and defiant, and "were I to send him to you in chains, I would transgress nothing of the pub-

---

[397]   Silver, *Gaines,* viii.

[398]   Gaines to Calhoun, December 4, 1817, ASPMA, V. 1, 688 ("poisonous cup" quotation; Gaines to Calhoun, October 117, 1819, AGO, RG 94, M566, R0121 ("patriotic citizens" quotation).

[399]   Silver, *Gaines, 93;* Gaines to Troup, July 10, 1825, ASPIA, V. 2, 800 ("acts of violence" quotation); Gaines to Troup, July 28, 1825, ASPIA, V. 2, 802 (quotations).

lic law."[400] Adams tempered the feud somewhat by insisting both men behave themselves and act professionally. War was averted, but Gaines had chillingly foretold the Indians' fate: "the white people will cheat them out of their lands, get all their money, and then kick them to hell."[401] By 1842, Gaines had fully metamorphosed: My "views are based upon the great principle of civilization," that the Indian must be treated well, "by ministering to his comfort, by feeding him when he is hungry, and clothing him when he is naked."[402]

Gaines, unfortunately, was one of the few frontiersmen whose exposure to reality was enough to overcome his prejudices. If the Indians were going to be treated fairly and respectfully, it would have to be done by West Point graduates, who, after 1820, came mostly from the East and did not have the typical frontier hatreds. The new officers, socialized in conservative nationalism and legalism, sought to uphold the law, social order, and national stability. In their eyes, violent frontiersmen, filibusters, and swindlers who would cause havoc in the young nation were simply desperate adventurers, deranged law violators, and even nineteenth-century sociopaths.[403]

The West Pointers, who were only fifteen percent of the army in 1817, grew to forty percent by 1824. Their civilizing influence on the white frontier grew more significant, and they became a moderating influence on an often rampant Jacksonian white supremacist democracy. The officers could be the thin line of reason and compassion separating the Indians from a violent white culture, even if at times it seemed that the empathy was a mere surreptitious cover of humanitarianism to protect the reputations of the politicians and country in the court of international opinion.[404]

Because of the officers' education, exclusiveness, and elitism, at least in the eyes of many anti-intellectual frontier people, they became objects of derision and hatred. To be rid of the men who kept trying to spoil the frontiersmen's fun, West Point itself had to go. Congress often debated its fate. In 1820, Tennessee Representative

---

[400]   Troup to Adams, August 31, 1825, ASPIA, V. 2, 815.
[401]   Iveson Brooks affidavit, October 17, 1825, ASPIA, V. 2, 850.
[402]   Gaines to Jones, April 21, 1842, AGO, RG 94, M567, R0251.
[403]   Watson, *Peacekeepers and Conquerors*, 18, 184.
[404]   Watson, *Jackson's Sword*, 246, 269.

Newton Cannon motioned that the House pass a bill to abolish the Academy, repeal all laws relating to it, and sell all the property to the highest bidder. After much argument, the committee voted, eleven to six, that it was inexpedient to demolish it at that time; however, one representative who voted to keep it recommended that half the students and half the expenditures ought to be cut.[405]

Many viewed the Academy as a school for the children of wealthy elites. Westerners argued that high entrance standards discriminated against their section—a legitimate complaint perhaps, but a self-inflicted one given the Jacksonian common man's disdain for education. This sticking point was smoothed somewhat when appointment control was given to congressmen and regulated by the total number of representatives of the states and territories, thus ensuring appointees with a more equitable distribution of wealth, class, and politics.[406]

It was never enough to stop complaints. In 1833, Tennessee protested that too much money was being spent on West Point, and congressmen still favored "a few young men, sons of distinguished and wealthy families." It was an "aristocratical institution" that excluded talented and meritorious people who did not have the luxury of a fine education. Besides that, a government school was not mentioned in the Constitution. The next year, Ohio sent a resolution that a military academy supported by public funds "was wholly inconsistent with the spirit and genius of our liberal institutions," so it must be abolished and any further appropriations ended.[407]

The *Army and Navy Chronicle* discussed causes of the vitriol. It found that most of the Academy's adversaries came from the West. One instance apparently stemmed from the days when civilian contractors were clearing forest and building the Cumberland-National Road through Ohio and Indiana. The civilians, "who were rather more sedulous for their own interests than for the public benefit," were making plenty of money building poor roads. When the government directed young army engineers to oversee and correct their

---

[405]   NWR, March 18, 1820, V. 18, No. 3, 54–55.

[406]   Skelton, *American Profession of Arms,* 139, 142

[407]   Tennessee Resolution, November 26, 1833, ASPMA, V. 7, 89; Ohio Resolution, March 3, 1834, ASPMA, V. 5, 307.

errors they did not appreciate it. The scrutiny, integrity, and honesty put an end to "their lucrative prospects and schemes for profit."
Therefore, the Academy became "a Nursery of a Military aristocracy," and Ohio called for its abolishment.[408]

Complaints spiked during the Second Seminole War. In
1836, 117 regular officers, about seventeen percent, resigned their
commissions. They quit for a number of reasons, including a rapidly
expanding economy that lured officers into other professions, because the Jackson administration had put the squeeze on liberal leave
policies, and because the Florida war was becoming a quagmire.
Some saw the rise in resignations as an indictment of the Academy,
but they failed to realize that many of the officers who quit were not
Academy graduates. Civilians, however, saw the officers simply as
cowards trying to avoid fighting.[409]

General Jesup, another non-West Point holdover from a previous generation, knew regulars were more efficient than volunteers,
but he couldn't help speaking out against a few of them who left
active duty in Florida to take posts as teachers at the Academy. "It
may truly be said," he wrote, "the spirit of the service is gone, or
fast going, when officers of respectable standing can be found ready
to abandon the high and honorable duty of their profession to become schoolmasters at West Point." His letter prompted protests.
One officer said that not everyone is a born soldier, and while Jesup
disparaged the graduates, he continued to employ them as his aides,
adjutants, engineers, quartermasters, and commissaries. The officer
reminded Jesup that seventeen graduates had already been killed
fighting in Florida, "and none but a prejudiced mind will say that
the 'spirit of the service'" was gone from such men. Another officer
challenged Jesup to explain what was wrong with being a schoolmaster. "Had these remarks fallen from some overgrown dolt, in a
country school, where the ignorant boor sometimes consoles himself
for his want of brains" by disrespecting the instructors, it might be

---

[408]   ANC, V. 2, No. 11 (March 17, 1836), 164–65.
[409]   ANC, V. 11, No. 12 (September 17, 1840), 182; Skelton, *American Profession of Arms*, 216–17.

understood, but Jesup ought to know better.[410]

Jesup was enmeshed in Jacksonian America, a world of anti-intellectualism, but one where many of the officers were bastions of the dying eighteenth-century Enlightenment in a losing fight with the growing nineteenth-century Romanticism that embraced Anglo-Saxon racism, bigotry, and xenophobia, bolstered by "awakenings" of evangelical religion. The atmosphere was hostile to army officers who were more educated and cosmopolitan, and who politically tended to be Whigs. They were united because of civilian criticism, and more so because of the frustrating experience of trying to keep the peace between belligerent frontiersmen and the Indians.[411]

A *Charleston Courier* correspondent, signed as "P," trashed the army, stating that the Academy led to "an odious *military aristocracy*," and it was clear to all that education "NEVER MADE A HERO." Using Scripture as a guide, he claimed that victory in battle was not to the strong, nor the race to the swift, "but to him who abideth in *the faith*." The army was said to be infested by men of poor nature who would never change because of an education, and who were inveterate gamblers who never knew an honest dollar not derived from the public treasury. He claimed that civilians made the best soldiers, and that the publically educated "grovelings" did not represent the military genius of the nation. "P" could not provide "specific facts," but the readers were to take his word. The current system of educating officers, he said, did nothing but bring into the army "a number of mere Namby Pambys of buckram... whose only energy or aptitude for service evaporated with the *wilting* of their *starched shirt collars*." The army was a clumsy machine because the officers were "drones, fops, and coxcombs," who tried to apply "too much *science*."[412] The attack was answered by an officer signed as "Agricola," who countered "P's" contumelies, called them "precious dogmas," and decried the fact that new regiments were being officered "by

---

[410] ANC, V. 6, No. 6 (February 8, 1838), 93 ("become schoolmasters" and "prejudiced mind" quotations); ANC, V. 6, No. 9 (March 1, 1838), 138 ("brains" quotation).

[411] Watson, *Jackson's Sword,* 279; *Reginald Horsman, Race and Manifest Destiny: The Origins of American Racial Anglo-Saxonism* (Cambridge, MS: Harvard University Press, 1981), 1–2.

[412] ANC, V. 5, No. 12 (September 21, 1837), 181–83.

citizens, by decayed editors, stale politicians," or by young men who had flunked out of West Point. The vile aspersions cast on the army should elicit feelings of "utter disgust."[413]

The dispute was unending. One officer complained that those who spewed the most rancorous hostility towards West Point did so out of personal profit motives or because they were uneducated. Civilian applicants had merely to pass the most rudimentary test, yet they complained of the tough questions. An irritated observer decried the spelling of one applicant: "sugar with an *h*, and musket with *tt*."[414]

Officers were not the only ones defending their cohorts. Foreign visitors observed the tension and often sided with the army. Alexis de Tocqueville believed that officers needed to sever ties with civilians because they had such opposing viewpoints. "If I am not mistaken," he wrote, "the least warlike and least revolutionary section" of the army were its leaders, while the civilian non-commissioned officers longed for war.[415]

English farmer Patrick Shirreff visited America in 1835. While traveling from Detroit to Chicago he rode for a time with an officer he called "Major W," a prim individual who "seemed as if carrying the dignity and honour of the whole army on his shoulders." The major appeared diffident, but hard as nails, and certainly one you would want on your side in a fight, yet his countrymen, agitated by his demeanor, considered him "very repulsive."[416]

Another English visitor, Charles Latrobe, wrote that while at Fort Dearborn (Chicago), he met several West Pointers, exiled for long years on the frontier, far removed from cultivated society, "and in daily contact with the refuse of the human race." Their sensibilities and graces were taxed, but wherever Latrobe met them he found them always to be "good friends and good company." He did have an inclination why the regular army was viewed with jealousy and suspicion: it was on the frontier to "defend the Indian against

---

[413]   ANC, V. 5, No. 17 (October 26, 1837), 266–68.

[414]   ANC, V. 8, No. 4 (January 24, 1839), 50; ANC, V. 8, No. 8 (February 21, 1839), 122 (quotation).

[415]   Tocqueville, *Democracy in America*, 759–60.

[416]   Patrick Shirreff, *A Tour Through North America* (Edinburgh: Oliver and Boyd, 1835), 220.

the citizen" as well as vice versa, and because officers had to prevent "encroachments and nefarious dealings of the loose inhabitants of the boundary, he is sure to win the hatred of the latter, who, as a citizen, will always meet with a sympathy, which, however just the cause, will rarely be accorded to the officer."[417]

The antipathy to West Point and its officers was slow to dissipate. Even during the Mexican War, when more Academy-trained officers were needed, Congress cleaved to the old fears. Certainly some of the dispute was political. The *American Whig Review* chastised Democratic congressmen as "stump-orators and editors of the slang-whanger school," for their unreasonable disrespect of officers. "When Members of Congress deliberately characterize cadets as 'wasp-waisted vampyres,' and officers of the army as 'epauletted loafers,' it would appear hopeless to argue points of propriety in that quarter." Those who doled out "stale denunciations and gross misstatements" only proved their "wretchedly crude" notions about the military establishment.[418]

Jacksonian Democrats disdained what they saw as educated aristocrats, so West Point would have to go. In a people who professed to believe in equality and considered that no man was better than any other man, there was no room for the gifted. The myth of the universal frontiersman as savior of the land was surely taking hold.

---

[417]   Latrobe, *Rambler in North America*, 205, 320.

[418]   "Army Attack and National Defence," *The American Whig Review*, V. 4, No. 2 (August 1846), 147.

HUNS IN HOMESPUN

"Your children ought not to kill us"

A treasured saga of American history concerns brave frontier settlers who were constantly faced with capture, torture, or death
by savages lurking in the forest. The very verbs and adjectives used
are symptomatic of the myth: Indians torture and savages lurk,
while pioneers clear and settlers build garden out of desert. Our
history is replete with tales of painted Indians massacring innocent,
defenseless settlers. Of course, there were instances of whites slaughtering Indians also, but for most of our history those incidents were
not emphasized. Some infamous episodes made the books, such as
the Puritans killing hundreds of Pequots in 1637, militia murdering
ninety Delawares at Gnadenhutten in 1782, volunteers killing about
150 Cheyennes and Arapahos at Sand Creek in 1864, or the army
killing about 170 Blackfoot at the Marais River in 1870. There were
many more examples.

One study of "atrocities" throughout American history finds
that fifty-six percent of deaths were caused by Indians and forty-four
percent by whites. Another study concentrating on "battles" between
1850 and 1890 finds white casualties to be thirty-one percent, while
Indians casualties were sixty-nine percent.[419]

Although we will likely never be able to prove which side
did the most killing, it seems reasonable to say that the whites were
the perpetrators more often than the history books tell—one reason
being that so many incidents were not well-publicized, large-scale
massacres, but near-daily events that barely made notice in the local
newspapers.

In the time frame of this study, 1815 had just begun when a

[419]   William M. Osborn, *The Wild Frontier: Atrocities During the American-Indian
War from Jamestown to Wounded Knee* (New York, Random House, 2000), 294–307;
Gregory F. Michno, *Encyclopedia of Indian Wars: Western Battles and Skirmishes,
1850–1890* (Missoula, MT: Mountain Press Publishing Company, 2003), 353.

force of civilian rangers attacked friendly Pottawatomies near Fort Clark, Illinois Territory. War Secretary Monroe called it "a horrid and unprovoked murder," and directed that the guilty be immediately punished. They were not.[420]

Near Muscle Shoals, Mississippi Territory, a white man named Taylor had rented a field and cabin from the Cherokees. Allegedly some of the Indians came to the cabin and insulted Taylor's wife. He recruited seven whites to help him get satisfaction. On August 12, 1816, the demand for an explanation turned violent and the whites shot and killed two Cherokees.[421]

Some Georgians were fed up with the lawless whites who attacked the Seminoles, saying they "have been plundered, and one or two of them murdered, by a banditti (a remnant of the self-styled patriots) who infest a part of East Florida." "The atrocities of these miscreants" made matters worse, and the government of East Florida did not seem to have the means or desire to punish them. Georgia called for a military force at Trader's Hill, on the St. Mary's River, for protection "from red or white savages."[422]

Since the army had more important areas to allocate its scarce resources, Georgia militia moved to guard the "defenseless inhabitants of our southern frontier." "Major" Bailey found no depredating Indians, however, so he and twenty-four volunteers went west to the Suwanee River, supposedly following a trail of stolen cattle. On the evening of May 22, 1817, they crept up to a half dozen Indians around a campfire. Bailey had "no doubt [they] were a party fitted out to do mischief." Without investigating further, the volunteers waited until night and attacked, killing one man and wounding others, who got away. They took two guns and three horses and in the morning they followed a trail that led to the big bend of the St. Mary's and found another camp. Attacking at daybreak, Bailey's men killed two, wounded several, took two guns and sixteen horses, "two of which belong to our citizens." Bailey was proud of his deeds and was "happy to state that not one of our party received any inju-

---

[420]   Monroe to Clark and Edwards, January 13, 1815, TPUS, V. 17, 116–17.
[421]   NWR, September 21, 1816, V. 11, No. 4, 63.
[422]   NWR, April 12, 1817, V. 12, No. 7, 112.

ry."[423]

The Indians were Yuchis, who lived on the lower Chatta-hoochee and were on a hunting excursion. The Creek agent David B. Mitchell said they were peaceful and "had always been friendly to our government." But white men attacked, killed them, stole their horses, guns, "everything else they could carry off," and left four men wounded and dying. Mitchell wanted to know if the perpetrators were Georgians or Spanish subjects from Florida, so any retaliation "may be averted from our people." Mitchell, who had been governor of Georgia until he resigned to become Creek agent in March 1817, divined what the likely result would be: the First Seminole War began because of "these petty acts of aggression...by a set of lawless and abandoned characters" who lived by plunder—never mind that they were often state militia.[424]

Two whites went to the Choctaw Agency in Alabama and shot and killed the unoffending Nanta, an act that Agent John McKee called an outrage. Since the only witnesses were the murderers, McKee knew it was useless to try to prosecute. His only hope was that the government would make "pecuniary compensation to the family of the deceased Indian."[425]

Near Pecan Point in 1819, in what would become Oklahoma, two whites named Williams and Music illegally sold liquor to the Indians and engaged in numerous nefarious schemes. Music persuaded some Delawares to let him cultivate one of their fields, but when the crops were ready to harvest, he and Williams drove the Indians away and took possession of the land. The Indian factor, John Fowler, said that the two whites were the "worst characters" in the territory. Additionally, two Indians were killed at Music's house by "drunken whitemen." Fowler hoped that the army would drive out Williams and Music, but it never could staunch the mayhem caused by frontier whites.[426] Four years later, Lt. Richard Wash, 7th Infantry, was still trying. He presented notices to the settlers west of

---

[423]   NWR, July 19, 1817, V. 12, No. 22, 335–36.
[424]   Mitchell to Senate Committee, February 23, 1819, ASPMA, V. 1, 749.
[425]   McKee to Calhoun, April 15, 1819, TPUS, V. 18, 608–09.
[426]   Fowler to Jamison, June 1, 1819, Fowler to McKenney, June 14, 1819, TPUS, V 19, 74–76.

the Kiamichi that they had until December 1, 1823, to get out or be evicted. They ignored him. General Scott was also frustrated by the whites' "perfect contempt." They were "a band of lawless marauders" who were "in the habit of committing the most outrageous acts of robbery, violence, and murders." He suggested a fort be built on the Kiamichi River to control them.[427]

Frontier Huns did not only inhabit the southern and western borders. In Licking County, Ohio, "an outrage of the most atrocious nature was committed" on a band of about twenty Oneidas from New York who were seeking new homes. On the Indians' return journey, several women—one being pregnant—and their children had fallen behind the main party, "when they were way-layed [sic] by a parcel of ruffians and fired at." The bullets took effect, but although "it was undoubtedly the intention of the ruffians to have killed the whole of them," only the pregnant mother had expired at the time of the report.[428]

In 1820, at the Little Osage village in present-day Missouri, Chief Walk in Rain protested the killing of three of his people, saying that when American "children come among us we give them meat and corn, and tobacco, and treat them like brothers," but that when the Indians went among the Americans "your children ought not to kill us." Walk in Rain knew it was hard for Americans to "keep your young bad men from mischief," but the Osage "cannot walk in the good road and let your men walk in the bad road." "Your men make me cry," he said.[429]

Realizing that they could not live in proximity to whites, some Cherokees moved west years before removal was official policy. As one band traveled from Tennessee, a white gang attacked them and stole their horses. When they got to Arkansas they located a fine tract of land with a salt lick and spent considerable money and labor to develop it. Just before they could market the salt at one dollar a bushel, white men named Bean and Sanders, representing themselves as having government authority, ordered the Cherokees off the land, took over, and produced the salt, selling it at three dollars per

---

[427]   Wash to Arbuckle, October 31, 1823, AGO, RG 94, M567, R0006; Scott to Jones, January 16, 1824, AGO, RG 94, M567, R0012.

[428]   *Ohio Register* in NWR, October 16, 1819, V. 17, No. 7, 111.

[429]   NWR, October 14, 1820, V. 19, No. 7, 112.

bushel. The Cherokees futilely filed for injury and losses.[430]

In 1824, the *Indianapolis Gazette* reported "one of the most outrageous transactions that has occurred since the settlement of this state." A party of ten unnamed Indians (three men, three women, and four children), were hunting in Madison County near Fall Creek about thirty-five miles northeast of town. On March 22, five white men and two boys approached their camp and lured the three adult males away for the ostensible purpose of hunting cattle. After walking some distance, the whites treacherously opened fire and killed two of the Indians, while the third escaped badly wounded. They returned to the camp, made professions of friendship to the wary women, and proceeded to murder them and their children. Supposedly wanting to make it look like Indians had committed the murders, they scalped and mutilated the bodies. One of the white boys later confessed that a man in their party "killed one of the children by taking it by the heels and beating its brains out against a tree." Murder must have been the sole purpose, for the attackers left without plundering the camp; when other whites found the bodies the next day, nothing had been stolen. When they went to the authorities, other neighborhood vultures descended on the massacre scene, stripped the bodies of their clothing, and stole "every species of property" they could find. The story was revealed by "one of the lads," who said his father forced him to assist. Four of the white accomplices were arrested; one, a boy, was pardoned, but three were executed the following year.[431]

An 1829 incident along the Missouri-Iowa border showed just how severe Americans could be to Indians for the slightest perceived transgression. In 1824, the Iowa had ceded their land south of the present-day southern Iowa border, but bands roamed into northern Missouri, particularly along the Chariton River, where deer and elk were still plentiful. Big Neck loved the area and in June 1829, he and about sixty men, women, and children traveled downriver until they encountered settler cabins in what is now Adair County. As was

---

[430]   Jolly to Rogers, March 25, 1821, TPUS, V. 19, 341.

[431]   *Indianapolis Gazette*, March 30, 1824, in NWR, May 8, 1824, V. 2, No. 10, 152. It is noteworthy that a white man killed an Indian child by bashing its head against a tree, since there were many tales told by frontier whites how often Indians allegedly killed white children by the same method.

often the case, the whites, seeking trade advantages, plied them with liquor, and "cheated the Indians out of everything valuable, and retired, quite satisfied with their skill." When the Indians came to their senses, they tried to get their *"civilized friends"* to trade again, but they refused. Apparently the Iowas stole some cattle in revenge, or their dogs killed some hogs—in any case the whites demanded payment. Big Neck, who had not signed the land cession, protested that the whites were on Indian land and they should leave. The angry whites went for reinforcements.[432]

Big Neck may have been irritated that whites were living on his favorite hunting grounds, but he knew he should not get into a confrontation, so he pulled out, going north about ten miles before camping for the night on what would be called Battle Creek, northeast of present-day Connelsville. The settlers, in the meantime, had gathered twenty-six men under a Captain Trammell, and, per Missouri governor John Miller, rode after them to get "satisfaction for previous outrages."[433] On July 17 they approached the camp, but when Big Neck saw armed men riding in, he hurriedly packed up to leave. Brigadier General I. B. Owen of the Missouri militia explained that the whites merely rode into their camp "in a peaceful manner." When they saw "the squaws and children" trying to escape, they "endeavored to convince the Indians that they were friendly to them & had no hostile intentions & requested them to deliver up their guns." Armed whites demanding surrender of weapons was no way to prove friendship, and in response, one Indian allegedly cocked his rifle and pointed it at John Myers. Myers's son immediately fired and killed the Indian, which began a short, sharp melee. From three to twelve Indians were said to have been killed, while the whites lost three killed on the field, plus Captain Trammell, who later died of his wounds. The whites precipitously fled. Governor Miller first reported that from 150 to 200 Indians were on the warpath and he asked President Jackson for help.[434]

---

[432]   NWR, August 29, 1829, V. 1, No. 1, 1.

[433]   Eugene M. Violette, *History of Adair County* (Kirksville, MO: Densville History Company, 1911), 9–10; Miller to Jackson, August, 1, 1829, AGO, RG 94, M567, R0045 ("previous outrages" quotation).

[434]   Owen to Miller, July 25, 1829 (quotations), Miller to Jackson, August 1, 1829, AGO, RG 94, M567, R0045.

Tales of a great uprising quickly spread. I. B. Owen collected two hundred militia and rushed to the area, while Miller requested the army to hurry, for there were supposed to be fifteen hundred Indians rampaging in the state. When Owen got to the scene of the fight, Big Neck was long gone, having fled east to the Sauk village on the Mississippi. More volunteers arrived, found nothing to do, and reluctantly went home, having lost the chance to kill Indians. Nevertheless, Miller told Brigadier General Atkinson that "the most exemplary punishment ought & must be inflicted" upon the Iowas, for if they escape, "a general Indian war" will begin. Miller also requested that President Jackson pay the state's expenses of organizing the militia "to repel the invaders." He declared that no part of the country was more exposed to Indian depredation than the Missouri frontier, and wanted more forts and more troops.[435]

Colonel Leavenworth did not believe the Indians had any intention of making war. He hoped the militia would be disbanded because they had "a decided tendency to impede any arrangements for tranquilizing the frontier" and the settlers were "not in the least danger."[436] The colonel called for the Iowa, Sauk, and Fox in the area to repair west to Cantonment Leavenworth, more to get them out of harm's way than as punishment. Not only did they come in, but they "cheerfully agreed to surrender a number [19] of their chiefs and warriors as hostages for their good conduct," as well as to apprehend those who may have killed any whites. Leavenworth told Governor Miller that in justice he ought to take measures against the whites who were also to blame in starting the mess.[437] Thus ended the "Big Neck War."

Down in Florida, the Camp Moultrie Treaty of 1823 gave the Apalachicola Band of Creeks and Seminoles a reservation on that river. Middle Florida, however, was filling up with plantations and whites coveted the land. In 1832, Chiefs John Blunt and Davy signed an agreement to move west with all 256 of their people, for a payment of $13,000—$3,000 in cash and the remainder when they

---

[435] Violette, *History of Adair County*, 10; Miller to Atkinson, July 22, 1829, Miller to Jackson, August 1, 1829, AGO, RG 94, M567, R0045.

[436] Leavenworth to Thornton, August 10, 1829, AGO, RG 94, M567, R0045.

[437] Leavenworth to Miller, August 15, 1829, AGO, RG 94, M567, R0045.

made the move.[438] Blunt and several others traveled to Arkansas with Agent John Phagan to see if they liked the proposed tract. They did not, but Phagan maneuvered them into signing an acceptance. While Blunt was gone, whites, including Hugh Robinson, Silas Wood and others, "took violent possession" of the reservation. When Blunt got home, on the night of April 30, 1833, Philip Oaks, John Ralls, and George Stafford broke into his house, beat him and his family with clubs, and stole about $700 in cash and $300 in goods. One hundred dollars reward was offered for their capture, and they were arrested, but somehow escaped and fled to Alabama and Texas.[439]

Now penniless, Blunt could not and would not move, at least until his son and other boys of the town, who had been sent to an Indian school in Kentucky, were returned home. Events were at an impasse until the new agent, Wiley Thompson, met with the band in the fall of 1833. He was able to pay them $1,500 of the $10,000 still owed, for supplies and transportation for the migration. Agent Thompson complained to Governor DuVal of the whites who constantly swarmed in at the smell of money, "like so many hungry Vultures hovering over the dieing [sic] skeleton of some fallen animal." They were devoid of honesty, "guided alone by avarice," and "swindle them out of their horses, cattle, hogs, corn & peltry."[440]

Thompson's portrayal was dead on, but white civilians weren't the only deceivers. In October, acting governor James D. Westcott, Jr., of Florida learned that Yellow Hair, another chief in the Apalachicola reserve, also desired to move west. Westcott told him he could go in place of some of Blunt and Davy's people who had run away down the peninsula. Westcott then heard that Blunt wanted to go alone, to pocket the $10,000 for himself, but Westcott said he would be paid only for the proportion of the people he took. In other words, if the original 256 people did not remove and Blunt went alone, his portion would only be thirty-nine dollars.

An angry Blunt said that "the white people who said this

---

[438]   Kappler, *Indian Treaties,* 352.

[439]   DuVal to Sheffield, February 4, 1833 ("violent possession" quotation), Sheffield to DuVal, February 23, 1833, Westcott Proclamation, June 1, 1833, DuVal to Herring, November 29, 1833, ASPMA, V. 6, 456–57; Pope to DuVal, May 10, 1833, TPUS, V. 24, 846.

[440]   Thompson to Cass, December 2, 1833, TPUS, V. 24, 916–17.

were fools. Did they suppose he would go to Texas without warriors, unable to protect himself? It was not true." Besides, if any of his people ran away, it was Commissioner James Gadsden's fault, because he had broken promises, such as assuring them a boat and supplies, and telling him he would be compensated for the robbery. Now, Blunt found he was to pay for the move out of the money promised to him that he had not yet received.[441]

In January 1834, Blunt got his son back, but others had died of cholera while at school. As he had promised, Blunt and his people paddled down the Apalachicola to the sea. Agent Thompson learned that "a systematic plan is matured to rob Blunt on his passage," and believed that the freebooter Stafford had been bragging that "Blunt should not escape with his life and money." There was also another plot to steal Econchattamico's slaves, and the steamboat captains were bribed to steer the Indians into the white men's clutches.[442] Governor Westcott took the threats seriously and told an agent to accompany them at least as far as the Sabine River, "to protect them and their party from the depredations of scoundrels who may meet them along the coast, and rob them or force them to violence."[443]

The Indians sailed to New Orleans, followed by William Beattie of Columbus, Georgia, who was determined to steal their money. Wise to his plans, Agent Thompson took them to a bank in New Orleans, paid them another $8,000 of the promised treaty money, and told them to depart at once. Thompson returned to Florida, but Beattie found the Indians, and on April 8, 1834, filed a bogus claim against them and had them jailed. Not knowing what to do, they made a deal with Beattie to get out of jail by paying him $2,000 and giving him two slaves worth $1,000. Rushing to get out of the white men's grasp, they crossed Louisiana and arrived at the Trinity River in Texas. Forty-nine had died and others ran away, leaving only 152 to reach their new home. Blunt died shortly after.[444]

---

441   Westcott, October 23, 1833, USCSS, V. 4, 707.
442   Thompson to DuVal, January 20, 1834, ASPMA, V. 6, 451–53.
443   Westcott to Johnson, November 12, 1833, Westcott to Cass, November 13, 1833, USCSS, V. 4, 673.
444   Thompson to Herring, January 19, 1835, ASPIA, V. 6, 485; Foreman, *Indian Removal*, 323.

"A good thing to introduce the small-pox among them"

Indians who tried to escape often found their exit blocked by whites who wanted their property and annuities. The state militia that infrequently tried to defend them faced white backlash. In 1832, Georgia volunteers protected a band of emigrating Cherokees in care of Superintendent Benjamin F. Currey, when armed men from Tennessee forced their way into the camp, began a quarrel with the captain of the guard, and cursed him with "the most abusive epithets." They "presented a cocked pistol and bayonet at the breast of the officer, who, with the guard present, seized their muskets in their own defense, amidst men, women, and children." It appeared that bloodshed was imminent, but Currey and a few brave citizens intervened and convinced them all to calm down. The Tennesseans agreed to leave, but said they would raise more men and drive all of them back into Georgia. To protect the Cherokees from "abandoned and unprincipled white men, who...commit every kind of imposition on them, and succeed...in thwarting every kind of benevolent intentions of the Government," army regulars were essential.[445]

Whites assisting Creeks were also intimidated. William H. Moore helped twelve families removing from Georgia to reservation lands in Alabama, but local whites set up an ambush along the road. They stopped the Creeks, tied them up, "and most inhumanly whipped some of them, and drove the whole party back. Those white savages then entered into a written contract with each other to whip or kill any white man who should offer aid to the Indians in obtaining reservations in the country."[446]

The immigrants faced severe hardships, but those who got out early avoided the coming war in Florida. It was no secret that hungry Indians hunted for game and occasionally killed livestock, but not every Indian seen in the woods was guilty. On June 18, 1835, seven white men from Alachua County, Florida, found five Seminoles hunting game. The whites surprised them in their camp, took their guns, bound them, and "flogged them with their cow whips."

445   Davis to Cass, March 23, 1832, USCSS, V. 3, 272.
446   Moore to Cass, March 27, 1833, USCSS, V. 4, 148–49.

Two other Seminoles who had been hunting nearby heard the ruckus and came to investigate, but the whites shot and killed one and seriously wounded the other. At Fort King, Brigadier General Clinch and Agent Thompson found the settlers in an uproar. They met the Seminoles to learn what happened, but determined the Indians had committed an "outrage," and "a demand was made on the chiefs for an immediate surrender of all the Indians that had been engaged in the affair." The Seminoles were enraged to be forced to make amends for something they had not done. On August 11, Seminoles intercepted and killed Pvt. Kinsley Dalton as he carried mail from Fort Brooke to Fort King, which Clinch said was "to revenge the death of a relative of theirs, who was killed in the encounter" in June. The Indians were satisfied with the justice, but it was another step closer to war.[447]

In the Old Northwest, the Pottawatomies may have ceded their lands to escape the whites, but it was no compensation for those who relocated or those who remained. The emigrants to Wisconsin Territory after the Black Hawk War were in bad shape, not scheduled to remove west yet, but not having sufficient land to farm. Captain Edwin V. Sumner of the dragoons found white squatters already among them. They protested, and Sumner said, "I must confess, that it was a complaint, that I could not well answer, for the whites are actually starving them." He counseled them not to retaliate, and told the whites to avoid clashing with the Indians, "for the Government would not sustain them, in any act of violence."[448]

A Pottawatomie named Manitou made the bad choice of entering the village of Milwaukee, when, on the evening of July 16, 1836, Joseph Scott and Cornelius Burnett assaulted him, stabbed him in the chest, and left him to die. Coroner Enoch Darling said the whites were taken into custody and the Indians appeared satisfied, but "as we have no judiciary here," they would not be tried. He wrote to President Jackson and asked "as to the manner in which the prisoners shall be disposed of."[449]

---

[447] Clinch to Jones, June 30, 1835, ASPMA, V. 6, 76, 79; Clinch to Jones, September 15, 1835, AGO, RG 94, M567 ("revenge the death" quotation).

[448] Sumner to Atkinson, July 5, 1836, TPUS, V. 27, 610–11.

[449] Darling to Jackson, July 19, 1836, Coroner's Inquest, July 17, 1836, TPUS, V. 27, 625–26.

Other Pottawatomies traveling to their new homes were waylaid by a gang of horse thieves led by the Kitheroy Brothers, who had fled from the law in Kentucky and Tennessee and now operated in Missouri. The gang followed the Indians in Carroll County, feigned friendship, and sold them whiskey. At daylight the Indians awoke to find eight of their horses stolen. Five of them followed the tracks that led directly to the gang's camp. When one stepped up to claim his horse, the whites shot him dead and wounded another, but the other three charged and shot two whites. The gang fled, leaving one of their men dead on the ground and another wounded. The Pottawatomies recovered their horses and rode directly to Fort Leavenworth to turn themselves in. Colonel Kearny would not jail them or turn them over to white "justice."[450]

In Wisconsin Territory in 1837, hungry Winnebagoes killed and ate three hogs. Nineteen whites pursued and caught them near the Wisconsin River, tied them, whipped them, and stole their guns. Two hungry Winnebagoes went to the cabin of a Mr. Sutton to beg for food, but he chased them away and shot one. The agent blamed it on their "distressed situation"—anyone would steal rather than starve to death.[451]

English traveler Patrick Shirreff observed the Illinois locals in 1835. "The cruelty of many of the militia towards the poor Indian when once in their power, was only to be matched by the fear which they showed at meeting their enemy." Their cowardice was incomprehensible, for they would fight any neighbor to the death for the slightest offense, "while whole detachments fled at the sound of a solitary war-whoop." Yet, Shirreff said that these same men could only "with difficulty be prevented from killing the squaws and children when defenseless." Certainly some of them had grievances, but "it must be admitted, the first aggression is generally on the side of the white."[452]

After years on the frontier, Brigadier General John E. Wool also came to that conclusion. He had been tasked with protecting the Cherokees from predatory whites, but found it nearly impossible.

[450] Dougherty to Clark, July 14, 1836, AGO, RG 94, M567, R0116; ANC, V. 3, no. 7 (August 18, 1836), 125.
[451] Dodge to Harris, February 15, 1837, TPUS, V. 27, 735–36.
[452] Shirreff, *Tour Through North America*, 258–59.

The rights of the Indians, he said, "have been too often disregarded, too often trampled upon, and too often violated without cause or justification, with impunity, not to have sunk deep into their hearts." If it did not stop there would be war. Wool was specifically referring to white men "who reside among them and who seem bent on drenching the country with blood." Wool referenced the murder of a Cherokee known as Darkee near New Echota, Georgia, in March 1837. Three whites, John G. Smith, John O. Smith, and Jasper Griffin, walked up to his house in broad daylight and shot him down as he answered the door. Wool had them arrested and turned over to civil authorities, but "the prejudices of the people, stimulated by avarice," made him doubt justice would be done. "With these people it really seems to be no crime to kill an Indian."[453]

John E. Wool. *Library of Congress* General Wool tried to defend the Cherokees from avaricious whites, but faced a Court of Inquiry for his efforts.

Colonel Ethan Allen Hitchcock, who spent about fifty years on the frontiers from Florida to California, was an armchair philosopher, well-read, conscientious, concerned that Americans did not treat their fellow man with compassion, and was often disgusted with their behavior. He was convinced that "the presence of the whites is a blight on the Indian character," and that Americans go to war "not for 'liberty,' but for land." He shared the view with many other officers that "the government is in the wrong" for going to war in Florida. There were constant cries of Indian outrages, but, Hitchcock said, "The wrong came, as usual, from white men." "It is a hard case for the troops to know whites are in the wrong, and yet be compelled to *punish* the Indians if they attempt to defend themselves." In California, Hitchcock met a Methodist minister who put on the airs

---

[453]   Wool to Shaw, March 20, 1837, Wool to Poinsett, March 31, 1837 (quotations), AGO, RG 94, M567, R0154.

of a gentleman but was not one at all. He "had the audacity to say that Providence designed the extermination of the Indians and that it would be a good thing to introduce the small-pox among them!" Unfortunately, Hitchcock said, that sentiment was the same "opinion of most white people living in the interior of the country."[454]

When ministers also believed God wanted the Indians dead there was little hope. The atmosphere of anti-intellectualism opened a niche for the nascent evangelicals. As the Methodists, Baptists, and to a lesser extent Presbyterians, gained in numbers and power they increasingly sanctioned violence. According to author Jeffrey Williams, the Methodists in particular valorized violence against Native Americans, seeing them as legitimate targets for extinction if they stood in the way of progress. As such, the evangelicals were ahead of the Manifest Destiny curve that exploded in the 1840s. Methodists enthusiastically melded into the American imperial cultural mindset of national mission to carry Christianity around the globe as part of God's battle against evil. As Williams pointed out, Methodists beat their plowshares into swords, sanctioned violence against the Indians, and glorified pioneers as innocent victims who should rightfully kill infidel savages. As victims, pioneers were also justified to act in self-defense, even if self-defense meant pre-emptive strikes against people who were not at war—a mindset that still exists today. Since spreading the American way of life was a divine calling, and Indians attacked Christian pioneers, aggression was justified. Violence was a religious obligation. Bishop Francis Asbury, a Methodist, cried for revenge against the "barbarian" Creeks who made war on women and children. He ended his harangue with the words, "O God, save thy people from rage of the heathen!" but it was unclear which heathen he was referring to.[455]

Even while Americans moved west to take over lands they claimed were unused and free, the blatant land grab produced cognitive dissonance in a few people who still retained a conscience.

---

[454] Ethan Allen Hitchcock, *Fifty Years in Camp and Field: The Diary of Major-General Ethan Allen Hitchcock, U. S. A.,* W. A. Croffut, ed. (New York: G. P. Putnam's Sons, 1909), 71, 111, 120, 395, 396.

[455] Jeffrey Williams, *Religion and Violence in Early American Methodism: Taking the Kingdom by Force* (Bloomington, IN: Indiana University Press, 2010), 106, 114, 121–27.

Presbyterian preacher James Finley explained how he dealt with the dichotomy. His fantastic rationalization was that ever since the days of George Washington, the United States had only taken Indian lands by legitimate treaty. "We conquered them [the Indians] on the field not to usurp territory, but to place them in a condition to observe how much more their interest and permanent prosperity would be, and have ever been, promoted by the plow than the sword."[456]

In the world according to Finley the Indians were nearly exterminated and had their lands stolen in a grand experiment to see if the survivors would prosper better without the wars that were begun by the whites who stole their lands. Dissonance alleviated. The whites could continue with their pacification program.

The Second Great Awakening of the early nineteenth century drew the curtain on the Enlightenment. Evangelicals swarmed the country, and by the 1830s their churches and their peripatetic proselytizers had become the mainstream of American Christianity. Some historians may argue that the Second Awakening was a national, integrating, cohesive force that rescued the country from the brink of moral chaos. It may be more valid to see the Second Awakening as a reactionary attack on Enlightenment sensibilities that had threatened to short-circuit the American mind into actually believing that all men were created equal and could assimilate and live together in peace. That was more than enough to cause great cognitive dissonance. The Awakening was a means to reduce the dissonance by trashing the Enlightenment and dumbing down its intellectual aspects with a return to God. Dump the thinking for the emotion: it was the perfect opening for the Romantic Age, and the perfect vehicle to justify the egregious behavior of the frontier people.

They "wished to ravish her"

Civilians acting unofficially were a threat to law and order, but when organized as state militia, they were often legalized marauders. The great distinctions between the militia and the regular

---

[456] James B. Finley, *Life Among the Indians; or, Personal Reminiscences and Historical Incidents Illustrative of Indian Life and Character* (Cincinnati, OH: Methodist Book Concern, 1860), 126.

army was in training and discipline. The army was preponderant-
ly staffed by professional officers socialized, civilized, educated, and
enlightened at the Military Academy at West Point. Although often
despising the civilians they had to protect, they were the barrier between the backwoods ruffians and frontier mayhem.[457]

The militia elected their "captains," who were usually as untutored and reckless as the men they led. With the commencement
of the Second Seminole War, the conflict between militia and regular army was exacerbated. One volunteer unit under "General" Andrew Moore of Alabama claimed to have captured 250 Seminoles
and sent them to General Jesup, who then sent them to Col. William Walker. When Jesup made no mention of them, a newspaper
criticized him for not giving credit to Moore. Jesup asked Walker
if Moore delivered any prisoners; Walker said no. Jesup asked if
Moore captured any Indians; Walker said no. Jesup was confused,
so Walker explained that Moore had only detained the Creeks Jim
Boy and Elkahadjo and their warriors—Indians who "were actually
in the service of the United States and preparing to join you in the
campaign."[458]

As the war dragged on, more Indians became indiscriminate
targets. Creek Chief Big Warrior had commented that "all red men
are alike in appearance" to whites,[459] but despite their temporary
detention, Jim Boy and about seven hundred warriors continued
to assist the army. The Creeks were expected to remove west, but
these warriors and their families had been granted a reprieve until their term of service had expired. Although some warriors went
home, others agreed to stay and fight for Jesup, which was unacceptable to the whites who wanted their land immediately. Marine
lieutenant and Indian agent John G. Reynolds indicated that these
families, living mostly between Columbus, Georgia, and Tuskegee,
Alabama, were friendly and obedient, and if not for the "designing
white men," there would have been no trouble. In February, 1837, to
placate civilian complaints that the Indians were depredating, Reyn-

---

[457]   Skelton, *An American Profession of Arms*, xiii, xvi; Watson, *Peacekeepers and
Conquerors*, xii, xv, 3.

[458]   Jesup to Walker, Walker to Jesup, October 14, 1836, ASPMA, V. 7,
819–19.

[459]   Big Warrior to Bibb, NWR, June 13, 1818, V. 14, No. 16, 271.

olds confiscated their guns. Jim Boy's and Elkahadjo's warriors were wary, but complied.[460]

Instead of assuaging white fears, it only served to make the Indians easier targets. On February 9, militia under a Captain Harrold went to mixed-blood Anne Cornell's place and stole two free blacks, an Indian boy, her fodder stacks, property, and $300 in cash, and then set fire to her house. On the 19th, Reynolds heard that Capt. William Wellborn, "usually styled general," was approaching a Creek camp. He hurried there, "fearful some depredations might be committed upon the Indians," but he was too late; Wellborn had already taken them prisoner. Reynolds demanded to know under whose authority Wellborn acted: "His reply was THE PEOPLE." Reynolds protested, but was powerless to resist. He argued that if Wellborn held the men, at least he should provide protection for the women and children.

Wellborn gave Reynolds "positive assurance that they would not be molested," but the lieutenant soon realized the blunder of asking the fox to guard the henhouse, for he saw that Wellborn was "more anxious to gain the applause of his disorganized soldiery than the public good." After dark, Reynolds heard muskets firing in the direction of Jim Boy's town. Wellborn made no move until Reynolds reminded him of his promise to protect the Creek families. While he demurred, armed citizens from Russell County, Alabama, under a Mr. Park, invaded several homes. In one, they found the ninety-year-old infirm and deaf man, Loch-chi-Yahola, and the fifteen-year-old daughter of Texico, a warrior imprisoned by Wellborn. The whites broke into the house, saw the girl, and "wished to ravish her." The old man tried to stop the assault. They later found him, said Reynolds, "lying in one corner, shot in the breast, and his head literally stove in with, as I supposed, the butts of muskets." The girl got out and ran towards a thicket and they shot her in the leg. Park's men invaded other homes and stole finger-rings, ear-rings and blankets from the women. Reynolds demanded that Wellborn arrest Park's entire company, but Park consented only to apologize. When Reynolds threatened to inform General Jesup, the volunteers were unconcerned.[461]

---

[460]   Reynolds to Wilson, March 31, 1837, ASPMA, V. 7, 867–68.

[461]   Ibid., 868–69.

On February 5, Georgians under men named Garmigan and Morris raided Marine Lt. Thomas P. Sloan's Creek camp, and "captured" more men. Sloan protested their conduct as "inhuman" and contrary to government pledges. They pillaged the Indians' houses, stole guns, property, and money, and disappeared for two weeks. When they returned, this time with Park, they swept the area clean, taking the last of the mules and horses. Additional militia arrived and insisted on moving all the Indians to Tuskegee. Sloan was about to distribute provisions and begged for a reprieve until all could be fed. Instead, the militia broke into the supply house and stole all they could carry. Sloan totaled the losses, which included 145 horses, sixty cattle, two hundred hogs, one hundred bushels of corn, sixty-three guns, and assorted cooking and farming utensils, in the amount of $8,250.[462]

The militia shunted the Creeks down to Mobile as fast as they could, leaving Jesup to explain to War Secretary Poinsett that he was "not aware of the brutal treatment which those families had been compelled to submit to," until he heard from Reynolds and Sloan. All he could do was hope they would be remunerated.[463]

It seemed sensible not to antagonize the Indians, especially after they had agreed to emigrate, but the people of Alabama and Georgia were in a frenzy to grab all the land they could get. Georgia governor George R. Gilmer realized the Indians' "fate is a hard one, and should be softened, if possible." "Our citizens should not resort to force in obtaining possession of their lands," but should hold back at least until the army could get the Indians on the road and out of sight.[464] It was a hopeless plea.

"In the disguise of Indians"

Illegal whiskey sellers were a significant class of white Huns, and Indian Territory had more than its share, especially along its east edge from Fort Gibson to Fort Towson. In February 1837, a regiment of Arkansas volunteers was camped near Fort Gibson. Be-

---

[462]   Sloan to Wilson, March 31, 1837, ASPMA, V. 7, 869–70.
[463]   Jesup to Poinsett, April 11, 1837, ASPMA, V. 7, 867.
[464]   Gilmer, May 6, 1838, ANC, V. 7, No. 1 (July 5, 1838), 11.

cause there was little use for them, all but three companies were discharged. Some of them engaged in a "frolic" with the nearby Cherokees, involving liquor, gambling, and a bit too many freedoms taken with the Cherokee women. As a result, some of the volunteers "were handled 'with gloves off' by the red gentlemen, which rendered them unusable for duty the next day." In revenge, about twenty volunteers went after the Cherokees, but unable to find the actual participants, they "fell upon and severely beat a young Indian lad and several other Cherokees." This prompted Cherokee warriors to whip and cut off the hair of the women who had "frolicked," and when they vowed to punish their white consorts, the volunteers fled to the fort for protection.[465]

In Miller Country near Fort Towson, whites sold whiskey to some Shawnees, started a fight, and killed two. Lieutenant Josiah Vose, Jr. said that the locals were "adventurers from various parts of the U. States, and much addicted to gambling, drinking, and every other vicious propensity." Whiskey sellers near the Choctaw Nation do "not hesitate to take away everything from the Indians they can get hold of." Vose concluded that, "It is the interference of dissolute and irresponsible white people that has, in my opinion, caused nearly all the difficulties."[466]

Near Red River in April 1838, a Mr. Rogers sold liquor to the Choctaws and cheated them of their property. A few fleeced Indians went to the cabin of a Mr. Simmons and begged for a pipe and tobacco, but Simmons became enraged and smashed one of them with a shovel. They retreated, but returned with a few lengths of boards to give Simmons some of his own medicine. This time Simmons shot and killed one; nevertheless, the others attacked and beat him, plus a few other men at his house. A citizen committee went to Lieutenant Vose, reported the Choctaws had killed a man, and demanded he bring the offenders to justice. The chief delivered two men, and Vose confined them, but nothing was done to Simmons. Vose concluded that "the white people were undoubtedly the

---

[465]   NWR, April 22, 1837, V. 2, No. 8, 124–25 ("gloves off" quotation); Arbuckle to Jones, February 21, 1837, AGO, RG 94, M567, R0135 ("severely beat" quotation).
[466]   Vose to Macomb, July 7, 1837, AGO, RG 94, M567, R0153.

aggressors as is generally the case in all Indian difficulties."[467]

General Gaines wholeheartedly agreed. He was "convinced that more than nine-tenths of our conflicts with the Indians, during the last thirty-eight years, have arisen either directly or indirectly, from the lawless intercourse" between traders and Indians. The Indian, he said, was plied with liquor, sold his goods for a pittance, and awakened "to find himself stripped of every necessary and comfort of life, to feel himself disgraced and degraded to the condition of a miserable dog, bound to see his wife and naked children starve." Because of this "legalized fraud and treachery," the Indian was often provoked to violence. The army could not stop the illegal liquor trade, but a good start would be to "imprison all white men" caught in Indian country.[468]

Threats did nothing. In February 1840, about a dozen whites crossed Red River into Texas. They found and trailed a small band of Cherokees for a few days. After the Indians camped one night, the whites crept up, attacked them while they slept, and killed seven or eight. The Cherokees fought back and killed a white man before they escaped the surround. The white leader said they attacked first because they feared the Indians would attack them. The officers at Towson believed it was nothing more than "an outrageous and unprovoked murder." No white jury, however, would convict them.[469]

In the summer of 1842, it appeared that the Second Seminole War was at an end. President Tyler and his cabinet members were tired of the casualties, complaints, and cost. Brigadier General William J. Worth gathered the remaining chiefs and offered them a deal: those who went west would receive a rifle, money, and a year's rations; those who stayed would not be molested if they removed south of the Peace River. Worth declared the war over on August 14, and went on leave.[470]

Removing the Seminoles was left up to 4th Infantry Col. Josiah Vose, who faced the same challenge as his son at Fort Towson:

---

[467]   Vose to Arbuckle, April 12, 1838, AGO, RG 94, M567 R0156; Vose to Jones, April 13, 1838, AGO, RG 94, M567, R0177.

[468]   ANC, V. 6, No. 21 (May 17, 1838), 328.

[469]   ANC, V. 10, No. 12 (March 19, 1840), 188.

[470]   Missall, *Seminole Wars*, 201–202; Mahon, *History of the Second Seminole War*, 315–16.

belligerent, intractable whites. Scofflaw liquor sellers infested much of Florida, particularly around Fort Brooke and Tampa Bay. Vose directed Capt. Washington Seawell to get help from the marshal and boot them out, including civilians Collas, Jackson, and Warren, whom Seawell called "worthless drunkards." Vose went to St. Augustine on business, but when he returned he discovered the liquor sellers were still there. The marshal said he could do nothing without a directive from the territorial judge showing just cause. Vose was livid. The swindlers "are not only shielded from the action of the law by the imbecility of the civil officer whose duty it is to enforce it, but thereby encouraged to carry on the nefarious traffic in liquor by which they subsist."[471]

Suddenly, liquor sellers were the least of Vose's worry, as white gangs seemed determined to rekindle the war. In August 1842, the Perkins family was killed in Washington County, West Florida, and War Secretary John Spencer instructed Vose to punish the culprits, whom he assumed were Indians.[472] Creeks and Seminoles were then traveling down the peninsula to a reservation in south Florida. Some had certainly not yet received word of the recent peace. Perhaps an uninformed band was guilty of the murders, or maybe it was one of the white outlaw gangs that infested the area. Bishop Henry Whipple called Florida "the tip of the top for rascality and knavery," and said half of the populace were "rogues and scoundrels."[473]

White gangs had been operating along the Georgia-Alabama-Florida borders for years. In 1840, a gang jumped two 2nd Dragoon privates near Fort Reed, Florida, killed one and captured the other. They tied him to a tree and abused him for a week. They decided to shoot him, but several of their guns misfired just at the time a dragoon patrol rode by. The gang fled and the soldier finally worked himself free, reaching the fort after two weeks in the wilderness. He said the gang consisted of mulattoes, Indians, and white

---

[471]   Seawell to Barbour, September 4, 1842, Vose to Jones, September 8, 1842, TPUS, V. 26, 535–37.

[472]   Jones to Vose, September 12, 1842, TPUS, V. 26, 538.

[473]   James M. Denham, *"A Rogue's Paradise" Crime and Punishment in Antebellum Florida, 1821–1861* (Tuscaloosa, AL: University of Alabama Press, 1997), 108.

men.[474] James Avant, called "a monster in human form," was wanted for murder in Pensacola and Marianna. His gang had hideouts along the Apalachicola River, where he "perpetrated murder and robbery upon all who fell in his way." Avant was caught and lynched in 1845. The Burney Gang and the Yeomans Gang disguised themselves as Indians, stole slaves, and ran them north for sale. They robbed, murdered, and terrorized Florida's northern counties. Yeomans was lynched in 1846, but there were always others to continue the mayhem.[475]

In April 1840, on the road along the Suwanee River between Forts Fanning and Griffin, whites disguised as Indians attacked a wagon with a small army escort. Colonel Zachary Taylor, 1st Infantry, believed "the attack was made for purpose of plunder rather than to destroy the guard," for they were allowed to escape and the teamster reported that the leader was a white man in "pantaloons, calico shirt, black vest and whiskers," who ran up to the wagon and declared, "teamster, don't be frightened, we will not hurt you." When the teamster reached Fort Fanning he reported that he had seen the man before, and he was probably the conduit for ammunition being supplied to white desperadoes.[476]

The gangs operated along Indian routes through Florida. A veteran who did not identify himself wrote to the *Army and Navy Chronicle* about the marauding whites, who have never found "a better theatre for land piracy than poor Florida is now." Even if the Indians were gone, he said that the whites "would continually plunge into the woods, paint and dress as Indians, and plunder and kill." In 1842, the St. Augustine *News* editorialized about "intelligence so atrocious in its nature as hardly to admit of belief." There existed "bands of *white men*, who carry on a system of predatory and murderous warfare in the disguise of Indians," robbing wagons and stealing property all throughout Middle Florida. The paper concluded that much of the depredations in Florida during the war were either instigated or committed "by a white banditti, who, being intent

---

[474] ANC, V. 11, No. 12 (September 17, 1840), 190.
[475] Ibid., 190–92.
[476] Taylor to Jones, April 14, 1840, AGO, RG 94, M567, R0218; ANC, V. 10, No. 18 (April 30, 1840), 279.

on plunder, in their predatory attacks on unprotected citizens have shown themselves utterly reckless of all the claims of humanity." Authorities were searching the Tampa Bay region for one unnamed woman, the wife of a gang leader, who had been known to boldly enter towns with wagonloads of stolen dry goods, capes, gloves, suspenders, overcoats, shawls, and other items, and sell them to willing customers. Every time the authorities would close in, however, the newspaper lamented, "the bird had flown."[477]

Army officers would not have found the reports astonishing. They had been dealing with lawless, frontier miscreants for decades. In Florida, Lt. John W. Barry, 1st Artillery, said that frontier white men "are the most depraved, lying, cut-throat scoundrels I ever met with." In 1841, Capt. John B. Clark, 3rd Infantry, said that white frontiersmen did more to perpetuate Indians wars than anyone, and "I believe that two-thirds of the recent murders have [been] committed by the whites themselves."[478] When Captain Seawell learned that a Mr. McDaniels and his family were killed while traveling near Chocachatti, he immediately concluded that whites were to blame and advised the citizens not to retaliate against Indians. Secretary Spencer agreed and directed Seawell to "enjoin upon the settlers the absolute necessity of abstaining from all offensive acts towards the Indians." The Creeks were moving south through the area and frightened and angry whites were the last thing they needed.[479]

Vose investigated the Chocachatti incident and found that only two settlers contended an attack was made, and stories varied as to the amount of money allegedly stolen. Civilians had "pillaged a canoe" and stolen the Indians' food—just as Vose had expected, because "the whites are the aggressors" almost every time. Seawell heard of settlers' plans "to destroy the Indians wherever they may find them." Both officers feared the whites would attack the Creeks when they passed through.[480] The "spirit of implacable resentment towards the Indians in the vagabond class of the citizens of this

[477]   ANC, V. 11, No. 9 (August 27, 1840), 137 ("dress as Indians" quotation); ANC, V. 13, No. 8 (March 12, 1842), 125.
[478]   Watson, *Peacekeepers and Conquerors*, 139–40, 193.
[479]   Seawell to Barbour, September 14, 1842, Barbour to Seawell, September 17, 1842, AGO, RG 94, M567, R0260.
[480]   Vose to Jones, September 24, 1842, AGO, RG 94, M567, R0260.

Territory" deeply dismayed Vose. While the war was going strong, "not a man evinced a disposition to defend even his own fireside," but now that the Indians have made peace, "a most unaccountable desire" to kill had taken over the minds of the citizens.[481]

Among the Indians moving south were Octiarche, whose people had opted to remain in south Florida, and Tiger Tail, who had agreed to emigrate. Both said that they would not be the first to break the peace. When Secretary Spencer ordered Vose to punish Indians for murders that may have been committed by white gangs, he faced a quandary. Even if a renegade Indian was guilty, the majority wanted peace and had fulfilled "every promise they have made." Vose disobeyed the order. He adamantly stated that an attack would "forfeit every pledge" made to them, and felt the "most unprejudiced conviction that it will be for the good of the country" not to execute the secretary's instructions. The civilians may have wanted war, but the army did not. The War Department agreed with Vose.[482]

By October, many of the Indians had gathered at Tampa Bay. Vose was still concerned about hostile whites and wanted the army to escort Octiarche's party, but he did not want them. He had made peace and could not understand why anyone wanted to attack him. Vose could not get him "to comprehend that I have no control over the citizens of the country."[483]

Vose's 4th Infantry left Florida in October, and General Worth resumed command in November. The Indians, however, were moving too slowly for him, and Worth "captured" Tiger Tail and about 250 of his people and shipped them off to New Orleans. Tiger Tail, said to be either old, or sick, or drunk, had to be carried aboard on a litter. He died in New Orleans—in one respect, his journey completed.[484]

---

481   Vose to Jones, September 29, 1842, TPUS, V. 26, 552.
482   Vose to Jones, September 26, 1842, TPUS, V. 26, 548–49.
483   Vose to Jones, October 20, 1842, AGO, RG 94, M567, R0260.
484   Mahon, *History of the Second Seminole War,* 317–18.

Chehaw Village: Sand Creek of the East

"Massacres" on the American frontier were disgracefully commonplace, with whites being the aggressors in many more instances than Americans might realize or care to admit. From the Gnadenhutten Massacre in 1782, one year after the nation ratified the Articles of Confederation, to Wounded Knee in 1890, the year recognized as the closing of the frontier, whites and Indians had been slaughtering each other. One of the most infamous was the November 1864 incident at Sand Creek in Colorado Territory, when elements of the First and Third Colorado Cavalry killed perhaps 150 Cheyennes and Arapahos. In contrast, one of the least remembered was the 1818 Chchaw massacre in Georgia. Although it had many similarities to Sand Creek, it nevertheless faded away in America's collective memory.

The Chehaw, or Chiaha, of the Muskogean linguistic group, first appeared in the historical record as a few small bands living in what would become Tennessee, Georgia, and South Carolina. They joined with several other tribes to fight the South Carolina settlers in the Yamasee War from 1715–17, but being defeated, were forced to relocate, and settled along the Chattahoochee and Flint Rivers in southwest Georgia. There they became part of a loose confederation of tribes called the "Creek Nation," with the Lower Creeks generally in Georgia and the Upper Creeks in Alabama.[485]

During the War of 1812, the Upper Creeks fought American troops under Gen. Andrew Jackson in several bloody battles. The Lower Creeks tried to stay neutral, but some of their warriors joined Jackson in the fight. Jackson was victorious, and in the resulting 1814 Treaty of Fort Jackson, both the Upper and Lower Creeks lost much of their lands. Angry with this injustice, Lower and Upper Creeks slipped away to Florida and joined the Seminoles to resist further white encroachment.

Who "started" the subsequent First Seminole War is debatable. There was constant raiding and killing along both sides of

---

[485] "The Chehaw Indians," https://georgiagenealogy.org/lee/the-chehaw-indians.htm; "The Chiaha Indians," http://www.carolana.com/Carolina/Native_Americans/native_americans_chiaha.html.

the border. Lands said to have been ceded to the United States in southwest Georgia were also claimed by the Mikasukis, a Seminole tribe that insisted it was not part of the Fort Jackson Treaty. Tasked with clearing the area, Brig. Gen. Edmund Gaines attacked the Mikasuki settlement at Fowltown in November 1817, which is said to have sparked the war. Gaines, however, believed it began the previous February with settler killings in southeast Georgia. A Savannah newspaper acknowledged that some murders "were actually perpetrated by a gang of white desperadoes, who had assumed the dress and appearance of Indians," and although Gaines concurred that much trouble was caused by "evil disposed white persons," he still blamed the Indians.[486]

In fact, friendly Indians were helping the U. S. military fight the Seminoles and disgruntled Creeks. William McIntosh, a Lower Creek chief of Scots-American and Creek parentage, fought beside Jackson in the war of 1812 and currently had about one thousand warriors fighting the Mikasukis. The Chehaws had also sent a smaller contingent of men to assist the army. Jackson had an affinity for the Chehaws. He left Tennessee in January 1818 with his volunteers, but by the time they reached Georgia they were low on supplies. Jackson sought relief at Fort Early, but barely found a half a pint of corn and flour per man.[487]

Jackson complained about the dearth of supplies: "I have been so frequently embarrassed from the failures of contractors, that I cannot but express a hope that some other more efficient and certain mode of supplying our army may be adopted." The contractors must live up to their agreements or be subject to "severe and merited chastisements" in court.[488] At Fort Scott at the junction of the Flint and Chattahoochee Rivers, Lt. Col. Mathew Arbuckle and his men were also starving, and he begged Jackson for rations. Arbuckle was saved when friendly Indians gave him "ten poor beeves and five hogs." He worried that McIntosh and his Indians would also arrive

---

[486]   Missall, *Seminole Wars*, 32–33, 36; Gaines to Rabun, January 23, 1818, NWR, February 14, 1818, V. 13, No. 25, 412 ("evil disposed" quotation); NWR, August 15, 1818, V. 14, No. 25, 424 ("desperadoes" quotation).

[487]   NWR, May 23, 1818, V. 14, No. 13, 218; Remini, *Jackson & His Indian Wars*, 141.

[488]   Jackson to Calhoun, February 14, 1818, ASPMA, V. 1, 697.

"without a pound of provisions," and that the Tennesseans "will also proceed with the calculation of being supplied here."[489]

Thus Jackson was pleasantly surprised when he met the Chehaws just beyond Fort Early. He told Secretary Calhoun that "the necessities of my army were first relieved at the Chehaw village, and every act of friendship characterized the conduct of their old chiefs. The young warriors immediately entered, and were mustered into the service of the United States." He said the Chehaws were some of his best men.[490]

Thus fortified, Jackson marched to Florida, but on May 7, disturbing news arrived from Brig. Gen. Thomas Glasscock of the Georgia militia: there had been a massacre, with "the Chehaw town having been consumed."[491] Georgia governor William Rabun, "having received information through sources which cannot be doubted," heard that Chehaws were killing his settlers, and he ordered the militia to attack the towns of Chiefs Hopony and Philemme, "to effect their complete destruction." Rabun said that the "most profound secrecy should be observed," being the only way to defeat "an enemy who will not come in contact on equal terms."[492]

The previous fall, Rabun had raised five hundred men to help reduce the smuggling base at Amelia Island, Florida, but since Gaines had already captured it, Rabun's militia were all dressed up with nowhere to go. Captain Obed Wright was nearby with his company from Savannah, and Governor Rabun directed him to take command of two cavalry and two infantry companies and attack the Chehaws.[493]

Wright left Hartford on April 21, with Captains Jacob Robinson and Timothy Rogers and their "mounted gunmen," and Captains Dean and Childe with their infantry, plus two smaller infantry detachments, totaling about 270 men.[494] On the march to Fort Early,

---

489   Arbuckle to Jackson, March 5, 1818, AGO, RG 94, M566, R0102.

490   Jackson to Calhoun, May 7, 1818, ASPMA, V.1, 776.

491   Glasscock to Jackson, April 30, 1818, ASPMA, V. 1, 776.

492   Rabun to Wright, April 14, 1818, NWR, May 23, 1818, V. 14, No. 13, 219–20.

493   Rabun to Calhoun, June 1, 1818, ASPMA, V. 1, 774.

494   Wright to Rabun, April 25, 1818, NWR, May 23, 1818, V. 14, No. 13, 218.

Wright heard that Hopony had moved into Chehaw town. At the fort, Wright asked Captain Bothwell, then in the service of the United States, to accompany him. Bothwell declined, told Wright that the Chehaws were friendly, and that very day Hopony had returned a stray government horse. Said General Glasscock, "This availed nothing; mock patriotism burned in their breasts; they crossed the river that night, and pushed for the town."[495]

Wright approached the village before noon on April 23, 1818. Lying near Muckalee Creek, it consisted of a cluster of wooden structures, a summer and winter house, and buildings for storage of animal furs and supplies. There was a council house on a public square, said to have been flying a white flag. The matrilineal extended families lived in about fifteen to twenty cabins, much as the white pioneers of the day. The Chehaws, like the other Creeks, were mainly farmers, growing corn, beans, and squash. They learned livestock raising from the whites, and had a number of fenced fields, with cattle, horses, and hogs.[496]

The livestock were provocative. The Indians assembled substantial herds when many whites had none, which to them intimated they were stolen. Half a mile from the village, Wright captured an Indian herding cattle; some were said to have "white people's marks and brands," and a man named McDuffee claimed one cow belonged to his father. Captain Robinson said that before the discovery the militia "was actually friendly," but finding the cow was proof of Indian thievery. Wright attacked toward the center of the town and Robinson hit from the right. Robinson said the Chehaws fired first, from sinks or caves hidden along their approach path. He claimed that some of the Indians were painted red for war.[497]

The attack was vicious, but the eyewitnesses told conflicting stories. A Mr. Pearre said that the militia carried a white flag into the village, lulling the Chehaws into a false sense of security, and "while the hand of friendship was extended to them," fired and shot them down. Captain Rogers vehemently countered that "the

---

[495]   Rabun to Mitchell, May 20, 1818, NWR, June 13, 1818, V. 14, No. 16, 268; Glasscock to Jackson, April 30, 1818, ASPMA, V. 1, 776.
[496]   "The Chehaw Indians," https://georgiagenealogy.org/lee/the-chehaw-indians.htm
[497]   Robinson, April 30, 1818, NWR, May 23, 1818, V. 13, No. 13, 219.

detachment never entered the town as friends." In fact, a Chehaw approached them and "held out the flag," but Indians inside the houses perfidiously fired at them, so the flag-bearer was shot and killed.[498] The person with the flag may have been an old man named Howard, who was William McIntosh's uncle. Glasscock said that Howard "stepped from within his doors in front of the line, with the flag of friendship; it was not respected; a general fire was made; he fell and was bayoneted." Local settler Timothy Barnard said both chiefs were known "always to be friendly to our color, ever since I have been in this land," and lamented that the soldiers only killed old men and women, while stealing all the horses they could find.[499]

Captain Wright said he gave "positive orders not to injure the *women*, or *children*," but to no avail—notwithstanding Captain Robinson's assertion that the order "was strictly enforced by the officers." The militias' blood was up. The few Indians who had come outside were killed, and while some cowered within, others managed to shoot at the rampaging soldiers from between the chinks in the logs of their cabins. Because the whites were unable to breach the sturdy doors, the dwellings, Wright said, "were set fire. The consequence of which, numbers were burnt to death in the houses; in all probability from 40 to 50 was their total loss."[500]

Robinson and Wright claimed that as the dwellings burned, some of them exploded because they were loaded with gunpowder, and that they found a considerable number of British muskets and carbines, along with opened letters addressed to General Gaines, thus proving Chehaw treachery. They said a large number of warriors escaped into a swamp, but Glasscock held that of the eighty men who resided there, fully forty of the young warriors had gone with Jackson. The militia spent nearly two hours torching the buildings and shooting down anyone who did not immediately surrender. Wright said they killed twenty-four warriors in addition to those

---

498   Rogers, May 15, 1818, NWR, June 6, 1818, V. 14, No. 15, 247.

499   Glasscock to *Georgia Journal*, May, 2, 1818, NWR, May 30, 1818, V. 14, No. 14, 236; Barnard to Mitchell, April 30, 1818, NWR, June 13, 1818, V. 14, No. 16, 268.

500   Wright to Rabun, April 25, 1818, NWR, May 23, 1818, V. 13, No. 13, 219; Robinson, April 30, 1818, NWR, May 23, 1818, V. 13, No. 13, 219.

burned to death, and Robinson said they "burnt the town agreeable to orders," which contradicted his assertion that the officers strictly followed orders not to injure the women and children. For all the bullets allegedly fired at them, the whites were unscathed. "The town is laid completely desolate," said Wright, "without the loss of a man." The destruction complete, Wright marched back to Fort Early the same evening. He wrote to Governor Rabun, "The conduct of the officers and soldiers on this occasion… was highly characteristic of the patriotism and bravery of the Georgians in general."[501]

While Wright was at Chehaw village, Glasscock, with his own hungry militia contingent, was marching to Fort Early. Four days after the massacre he arrived at Chehaw village where he had hoped to get food, but found only desolation. Eventually some Chehaws came out of hiding and Glasscock assured them he meant no harm. They gave him twenty-four head of cattle that they had hidden from Wright. Glasscock left several of his sick men with the Chehaws, who, rather than taking vengeance, fed and cared for them. Glasscock called the attack a "transaction calculated to blast the reputation of the state."[502]

Two days after the massacre, Lower Creek Chief Little Prince wrote to Indian agent D. B. Mitchell, that "One of our friendly towns, by the name of Chehaw, has been destroyed." The whites had killed the head men, women and children, and burnt all the houses. All the fighting men were gone with General Jackson and only a few were left on guard. "Men do not get up and do this mischief without there is someone at the head of it, and we want you to try and find them out." Mitchell then wrote to Governor Rabun, asking "by whose order this unwarrantable and barbarous deed had been done."[503]

Jackson first heard of the trouble when William McIntosh

---

[501]   Wright to Rabun, April 25, 1818, Wright to Robinson, April 30, 1818, NWR, May 23, 1818, V. 13, No. 13, 219; Glasscock to *Georgia Journal,* May, 2, 1818, NWR, May 30, 1818, V. 14, No. 14, 236.

[502]   Glasscock to *Georgia Journal,* May, 2, 1818, NWR, May 30, 1818, V. 14, No. 14, 235–36.

[503]   Little Prince to Mitchell, April 25, 1818, NWR, June 13, 1818, V. 14, No. 16, 268; Mitchell to Rabun, May 6, 1818, NWR, June 13, 1818, V. 14, No. 16, 267.

and his warriors met him at the Creek town of Coweta on May 5. He told Jackson that his Uncle Howard and his family had been murdered and the town destroyed. "If an Indian kills a white man, I will have him punished—if a white man kills an Indian, he ought to be punished." He asked Jackson to find out who had done it and why.[504]

Jackson was irate and fired off two letters. He told Calhoun of the outrage "committed upon the superannuated" men and women of Chehaw town, whose sons were then serving the United States, and said he had ordered Captain Wright "arrested and ironed." He lashed the governor with his fury, calling the act "a base, cowardly, and inhuman attack," and questioned by what right Rabun made war on peaceful Indians "under the protection of the United States." Jackson said it was unconscionable that there existed a man—"a cowardly monster in human shape"—who would "violate the sanctity of a flag, when borne by any person." He said that Rabun had no right to give an order to the militia while Jackson was in command, and Wright—"this hero"—did not go after hostile Indians, but attacked old men and women. "Capt. Wright must be prosecuted and punished for this outrageous murder."[505]

Letters of recrimination flew. Rabun gave Calhoun his version of events, and told Jackson that if he had been "in possession of the facts" he would not be speaking in such "a very haughty tone." Wright was under Rabun's command, and as governor of Georgia, he had the right to call out the militia. Rabun had directed Wright to attack Hopony and Philemme, and since he disobeyed, he had ordered his arrest. To Agent Mitchell, Rabun rationalized that as governor, it was his duty to "defend the cause of the whites"—besides, he didn't believe the Indians. It was unfortunate that innocent people had died, but that was "one of the misfortunes attendant on war."[506]

Rabun may have ordered Wright's arrest, but Jackson beat

---

[504] McIntosh to Jackson, May 5, 1818, NWR, June 20, 1818, V. 14, No. 17, 292.

[505] Jackson to Calhoun, May 7, 1818, ASPMA, V. 1, 775–76; Jackson to Rabun, May 7, 1818, ASPMA, V. 1, 777.

[506] Rabun to Jackson, June 1, 1818, ASPMA, V. 1, 775; Rabun to Mitchell, May 20, 1818, NWR, June 13, 1818, V. 14, No. 16, 268.

Andrew Jackson. *Public domain* President Jackson was condemned by many for his Indian removal policy, but in 1818, he was irate when Georgia militia violated the "sanctity of a flag" and massacred Chehaw men, women, and children.

him to it. Major John M. Davis arrested Wright on May 24, in Dublin, Georgia, and took him to the capital at Milledgeville, where the court, "deeming that no sufficient cause is shown for his detention," served Davis with a writ of habeas corpus and set Wright free.[507] His freedom was short-lived, however, for he was arrested the next day on Rabun's order. In confinement, Wright no doubt learned the seriousness of the potential charges against him. The *Georgia Journal* printed that Wright would be tried for breaking the Trade and Intercourse Act, which stated that any person who murdered an Indian in a tribe in amity with the United States, "on being thereof convicted, shall suffer death."[508]

A U. S. marshal was authorized to take Wright into custody, and as the days passed, he increasingly dreaded the death penalty or "a long and loathsome imprisonment." On July 26, Wright wrote to Rabun that he had been confined for a month, but had not yet been charged with anything, and "I therefore pray that your excellency would withdraw the arrest." With the marshal due to arrive, and not waiting for an answer, Wright somehow escaped the next day. Rabun issued a proclamation, offering $500 for his apprehension. Wright was said to be about thirty years of age, five feet, eleven inches in height, slender, with fair complexion, light blue eyes, and light brown hair. He evaded capture, fled to St. Augustine and gained Spanish protection, then sailed to Havana, Cuba.[509]

In addition to verbally flaying Governor Rabun and protest-

---

[507]   Court order, and Davis to Rabun, May 29, 1818, ASPMA, V. 1, 778.
[508]   *Georgia Journal,* July 14, 1818, NWR, August 15, 1818, V. 14, No. 25, 416.
[509]   NWR, August 22, 1818, V. 14, No. 26, 439–40; NWR, September 19, 1818, V. 15, No. 4, 63.

ing to Secretary Calhoun, Jackson went into damage control. He told the Chehaws that the attack "fills my heart with regret, and my eyes with tears," and said he did not suppose "there was any American so base as not to respect a flag, but I find I am mistaken." He said he could not bring the dead back to life, but he had ordered Wright's arrest and would see that they were compensated—"Justice shall be done to you." The government sent Agent Mitchell $10,000 to remunerate the Chehaws for their losses."[510]

Jackson's dispute with Rabun eventually faded to the back pages as President Monroe's administration appeared reluctant to take sides.[511] Jackson, who is often depicted as virulently anti-Indian, especially given his support of Indian removal in the 1820s and 1830s, was genuinely upset that his friends had been dealt with so treacherously. Glasscock had said the massacre would tarnish the state's reputation, and Jackson concurred: "This act will, to the last ages, fix a stain upon the character of Georgia." Governor Rabun dismissed it as a tempest in teapot merely because militia may have "mistaken their orders." He believed the affair was "shamefully misrepresented" by people whose "delicate feelings" seem to have made them forget that they were white men after all.[512]

In the end, Jackson's fury dissipated and most people forgot the Chehaw massacre. Many others occurred to make sensational splashes in the newspapers before fading from memory. By the time of the infamous incident at Sand Creek, Colorado Territory, in November 1864, no one remembered the Chehaw affair to consider the similarities. Although the exact details are arguable, in both instances exaggerated hatred and fear of Indians expedited a governor's calls for volunteers to go to war. Having been mustered and supplied, the soldiers needed a fight to justify the expense of their organization. Although there may have been warring Indians in both villages, the majority were innocent. A case has been made in both instances that the Indians were under army protection. Testimony was given in both situations that the Indians fired first. Eyewitnesses in both

---

510   Jackson to Chehaws, May 7, 1818, ASPMA, V. 1, 776–77; NWR, August 15, 1818, V. 14, No. 25, 416.
511   Remini, *Jackson & His Indian Wars*, 159.
512   Jackson to Rabun, May, 7, 1818, AAPMA, V. 1, 777; Rabun to Mitchell, May 20, 1818, NWR, June 13, 1818, V. 14, No, 16, 268.

incidents said that the Indians flew either white flags or American flags and they were not honored. The Indians either offered no resistance or were tenaciously defending their homes. One or more chiefs were killed. There were great discrepancies in the estimates of Indian casualties. The villages were destroyed. Indian possessions were destroyed or stolen. White reaction was either sympathetic or censorious. A culprit was sought to take the blame. Both men in charge during the massacres ultimately escaped punishment.[513]

Some dissimilarities were in the number of soldier casualties: seventy-six at Sand Creek and none at Chehaw. As for the governors, John Evans of Colorado Territory was accused of covering up the affair, and President Andrew Johnson demanded his resignation. On the other hand, the Georgia legislature declared that Governor Rabun was not at fault, and that Captain Wright, then safely ensconced in Cuba, acted contrary to orders and was wholly to blame.[514]

The Chehaw massacre is largely forgotten. It has been said that Americans have a short memory. Our founding documents insist that our rights include justice, tranquility, and the pursuit of happiness. Given a history that is replete with rapacity, deceit, injustice, and war, we are more likely to reach that tranquil, happy, dissonance-free state of mind through the pursuit of forgetfulness. We do not remember our history or learn from it because many of us are in a constant struggle either to forget it or whitewash it.

---

[513]   For Sand Creek details, see Gregory Michno, *The Three Battles of Sand Creek: In Blood, In Court, and as the End of History* (New York: Savas Beatie, 2017).
[514]   Harry E. Kelsey, Jr., *Frontier Capitalist: The Life of John Evans* (Denver, CO: State Historical Society of Colorado, 1969), 152; NWR, December 12, 1818, Supplement to V. 3, No. 15, New Series, 266.

THE FRONTIERSMAN AS TERRORIST

"One of the most dangerous": Hardeman Owen

Frontiersmen could be incorrigible villains. American colonial and Revolutionary history had their share of hard cases. Men like Simon Girty, a white captured by Indians who lived and fought with them, and allegedly tortured and slaughtered white pioneers by the score, was the stuff of frontier myth. Not so well-known were the white frontier rogues who lived as more or less respectable men in white communities, but terrorized Indians as well as whites. One such scoundrel was Hardeman Owen.

Owen lived for a time in Columbus, Georgia, and then moved south to Russell County, Alabama, near Fort Mitchell. A stipulation in the Cusseta Treaty of 1832, which ceded more than five million acres of Creek land to the United States, called for removal of white intruders, but not if they had already made improvements on the land. Hundreds of whites moved in, claimed they had made improvements, or drove Creeks from their farms and took over. Hardeman Owen stole a Creek farm and justified it by saying that the Creeks were prejudiced against the whites and that they didn't really want their land and wished to emigrate—he would help them along.[515]

At the same time, the army, tasked with driving out white intruders, found it difficult to distinguish between intruder and legitimate landholder. When the army destroyed a warehouse in Pike County, Alabama, the sheriff served a warrant on one of the officers, and in the altercation a soldier bayoneted the sheriff. While marshals assisted the army and drove out intruders from Indian homes, sheriffs served warrants on marshals and the army, and drove out Indians who had re-occupied their homes from intruders.[516]

[515]   Winn, *Triumph of the Ecunnau-Nuxulgee*, 350; Owen to Gilmer, June 10, 1831, USCSS, V. 2, 489–90.

[516]   Irwin to Cass, July 30, 1832, USCSS, V. 3, 410; Crowell to Cass, August 3, 1832, USCSS, V. 3, 413.

Whites seized the Indian town of Eufala on the Chatta-hoochee River, burned most of the dwellings, confiscated the fields, and built the small town of Irwinton. In August 1832, Robert L. Crawford, marshal for the southern district of Alabama, called these whites "the most lawless and uncouth men I have ever seen; some of them refugees from the state of Georgia, and for whom rewards are offered; and these are some of Mr. [William] Irwin's *best citizens.*" The whites burned Indian houses and corn, defrauded them, and did "violence to their persons." He evicted eighteen intruders, received death threats, and asked for protection from troops at Fort Mitchell.[517]

Captain Philip Wager, 4th Infantry, sent Capt. John Page, Lt. Charles H. Larned, and twenty-five men to assist Crawford. The intruders in and around Irwinton were "represented as being a desperate set of rogues" who mustered "upwards of a hundred sturdy scoundrels all ready for a fight and swearing vengeance against the United States troops." Page confronted them and they backed down, but Wager explained, "[I]n a community like this, it is no difficult matter for one thief to procure another thief, to swear for him," and prove anything. Marshal Crawford and the troops destroyed houses and drove families out; Lieutenant Larned and fifteen men stayed behind to keep the peace. Almost immediately the whites and the sheriff returned with writs of trespass, and Wager pulled the troops from harm's way. The more he tried to protect the Indians, "it only seems to make their condition more wretched than ever." The *Columbus Enquirer* caustically wrote that the great battle of Irwinton ended when the army demanded surrender of the "fortress" and the inhabitants ran away. "This terminated the storm, capture and burning of Irwinton. Short its existence, but brilliant its history."[518]

The episode was not over. Georgia governor Wilson Lumpkin believed the idea of Cherokees and Creeks being oppressed people was preposterous, yet he admitted that it was "impossible to preserve the rights and interests of the Indians from the corrupt and

---

[517]   Crawford to Robb, August 31, 1832, Crawford to Robb, September 15, 1832, USCSS, V. 3, 440, 453, 454 (quotations).
[518]   Wager to Macomb, August 4, 1832, AGO, RG 94, M567, R0077; *Columbus Enquirer,* July 28, 1832, in Winn, *Triumph of the Ecunnau-Nuxulgee,* 328.

lawless depredation of abandoned and unprincipled white men." Although the state had laws, they were useless to control whites of deficient character; no one could "give moral force to the administration of the laws."[519]

In November, a number of Creeks petitioned War Secretary Cass to protect them from whites who had stolen their property, and even taken their women as "wives" so they could claim more Creek lands. The very next day the whites remaining in the Irwinton area petitioned Cass for the suspension of orders to remove them, stating that it was in the Creek's interest to have whites there to do business. In fact, all their past differences were rectified, "and, at the present, all is perfect peace and good humor between us."[520]

All was not peace and humor. The wearied Marshal Crawford sent Deputy Marshal Jeremiah Austill to continue the job, but he demurred, claimed that there were two thousand white families in the area and he wanted at least two hundred troops to accompany him. Wager told General Alexander Macomb that there were simply too many whites to drive out, while Crawford admitted to Cass, "I am at a loss how to act." The marshals and the army could not handle it, and appeared to be seeking a way out of an impossible situation.[521]

In this mix was Hardeman Owen, one of the leading racist, bigoted agitators. Almost everyone in the area knew of him and by the summer of 1833, he was one of the informal leaders of a gang of white terrorists. Deputy Marshal Austill wrote to Secretary Cass about him, but left his name blank, as if he were afraid Owen would retaliate. The Indians complained about Owen and his cronies "as being obnoxious, quarrelsome, and abusive to them...for having burnt up their cabins and threatening their lives." Owen raised a force to drive Austill and the troops away, so the deputy counseled the Indians that it might be better for them to submit than to be

---

[519]   Lumpkin to Cass, September 22, 1832, USCSS, V. 3, 460.

[520]   Eneah Micco, et al. to Cass, November 15, 1832, Packer, et al. to Cass, November 16, 1832, USCSS, V. 3, 527–28, 529 (quotation).

[521]   Austill to Wager, November 12, 1832, Wager to Macomb, December 6, 1832, AGO, RG 94, M567, R0077; Crawford to Kurtz, December 6, 1832, USCSS, V. 3, 546–47; Crawford to Cass, December 11, 1832 USCSS, V. 3, 549 (quotation).

burned out or sued in the state courts and lose everything. He complained that state officers had arrested Indians on false reports with false writs, threw them in jail, and compelled them to surrender their land if they wanted to get out of jail. It seemed that everyone was "trying to fleece the Indians." Austill too, was threatened with arrest or death, but he vowed to persevere.[522]

By the end of July, Austill was fed up with Owen's terrorism. Residing about twenty miles from Fort Mitchell, Owen had procured a postmaster position as a respectable cover for his other activities. Creeks pled with Austill to protect them from Owen and his raiders, who killed their hogs and horses, and beat them unmercifully. As Owen's notoriety spread, the *Charleston Courier* printed that he and his gang settled among the Indians in order to cheat them out of their land and their slaves. "It was proved" that he dispossessed one man of his farm, "and a young girl of another farm of one hundred acres of valuable land, and broke her arm for complaining." Owen and a partner, allegedly a dentist, dug up Indian graves like ghouls—"the dentist, for the teeth, and Owen, for the silver ornaments and beads...and these he afterwards *sold in his shop*." The *Courier* said Owen was an outlaw and desperado who committed outrages "with a ferocity belying his lineage that paid no respect to sex, and a greedy avarice that invaded even the sanctuary of the dead."[523]

On July 29, Austill visited Owen again and ordered him out, but Owen said he would die before leaving. Realizing he would need troops to back him, Austill headed down the road when some Creeks overtook him and begged him not to go, because Owen had just drawn his knife on them "and swore he would kill some of them" if they cooperated with the marshal. Soldiers from Fort Mitchell accompanied the deputy on his next visit. He arrested Owen, but he "begged, and promised to leave in peace"—Austill fell for it and gave him another chance. The deputy was only fifteen miles down the road when the Creeks caught up and said Owen had just "threat-

---

[522]   Austill to Cass, July 8, 1833, USCSS, V. 4, 461 ("obnoxious" quotation); Austill to Cass, July 12, 1833, USCSS, V. 4, 469; Austill to Cass, July 26, 1933, USCSS, V. 4, 487 ("fleece" quotation).
[523]   Austill to Cass, July 31, 1833, USCSS, V. 4, 493; *Charleston Courier*, in NWR, October 26, 1833, V. 9, No. 9, 143.

ened he would burn their houses and kill all those who dared to come upon the fields" he had stolen. Austill returned, but this time Owen defiantly ordered him off his property. The deputy warned him that the soldiers were coming, and this time they would take him. Owen sent his family into the woods, and, said Austill, "set a mine in his house." Apparently he had it prepared beforehand, because the troops soon arrived, and Owen's demeanor had radically changed. Said Austill, "he very politely asked us to come in." Austill neared the front gate about fifty paces ahead of the soldiers, when a Creek called to him that "there was powder in the house." When Austill turned his horse to leave, Owen ran into the woods. Austill called for the soldiers to arrest him, but to stay out of the house, "and in a few seconds it blew up." The explosion sent wood fragments shooting through the air while the soldiers dove for cover. In the chaos, Owen turned to shoot once at Austill before he escaped. Incredibly, he circled around to confront the deputy a mile from the house and called to him from behind the trees, "swearing he would kill me on sight," and said if the soldiers were not so close "he would have shot me before he sprung the mine." Austill had enough, and told the Creeks that if Owen came among them again, "to shoot him down." The deputy wrote to Secretary Cass, "He is the most daring man I have ever met with, and one of the most dangerous."[524]

Owen's reign of terror was nearly over. In a few days, Austill and eight soldiers found him. He tried to shoot Sgt. Frank Borger, but Pvt. James Emmerson was faster, firing a musket ball into Owen's head.[525] Far from easing matters, the killing prompted a vociferous protest from Alabama governor John Gayle. He accused the marshals and the army of illegally usurping state powers and injecting armed forces into their peaceful society. He said federal attempts to remove settlers were illegal, and any land disputes between whites and Indians needed to be settled in Alabama courts. Local newspapers began calling Owen a victim, a hero, and a freedom fighter for the rights of Alabama citizens. The *Columbus Enquirer*

---

[524]   Winn, *Triumph of the Ecunnau-Nuxulgee, 350–51;* Austill to Cass, July 31, 1833, USCSS, V. 4, 493.
[525]   Pickett to State of Alabama, October Term, 1833, USCSS, V. 4, 616.

called the soldiers murderers and cries arose for their arrest.[526] Farther removed from the uproar, the *Charleston Courier* took an opposing view. The killing was justifiable. Some people claimed Owen was a hero, not an outlaw, but the newspaper said that a robber, a man of violence who preyed on the defenseless, shot at law officers, and blew up houses, was worse than an outlaw.[527] The *Courier* did not have the word that would be common in the twenty-first century: Owen was a terrorist, and frontier people who behaved in a like manner were also terrorists.

Indian agent Luther Blake said the people "make much noise about Owen; he ought to have been killed."[528] But the majority of civilians were outraged, and Austill's, Crawford's, and the army's troubles were just beginning. The anti-federal government spirit was high. South Carolina had just "nullified" the Tariffs of 1828 and 1832, argued that states' rights took precedence over law, and brought on a crisis that nearly led to a civil war. Alabama threatened to drive out U. S. troops if they continued to remove intruders. In this atmosphere, Austill found it was necessary to carry a weapon at all times to protect himself. To be threatened with death, to face arrest, and to be "tried by an infuriated set of mad men would be folly," for "*neither law, testimony, nor justice could save my life.*" The deputy said that he and Marshal Crawford both had been threatened, and that "public declarations are made by the settlers that they will take my life on sight."[529]

Governor Gayle declared that the marshals could not legally remove intruders, that it was a state issue to be decided by Alabama courts, and that Crawford must desist. Secretary Cass gave conflicting orders, telling Crawford to remove intruders, but to avoid force—simply order them out, and a district attorney would prosecute the non-compliers. Cass protested to Gayle that the state's judicial system was weighted against the Indians, they would rarely get to court, they could never prove their cases, and no jury would ever

---

[526]   Ellisor, *Second Creek War,* 85; Winn, *Triumph of the Ecunnau-Nuxulgee,* 355

[527]   *Charleston Courier,* October 15, 1833, in NWR, October 26, 1833, V. 9, No. 9, 143.

[528]   Blake to Herring, September 11, 1833, USCSS, V. 4, 557.

[529]   Austill to Cass, August 10, 1833, ASPMA, V. 6, 633; Austill to Cass, October 26, 1833, ASPMA, V. 6, 634 (quotations).

rule in their favor. Then again, he agreed to allow intruders who had already planted crops to remain until they could be harvested—the same old concession that had been granted scores of times.[530]

In the meantime, Owen's widow filed for damages. In a completely twisted version of events, it was alleged that the Creeks destroyed Owen's "fine crop," and she was left with her children and no property, seemingly oblivious to the fact that her husband blew up her house. Cass replied that Owen's death was "much to be deplored," but there was no measure the president could take for her relief. The situation certainly did not fall within the precepts of the TIA and she would have to petition Congress.[531]

Like other federal government representatives, Marshal Crawford looked for a way out of the mess. He believed that only military force would remove the intruders and he was concerned for his own safety. "Threats have been made to shoot me," he said, and wondered what he was to do when the sheriff served a warrant against him. He would yield if so directed, but said, "I should dislike to be tried by those who are entirely interested" in harming him.[532] By late October, Crawford wanted out. He rationalized that removal caused too much bloodshed, and besides, he calculated that there were only eighteen or twenty people who actually took over Indian farms, and they were hardly worth the trouble. A warrant was issued for Austill and the soldiers who killed Owen, and he was afraid he would be indicted "if I attempt to remove a single person." He asked Brevet Major James S. McIntosh, 4th Infantry, commanding at Fort Mitchell, for fifty soldiers, but McIntosh said he did not have sufficient ammunition. "I do not wish to risk my life without full protection," Crawford said. He rationalized that only "a few designing white men" caused all the trouble, and although some Indians had

---

[530] Gayle to Cass, August 20, 1833, USCSS, V. 4, 529–30; Gayle to Crawford, August 20, 1833, USCSS, V. 4, 534; Cass to Crawford, August 26, 1833, USCSS, V. 3, 758–59; Cass to Gayle, September 5, 1833, USCSS, V. 3, 763–66.
[531] Gilmer to Cass, September 5, 1833, USCSS, V. 4, 541–42 ("fine crop" quotation); Cass to Gilmer, September 16, 1833, USCSS, V. 3, 769 ("deplored" quotation).
[532] Crawford to Cass, September 23, 1833, USCSS, V. 4, 573 ("shoot me" quotation); Crawford to Cass, October 3, 1833, USCSS, V. 4, 593 ("should dislike" quotation).

been abused, "I do not believe their injuries have been near so great as have been represented by them."[533] Cass worried Crawford even more when he instructed him to "submit to any legal process which may be served upon you," and the district attorney would try to move the case to a United States court.[534]

Major McIntosh was caught in a dilemma. He was ordered to give all necessary aid to the marshal and deputy for removal, but admitted that "where one intruder is dislodged... about one hundred are left unmolested."[535] Nevertheless, he continued until early October, when a grand jury indicted Austill, Lt. David Manning, James Emmerson, Frank Borger, James King, plus five other unnamed soldiers for the murder of Owen. The charge against Austill and Manning was for "not having the fear of God before their eyes, but being moved and seduced by the instigation of the devil" to aid and abet the soldiers. Among the jurors were two intruders: one specifically named by the Creeks as particularly vexing, and the other a member of the Columbus Land Company and a friend of Owen.[536]

McIntosh would not stand for it. He was not to engage in direct conflict with state authorities, but, on October 14, when Russell County Sheriff Ed Crowell arrived to arrest his soldiers for murder, he stated, "I'll be damned if I give up a man." Nevertheless, McIntosh let Crowell search the fort. He could not find the soldiers, but served a subpoena on Lieutenant Manning, who replied, "I shall not go." Crowell returned the next day and handed a contempt of court citation to McIntosh, but he replied, "You shall not touch me," and said the court had no authority over him. Crowell left, and told the court the State did not have the power to take on the army.[537]

McIntosh wrote to General Macomb for advice. He said he did not surrender the soldiers because they were legally performing their duty, and that Governor Gayle was assembling a "sufficient military force to arrest me." What was to be his response if State

---

[533]   Crawford to Cass, October 23, 1833, USCSS, V. 4, 615.

[534]   Cass to Crawford, October 19, 1833, USCSS, V. 3, 793.

[535]   McIntosh to Jones, September 9, 1833, AGO, RG 94, M567, R0086.

[536]   Pickett to State of Alabama, October Term, 1833, USCSS, V. 4, 616–17; Winn, *Triumph of the Ecunnau-Nuxulgee,* 361.

[537]   Crowell to State of Alabama, October Term, 1833, in NWR, November 16, 1833, V. 9, No. 12, 190.

troops marched against him? He did not have enough soldiers to continue to remove intruders and protect the fort. McIntosh received his answer: the military will not battle with civil authority and the major will "interpose no obstacle to the service of legal process upon any officer or soldier under your command."[538]

President Jackson and Secretary Cass realized they must intervene to obviate a civil war, and dispatched Lt. Col. John Abert, who was currently engaged in sorting out the land frauds that contributed to the crisis, and Francis Scott Key, author of "The Star-Spangled Banner" and a Washington, D. C. attorney. They were given much latitude to mediate among the army, Alabama, the civilians, and the Indians. Abert believed that the trouble began because the United States was too lenient. If removal had at once been carried out with force and with no concessions, the intruders would not have been emboldened. Conversely, he said many of the intruders were enterprising, "well informed and courteous gentlemen." Key, on the other hand, said some intruders were peaceable, but "most of them are violent and clamorous."[539]

Key talked to the soldiers at Fort Mitchell and advised Lieutenant Manning and the indicted soldiers to submit to legal civilian authority and offer bail; if bail was refused, they must remain in jail until the federal attorneys could defend them. It was harsh advice to swallow. Sometime in early November, James Emmerson deserted. Manning requested to be sent to another post, but Cass said it was improper, and better to remain on station than leave with an indictment hanging over him.[540]

As in Georgia in 1826, the situation in Alabama had grown to the point of civil war between federal and state jurisdiction over disposal of Indian lands. The government blinked first. It instructed the army to submit to civilian judicial processes, President Jackson declared that settlers who had not interfered with Indian property could remain, and Indian reservations would be delineated by Jan-

---

[538] McIntosh to Macomb, October 21, 1833, AGO, RG 94, M567, R0086; Cass to McIntosh, October 29, 1833, USCSS, V. 3, 807.
[539] Abert to Cass, November 5, 1833, USCSS, V. 4, 649; Key to Cass, November 15, 1833, USCSS, V. 4, 703.
[540] Key to Cass, November 14, 1833, USCSS, V. 4, 702; Cass to Manning, October 29, 1833, USCSS, 3, 809–10.

uary 15, 1834, meaning that settlers outside the reserve lines would not have to leave. Abert informed the settlers of the deal while Key told Governor Gayle that the government would yield. Gayle agreed that if the army ceased removing whites, the state would cease serving writs, and thus, said Key, "The prosecutions, I am satisfied, will not be pressed."[541]

The situation worked out well for Alabama, but appeared to be a capitulation by the federal government. The TIA obligated the army to remove white intruders and protect the Indians in their homelands. The Indian Removal Act of 1830 was effectively a contravention of the letter and spirit of the TIA and the military had to decide which one should take precedence. It was apparent that many officers were mortified by the inconsistencies. Enforcement of the TIA led to civilian conflicts, lawsuits, even killings. With dubious backing by its "employer," many officers chose the easier path and overlooked civilian misconduct. No doubt when their own belief system differed from their behavior, their cognitive dissonance increased. To remedy this, the classic response was to alter either the belief or the behavior. Since past behavior could not be changed, the belief system had to. Accepting the new regime—rationalizing the transformation—greased the slide into abandoning their role as Indian protectors. Major McIntosh breathed more easily in the new atmosphere. If the army was not to remove squatters or to interfere with the legal processes, fine. He could lay low at the post. As a result, he said, the excitement "has almost entirely subsided."[542]

Captain Wager wanted desperately to get away from Fort Mitchell and the Southeastern Frontier. He believed he would be sent to New York on recruiting service, but discovered to his chagrin that his company was slated for the Chickasaw Agency. He protested. They had been on the frontier for more than five years and had built four sets of quarters, "not to speak of our operations against the intruders, the Indians, the gold diggers, and the Nullifiers." Why couldn't some other company have the pleasure of that service? He apologized for complaining, but said, "I am unable to remain

---

[541]   Key to Cass, November 30, 1833, Key to Gayle, December 16, 1833, Gayle to Key, December 16, 1833, Key to Cass, December 18, 1833, USCSS, V. 4, 741, 761, 762, 764 (quotation); Winn, *Triumph of the Ecunnau-Nuxulgee*, 366–68.
[542]   McIntosh to Cass, November 30, 1833, AGO, RG 94, M567, R0086.

silent."[543] Wager wanted out, as did other officers who resigned in growing numbers during the 1830s.[544] No paper laws and no physical barriers would keep out white intruders, so why try? The terrorists were winning.

The Jacksonian Age of Riot

The Jacksonian common man rarely had common sense. He feared and hated Indians, but Indians were not the sole victims of his terrorist activities—for the Jacksonian Era was also a time of racial, ethnic, and religious persecution. After Nat Turner's rebellion in 1832, fears of slaves rising up to kill their owners in their sleep were magnified. Blacks had been lynched for decades, but after the paroxysm of the Turner revolt there was a lynching lull for a few years, almost as if the country waited to catch its breath. The great exhale came from 1834 to 1837, years that may have seen the most rioting and mob violence in American history. This fierce undercurrent was endemic. Historian Paul Gilje said that unless we understand the scope and impact of rioting, "we cannot fully comprehend the history of the American people." Colonials had rampaged, especially during the religious "Awakening" years in the 1730s and 1740s. America, born the child of riot, became incorrigible after the Revolution. The latest mobs were most concerned with ethnicity, class, and race. Whereas most riots of the eighteenth century targeted property and sought to preserve an imagined Eden, those in the nineteenth century were split by internal divisions and enmities, were individualistic, and targeted people. The democratic, egalitarian age of Andrew Jackson was riven with class and ethnic strife. As capitalism reared its often ugly head, rioters no longer shared the same values, community allegiance was low, and race and class consciousness was high. The new democratic man was an individual and acted solely for his own benefit. The government was no longer

---

[543]   Wager to Macomb, February 25, 1834, AGO, RG 94, M567, R0102.
[544]   Skelton, *An American Profession of Arms*, 216. Skelton assigns a number of reasons for the increasing resignations, from economic conditions to the Florida wars, but the growing gap between obligation of duty and expectation of support was certainly a factor.

a protector of the common good, but a referee between competing interest groups. Man may have been common, but he was not communal.[545]

Anti-intellectualism grew with popular democracy, reinforcing beliefs in the superiority of inborn, intuitive folk wisdom. Just as evangelicals discarded a learned clergy, politics abandoned intellectuals in favor of the supposed practical sense of the common man. Historian Richard Hofstadter argued that the Jacksonian era evidenced the first widespread anti-intellectual movement in American politics with its dislike of big government and educated experts. John Quincy Adams was the last nineteenth-century president who wanted the federal government to promote science and the arts, while Jackson, the wise natural man, believed it was hogwash. Adams could write, but Jackson could fight.[546]

The vulgar and the unschooled used log cabins, hard cider, rail-splitting, and bare knuckles to determine fitness for the presidency. The good old boys had taken over the country. You didn't need education to grin down a b'ar or to bust open your neighbor's head when he disagreed with you. The Jacksonian period was characterized by a great amount of collective violence and disorder, from anti-abolitionist mobs in the 1830s, nativist riots in the 1840s, vigilante movements in the 1850s, increasing anti-black riots and lynching, and the almost continuous killing and driving out of Indians from the 1810s to the 1840s.[547]

Jacksonian America's nativism had its religious overtones. The increasing number of Irish Catholic immigrants were another source of fear to the majority Anglo-Saxon Protestants. Lyman Beecher had been writing his book, *A Plea for the West*, about the dire threat of Catholicism taking over the country. He preached that Protestants should fight Catholics with "Bibles, and Sabbaths, and schools, and seminaries," while keeping their children out of Catholic schools that infected them with popish demonologies. Beecher

---

[545]   Paul A. Gilje, *Rioting in America* (Bloomington, IN: Indiana University Press, 1996): 1, 62–64.

[546]   Richard Hofstadter, *Anti-Intellectualism in American Life* (New York: Vintage Books, 1962), p. 54–58.

[547]   Michael Feldberg, *The Turbulent Era: Riot and Disorder in Jacksonian America* (New York: Oxford University Press, 1980), 82.

called it treason to commit "republican children" to Catholic influences. Catholics were anti-intellectual, unthinking, and superstitious. "The population which can be governed thus by the power of superstition is a dangerous population." Preaching in Boston, Beecher said that Europe planned to send all its paupers and criminals to America to take over the country. The government had to stop this immigration because America was for Americans.[548]

Beecher spread his bigotry in three sermons in Boston on the night of August 10, 1834, exhorting audiences to take action against popery. The previous night, Charlestown selectmen visited the Catholic Ursuline convent and demanded to inspect the premises after hearing rumors that a woman, Elizabeth Harrison, had been kidnapped and kept there in a torture chamber. The mother superior refused entrance, but allowed Harrison to tell them that she was "entirely satisfied with her present situation, it being that of her own choice; and that she has no desire or wish to alter it." The disappointed selectmen went home. Harrison's story was printed in the newspapers, but one day too late. On the night of August 11, a Protestant mob carrying banners and shouting "No Popery" and "Down with the Cross," "disguised by fantastic *dresses* and painted faces," surrounded the convent at midnight and broke open the door. One dozen sisters hurried the children out the back door while the mob torched the school and a nearby farmhouse. The mob stopped fire companies from quenching the flames. Early the next day the bishop called on the area Catholics to remain calm and allow the law to take its course. The law did nothing. The next night the mobs were back, burning everything that had survived the first attack. The *Boston Daily Advertiser* shouted: "*Disgraceful outrage.* We are called on to record one of the most scandalous acts of popular violence which was ever perpetrated in this community." The Ursulines rebuilt the convent, but by then few pupils were brave enough to attend, and in 1838 they closed down and moved to Canada where prejudices weren't so brutal. The rioters went to trial, but they were acquitted

---

[548]   Lyman Beecher, *A Plea for the West* (Bedford, MS: Applewood Books, nd. First published Cincinnati, OH: Truman & Smith, 1835), p. 10, 54, 96, 106, 114, 128, 175.

to "thunderous applause" in the crowded courtroom.[549]

The Charlestown incident was noteworthy, but not exceptional. Rioting increased all across America in the 1830s. During the
Charlestown episode, white rioters surged through Philadelphia, the
city of "Brotherly Love," beat and killed blacks, and burned down
their houses. After the third night of rioting, the *Philadelphia Inquirer*
wrote that the outrage must cease, for the victims were "unoffending
blacks, against whom not a shadow of offense was ever alleged."
Philadelphia experienced anti-abolition or anti-black riots in 1834,
1835, and 1838. Riots occurred in New York City in 1834, 1835,
and 1836; in Alabama in 1835; in Connecticut in 1833, 1836, and
1837; in Georgia in 1831 and 1835; in Illinois in 1836 and 1837; in
Kentucky in 1834; in Louisiana in 1834, 1837, 1838, and 1840; in
Maine in 1835; in Maryland in 1835, 1836, and 1839; in Massachusetts in 1834, 1835, and 1836; in Michigan in 1833; in Mississippi in
1833, 1835, 1836, and 1837; in Missouri in 1836, 1838, and 1840;
in New Hampshire in 1835; in New Jersey in 1834 and 1835; in
North Carolina in 1830, 1831, and 1840; in Ohio in 1836, 1837,
1839, and 1840; in South Carolina in 1835; in Tennessee in 1834,
1835, and 1836; in Texas in 1838, and 1839; in Vermont in 1835;
and in Virginia in 1831, 1835, and 1838.[550]

What was going on in America? Every state saw some type
of mob action during the decade of the 1830s. The *Niles Register* in
1835 believed some malady had taken over the nation. "Many of
the people of the United States are 'out of joint.' A spirit of riot or
a disposition to 'take the law into their own hands,' prevails in every
quarter." There were political riots, anti-black riots, anti-immigrant,
anti-Catholic, anti-Protestant, anti-Irish, anti-Mason, anti-abolitionist, anti-slavery, anti-labor riots, and an increase in lynching. "What
is the cause of it?" the *Register* asked.[551]

---

[549]   Ray Allen Billington, *The Protestant Crusade 1800–1860: A Study of the
Origins of American Nativism* (Rinehart & Company, Inc.), 1952), 72–76, 87–88;
NWR, August 23, 1834, V. 10. No. 26, 436–37 ("fantastic dresses" and "Dis-
graceful outrage" quotations).

[550]   NWR, August 23, 1834, V. 10, No. 26, 435; David Grimsted, *American Mobbing, 1828–1861: Toward Civil War* (New York: Oxford University Press,
1998), 357–72.

[551]   NWR, August 22, 1835, v. 59, No. 25, 439.

Samuel F. B. Morse, well known as the inventor of the telegraph, but less known as the conspiracy-minded anti-Catholic that he was, saw the riots stemming from evil foreign influences. "If there is nothing intrinsic in our society which is likely to produce so sudden and mysterious effect [as rioting], the enquiry is natural, are there not extrinsic causes at work?" Historian David Grimsted suggested that strains in societies undergoing changes toward democracy, industrialization, urbanization, modernization, and a market economy may foster conditions of collective violence, yet he said there were few explanatory clues for the rising riot patterns.[552] On the other hand, maybe Morse's basic premise was wrong. Perhaps there was nothing to blame in the wilderness, or in the soil, or in an immigrant, but there was something intrinsic to blame in our very culture and character. Maybe the disease was not from insidious foreign sources, but from the hearth and the heart.

Burning schools or killing Catholics or blacks in the North was as likely to be punished as was killing blacks or Indians in the South or West—virtually not at all. Beecher and his fellow preachers revealed that their role in the natural world was to fan fear, intolerance, and hatred of the "Other"—to warn of the fires of hell while instigating their flocks to fire the earth. Terrorism came in many packages.

"God take my life":
The Beginning of Spectacle Lynching

The year 1835 might have been the most lawless year in American history, with at least 147 riots, 68 in the North and 79 in the South. Forty-six of them were proslavery riots, with 35 of those against abolitionists and 11 in response to non-existent insurrection scares. There were also 15 race riots—at this time a "race riot" meant white gangs beating and killing blacks. In these riots, eight were killed in the North, while 63 were killed in the South. Forty-eight of the victims were executed outright by mobs or died while undergoing tortures. In the South, many riots included "whipping-out" victims until they confessed to some crime. The occasional

---

[552]   Grimsted, *American Mobbing*, 9–10.

white victim was often killed for skepticism or defending black men, much as several 1692 Salem victims like Rebecca Nurse or John Proctor were viewed as guilty for doubting the procedures of the witch hunt. The murdered abolitionists can also be seen as "witch defenders," thus making them candidates for fatal reprisal. There were several incidents of slave burnings. Sadism was definitely a factor in one-quarter of the incidents.[553]

After the Nat Turner episode, more abolitionists were getting blamed for starting slave rebellions, although Turner clearly stated that God had motivated him. On the other hand, Southern evangelicals searched their bibles for passages that proved God was pro-slavery. They believed their monsters were outside agitators, never realizing that their demons came from within. Abolitionists may have printed inflammatory pamphlets, but Southerners added to their own chaos. In the early 1830s, John A. Murell, a notorious highwayman who operated along the Natchez Trace, worked a scheme worthy of his fellow frontiersmen who found unique ways to cheat Indians: he helped slaves escape from plantations, and then captured them and sold them back to their owners. Murell was also a fire and brimstone preacher known as the "Reverend Devil." After he was captured and jailed in 1834, one of his confederates wrote a sensational booklet of Murell's life, part of the title which read, "Together with His System of Villainy, and Plan of Exciting a Negro Rebellion." The booklet was a big hit, and it warned of a massive slave uprising planned for Christmas 1835.[554]

Frightened whites saw boogeymen everywhere. In June a female slave on a plantation at Beattie's Bluff along the Big Black River in Mississippi was said to have disrespected her white masters and fantasized about killing white children. White men in Livingston, about nine miles away, smelled an insurrection. The inevitable whipping of slaves produced a few names, but no solid evidence of any mischief. At Beattie's Bluff a mob "interrogated" two slaves. One named Weaver refused to name anyone even while being whipped. Refusal to talk certainly proved guilt, so Weaver was hanged. The

---

[553]   Grimsted, *American Mobbing*, 4, 13–16.
[554]   Philip Dray, *At the Hands of Persons Unknown: The Lynching of Black America* (New York: The Modern Library, 2003), 22–23.

218

second slave, Jim, after being lashed, decided hanging was not for him and named all the names the whites wanted. The mob hanged five more slaves.

Planter Ruel Blake was angry when some of his own slaves were killed. Too angry. The mob suspected he might be in on the "plot" and he fled to save his life. In Livingston, whites strung up three slaves, and the next day 160 citizens formed a vigilance committee to guide future hangings. They caught and whipped two white men, Joshua Cotton and William Saunders, who were believed to have been trading with blacks in stolen property. They assumed if they confessed and named others, they could save their lives, but with so many confessions the mobs were not getting enough rope action, and the two men were hanged anyway, on July 4, from the bars of the jailhouse windows.

Several other white men were flogged, tarred, or banished, while another dozen or more slaves were hanged in the Livingston-Beattie's Bluff area. On July 8, the vigilantes hanged a white man, Albe Dean, whose only crime was to have known Cotton and Saunders. Then they hanged another white man, Angus L. Donovan, a corn trader from Kentucky, whose only crime was protesting the bloody beatings of the slaves. The vigilantes were apparently "satisfied from the evidence before them that Donovan was an emissary of those deluded fanatics at the north—the ABOLITIONISTS." On July 10, Ruel Blake was caught and hanged for protesting the killing of his slaves. In Warren County near Vicksburg, a mob caught John and William Earle. They tortured and beat William senseless, revived him, swung a tomcat by the tail, let the frenzied creature dig his claws into the man's back, and then poured sealing wax onto his wounds. When put in jail, William hanged himself. The mob then hanged John Earle in the morning. Their only crime was being related to another man who was wanted by the mob. Two months later the mobs caught and hanged the slave Ned Hudnold, who had been hiding out since June.

About eight whites and twenty-four blacks were murdered. The eight white victims were poor men viewed as criminals or "Yankees." The entire episode was driven by white fear, but now, poor whites could be the victims as well as poor blacks. Worse yet, abolitionists were said to be inciting slaves to throw down their shovels and pick up a gun, and Southern slave owners had another bugbear to contend with. Six of the eight whites killed had never lived in the area and two were only passing through. They were the "outside agitators" the South would fear for another century and a half. Murell's plot to incite the slaves was a fantasy; Mississippi politician John H. F. Claiborne called it "one of the most extraordinary and lamentable hallucinations of our time."[555]

Racism, fear, and hatred increased between 1815 and 1845 as the Romantics destroyed the humanistic ideals of the Enlightenment. The eighteenth century emphasis on race progress was replaced by the nineteenth century emphasis on distinct races and their unequal qualities. As the "sciences" of craniology and phrenology came into vogue, Caucasian Anglo-Saxons viewed themselves as the superior race. After 1815, theories of American superiority coupled with rationalizations like Indian removal and Manifest Destiny meant that Indians and blacks would be plowed under. The idea of the "noble savage" was dead by the 1840s. The East was cleared of Indians, but the blacks remained behind to grow into the most monstrous white nightmare. The antebellum world was not transformed by new ideas as much as by race.[556]

Indians and blacks always populated the recesses of white nightmares, and were depicted as devils, witches, and monsters, the sinister "Others" who were shunned, persecuted, and even destroyed. A horrible method of purging, called spectacle lynching, became notorious in the late nineteenth century, but this brand of persecution/entertainment made an early appearance in 1836. New England witch trials in the 1600s had been mostly legal affairs; executions of alleged black rebels in the 1700s were generally accompanied by judicial trappings; but by the 1800s the façade of legality evaporated along with its sense of solemnity and sorrow. Judge Lynch operated under new rules of sadism, torture, cheering crowds, and even group participation.

---

[555] Christopher Waldrep, ed., *Lynching in America: A History in Documents* (New York: New York University Press, 2006), 65, 66 ("deluded fanatics" quotation); Grimsted, *American Mobbing*, 145–48, 149 ("hallucinations" quotation).
[556] Horsman, *Race and Manifest Destiny*, 43, 44, 56, 115, 146, 303.

A case in point was the burning of Francis McIntosh. Only two months before, in March 1836, Davy Crockett, Jim Bowie, William Travis and their cohorts had died under swift Mexican justice at the Alamo in Texas, supporting, among other things, their right to keep slaves. In May, a free black in St. Louis, Missouri, got a taste of American justice. Fear and hatred of blacks was never limited to the Deep South. A witness, known only as M. C., described the harrowing incident. McIntosh, a mulatto called a "yellow fellow," had committed some offense, was arrested, tried, and was being taken to jail when he allegedly pulled a knife and stabbed the deputies escorting him. He broke free and ran, but was quickly caught. Determined that McIntosh should die immediately, a mob rushed the jail and took him to a pasture outside the city. They were about to hang him when a number of people began shouting "Burn him," and "Let the fire be slow." About five hundred people gathered, collected kindling and logs, and piled them three feet high around the struggling man. When matches were applied, said M. C., "the murderer commenced singing a hymn, which he continued until the heat became intense, and then these few half-smothered words escaped him, 'God take my life!'" M. C. got into the front row, transfixed, "as if some horrid fascination chained me to the spot, and I witnessed all his agony." He burned for fifteen minutes. M. C. was mesmerized by "the boiling blood gushing in torrents from his mouth—his legs burnt to a crisp—yet his head moving from side to side, and occasionally a half uttered groan. But I will not, I cannot, further enlarge upon a sight so horrible—I feel a sickness in my heart, a dizziness in my head, occasioned by witnessing that terrific sight; but I was rooted to the spot, I could not withdraw my eye from the sight before me."[557]

Terrorism had entered a new phase.

A mob had just murdered a man, but would the law do anything about it? Shortly afterwards, a judge with the ironical name of Luke E. Lawless, charged a local grand jury not to indict anyone, pleading, "Is not something to be allowed for human sympathies in those appalling circumstances?" Lawless focused on McIntosh and not his murderers, and argued that perhaps if one or two men had done the deed, prosecution would be warranted, but when a crowd

---

[557]   Waldrep, ed., *Lynching in America*, 53–55.

"is seized upon and impelled by that mysterious, metaphysical, and almost electric phrenzy, which, in all ages and nations, has hurried on the infuriated multitude to deeds of death and destruction—then, I say, act not at all in the matter—the case then transcends your jurisdiction—it is beyond the reach of human law." Lawless believed mob burning of criminals was sanctioned by God, and he turned McIntosh into a symbol of black insurrection. "His rabid denunciations of the white man—his professions of deadly hostility to the whole white race"—accusations totally unfounded—openly betrayed his "incendiary cause." McIntosh was "only the blind instrument in the hands of the fanatics." To Lawless, the abolitionists were inciting the blacks to ally with Indian "savages" on the frontier "to assail the white population."[558]

No one was tried for McIntosh's murder, but at least one man was appalled by the burning. Elijah P. Lovejoy, editor of the *St. Louis Observer,* had passionately argued that slavery was a sin and treacherous to the cause of liberty. Lawless verbally trashed Lovejoy, and Lovejoy answered Lawless by accusing him of cowardice and perpetuating injustice. A short time later a white mob destroyed Lovejoy's printing presses. He abandoned St. Louis and moved twenty miles upriver to Alton, Illinois, but his progressive views were not welcome there, either, and people vandalized his office three times. When a new press was being delivered by steamboat up the Mississippi River on the night of November 7, 1837, Lovejoy and a few employees waited for it in a dockside warehouse. A mob gathered and trapped them inside. Someone crawled on the wooden roof and set it on fire. When Lovejoy emerged from the smoking building to challenge the arsonists, they shot and killed him. He became an abolitionist martyr. Wendell Phillips said the episode "stunned a drunken people into sobriety" and was almost an opening shot in the coming Civil War.[559]

The Lovejoy murder showed that Northerners would also kill when their fear and bigotry reached a boiling point. Still, the Southerners led the charge. David Grimsted calculated that there were

---

[558]   *Missouri Republican,* May 26, 1836, cited in Waldrep, ed., *Lynching in America,* 55–57.
[559]   Waldrep, ed., *Lynching in America,* 57; Dray, *At the Hands of Persons Unknown,* 28–29.

thirty-five instances of alleged insurrection plots between 1828 and 1861, although he also assigns the great majority of them to white fear rather than black rebellion. Southerners killed twenty-five abolitionists, but they also killed 448 people in quashing real or imagined insurrections, including twenty-six whites, eight free blacks, and 414 slaves.[560]

The distinction between terrorists and vigilantes was in the eye of the beholder. There were scores of episodes that blurred the line. In 1841, the *New Orleans Picayune* ran a story about Arkansans who believed a gang of counterfeiters was operating from a base along the Mississippi River near Helena. About one hundred "good" citizens set a trap for the gang when they next came to town to buy supplies with counterfeit money. Twenty-seven were caught when the trap was sprung. "They were tied hands and feet, and... drowned in the Mississippi." Not satisfied, the citizens caught, shot, or drowned from fifty to seventy-five other alleged gang members, "after which the executioners proceeded up and down the river, burning the houses lately occupied by the victims of their vengeance, and ordering their families to leave their homes forever." Papers called it a dark and bloody outrage and "a whole sale exercise of Lynch Law."[561]

In *Beyond Good and Evil*, Friedrich Nietzsche said, "He who fights monsters should see to it that in the process he does not become a monster. For when you gaze long into an abyss, the abyss also gazes into you." Americans were engaging in behavior that would become standard fare in horror films of the late twentieth century, and, as in those plots, the phone calls were coming from inside the house.

---

[560] Grimsted, *American Mobbing*, 134–35. In the four years after the Civil War, from 1866 through 1869, with the formation of the Ku Klux Klan, American terrorists, mainly in the rural South, lynched/murdered 3,270 blacks and "Others." 1868 stands as the worst year of all, with 2,014 killings. Gregory F. Michno, "Lynching and Christianity: A Three-Century American Witchhunt," TMs, 2014, 212.

[561] NNR, September 4, 1841, V. 11, No. 1, 3.

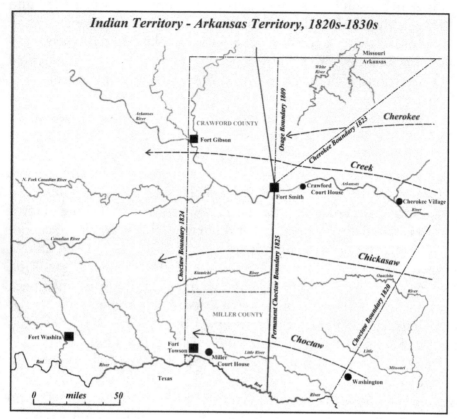

Indian Territory - Arkansas Territory, 1820s-1830s

Elizabeth Rosenberg

THE FRONTIERSMEN
VS. THE ARMY

"Where every man is an intruder"

The end of the War of 1812 exacerbated the hostility between the army and civilians because millions of acres of Indian land appeared free for the taking, but the TIA tasked the army to keep whites out. Even before word of the treaty ending the war had filtered to the frontiers, Americans were breaking the law. Cherokee agent Return J. Meigs complained that large numbers of whites were driving in stock and building cabins on Indian land. Past practice was to remove them, but treat them with "humanity & tenderness." Unfortunately, they would simply return once the army was gone, and Meigs said that some other method was needed—perhaps prosecution would work better than burning cabins. Meigs said the backwoods ruffians were unrestrained, poor citizens, and dangerous malcontents, but believed that fines and jail time would "repress the licentious disposition to intrude." Even a marshal, however, took his life in his hands if he interfered. The best lands available in Mississippi Territory, a land agent told Meigs, were "occupied by intruders who threaten with assassination" any person who dared bid for the land or tried to remove them.[562]

Mississippi Judge Harry Toulmin took the opposite view from Meigs: a jury would never "convict a man of intrusion—where every man is an intruder." In Missouri Territory, Marshal A. McNair said he could not distinguish between them. The gist of the problem was that most of the people living on public lands had "borne the storm of the Indian War," and they figured it was their right to take the land. He believed "that five Militia men of this territory would

---

[562]   Meigs to Winston, January 12, 1815, TPUS, V. 6, 492–93 ("humanity" and "licentious" quotations), Sewell to Meigs, December 8, 1815, TPUS, V. 6, 599 ("assassination" quotation).

not march against intruders on public lands."[563]

In December 1815, Governor William Clark of Missouri Territory issued a proclamation that "all white persons who have intruded and are settled upon the lands of the Indians within this territory, depart therefrom without delay." An optimistic War Secretary Crawford told Clark that he did not expect that regular troops would be necessary for enforcement. Michigan Territory apparently was different, for there, Crawford instructed Gen. Alexander Macomb that "evil disposed persons" continued to violate the law and directed him to remove them with military force and destroy their habitations. Pleas, proclamations, and threats made no difference, as intruders everywhere ignored the government and the army.[564]

On the Michigan frontier, General Duncan McArthur knew it was impossible to pacify or remove American or Canadian inhabitants. Previous military failures to take Canada or Mackinac "may justly be attributed to the Citizens of Detroit." They ignored the Territorial laws, they were treacherous, treasonous, greedy, and "would not spare a pound for the Army." He said he could never get volunteers from Kentucky or Ohio to go to Detroit again. They were convinced the Michiganders "were the most dangerous of our enemies."[565]

Crawford's optimism soon faded. He appealed directly to the Tennessee Cherokees to take matters into their own hands, saying he knew "disorderly white men have settled among you, who have harassed and vexed the peaceable inhabitants," and he told the Cherokees to kick them out. If they could not, their agent or the army would deal with them.[566]

Whites hired lawyers to argue that they were not really on public land, but on Indian land, and exempt from the law. Crawford was incensed. The intruders' assertion that they "are ready to remove

---

[563]   Toulmin to Madison, January 20, 1816, TPUS, V. 6, 647; McNair to Meigs, January 27, 1816, TPUS, V. 15, 112.

[564]   Clark Proclamation, December 4, 1815, TPUS, V. 15, 191–92; Crawford to Macomb, January 27, 1816, TPUS, V. 10, 619; Crawford to Clark, February 5, 1816, TPUS, V. 15, 113.

[565]   McArthur to Monroe, February 16, 1815, TPUS, V. 10, 504.

[566]   Crawford to HEADMEN of the Cherokee Nation, May 13, 1816, ASPIA, V. 2, 110.

from their settlements as public property, but not as Indian lands, is too shallow a device to deceive the most inconsiderate." They knew what lands they were on and knew they were in violation of the law. "This delusion must be terminated," Crawford told General Jackson. Unfortunately, Jackson was not disposed to drive away Tennesseans with Tennesseans, especially since the Cherokees had complained about depredations committed by his soldiers. Return Meigs tried to stroke Jackson's ego: "Your character...cannot be even touched by the conduct of some unruly, insubordinate men," whose actions did not detract from the character of the general or his army any more "than the spots in the sun destroy the splendor of that luminary." Having disgorged those obsequious lines, Meigs wrote to Crawford that the Cherokees were promised the land they occupied, were due reparations for the spoliations done by the whites, and any attempt to redefine the treaty was "a monstrous perversion of language."[567]

When Jackson did remove intruders they retaliated. John McCartney of Alabama filed a claim alleging that in 1817, Lt. Sam Houston, under Jackson's orders, not only destroyed his house, but confiscated fifty-one cattle and a horse. McCartney wanted compensation. Treasury Secretary Crawford said that the order was to destroy houses, not to confiscate property; however, there was no evidence that McCartney had lost any stock, and even if he had, Jackson was responsible, not the government.[568]

In Georgia, Capt. David E. Twiggs, 7th Infantry, had been removing intruders near Fort Hawkins, "having destroyed their houses, [illegible] & crops as far as it was practicable." Even without a cooperative local guide to assist him, Twiggs destroyed all he could find.[569]

Indian agents from Georgia to Arkansas asked for army help to extricate intruders, but General Gaines, for one, acknowledged that the frontiersmen's belligerent character preordained resistance,

---

[567]   Crawford to Jackson, July 1, 1816, ASPIA, V. 2, 112–13 ("shallow a device" and "delusion" quotations); Meigs to Jackson, August 8, 1816, ASPIA, V. 2, 113 ("spots in the sun" quotation); Meigs to Crawford, August 19, 1816, ASPIA, V. 2, 114 ("perversion" quotation).

[568]   Crawford to Williams, December 15, 1820, ASPC, V. 1, 753–54.

[569]   Twiggs to Gaines, September 20, 1819, AGO, RG 94, M566, R0128.

and he was uncertain if military force would have any effect.[570] Militia and volunteers would not remove their own friends if they could help it, and Secretary Crawford realized the government was fighting a losing battle. "Experience has sufficiently proven that our population will spread over any cession, however extensive," and will demand protection, "embarrassing the government by broils with the natives, and rendering the execution of the laws regulating intercourse with the Indian tribes utterly impossible."[571]

Intruders fought back with petitions. Responding to the order that all intruders were to leave the Cherokee Nation by July 1, 1819, supplicants told War Secretary Calhoun that they "are poor but industrious farmers," and to force them out into the wilderness at that time of year would leave them destitute. Where, they asked, "will your petitioners apply for bread to support their starving families?" Since they must subsist somewhere, "they will thus become unwelcome guests to the frontier counties to beg (for they cannot buy) something for their little children."[572] The Committee on Public Lands had addressed that argument many times: intruders always had a crop growing that they had to harvest or they would starve, and when granted a reprieve, the following year there was always another crop to plant. It recommended to stop indulging trespassers, for it would only injure the government as well as legal purchasers.[573] The people of Prairie de Chien, Michigan Territory, were more demanding. After being forced out of their houses and subjected to "severe and grievous losses by the illegal acts of Military Officers," their rather perplexing remedy was that in order to avoid asking for government charity, they would rely on the "Justice and liberality of the Government" to give them free land elsewhere.[574]

---

[570]   Mitchell to Gaines, February 5, 1817, ASPMA, V. 1, 748; Jamison to Graham, March 31, 1817, TPUS, V. 15, 258; NWR, March 27, 1819, V. 4, No. 5, 84.

[571]   Crawford to Clark, September 17, 1816, TPUS, V. 15, 175.

[572]   Memorial to the Secretary of War, nd, 1819, TPUS, V. 18, 613.

[573]   Committee on Public Lands, April 23, 1824, ASPPL, V. 3, 619.

[574]   Petition to Congress, December, 24, 1821, TPUS, V. 11, 212.

"Whipped his back almost to a jelly"

White borderers not only battled the government with petitions and lawsuits, the antagonism often escalated into beatings and murders. Major Talbot Chambers, commanding Fort Howard near Green Bay in 1816, got into a scrape with civilians at the post. Indian agent John Bowyer claimed that his "Mulato boy," an assistant to the blacksmith, Younglove, killed two of Chambers's pigs, and Chambers allegedly promised a soldier a half-gallon of whiskey if he would give the boy fifty lashes. When Younglove interfered, the soldier tried to whip the blacksmith, who clubbed the soldier with his own gun. Chambers heard that Younglove had killed the soldier, and the commander and captain of the guard rushed to the scene. The captain attacked Younglove "with his naked sword, and wounded him severely in the shoulder," while Chambers punched and kicked him. Bowyer claimed that Younglove was thereafter disabled and he had to pay passage to send him and the boy back to Detroit. He demanded an investigation.[575]

Mobile, Alabama, had its share of army-civilian encounters. Some of them stemmed from the War of 1812, when, according to civilian petitioners, the army and militia got the idea "that the property of the inhabitants was free plunder." They scoured the countryside and "destroyed the cattle at their pleasure"—the Tennessee militia being particularly culpable. Hunger was not an issue, for the petitioners claimed that they shot down cattle "from mere wantonness, leaving the carcasses as food for the birds and beasts of prey." The people demanded reparations.[576]

When the army captured Fort Charlotte in 1813, Mobile was a small town, but growing. The fort was not enclosed, a road went right through it, and Capt. George P. Peters spent much of his time trying to keep the locals out. Civilians used it as a thoroughfare and apparently behaved much as had the militia that they petitioned against. Peters said the fort was "exposed to the depredations of horses, cows, sheep and hogs," as well as thieves, all of which "were

---

[575]   Bowyer to Crawford, October 29, 1816, TPUS, V 17, 419–20.
[576]   Petition to Congress by the Inhabitants of Mobile, January 16, 1817, TPUS, V. 6, 751.

continually defacing and demolishing the works." In 1816, Peters built a fence and a gate, but the locals issued an indictment against him, stating that they had a right to the land, "founded on *Ancient Usage!*" In addition, the civilians claimed a right to all the public land in the county, and they wanted the fort demolished as a nuisance. Peters pleaded for help for he did not have the money to engage a lawyer.[577]

The army was custodian of public land, but the people of Mobile built a jail on a prime lot, and Lt. Robert Beall was tasked with getting them to remove it. After an unsuccessful appeal to the town and courts, Beall planned to remove the prisoners, secure them at the fort, and demolish the jail. A mob gathered to oppose him, and, as Beall's detachment was unarmed, the threat of violence caused him to return to the fort for weapons. Reports varied, but Beall was said to have taken muskets, artillery, and a band, which, said the *Mobile Gazette*, was calculated "to excite the inhabitants to arms, and to deeds of bloodshed and horror," and was an attack upon their "sacred rights." Some said Beall fired and some said it was Beall who was menaced and showed no disposition to fight. Apparently no one was killed, but the townsfolk wanted Beall disciplined, and he was cashiered in 1819.[578]

About the same time in East Florida, a man named Miller, an army deserter and at the time a captain in the Florida militia, accosted artillery Sgt. Augustus Santee, on leave and heading to St. Johns with his brother and another man. The reason for the confrontation was unknown, but Miller's men fired and wounded Santee's companions, then arrested all three and marched them to jail in St. Augustine. General Gaines demanded the governor release the men and punish the perpetrators.[579] Six months later, in September 1819, Colonel Duncan Clinch, 8th Infantry, told Gaines that two of them had finally been released with a writ of habeas corpus, but one was still confined. The locals believed the soldiers were outlaws. Per Clinch, "there has been so many outrages committed on this frontier

---

[577]   Peters to Jesup, November 30, 1816, TPUS, V. 18, 119–21. Fort Charlotte was sold and demolished in 1820.
[578]   NWR, August 22, 1818, V. 2, No. 26, 440 (quotations); NWR, September 12, 1818, V. 3, No. 3, 43.
[579]   NWR, March 27, 1819, V. 4, No. 5, 88–89.

by this group of vagrants" that every honest citizen wanted them all brought to justice.[580]

In Michigan Territory in 1823, Agent Henry R. Schoolcraft ordered his employees to cut down trees around Fort Brady to construct buildings for his agency. When Lt. Col. William Lawrence, 2nd Infantry, commanding the post at Sault Sainte Marie, discovered the cutting, he angrily threatened to flog them and throw them in jail. When they said they acted under Schoolcraft's order, Lawrence did not believe Schoolcraft was "such a fool," and he would be damned if he would let any man cut the government trees. Schoolcraft was away at the time, which precluded further conflict, but he complained to the secretary of war that he had never heard of "so violent, injurious, and extraordinary a proceeding." Judge James D. Doty, later governor of Wisconsin and Utah Territories, wrote to Schoolcraft that he had similar troubles with the army, and as citizens "we are bound to unite in defending ourselves against the outrages of these military tyrants and oppressors." He warned Schoolcraft to be careful, because "you are not dealing with men of honor." Stay out of their reach, Doty said, for they only pretended to be gentlemen because of the epaulettes they wore.[581]

Similar confrontations occurred at several frontier posts. Settlers around Green Bay interfered with the emigration of the New York Indians by inciting the Winnebago and Menominee against them. Commissioner of Indian Affairs Thomas L. McKenney told the Indian agent that the settlers' conduct "is highly reprehensible, & cannot be suffered by the Government with impunity." He was to take strong measures to suppress them and seek military help if necessary. At nearby Fort Howard in 1828, post commander Major David Twiggs fought settlers who cut reservation trees and hay, made bricks, and set up grog shops. Their claims, said Twiggs, "are founded on trespass." He refused to let surveyors run lines or allow anyone else in, because keeping civilians and the military separate was the only way to preserve harmony.[582]

[580]   Clinch to Gaines, September 25, 1819, AGO, RG 94, M566, R0017.
[581]   Schoolcraft to Calhoun, August 6, 1823, TPUS, V. 11, 396–98; Doty to Schoolcraft, October 15, 1824, TPUS, V. 11, 594–95.
[582]   McKenney to Brevoort, March 8, 1825, TPUS, V. 11, 657–58; Twiggs to Porter, August 23, 1828, TPUS, V. 11, 1204.

Commissioner McKenney directed Superintendent Lewis Cass at Detroit to drive out the white intruders. "The evil of their presence is felt to such a degree" that it inflamed both Indians and civilians. The border landers were a pestilence; they were "lazy—dishonest, intemperate—setting vicious examples before the Indians," and pitting them against each other and the authorities.[583] McKenney's attitude was not unique. A remarkably candid remonstrance was sent to Congress by the "respectable" people of Michigan Territory regarding a proposal to lower land prices for newcomers. They said it would be unfair to the old settlers who had made improvements. The old system "produced the happiest results in establishing a moral population in Michigan," while the new proposal would admit "squatters who are a pest to society." The door would open to undesirables, "thus enticing the dregs of community from the old states." If Congress wanted "to establish a place of refuge for the refuse of society…that portion of the people who are a nuisance to any country," it ought to be far out in the interior of the Northwest Territory, "but we beg that Michigan may not be selected for that object." The petitioners said that the proposed bill would result in "the destruction of the moral character of new countries."[584] In effect, they said, "Not in my backyard." Since they very likely came from the same classes of immoral dregs and squatters that they now abhorred, they knew well of what they warned against.

While Michigan wanted newcomers out, Alabama wanted them in. At Fort Mitchell in 1830, Capt. Philip Wager, 4th Infantry, issued a proclamation that all white men living within Creek lands without permits or Indian wives were to vacate. Alabama countered "that there is no law to authorize the said Philip Wager issuing this proclamation," and the whites should stay right where they were. The Creeks and whites were subject to Alabama law and the military was to mind its own business. The army decree was against the law and "the peace and dignity of the state of Alabama."[585]

Wager and the nearby people of Columbus, Georgia, were in continuous turmoil. In March 1831, soldiers were accused of murdering an Indian. Wager arrested them, but refused to give them

[583]   McKenney to Cass, February 17, 1829, TPUS, V. 12, 23–24.
[584]   Remonstrance to Congress, March 10, 1828, TPUS, V. 11, 1175–76.
[585]   NWR, May 8, 1830, V. 11, No. 11, 204.

up to civilian justice. When whites seized a Chattahoochee River ferry owned by the Indians, Wager tried to get it back, only to be threatened with a lawsuit. William Bailey of Columbus, whom Wager called a third-rate lawyer and "despised as a coward and a liar," wrote to President Adams that the army confiscated a ferry owned by the town of Columbus. A Georgia court ruled against the Indians. Wager, all the while, begged for clear direction from the War Department as to how to remove one thousand white intruders from Creek lands, because if he used force he would wind up in court, or worse.[586]

Creek Chief Eneah Micco begged the secretary of war to keep the whites out. He said they fought with the Indians, and while the Indians brought their people to justice, "the whites go unpunished. We are weak, and our words and oaths go for naught; justice we don't expect, nor can we get." The whites "bring spirits among us for the purpose of practicing frauds; they daily rob us of our property." Eneah Micco could only "pray that our father, the President, will...protect us from such intruders."[587]

Far south at Key West the small civilian population was often harassed by raiding pirates and it wanted army protection. Arriving in February 1831, Maj. James M. Glassell, 4th Infantry, quickly learned it was to be no tropical vacation. The land he thought would be sandy was just "pulverized shells," and there were few trees with which to build a post. Worse, the civilian proprietors, who offered the army a site for a fort, "do not think they are *now* bound to the United States on the offer formerly made." Glassell was not authorized to contract for land, had no shelter, and was "at a loss what to do."[588]

Forced to improvise, Glassell built a rudimentary post and struggled to supply his men with food. Constantly hungry, the soldiers hunted for game and occasionally shot a cow. Pardon C. Greene, said to be the senior militia officer of the county, complained to the secretary of war that soldiers were running riot, destroying property, and assaulting the civilians. Glassell countered that Greene was a

---

[586] Wager to Macomb, March 10, 1831, May 1, 1831, (quotation), May 25, 1831, AGO, RG 94, M567, R0065.

[587] Eneah Micco et al. to Eaton, April 8, 1831, USCSS, V. 2, 425.

[588] Glassell to Jones, February 28, 1831, TPUS, V. 24, 504.

crook who had defrauded his creditors, was a slave trader, and came to Florida to speculate in lands. Glassell had already apprehended the soldiers who shot the cow and offered to pay for damages, but Greene demanded that he confiscate their weapons and keep them out of town. Glassell protested that they would not go to town were it not for the fact that "every third house is kept as a grog shop by the most depraved of men." On October 8, 1832, a sergeant crept out at night and went to one of the shops, where Greene found him, attacked him from behind, and bludgeoned him "to such a degree that his life was much endangered." Glassell tried to get a judge to form a jury but was told he had to wait until the following spring. The angry major said that if a soldier had committed the assault, they would "try cases on the first report, without evidence, & make up their minds, which they have no wish to change."[589]

Early in 1833, a civilian named Harris concocted a scheme with one of the soldiers and convinced him to desert. Following Harris's direction, the soldier tried to take a small boat owned by the sheriff, but the sheriff was informed and caught the soldier in the act. The posse tied him, stripped off his shirt, and, per Glassell, "whipped his back almost to a jelly." Irate soldiers went to town and caught the sheriff and Harris at a grog shop; the sheriff escaped, but they beat Harris, prompting Greene to complain that Glassell's soldiers had assaulted civilians, and as senior militia officer, it was his duty to protect them from the army. Glassell admitted that he did not have enough sentinels to ring the quarters at night, but he wondered why authorities never prosecuted the scofflaws who illegally sold the liquor. He asked Greene why the sheriff, who was supposed to be "quite stout hearted," ran away from the fight when he was so brave in a mob. Should any civilians perpetrate any similar outrages, Glassell said, he "cannot be answerable for consequences."[590]

Out in Arkansas Territory that same year, soldiers and whiskey sellers continued their love-hate relationship. At Fort Smith, Capt. John Stuart spent much of his time chasing whiskey smug-

---

[589] Greene to Cass, October 15, 1832, TPUS, V. 24, 743–44; Glassell to Jones, December 14, 1832, TPUS, V. 24, 762, 763.

[590] Greene to Glassell, January 8, 1833, TPUS, V. 24, 796; Glassell to Greene, January 13, 1833, TPUS, V. 24, 797; Glassell to Jones, January 15, 1833, TPUS, V. 24, 795 ("jelly" quotation).

glers. Jonas and George Bigelow, whose store was only 150 yards from the fort, were some of the most notorious. Stuart never could catch them, because it seemed for every soldier who wanted to shut them down, there was another who kept them in business. On August 26, 1833, Captain Stuart went to Nowland and Scott's store, next to Bigelow's, where George Bigelow beat Stuart with a club and knocked him unconscious. Dr. David Holt found Stuart on the floor "in an insensible state with a severe wound on the upper part and right side of the forehead extending upwards and backwards about two inches and reaching to the skull-bone. The Captain's right ear was cut through entirely... and the right side of his head was much bruised." Stuart was carried to the fort.[591]

Lieutenant John P. Davis abruptly left his dinner and hurried to Stuart's room where he found him "most horribly mangled, the blood apparently gushing from all parts of his head." No one believed he would live. Davis called Bigelow's attack "one of the most fiendish acts" ever recorded. As Stuart fought for life, Davis walked through the garrison and heard the men discussing revenge. After midnight, soldiers wheeled out an artillery piece toward Bigelow's, and about three o'clock in the morning an explosion jostled Davis awake. He ran to the door, saw a flash and heard another explosion. Gunshots cracked and one ball slammed into a post near his head. Davis had long roll beaten and summoned all the men. The moon was down and he could hardly see a man ten yards away. All appeared to be present, however, and acted as if nothing had happened. No one would reveal who had fired a couple of six-pound balls into Bigelow's store. All Davis could do was report that Bigelow's was a public nuisance and injurious to good order, as "Indians, negroes and the lower order of white people" commingled there in rioting, dissipation, and "beastly intoxication."[592]

Sometimes the "frontier" came to Washington, D. C. On February 26, 1835, after the House had adjourned, Indiana Representative John Ewing walked down the street and was met by Lt.

---

[591]   Stuart to Cass, September 20, 1833, TPUS, V. 21, 797–98; Holt to Weener, December 18, 1833, AGO, RG 94, M567, R0099.
[592]   Davis to Moore, June 12, 1834, AGO, RG 94, M567, R0099. It took Stuart nearly three weeks before he could return to duty.

John F. Lane, 4th Artillery. Apparently Ewing had made disparaging comments about members of Lane's family and Lane sought satisfaction. After a few words, Ewing reached into his pocket. Lane assumed he was going for a gun and he struck Ewing in the face with a "slender iron cane." Ewing carried a cane-sword, which he drew from its case and sought "to revenge himself with the naked blade." The two thrusted and parried for a time; Lane blocked the sword with his arm and managed to grab Ewing by the hair. As neither of them gained further advantage, the fight ended. However, there was the matter of the Fifth Article of War, which stated that no officer could use disrespectful words against a congressman under penalty of court martial. They had fought, but no one could prove Lane had verbally abused Ewing. Still, he could not go unpunished. He was given a reprimand, removed from duty in Washington and returned to his regiment.[593]

"You will take them over our dead bodies"

On Missouri's western border the Osage were being squeezed by whites and Indians arriving from the Old Northwest Territory. The Osage called for army protection, but the whites called louder. In the summer of 1837, Lewis F. Linn and Albert G. Harrison, Missouri members of the Senate and House, respectively, chided Col. Stephen W. Kearny, 1st Dragoons, for doing a poor job protecting them. They sarcastically said how impressed they were at his length of service and his knowledge of the frontier and the Indians, but wondered how the government could spend millions of dollars on numerous other projects and leave the frontiers vulnerable. They asked how the government could open lands to white settlement and place "thousands of the most restless and implacable enemies" among them. "The government itself is guilty," they said, while white men were "innocent of the causes" that necessitated their protection.[594]

---

[593]   ANC, V. 1, No. 10 (March 5, 1835), 76; ANC, V. 1, No. 16 (April 10, 1835), 121–23. Lane was promoted to lieutenant colonel to command the Creek Regiment in the Seminole War. Suffering fevers and headaches, he ran a sword through his right eye on October 19, 1836 (Foreman, *Indian Removal*, 348n15).
[594]   Linn and Harrison to Kearny, June 3, 1837, ASPMA, V. 7, 960.

Kearny begged to differ. The army was small and he had only his allotted force to work with, but given the resources, he believed it had done a commendable job. The gentlemen from Missouri had forgotten a salient point: "most of the difficulties we have had with the Indians may be traced to the lawless acts of some white men" and the reluctance of civilian courts to prosecute them. He suggested that if the army would be allowed to apprehend intruders as stated in the TIA, and try them in military courts, it would do "more to preserve peace on the frontier than many additional regiments."[595]

Stephen Watts Kearny. *Graham's Magazine,* July 1849. *Public domain* While frontier civilians claimed their innocence, Colonel Kearny asserted that almost all Indian problems stemmed from lawless acts of white men.

Missouri simply did not want Osages within its borders and the white troublemakers were out in force. In October, Governor Lilburn W. Boggs called out two militia brigades under Maj. Gen. Samuel D. Lucas in order to drive out alleged depredators. Instead of four hundred raiding warriors, Lucas found only peaceful camps. Alarms poured in that Indian raiders were attacking everywhere, but wherever Lucas searched, the raiders disappeared. He suspected that a French community near Harmony Mission in Bates County was alerting the Osage so they always kept one step ahead. Lucas went there and "captured" about three hundred, who submitted without a fight and wondered why so many white men were chasing them. Lucas couldn't understand why the smoke from the raiders' campsites was always just over the next horizon. He was certain the local whites were telling him the truth, as there were only "respectable people" on that frontier, "men of exemplary habits and good moral character," and "temperance men" who deserved security. The dragoons, he said, "have afforded

---

595   Kearny to Linn and Harrison, June 20, 1837, ASPMA, V. 7, 961.

them no protection whatever," so they had to depend on the state militia.[596]

One of Lucas's brigade commanders, Col. M. G. Wilson, was certain that western Missouri would be "overwhelmed in a general war," especially since the Osages were "committing outrage after outrage" on the frontier citizens. Wilson said that one of the greatest evils was that a number of French liquor-sellers lived near Harmony Mission and had "full-blooded Osage Indian squaws as pretended wives." That status apparently affronted white religious and racial attitudes, so Lucas ordered the women to be expelled from the state. Riding south from Fort Leavenworth was Capt. Edwin V. Sumner, with Companies A and B, 1st Dragoons, under Colonel Kearny's orders to prevent the eviction. Sumner, nicknamed "Bull Head," was born in Boston in 1797, and joined the army as a second lieutenant in 1819. Legend says that a musket ball once bounced off his forehead without harming him, but temperament rather than thick skull may have been the reason for his moniker. Sumner sent a message to Lucas to stay away from the Indians until they could talk, "before any blood is shed by your command." Before he arrived, a Captain Mitchell went to Harmony Mission and forcibly took five Osage women from their husbands.[597]

Sumner reached there on the morning of November 2, 1837, and "was astonished to learn that a detachment of Militia, had the night before made prisoners of five Osage women who were living with white men in that vicinity, some of them having been married for fifteen or twenty years." "After mature reflection," Sumner decided to rescue them. He caught up to the sixteen kidnappers riding in front and behind "five helpless and frightened women," and called it "the most contemptible sight I ever saw or ever expect to in the course of my life." Sumner told Captain Mitchell to release them and he would take responsibility for their safety. Mitchell reluctantly did so. In Colonel Wilson's words, Sumner, "with force of arms, took said squaws and ordered them back" to the mission. There, Sumner

---

[596] Robert A. Glenn, "The Osage War," *Missouri Historical Review*, V. 14, No. 2 (January 1920), 204–207.
[597] Wilson to Harrison, November 25, 1837, ASPMA, V. 7, 961; Sumner to Lucas, October 30, 1837, AGO, RG 94, M567, R0143.

posted Sgt. M. Hancock and three privates to guard them and rode to notify Lucas. He told the general that he had taken the women and protested that "they had as much right to feel at home in that state as we had ourselves." Lucas explained that Governor Boggs had ordered their removal, but Sumner said Colonel Kearny had given him orders that did not include breaking up families. Lucas did not wish to fight the dragoons, so he agreed and they parted ways.[598]

Edwin V. Sumner. *Library of Congress* Captain Sumner rescued Osage women from the Missourians while four of his dragoons defied the volunteers' efforts to take them back.

Colonel Wilson arrived near Harmony Mission the next day, where Sergeant Hancock watched them ride up, armed with guns and swords. Wilson handed Hancock a letter that read the guard "is hereby dissolved by order of Captain Sumner," but it was signed by Lucas. Hancock returned the letter and told Wilson "it was no good," that he could not obey it, and he "did not know General Lucas from the Devil." Another officer brandishing a sword approached Hancock and demanded to see his orders, but the sergeant said his orders were his own and he would not turn them over to anyone. The officer said he understood his business, but Hancock countered that he understood his too. Wilson reiterated that his orders were for Hancock to break up the guard and give Wilson the women.

"I will not give them up," Hancock said.

"I will take them," Wilson replied.

"If you take them," Hancock said, "you will take them over our dead bodies."

Wilson asked if he disobeyed Lucas's direct orders, and the sergeant replied, "I obey Captain Sumner's orders."

Wilson again demanded the women, and Hancock explained that he assumed Wilson had some good and brave men in his com-

---

[598]   Sumner to Kearny, November 23, 1837, AGO, RG 94, M567, R0143; Wilson to Harrison, November 25, 1837, ASPMA, V. 7, 961.

mand, and in all probability even "some Gentlemen among them." He also said that in the future perhaps they could meet again as friends, but right now it was a shame that Wilson had brought his men "into danger and that if any blood was spilled I would have his first."

The other officer with the sword then rode up close to Hancock and said, "I like your spunk and it would be a pity to kill such men as you."

"I am not dead yet," Hancock retorted, "and when I am killed there will be some empty saddles in your party." Realizing they could not bluff the dragoons, Wilson and his command wheeled about and rode off.[599]

Dealing with civilians exasperated Sumner. He had learned that some Osages "were most severely flogged by a party of militia" while removing them from the state. He had no proof of it, but said that if true, the culprits ought to be "held to a fearful account," for their actions could start a war. Sumner informed Lucas of Kearny's directive: the volunteers "are not required and have not been to preserve peace on this frontier."[600]

So ended the "Osage War." The skeptical *Missouri Republican* printed an acerbic account that said hordes of Osages had crossed the line and may have killed a few hogs. In response, the governor called out 560 officers and men, including "one major general, two brigadiers, four full colonels, besides *lots* of lieutenant colonels, majors, captains, lieutenants, chaplains, surgeons, etc."—ninety-eight officers to command 462 privates—"to expel from our borders these *murderers of hogs!*" These brave soldiers so expertly surrounded camps of Indians loaded with women and children that "not a papoose escaped." General Jesup in Florida may have captured Osceola, the paper said, but that "falls vastly short of this achievement." As Lucas escorted the captured Osages out of the state, the brave Colonel Wilson had some of the males "*stripped and severely scourged! Oh shame! Where is thy blush?*" Thus "was an end of this *glorious* campaign."

---

[599]   Hancock to Sumner, November 24, 1837, AGO, RG 94, M567, R0143.
[600]   Sumner to Kearny, November 23, 1837, AGO, RG 94, M567, R0143 ("flogged" and "fearful account" quotations); Sumner to Lucas, November 2, 1837, AGO RG 94, M567, R0143 ("not required" quotation).

Just as after the Black Hawk War, most of the damage was done by civilians. The *Republican* said that the militia, plus the dragoons, "made furious attacks on the corn fields and crops, beeves and hogs of the settlers" who had little to spare. "The Indians in ten seasons would not have created as much distress as this two weeks' campaign has."[601]

They "lie like pickpockets"

Americans almost universally believed the army existed to protect them from the Indians, but after decades of civilian abuse, the army, at least, got an attitude adjustment. A young officer stationed at Fort Heileman, Florida, wrote that people had no conception of the severe time they had living in swamps, eaten by insects, low on supplies, constantly wet, suffering diseases, often barefooted, with pants shredded at the knees, doing their best to protect the white inhabitants, "whose presses teem with abuse upon the army." The officers were alienated from home and friends, as well as from those "who would suffer much in comparison with the savage."[602]

The hostility was evident on higher levels. War Secretary Poinsett wrote to President Van Buren that it was impossible to deal with Florida territorial governor Richard Call. Successful conclusion of the latest Seminole campaign depended on his cooperation with the army, which "cannot be expected" while he remained in power. The animosity between the army, civil authorities and volunteers was having "unpleasant and disastrous consequences." Poinsett asked for Call's removal, which took place December 2, 1839.[603]

Malicious civilian-army animosities often appeared in print. In the May 12, 1840, *New Orleans Bee*, "Viator," perhaps a pseudonym for Vicksburg lawyer John M. Chilton, railed against the army on the Arkansas frontier and accused them of trying to start an Indian war to "retrieve a reputation lost in the swamps of Florida." Viator called General Arbuckle an imbecile and a coward, and accused him of sending troops from Fort Leavenworth to Fort Gibson

[601]   *Missouri Republican*, November 20, 1837, in NNR, December 2, 1837, V. 3, No. 14, 213.
[602]   ANC, V. 7, No. 7 (August 16, 1838), 105.
[603]   Poinsett to Van Buren, November 29, 1839, TPUS, V. 25, 656–57.

because he was "startled, terrified, and bewildered by the fear of immediate massacre—forgetting honor, policy, and the high bearing of a soldier, and intent on securing his own personal safety." Arbuckle allegedly used dragoons as a personal bodyguard to surround his house. When they were withdrawn from Leavenworth, Viator claimed that the Indians immediately began to plunder and depredate "with that vile class of our own countrymen who are ever hovering on our frontiers." He said Arbuckle was too incompetent to manage soldiers and civilians, and since he was afraid of Indians, it only increased their contempt for him, as well as with "the vicious whites who carry on contraband trade with them." Viator hoped Arbuckle would be "the first victim that joins the number of whom his folly has already consigned to the grave, or that his friends, pitying the exposure of dotage, may induce him to retire on half-pay, and give place to a successor more capable." Arbuckle shot back, calling the editorial "a most foul, slanderous and malicious production against the Government of the United States and myself."[604] It was indicative of the acrimony between frontier people and the military during the years between the War of 1812 and the War with Mexico, and there was little anyone could do about it.

As the frontier expanded across the Mississippi River and traders headed west along the Santa Fe Trail, there were the usual confrontations with Indians, but also attacks by civilian marauders from Texas. After the failed 1841 military and commercial Texan Santa Fe expedition to secure New Mexico, and the failed Mier expedition of 1842, Texan Jacob Snively secured permission to launch a retaliatory foray to capture Mexican caravans on the Santa Fe Trail. Snively assembled nearly two hundred men and marched north to the Arkansas River to await a wagon train. Long days of inactivity brought discontent, and the band divided into opposing parties. On June 30, 1843, dragoons under Capt. Philip St. George Cooke ran into one of the parties and disarmed it, leaving them only ten muskets. He learned that they also planned to attack Mexican settlements, but did not believe the Texas president knew of it, or "he would pronounce them banditti!" They were, said Cooke,

---

[604] *New Orleans Bee,* May 12, 1840; Arbuckle to Mason, June 6, 1840, AGO, RG 94, M567, R0201.

"cutthroat outlaws & their principal men lie like pickpockets on all subjects." Although he treated them as "inveterate enemies," Cooke allowed forty-two of them to join him in the march back to Independence, Missouri, rather than trail back through Comanche country. The rest of Snively's men rejoined, fought with the Comanches, and then returned to the Santa Fe Trail to follow a Mexican caravan. When they found the escort was too strong, they finally gave up and went home.[605]

General Gaines approved of Cooke's action to disarm and foil "one hundred Texians," and suggested that the only way to guarantee protection to travelers and traders on that route was by the establishment of permanent military posts along the Great Bend of the Arkansas or beyond. They had to be strong enough to protect against Indians "as well as predatory bands of civilized men disposed to violate the laws of war by violating the principle of free trade."[606]

Snively's was not the only band operating along the Western trails. Missouri borderers had engaged in mayhem long before their appearance in "Bleeding Kansas" in the 1850s. Attacking wagon trains heading to and from Santa Fe was almost a pastime. Two gangs made the news in 1843. The McDaniel-Mason Gang of about fifteen men intercepted the wagon train of Antonio Charvis on its way to Independence, murdered Charvis, and stole $35,000 in gold and silver. Some of the money went to accomplices in Clay and Jackson Counties, Missouri, and $1,500 was recovered from the desk of the Clay County clerk. Another gang of about forty-five men under a "Colonel" Warfield, a merchant from New Orleans, also raided the Santa Fe Trail. Warfield apparently believed he was a type of Robin Hood, declaring that he was "merely a *land privateer* against Mexico," and would not harm Americans. He "declared a war or rather a *hunt*, of extermination against the Mexicans, both in their lives and property." The *Niles National Register*, citing several

---

[605] Gregory F. Michno and Susan J. Michno, *Forgotten Fights: Little-Known Raids and Skirmishes on the Frontier, 1823 to 1890* (Missoula, MT: Mountain Press Publishing Company, 2008), 64–65; *Cooke Journal,* June 22, 1843, June 30, 1843, July 8, 1843, AGO, RG 94, M567, R0267.

[606] Gaines to Jones, July 26, 1843, AGO RG 94, M5676, R0269.

newspapers, claimed that such depredations had been occurring for years, as "the frontier men of Missouri" have stolen immense sums from the Mexicans and Indians. It sarcastically added that the gang's barbarism and ferocity notwithstanding, there was never a "more honorable race of men." Sure they robbed and assassinated, "but their *patriotism* is unquestionable—they will never touch one of their fellow citizens." If Americans were unmolested, it was no crime to kill a Mexican or a Comanche, to "burn up his wigwam and its inmates and carry off his mules." Said the *Register*: "And these outrages have been perpetrated for years and years, without attracting any attention at the seat of government, while the local magistrates are either too feeble to interfere, or else bribed to wink at such infamous acts."[607]

Missourians and Texans raided into Indian Territory, Mexico, and even Louisiana. At Fort Jesup in May 1844, Colonel Twiggs was concerned with "outrages committed by armed bodies of men, said to be citizens of Texas, upon the persons and property of...citizens of the United States." About thirty mounted, armed men, allegedly looking for outlaws, crossed the Sabine into Louisiana, rode to Caddo Parish, killed one man and captured another. Instead of taking him to the local magistrate, said a jury member in Sabine Parish, they crossed the river and "hung him without giving him any trial." The raiders rode through several towns "pretending" to search for other criminals while threatening and abusing the people. Twiggs authorized troops to search for them and if necessary, call upon the local magistrate to raise a posse comitatus.[608]

Texan unruliness was dampened somewhat after they joined the Union in 1845. Then again, perhaps they simply shifted their focus—cheating, robbing, and murdering U. S. citizens was more frowned upon than similar actions against Mexicans or Indians.

General Gaines's request for security along the Western trails was based on a reality we are virtually unacquainted with today— most of the forts built between 1815 and 1845 were not built to protect whites from Indians, but to protect Indians from whites. Forts

---

[607]   NNR, June 10, 1843, V. 14, No. 15, 235.
[608]   Twiggs to Jones, May 14, 1844, AGO, RG 94, M567, R0291; Estes deposition, May 14, 1844, AGO, RG 94, M567, R0291.

Gratiot and Brady in Michigan; Forts Dearborn and Armstrong in Illinois; Forts Howard and Crawford in Wisconsin; Forts Sanford, Des Moines, and Atkinson in Iowa; Forts Gibson, Coffee, Towson, and Washita in Oklahoma; and Fort Snelling in Minnesota, were all built primarily for the protection of Indians and the expulsion of white intruders. Army inspector general George Croghan spent many years examining forts and commenting on their usefulness—and uselessness. The value in Fort Armstrong, he said, was to protect the Sauk and Fox "against the frontier whites." Forts Brady, Atkinson, and Howard, Croghan said, would never be used against Indians, but against whites "who would deprive them of all merit of good faith and common honesty." Croghan inspected all of the above-mentioned posts, and came to the conclusion that most were boondoggles to bilk the government, and he wondered why any of them needed "garrisons of such strength when surely no attack from the Indians…can be apprehended?"[609]

Lieutenant Colonel William Whistler wrote from Fort Coffee that it and Fort Gibson were good locations in Indian country to give the tribes "a military protection, which they confidently expect," as well as for "enforcement of the 'intercourse law.'" The Arkansans "who believe or pretend to believe that the tribes" would make war on them were badly mistaken. Forts were necessary to keep the whites away from the tribes, because "The abandoned and disorderly portion of them would at once commence their lawless aggressions on the persons and property of the Indians. They would steal and kill their stock, and trespass upon them in various ways, calculated in their nature to arouse the Indians to acts of violence in self-defense."[610]

One place where hostility among the frontiersmen, army, and Indians reached a boiling point was at Cantonment Towson—a post that was essential to protect the army from white frontier terrorists.

---

[609]   Francis Paul Prucha, ed., *Army Life on the Western Frontier: Selections from the Official Reports Made Between 1826 and 1845 by Colonel George Croghan* (Norman, OK: University of Oklahoma Press, 1958), xxx, 4–5, 14–15, 18, 22.

[610]   Whistler to Macomb, September 30, 1837, ASPMA, V. 7, 978–80.

Ground Zero: Cantonment Towson

The frontiersmen and the army were at each other's throats for decades, but the situation around Cantonment Towson in Arkansas Territory from 1824–1828 may have been the benchmark chapter. Uncertain where to place Indians removed from the East, the government set aside lands in numerous locations, only to continuously adjust the boundaries as the situation changed. One solution was to place the Indians in Arkansas Territory upon land where whites had already "squatted," seemingly unaware of the trouble that would follow.[611] To fix the error, the Arkansas borders were shifted several times, sometimes leaving white settlers on the wrong side of the fence.

Squatters began moving into what would become southeastern Oklahoma shortly after the War of 1812. In May 1819, 7th Infantry Maj. William Bradford removed two hundred families that were west of the Kiamichi River, but they moved back after he left. Civilian Thomas Nuttall described the intruders: "These people… bear the worst moral character imaginable, being many of them renegades from justice, and as such have forfeited the esteem of civilized society." Even those who had moved east of the Kiamichi were still on Choctaw land per the 1820 Treaty of Doak's Stand, which placed the boundary 100 to 150 miles to the east. Since it was easier for the government to move the boundary than to evict the squatters, in 1824 the line was moved west, leaving the Kiamichi River near the western boundary. Thus, the settlers were once again out of Indian Territory—until 1825—when the line was moved east to the present Arkansas-Oklahoma state line, making the settlers illegal again.[612]

A constabulary army was needed to enforce the boundaries and tenets of the TIA. In May 1824, Maj. Alexander Cummings, 7th Infantry, went to the hot spot, building Cantonment Towson east of the Kiamichi River and six miles north of Red River, to secure

---

[611]   Abel, "History of Events Resulting in Indian Consolidation," 367.

[612]   Bradford, March 25, 1824, ASPIA, V. 2, 556–57; Thomas Nuttall, *Travels into the Arkansas Territory,* in R. G. Thwaites, *Early Western Travels,* XIII, 221–22, cited in Rex W. Strickland, "Miller County, Arkansas Territory, the Frontier that Men Forgot," *Chronicles of Oklahoma,* V. 18, No. 1 (March 1940): 32.

the frontier for the Choctaws and Chickasaws relocating there, as well as for the legal white settlers. As for the illegals, the Committee on Public lands expressed its opinion in April 1824: "It cannot be perceived by what principle persons having no color of title, should, after lands on which they settled were known to belong to the United States," claim them as preemption rights. If allowed to do so it would encourage "a certain description of our population" to steal public land without regard for boundaries and with "very little respect for the rights either of the Government or their Indian neighbors."[613]

Laws and declarations did little to deter intruders. By mid-1825, southwest Arkansas Territory was filling up fast, with the large Miller County already containing about 2,500 whites, 8,500 horses, and 55,000 cattle.[614] Cummings had to move settlers east as well as prevent them from going west into Indian country to hunt, trap, and sell liquor. In November 1824, Cummings sent Samuel C. Roane, U. S. District Attorney for Arkansas Territory, the names of twenty-two violators and urged their prosecution. Roane replied that he did not have a copy of the law and could not take action.[615]

While Cummings waited, Caddo agent George Gray at Sulphur Fork on Red River wrote to Cummings that he was having similar problems: the "lower class of frontier Whites" were trading whiskey to the Indians, intruding in their territory, and the army had to drive them out. Cummings replied that he had no orders allowing him to help. Gray complained to Secretary of War John C. Calhoun. Those "lawless fellows, can, commit any outrage of the Indian Laws, and make their escape into Texas before I can receive any assistance from Camp Towson."[616]

Cummings had no time to deal with Gray's problem, because everything exploded around him. He drove out intruders and

---

[613] Robert W, Frazer, *Forts of the West: Military Forts and Presidios and Posts Commonly Called Forts West of the Mississippi River to 1898* (Norman, OK: University of Oklahoma Press, 1965), 125; Committee on Public Lands, April 23, 1824, ASPPL, V. 3, 619.

[614] Census of Miller County, July 10, 1825, TPUS, V. 20, 92.

[615] Cummings to Roane, November 24, 1824, Roane to Cummings, November 25, 1824, AGO, RG 94, M567, R0013.

[616] Gray to Calhoun, January 13, 1825, TPUS, V. 19, 745; Gray to Barbour, September 30, 1825, TPUS, V. 20, 119–20.

destroyed their stills, but when someone exposed his list of names, it produced "among the settlers in this neighborhood a hostility to the garrison."[617] Trouble began early in 1825 when post quartermaster Lt. Charles Thomas borrowed a horse from James Brice to ride to Miller Courthouse for the mail. The animal was injured during the trip and Brice wanted compensation of thirty-five dollars. Thomas refused. Brice brought suit in John Bowman's court, but Thomas did not appear, and a jury awarded damages of forty-five dollars. Thomas refused to pay, and Deputy Constable James Garner seized Thomas's horse and locked it up in William Brice's stable.[618]

On the night of January 19, eleven soldiers[619] slipped away from the post and went five miles to James Garner's and William and James Brice's cabins. One or both places were known to operate stills, and Garner had taken Thomas's horse, while the Brices were on Cummings's list of illegal hunters. They broke into Garner's cabin "in the dead of night," and swinging clubs and fists, they pummeled Garner, Warren Pearson, and Morris Pendergrass. Pearson said that Jernigan "did sorely beat & whip" him "to the terror of the women and children" present.[620]

The soldiers next went to William Brice's, broke into the stable and took Lieutenant Thomas's horse. Said Brice, they "entered my house with cocked guns and threatened my life, rummaged the house and throwed down a bed and raised the floor." Brice protested, and the soldiers said that Major Cummings had given them authority to recover the horse or "burn my house and beat out my brains," and further "to whip James Brice and James Garner to death." After roughing up the occupants, the soldiers went to Justice John Bowman's place and told him they had taken Thomas's horse.[621]

---

[617]   Gray to Morton, February 2, 1825, AGO, RG 94, M567, R0013.

[618]   Bowman, January 20, 1825, TPUS, V. 19, 777; Rex W. Strickland, "Establishment of 'Old' Miller County, Arkansas Territory." *Chronicles of Oklahoma,* V. 18, No. 2 (June 1940): 168.

[619]   Sgt. Henry L. Jernigan, Jacob Switzer, John Callender, Francis Baker, Samuel Lofton, Jacob Page, William McMahon, John Noakes, William White, Michael McDevitt, and John Wither.

[620]   Cummings to Many, January 30, 1825, AGO, RG 94, M567, R0013; Brice, Garner, and Pendergrass, January 20, 1825, TPUS, V. 19, 776, 778.

[621]   Pendergrass, Brice, Reed, Bowman, January 20, 1825, TPUS, V. 19, 776–77.

Sergeant Jernigan and his men, apparently not realizing the seriousness of what they had done, spent the rest of the night at Samuel Brice's, partaking of his homemade brew. Meanwhile, Bowman and Justice Joshua Ewing issued battery and burglary warrants. They deputized Charles Moore, and he, with a posse of civilians, went after the soldiers.[622]

Jernigan was eating breakfast about seven in the morning when a mob of men walked in. One of them punched him in the mouth while others tied him up. John Callender stood by the fire when Warren Pearson "put a pistol to my breast." The others went after the sleeping soldiers. Jesse Cheek told Jacob Page that if he moved "he would blow my brains out." Cheek "snapped his rifle two or three times" at Jernigan, but it did not fire. Frustrated, he swung it like a club and smashed Michael McDevitt in the head. When he hit the floor, James Brice stomped on him. Pearson told the soldiers to stand still "or they would blow us through." William Brice beat Callender so hard that he "broke the club in two." William McMahon said that "after abusing us and knocking several of us down took us out and tied us, and then proceeded to Squire Ewing's." Constable Moore said that the affair was a "severe struggle."[623]

Their treatment did not improve on the march. John Noakes dropped back into the woods to relieve himself, but Cheek forced him back in line. Jernigan protested that this was "acting contrary to the law of nature," but another man struck Noakes while Cheek called Jernigan a "damned rascal" and clubbed him in the head. The walking soldiers could not keep up with the riding civilians. Cheek and Moore whipped the soldiers with their rifle ramrods to speed them up. Jernigan tried to lead his men around a marsh, but the guards forced them into the water. When Jernigan protested, Moore rode his horse over him and Cheek "sunk me entirely under the water." Cheek said "he wished he had killed Sergeant Jernigan for he would rather shoot him than a rattlesnake, and if he ever got

---

[622]   Ewing, January 20, 1825, Moore, February 2, 1825, TPUS, V. 19, 775, 779. The posse included William and James Brice, James Garner, Warren Pearson, Morris Pendergrass, Jesse Cheek, John Bowman, and men named Satterway, Ambrose, Morton, and several others.

[623]   A. Cummings, C-41-1825, soldier statements, nine undated pages. AGO, RG 94, M567, R0013; Moore, February 20, 1825, TPUS, V. 19, 779.

a chance he would kill him."[624]

Noakes was exhausted, but when he slowed, Ambrose rode him down. Noakes rebuked him for abusing a bound man, so Ambrose "jumped off his horse and struck me across the neck with his rifle and knocked me down." Then Ambrose had a change of heart and told Noakes he would let him ride if he paid him a dollar. Noakes paid and was able to ride the next three miles to Ewing's. William Brice announced that "he would raise the militia and come and take the garrison and blow it and Major Cummings to hell," because he was "a thief and a damned rascal." He swore that "he had as much money and Negroes as old Cummings, and would have him hoisted out of the place he was in, and he would get a petition from the inhabitants of the county…and if that failed he could raise men enough… to take the garrison."[625]

The civilians had just dragged the soldiers to Ewing's house where a kangaroo court was hurriedly assembled, when more men appeared outside. It was Lt. James R. Stephenson and fifty soldiers coming to the rescue. The lieutenant produced a written order from Major Cummings demanding the soldiers be released, and the cowed civilians acquiesced. By that evening they were all back at Towson. The next morning, Constable Moore and Deputy Sheriff John G. W. Pierson rode to the post and demanded that Cummings return the prisoners. He refused.[626]

The situation was at an impasse, but Cummings knew this would not be the end of it. He wrote to his superior, Lt. Col. James B. Many, at Fort Jesup, and sent his soldiers' statements "in order that you may have an idea of the disposition of the people among whom we are located." He said that he was hogtied by the civilians and the uncooperative district attorney, and was sure Roane had leaked his list of trespassers. Cummings knew this would "produce endless lawsuits with all the lawless banditti who inhabit this frontier, some of whom have threatened to attack the post."[627]

---

[624]   A. Cummings, C-41-1825, soldier statements, nine undated pages. AGO, RG 94, M567, R0013.

[625]   Ibid.

[626]   Moore, February 2, 1825, TPUS, V. 19, 779.

[627]   Cummings to Many, January 30, 1825, AGO, RG 94, M567, R0013.

On February 2, Cummings wrote to Roane that "about 200 men assembled... for the purpose of making an attack on the post; the principal ringleaders... were William Brice, John Bowman, and [Jacob] Pennington." Cummings's letter was inexplicably returned to him two weeks later, "either by mistake or design," and all "crumpled and torn"—evidently having been pigeonholed by the postmaster at Miller Courthouse. Cummings wrote again, and this time Roane responded. He said he had not prosecuted anyone for violating the TIA because it was "utterly impossible" to catch them; besides, they committed crimes in Indian country, which was the military's responsibility. He would not assemble a grand jury for Brice, Bowman, Pennington, and others, only on the officers' unsworn statements. And, Roane warned, the civilians were signing petitions to indict the army, "and possibly against yourself for resisting the civil process."[628]

Cummings knew that local juries were overwhelmingly hostile. Acting territorial governor Robert Crittenden wrote to Secretary Calhoun that he had information from Moore and Brice, "highly respectable" men, that the army was running amok, and "the people are all in a flame and talk loudly of *investing* the post." Crittenden asserted, "Nothing less than the surrender of all concerned to the civil authority, and their *formal arrest* and trial will appease the public."[629]

James Barbour, the new secretary of war appointed by the incoming John Quincy Adams administration, responded: "This morning I have directed that the Officers and soldiers implicated in the affair...be delivered up to the Civil authority for trial—that the Commanding Officer of Cantonment Towson should be changed, and that a Court of Inquiry should be forthwith held upon him, to investigate his conduct, complained of by the Citizens."[630]

Cummings fought back. In a letter to Western Department Commander Brig. Gen. Henry Atkinson, he claimed the civil authorities were obstructing the military, and that Roane would not prosecute anyone, although he had provided their names and places of residence. But "the good government" of Arkansas Territory

---

[628] Cummings to Roane, February 2, February 16, 1825; Roane to Cummings, March 30, 1825, AGO, RG 94, M567, R0013.

[629] Crittenden to Calhoun, February 14, 1825, TPUS, V. 19, 774.

[630] Barbour to Crittenden, March 18, 1825, TPUS, V. 20, 11–12.

"forbids an investigation of the subject. The Act of Congress therefore cannot be enforced."[631]

In April, Cummings received an old *Arkansas Gazette*, and learned that a court martial was to be held in Little Rock. He "could scarcely believe" it, because it was three hundred miles away, he would have only one officer left at the post if all those accused attended, and the newspaper had been printing stories "to prejudice the public against us"—editorials "destitute of truth" and full of "calumny, misrepresentation, & falsehood."[632]

Atkinson agreed to change the venue and the inquiry convened at Towson on May 17. The judging officers were much more sympathetic than a civilian jury would have been; Cummings was acquitted of resistance to civil authorities. Even so, he was removed from command and sent to Cantonment Gibson. He protested: "I cannot believe that it is the intention of the commanding general to inflict punishment when no offence has been committed."[633]

Arkansas territorial governor George Izard was not satisfied and protested to Gen. Winfield Scott, stating that principal civilian witnesses did not attend "under apprehension of violence" if they testified. Izard cited the *Arkansas Gazette*, which used inflammatory language "highly derogatory from the character of the military officers." He believed the officers and garrison had to be replaced by "a detachment uninfected with the animosity which evidently prevails among the troops there." In addition, Jesse Cheek had been gathering petitions to have charges brought against Cummings in Territorial Court, as well as to have Towson closed down.[634]

Scott tried appeasement. Because of "the temper and feeling evinced by the inhabitants of Miller County," he recommended abandoning the post.[635] But because of that very heated, unsettled situation, the army had to stay, and because there were plenty of

---

[631]   Cummings to Atkinson, April 8, 1825, AGO, RG 94, M567, R0013.
[632]   Cummings to Atkinson, May 3, 1825, Cummings to Nourse, May 3, 1825, AGO, RG94, M567, R0013.
[633]   Strickland, "Establishment of Old Miller County," 169; Cummings to Jones, June 30, 1825, AGO, RG94, M567, R0013.
[634]   Izard to Scott, July 16, 1825, Cummings to Atkinson, April 8, 1825, AGO, RG94, M567, R0013.
[635]   Scott to Jones, August 18, 1825, AGO, RG 94, M567, R0013.

voices calling to let the settlers stay, the situation would not improve. Territorial delegate Henry S. Conway opined that removal would cause hardship. The people, "industriously engaged in agricultural pursuits," needed time to harvest their crops in the fall. Secretary Barbour fell for the old argument again, granted a reprieve for "humanity," and agreed to let them stay until January 1, 1826, but "no indulgence beyond this period can be granted."[636]

The people of Miller County formed into military and anti-military factions. Aaron Hanscom, who had supported Major Cummings, was the choice of the military faction for the House of Representatives against the notorious Jesse Cheek and James Hanks of the opposition. Hanscom beat Cheek by forty-seven votes; Cheek cried foul and gathered another protest petition. Hanscom examined it, saw that almost all the names were in the same handwriting, and believed Jesse Cheek forged them.[637]

Cheek was a scalawag who had fled St. Louis to avoid prison for embezzlement and counterfeiting. Captain Russell B. Hyde, now in command at Towson, brought charges against Cheek for selling whiskey. Cheek was subpoenaed to appear in the court of John Bowman—the same man who had allied with Cheek against the soldiers in January—to answer Hyde's charges. On August 11, Cheek appeared for trial, but refused to limit his vituperative comments, and when Hyde objected, Cheek somehow produced a club and beat the captain senseless, raining down blows until others restrained him. Bowman only fined Cheek fifteen dollars, but he never paid. Somehow he escaped to Little Rock to tell the governor his version of events. Cheek contended he was "an outraged and oppressed man, avoiding the vengeance of a set of lawless men, who have insulted the constituted authorities, trampled upon the laws of the land, and recognize no restraint to their own wild passions and vengeance."[638]

Petitions proliferated. In the summer of 1825, 270 citizens

---

[636]   Conway to Barbour, March 15, 1825, Barbour to Conway, March 16, 1825, TPUS, V. 20, 8–10.

[637]   Hanscom to William Woodruff, October 31, 1825, in the *Arkansas Gazette*, November 1, 1825, cited in Rex W. Strickland, "The Final Breakup of 'Old' Miller County, *Chronicles of Oklahoma*, V. 19, No. 1 (March 1941): 40–41.

[638]   *Arkansas Gazette*, August 30 and September 6, 1825, cited in Strickland, "Establishment of Old Miller County," 170.

of Miller County sent one to President Adams, complaining of injustices done to them through the inconsistent policies of allowing them to pre-empt lands in some areas and forbidding it elsewhere. How could the government force people from their farms "to give a place to Indians! An act that would have no example in any civilized Government."[639] Some civilians refused to vacate after the January 1826 deadline, hoping that the government would relent once again. Others crossed south of Red River, preferring to become subjects of Mexico rather than pay taxes for property they might have to abandon. Of fifty delinquent taxpayers in 1825, two were insolvent and the other forty-eight crossed the river to avoid the collectors.[640]

Not everyone wanted the army out. In November, Major Cummings was at Fort Jesup where he received a petition signed by one hundred inhabitants of Miller County, "with a view of counteracting the designs of a scoundrel by the name of Jesse Cheek, who has been the cause of the disturbances." The petitioners said that Cheek had been spreading falsehoods contrary to "the thinking and respectable part of the citizens of Miller County." The conduct of the soldiers at Towson was admirable and the settlements in the area "have received much benefit from the establishment of the post." Two other citizens wrote that Cheek's petition was forged. County Clerk John Fowler concurred, stating that Cheek was circulating another "ridiculous" petition that complained of the officers and demanded that the post be abandoned. Some of the signatories lived fifty or more miles away and knew nothing of the situation. In addition, the Indians had not been depredating since the post was established. The informed citizens wanted the soldiers to remain.[641]

Settlers and delegates could protest, but the latest Choctaw treaty only meant that the legitimate settlers would move, leaving the frontier scoundrels in the majority. In October, Captain Hyde, recovering from his beating, wrote to Governor Izard that whites were still hunting and trapping in Indian country, but he was powerless to stop them. He did not have enough soldiers to chase the offenders,

---

[639]   Petition to the President, TPUS, V. 20, 138–39.
[640]   Strickland, "Final Break up of Miller County," 37.
[641]   Cummings to Jones, November 12, 1825, Fowler to Barbour, October 24, 1825, AGO, RG94, M567, R0013.

and he was "unable myself to get about in consequence of a blow received from an assassin." Plus, Roane still refused to prosecute, which let the violators—fully one-half of the inhabitants—"believe that they might hunt with impunity." Roane would not indict the locals, "but when a fracas occurred between some worthless citizens and drunken soldiers, he was the first to advise a prosecution."[642]

Meanwhile, Agent George Gray at Caddo Prairie was having the same difficulties he had for the past two years. "There is scarcely a week passes but what some depredations are committed, by the lower class of Whites...on the Indians, belonging to this Agency." He wanted troops stationed there, but there were none to spare.[643]

When 1826 arrived, many settlers in Miller County still did not believe the government would evict them. The Committee on Public Lands cautioned the House of Representatives that frontier whites did whatever they pleased, while "legal prohibitions are entirely inadequate to repress trespasses." Intruders were never removed because they always played the victims. Squatters viewed legitimate purchasers as enemies and used "whatever combination, violence, and artifice" they could employ to drive them away. "Experience has shown that those who fasten upon the public lands with one moment's encouragement can never afterwards be loosened from their hold." The Committee would not fall for the old tale of woe—but not Congress, whose constituents cared little for the army or the Indians. Delegate Henry Conway constantly sent petitions praying "that the President will interpose—adopt some measure for their relief, and save them from ruin." Washington gave in and allowed the settlers to remain for another year.[644]

While the intruders rejoiced in their victory, in January, Major Cummings was back in charge at Towson and reported that Indians had settled on Red River about one hundred miles above the post. Even that was not far enough away from the evil influence of the whites, said Cummings, "many of whom, cannot be classed

---

[642]   Hyde to Izard, October 11, 1825, TPUS, V. 20, 123.

[643]   Gray to Barbour, November 30, 1825, TPUS, V. 20, 154.

[644]   "Settlers on Public Lands," January 18, 1826, ASPPL, V. 4, 468; Conway to Barbour, December 13, 1825, TPUS, V. 20, 162.

much above the savage."[645] Scofflaws continued to invade Indian country to hunt, trap, and rob. Either Pawnees or Osages intercepted one horse-stealing expedition and killed three of the would-be thieves, and now, incredibly, they expected the army to get back their stolen horses. General Gaines had a different idea. He ordered Colonel Arbuckle not to retaliate, but "keep the peace—quietly if you can, but forcibly" if necessary to assist the inhabitants, "whether of the red skin or the white."[646]

Taking advantage of their reprieve, many frontiersmen continued to distill and sell liquor, hunt and trap on Indian lands, and depredate. The situation deteriorated. In June, Cummings reported that the citizens were organizing a war party to attack the Pawnees. He believed that "unless some measures are taken to put a stop to the lawless practices of some of the frontier settlers, we shall ere long have an Indian war." He complained once again that he had been trying to curb white aggression, but "finding that they have nothing to apprehend from the civil authorities, are more open in their transgression now, than they were formerly."[647]

The soldiers of Towson continually clashed with the locals as well as with District Attorney Roane. Lt. Joseph Cadle allegedly thrashed Morris Pendergrass, one of the civilians involved in the January 1825 fracas. Cadle "was indicted for the crime of maiming" him. Shortly before the June 1826 trial, the main witness against Cadle disappeared and Roane had to enter a *nolle prosequi*. He charged that Cadle had bribed the witness to abscond and called his conduct "ungentlemanly." Cadle fired back: "I therefore assert the observation made by you, to be entirely destitute of truth & that you are an infamous Coward, as you would not have dared to have made any remark, whatever concerning my conduct, in my presence." Adjutant General Roger Jones labeled this a personal matter and suggested "no farther notice be taken" of it.[648]

Increasing white belligerence and increasing Indian com-

[645]   Cummings to Jones, January 18, 1826, TPUS, V. 20, 185.
[646]   Cummings to Lowndes, April 27, 1826, AGO, RG94, M567, R0013; Gaines to Arbuckle, March 28, 1826, TPUS, V. 20, 219.
[647]   Cummings to Gaines, June 22, 1826, TPUS, V. 20, 267.
[648]   Cadle to Roane, June 14, 1826, Roane to Barbour, June 26, 1826, TPUS, V. 20, 269–70.

plaints spurred army determination to get the intruders out. By the end of 1826, the House of Representatives wanted to know how many whites were still illegally in the Choctaw Nation and if the Indians had "remonstrated against the encroachments." Commissioner McKenney estimated 375 families remained, affirmed that the Indians complained many times, and said they were upset that lands granted to them were under consideration to be repurchased to give to white trespassers who had no business being there.[649]

The intruders may have hoped for another reprieve, but their days were numbered. The army evicted some, but most vacated Miller County on their own accord. Mid-way through 1827 the population had dwindled to 751—the most intractable among them still giving Major Cummings fits. In April 1827 near Red River, Judge John Bowman and James Roberts "tied up a Cherokee Indian and whipt him very severely, and a few nights afterwards" they shot another Cherokee "down at his own door, and [he] died in half an hour after."[650]

Agent George Gray's troubles were unending. Whites were flagrantly breaking the TIA and enrolling in a "Corpse" to fight the Indians, and "their character is of the worst description & their object is plunder & robbery." While desperados recruited men into their gangs, Gray wanted to arrest the leaders, but because of their "desperate character...I have thought it best to wait for aid." He again wrote to Cummings for help, but the major remained handicapped with too few soldiers, too much territory, and too many problems of his own. Cummings wanted a stronger force "to awe the disorderly & disaffected persons in the neighborhood both white and red." There were Indians in the area, and "the whites, most of whom are no better than the savages, are constantly coming in collision with them, and numerous complaints are made of horses being stolen, or property plundered." Innocent people suffer, but "the rogues and horse thieves seldom have anything to lose." Cummings concluded: "I will do the Indians the justice to say, that so far as I can

---

[649]   McKenney to Barbour, January 4, 1827, ASPIA, V. 2, 703. McKenney estimated seven people per family, which meant the total of 2,625 was even more than the 2,500 estimated two years earlier.
[650]   Strickland, "Final Break up of Miller County," 42; Cummings to Arbuckle, April 3, 1827, TPUS, V. 20, 457.

learn, they are the more sinn'd against than sinning."[651]

The ongoing chaos brought Colonel Arbuckle to Towson, but he reiterated what so many other officers had discovered: the number of Indians were few and they had no intention of attacking. "Yet they are much mixed with the worst description of our citizens," and thus, disorder may arise, "which will, as I believe, be as often produced by the improper conduct of our people."[652]

In September 1827, Charles Burkman and Nathaniel Robbins, operating in the vicinity of Pecan Point, a notorious hangout of malcontents on Red River, represented themselves as Mexican officers and recruited Americans for the ostensible purpose of attacking the Comanches. Major Cummings dispatched Lt. William S. Colquhoun to investigate, and he warned the leaders to desist. When Secretary of State Henry Clay threatened prosecution and when the volunteers learned that the real intention was not to attack Indians, but to plunder Mexican caravans, it disbanded.[653]

The remaining settlers would not give up. Territorial delegate Ambrose H. Sevier[654] forwarded a petition from Miller and Crawford Counties to President Adams. The people demanded relief "for our unoffending and Suffering Citizens" who were approaching "speedy and certain ruin." They had been sold out to the Indians and "paralyzed in their agricultural pursuits." If they were originally trespassers and violated the law, so did half the Territory. It wasn't fair. The solution must be either to end Indian title to the land or pay the whites "for the years of labour they have spent in opening the country." There were two thousand citizens "who have committed no moral crime and who if they have infracted the laws of the land have done it in common with fifty thousand settlers in the new States, who have been rewarded for the same offence." Se-

---

[651]   Gray to Barbour, July 3, 1827, Cummings to Jones, September 1, 1827, TPUS, V. 20, 500–01, 526–27.

[652]   Arbuckle to Gaines, August 27, 1827, AGO, RG 94, M567, R0025.

[653]   Clay to Izard, September 6, 1827, Izard to Clay, October 16, 1827, TPUS, V. 20, 529–30, 543; Grant Foreman, *Indians & Pioneers: The Story of the American Southwest Before 1830* (Norman, University of Oklahoma Press, 1936), 217–18.

[654]   Sevier was elected as delegate after Henry Conway was killed in a duel with Arkansas Secretary Robert Crittenden on November 9, 1827.

vier backed the squatters, sending his missive to Secretary Barbour with a threat: "Should their farms and improvements be given up to the Indians, it will require the strong arm of the United States to restrain them from violence against the Cherokees."[655]

Sevier's entreaty had been addressed by the Committee on Public Lands numerous times. Squatters knew they were in the wrong, but believed the government would continue to bail them out. No longer. The committee would not "recommend any relief to these unfortunate people without…establishing a dangerous precedent, awarding a premium for the violation of the law."[656]

As if the army didn't have enough worries, national events spilled into Towson's little corner of the world. The late 1820s saw a flare-up in anti-Masonry across the country. The Freemasons were a fraternal organization with secret passwords, initiations, ceremonies, and lodges. Their closed system of law and loyalty made them anathema in Jacksonian America with its appetite for popular democracy and egalitarianism, and the presence of a secret society was fodder for conspiracy zealots. Wealthy Masons were said to control business, press, politics, and the judicial system. And if a fellow Mason was in distress, his compatriots would come running. An anti-mason handbook of 1829 claimed they were "dark, unfruitful, selfish, demoralizing, blasphemous, murderous, anti-republican, and anti-Christian."[657]

The incident that sparked the anti-Mason surge began in western New York with the 1826 disappearance of ex-Mason William Morgan, who, when denied membership in a new lodge, threatened to write a book revealing Freemasonry's secrets. This could not be allowed. Morgan disappeared, said to have been abducted and killed by other Masons. Newspapers spread the story that his life had been "secretly sacrificed" by demonic Freemasons. Outrage grew. Four members were arrested and tried, but without a corpse there

---

[655]   Memorial to the President, December 24, 1827, Sevier to Barbour, February 18, 1828, TPUS, V. 20, 573–75, 605.

[656]   "Settlers on the Choctaw Lands in Arkansas," February 27, 1827, ASP-PL, V. 4, 959.

[657]   *Light on Masonry* (Utica 1829), iii, x, cited in Richard Hofstadter, *The Paranoid Style in American Politics and Other Essays* (New York, Vintage Books, 1967), 14–16.

was not enough evidence for conviction. That changed on October 7, 1827, when Morgan's remains washed ashore on Lake Ontario. The newspapers screamed, books were published, and the anti-Mason furor exploded.[658]

A search began for the suspects. Three days after the discovery of the body, New York governor DeWitt Clinton asked Secretary Barbour if he had information as to the whereabouts of suspect William King, who was said to have been an army sutler in Arkansas Territory. "I wish this request to be kept secret," he wrote. When leads pointed to King being at Towson, Clinton asked if Barbour would order the commander "to furnish all the proper facilities in his power" to assist in his arrest.[659]

Clinton's agents, Joseph Garlinghouse and Phineas Bates, armed with an authorization from Governor Izard for King's arrest, traveled to Cantonment Gibson, where Arbuckle gave them Barbour's correspondence to pass to Captain Hyde, who was now back in command at Towson. The agents reached the post on February 14, 1828. To prevent suspicion, only Garlinghouse and his guide, Clark Landers, entered the post grounds. Hyde looked at the letters, but refused to make an arrest: "I do not consider it an order and if it was I would not obey it; for the Secretary of War had no business to make such an order." There was no arrest warrant and the paperwork indicated Hyde was only to assist the civil authorities. Garlinghouse asked for a military escort, but the captain refused because he had no men to spare.

Garlinghouse would make the arrest alone, but he did not know what King looked like, so Hyde sent for Lieutenant Colquhoun to take him to the sutler's store about two hundred yards from the post. They were unsuccessful, said Hyde, because King got word that strangers were in camp looking for him and he disappeared. Garlinghouse had a different recollection: Hyde sent for Colquhoun but was told he could not be found. Landers, however, knew the lieutenant and said he saw him furtively pass by the window. After

---

[658] Mark Stein, *American Panic: A History of Who Scares Us and Why* (New York: Palgrave Macmillan, 2014), 39–42.
[659] Clinton to Barbour, October 10, 1827, November 6, 1827, TPUS, V. 20, 540.

a few minutes, Hyde got Lt. Silas Casey to take Garlinghouse and Landers to the store, where a clerk told them that King had gone out with Lieutenant Colquhoun. Landers was sure the intention was "to blind and deceive Garlinghouse." Phineas Bates, Garlinghouse's partner, said that Colquhoun later told him he had warned King, and King's clerk brought his horse to the woods behind the store so he could escape. Hyde insisted that King knew agents were coming for him ten days earlier and had already vacated the premises. In fact, the night before the agents left, a man who lived thirty miles from the post arrived to tell Hyde that King came to his house, lost and famished. The house was on the road to Natchitoches, so the agents headed that way. A few days later, King returned to Towson, settled up his business, and told Hyde that he was going to New York to try to clear his name.[660]

There was further uproar when the agents made their report. Adjutant General Roger Jones demanded to know why Hyde did not help arrest the fugitive. Nathaniel Pitcher, who became New York's governor when Clinton died in office on February 11, 1828, sent a concerned letter to President Adams, stated that Captain Hyde and Lieutenant Colquhoun willfully communicated to King "timely warning & assisted him in his escape," their conduct being "extraordinary & reprehensible." The army issued an arrest order for Hyde for disobedience of orders.[661]

When Hyde learned a court of inquiry was to be held in New York, he asked if it could be held at Towson, "as I am totally unable to travel in consiquence of my lame ancle I have not been able to git about without a crutch for five months." Lieutenant Patrick H. Galt, 4th Artillery, verified Hyde's disability, stating the doctor believed his leg was so diseased "it cannot now be many months before it terminates in death." Taking this into consideration, the army

[660] Jones to Cummings, November 10, 1827, Izard proclamation, January 25, 1828, Arbuckle to Hyde, February 3, 1828, Landers certificate, February 15, 1828 ("blind and deceive" quotation), Garlinghouse to Barbour, April 30, 1828 ("such an order" quotation), Hyde to Jones, May 29, 1828, TPUS, V. 20, 600, 664, 667, 669, 691.

[661] Jones to Hyde, April 19, 1828, Pitcher to Adams, April 28, 1828, Barbour to Izard, May 13, 1828, TPUS, V. 20, 650, 659, 679.

held trial at Cantonment Jesup, Louisiana, in July 1829. Hyde was acquitted.[662]

While the officers at Towson were engaged in the King affair, Governor Izard received a complaint from citizens at Pecan Point that Shawnees were cutting timber, killing their hogs, and building in their cornfields. The letter said that if Izard would drive the Indians out, "we have the promise of the assistance of the troops at Cantonment Towson to cooperate with the Militia"—a pledge the officers never made. The missive was signed by J. G. W. Pierson, Major of the 9th Arkansas Militia, the same man who, as deputy sheriff in 1825, demanded that Major Cummings surrender his soldiers. Izard ordered Arkansas Territory Adjutant General Col. Wharton Rector to demand that the Indians remove immediately, and to take hostages under guard to Little Rock. Izard directed Rector to call on the officers at Towson to cooperate.[663]

Rector rode to Pecan Point and was told that belligerent Shawnees and Delawares had threatened to drive the whites from the south side of Red River. The problem was that south of the river was Mexican Territory, the Indians had obtained Mexican approval to be there, and it was the whites who were there illegally. Nevertheless, Rector confiscated the Indians' occupancy document and demanded that they move. The Delawares were amenable, but the Shawnees resisted, and Rector rode to Towson for reinforcements. On April 21, Rector demanded help, but Hyde refused, stating that *"Mr. Rector had declared war"* on peaceful Indians who did not reside in the United States. Rector did not care, because "he would chastise them at any rate for the trouble they had put him to & if they had gone he would follow them." Hyde was indignant: "If the Commanding Officer of this frontier is bound to furnish every man with troops who calls on him & who wishes to immortalize himself by plundering an Indian town & killing a few women and children, it will be necessary that the force in this section of the Country should

---

[662]   Hyde to Jones, June 25, 1828, Galt to Jones, August 5, 1828, TPUS, V. 20, 703, 725. Hyde stayed in the army until 1834 and died in 1851.

[663]   Pierson to Izard, March 22, 1828, Izard to Rector, April 7, 1828, TPUS, V. 20, 632, 640.

be considerably increased."[664]

Lieutenant Colquhoun was under arrest at the time, apparently stemming from an altercation with Hyde over King's escape, which Hyde called "the most outrageous act of mutiny there ever occurred in our service, a crime for which if tried before a civil court, would have sent him to the penitentiary for life." After Hyde denied assistance, Rector talked to Colquhoun and persuaded him "to break his arrest & clear out with him." Colquhoun apparently fled to Virginia.[665]

Rector complained to Izard about the lack of cooperation, and stated that there were plenty of soldiers to assist him, but it seemed "the principal duty which is done at that post is planting corn." Rector vented his anger to Assistant Surgeon John Thurston that the post and its soldiers were a sham, and "by God, he could bring five men that could butt it down with their heads." Trader Collin Aldrich asked what he would do with the Indians, and he said "he should drive them across the Sabine River or give them a damn whipping." An angry Rector then "called on the militia of Miller County, & very soon raised sixty-three well-armed men" to attack the Shawnees near Pecan Point. As they neared the village the Shawnee chief met them and told Rector that they would move, but needed a few days to collect their stock. The chief said if his people had done wrong, they did so innocently, for the Spanish had given them permission to stay there. Rector asked on whose authority, and the chief answered, "The Governor of St. Antonie (San Antonio)." Rector had the interpreter explain that if he caught the governor, "he would hang him on a tree by the neck like a dog." Rector gave him twenty days to get out.[666]

Commissioner McKenney pleaded that the United States

---

[664]   Rector to Izard, May 8, 1828, TPUS, V. 20, 677; Hyde to Arbuckle, May 6, 1828, Hyde to Jones, November 17, 1828, AGO, RG 94, M567, R0036.
[665]   Hyde to Jones, November 17, 1828, AGO, RG 94, M567, R0036; Hyde to Jones, April 23, 1829, AGO, RG 94, M567, R0044. Colquhoun was convicted of dereliction of duty and was cashiered on November 10, 1829.
[666]   Rector to Izard, May 8, 1828, TPUS, V. 20, 677, 722; Statements of John Thurston, Collin Aldrich, and Jesse Shelton, AGO, RG 94, M567, R0036. Rector charged the government $503 for his services. Both Rector and Colquhoun later became Indian removal agents.

must keep its promises to stop whites from starting a war, a task he knew was nearly impossible. The condition of the Arkansas Indians was "wretched," he said. "I need not speak of the hate which is cherished towards them by those new settlers." Meanwhile, Delegate Sevier championed his constituents, stating that giving land to the Indians would "ruin five thousand citizens of Arkansas," prompting Cherokee agent Edward W. Du Val to counter that Sevier showed "the most entire ignorance of the subject," and the government was too often influenced "by interested, prejudiced and irresponsible persons."[667]

The intruders ejected from Miller and Crawford Counties had to go somewhere. They and others filed for about fifty thousand acres in small land claims, with many of them, per Land Commissioner George Graham, "numerous forged & fraudulent." Adults registered their children at the land offices using the same inane trick of writing "twenty-one years" on a piece of paper and placing them in their shoes.[668]

Finally, the days of old Miller County were about over when on October 17, 1828, the Arkansas General Assembly abolished the county north of Red River and west of the Choctaw Treaty Line.[669] The local desperados, however, were still in business. Agent Gray had grumbled for years that white peddlers saturated his Caddoes and Quapaws with whiskey, that he was powerless to stop "outrages being committed by a set of lawless fellows, that are continually stealing horses from the Indians," as well as taking "stolen negroes" to Texas, and he wanted troops stationed at his agency or have the agency moved to Cantonment Jesup. Gray's troubles finally ended on November 2, when he abruptly died.[670]

In December, Lt. John E. Newell, temporarily in command at Towson, had his initiation with the white rogues who still plagued

---

[667] McKenney to Barbour, April, 12, 1828, Sevier to Barbour, April 22, 1828, DuVal to McKenney, April 22, 1828, DuVal to Barbour, April 24, 1828, TPUS, V. 20, 649, 651, 653, 655.

[668] Graham to Smith and Desha, June 3, 1828, Wharton to Graham, August 15, 1828, TPUS, V. 20, 695, 731.

[669] Strickland, "Final Break up of Miller County," 42.

[670] Gray to Porter, August 30, 1828, Dillard to Porter, November 4, 1828, TPUS, V. 20, 743, 774.

the land. He asked Atkinson what to do with the "troublesome" vagabonds infesting the area, when brothers by the name of Lawrence attacked the post sutler and "came very near destroying him & his property." Newell and Lt. Silas Casey interceded, which "caused them to threaten our lives, & [they] have actually laid [along] the roads & other outlets from this post, for the purpose of killing some of our officers." They kidnapped, "tied up, & whipped, & have even taken the lives of several who have opposed them." Newell captured two of the culprits, but did not know how to punish them since the territorial laws no longer applied. The only other recourse was the TIA, which called for removing all trespassers from Indian country and punishing those guilty of crimes, but he wondered how to proceed. "If this is an Indian Country all are aggressors & should be removed. If they are not removed there must be some restraining power or we shall be infested with numerous banditties." In response, the local thugs brazenly burned down the Miller post office and courthouse, destroying all the county records since 1821.[671]

With Miller County abolished and Cantonment Towson to be vacated in June 1829, the need for law enforcement was even more urgent. At Cantonment Jesup in May, Inspector George Croghan was "much disturbed by a dread of the probable consequences of the abandonment of Cantonment Towson." Croghan believed most frontier forts were unnecessary as white refuges, but he maintained that Towson was indispensable. White desperados did not want the army around, but legitimate settlers would be in jeopardy from lawless whites as well as Indians if the post was closed.[672]

The border ruffians' contempt for the government was echoed by Delegate Ambrose Sevier. Impertinently addressing new Secretary of War Peter B. Porter, he challenged him to evict the whites. "Will you institute actions of trespass against them?" The government had tried that hundreds of times and, Sevier taunted, "I should think would not be overanxious to try the experiment again." It was fruitless to try to keep the whites out, Sevier said, unless you guard "every vacant spot with an armed force—Are you disposed to

---

671   Newell to Atkinson, December 18, 1828, TPUS, V. 20, 816–18; Strickland, "Final Break up of Miller County," 43.
672   Prucha, ed., *Army Life on the Western Frontier*, 11.

pursue such a measure?" He finished, "Permit me to say in conclusion that your order will not be obeyed—that you will find yourself unable to enforce it."[673]

General Gaines, perhaps dodging the answer that a little introspection may have revealed, was troubled by white bellicosity as he contemplated the condition of the Indians. Why did they appear to become more debased and immoral after contact with the white man? It seemed that they, "like most others in the incipient stages of civilization, have learned many of the vices, but few of the virtues of their white neighbors."[674]

"Deciding between pecuniary ruin... and disobedience of orders": In Court

Perhaps the army's toughest task on the frontier was to enforce the Trade and Intercourse Acts. Stopping illegal liquor sales, keeping intruders out of Indian lands, and preventing white swindlers from cheating the Indians and despoiling their lands was a constant, frustrating battle. Many frontier people made a mockery of the law, but when the army tried to enforce it, the people exploited the same justice system they had scorned. For instance, when the army tried to stop illegal timber cutting, remove squatters and traders, or confiscate whiskey, they were often slapped with lawsuits. What was worse for the officers was that their own government seemed unwilling to support them. In 1817, Maj. Willoughby Morgan arrested two unauthorized traders in Missouri Territory and was immediately sued by their employer, Samuel Crooks and Company. The TIA stated that even to attempt unauthorized trade was a violation, and the men had a large quantity of merchandise they were taking to the Indians. The charge against Morgan said that the traders had not yet traded, and he had no authority to arrest them. When his defense attorney seemed unsure of the legal stance, Morgan justified his actions under the TIA, plus orders of his superior officer. "If I cannot offer this as a plea, before a court of Justice," he said, "certainly it will not be ineffectual, when addressed to my government; it will not

---

673   Sevier to Porter, February 10, 1829, TPUS, V. 20, 843.
674   Gaines to Barbour, July 20, 1826, TPUS, V. 20, 274.

permit me to suffer, in consequence of the discharge of my duty."[675] The government was not so certain.

Another impediment to enforcement was a reluctant justice system. A number of illegal traders were arrested in Missouri and Illinois Territories in 1818. They were caught red-handed and the evidence against them was overwhelming, but Judge Silas Bent on the Missouri Supreme Court, father of future traders Charles, William, and Robert Bent, ruled that they were not arrested within his jurisdiction and there was no legal evidence against them. Civilian intransigence led Brig. Gen. Thomas A. Smith to countermand arrest orders he had issued. If courts would not prosecute, he would not arrest. Secretary Calhoun, however, said that Judge Bent was plainly in error, and that Smith must continue to arrest violators of the Intercourse Acts.[676]

In 1819, Capt. George P. Peters of the Artillery Corps seized 3,800 cedar logs at Mobile, Alabama, that were cut from public lands. Almost immediately, the company of Johnson and Connally sued him, claiming that the cutting was done on private land. At the trial, which Peters was not allowed to attend by order of his superior officer, the verdict was that the defendant did not prove the timber was cut on public land and therefore Peters was liable for $611 in damages to the company. Peters pleaded for assistance, and Calhoun promised the government would help; however, Peters died later that year.[677]

In Florida, Capt. John R. Bell, 4th Artillery, incurred the wrath of the marshal, several officials, and businessmen of St. Augustine, by blocking their attempt to confiscate public property and refusing to allow them to erect private buildings on public land. Bell tried to compromise by allowing civilians to share some buildings with the army, but they wanted the army out. They threatened Bell, but he said, "I was not to be intimidated," and when a civilian tried "to carry off by force…a negro woman and her two children then in

---

675   Morgan to Calhoun, October 12, 1817, TPUS, V. 15, 313–16.
676   Ballard to Smith, April 3, 1818, Bates to Smith, April 9, 1818, Smith to Calhoun, April 18, 1818, Calhoun to Clark, May 13, 1818, Calhoun to Smith, May 13, 1818, TPUS, V. 15, 380–83, 393.
677   Peters to Calhoun, February 2, 1819, TPUS, V. 18, 551–52; Calhoun to Peters, February 11, 1819, TPUS, V. 18, 562.

possession of the law," Bell arrested him. An attorney sued Bell for $450 in damages. The captain claimed that he was not accountable to the civilian court, but to Andrew Jackson, the military governor of the territory. Jackson lent no support, and when President Adams said that the military should yield to the civil officers, Bell's defense was sunk. He was fined, but a group of sympathetic citizens who believed he had acted in the public welfare paid it for him.[678]

In a twist on the usual plot, citizens sometimes accused the army of cutting timber on private land. Major Enos Cutler, 2nd Infantry, commanding at Fort Brady in Michigan's Upper Peninsula, faced such charges in 1824. Cutler cut timber on the military reservation, when a man named Johnston claimed the land was his and filed a suit. Cutler asserted he had not cut a single stick of wood from the land Johnston claimed. In addition, he knew Johnston was a swindler "who will resort to any means to sustain his demand for damages, and he will find witnesses here enough to prove whatever he pleases." Cutler knew he would never win with a local jury, and "without the interference of the government in my behalf, I shall be involved in difficulties, from which I shall be totally unable to extricate myself." He begged the secretary of war for help, so "I may not be left to suffer for the acts of others." Cutler lost. Four years later, Secretary Barbour still sought justice, and asked the Michigan District Attorney to take his case—local courts simply would not rule in favor of the army.[679]

Attorney Henry S. Baird of Green Bay was well aware that any local jury would rule "not only against the commanding officer, but the whole world." He believed it would be much simpler to compensate settlers with money or equivalent land, if only they would agree to move. The military at Fort Howard made extra efforts to placate litigious settlers. Whenever it cut timber on lands where the ownership was in question, "they were glad to pay for the wood, so cut, & thereby avoid suits for the trespasses committed."[680]

---

[678]   Bell to Jackson, October 8, 1821, TPUS, V. 22, 245, 246, 269.

[679]   Cutler to Calhoun, July 10, 1824, TPUS, V. 11, 566–67 (quotations); Barbour to Le Roy, May 17, 1828, TPUS, V. 11, 1184–85.

[680]   Baird to Wing, October 18, 1828, TPUS, V. 11, 1234–35.

When officers and civilians got into physical altercations, it was almost guaranteed the officer would be found guilty. In 1825 at Fort Howard, Capt. William G. Belknap, 3rd Infantry, got into a row with two men. He was convicted of assault and battery and fined one hundred dollars. Territorial governor Lewis Cass reviewed the record and remitted the fine.[681]

When intruders moved near Cantonment Brooke at Tampa Bay, Lieutenant Colonel Brooke could do little to stop them from cutting timber and selling liquor. Here it was not a case of local courts ruling against the army—there were no courts at all. He never had enough men to arrest and transport violators to St. Augustine, and even if he did he "would subject myself & the army to the abuse of every newspaper in the Union." He asked for direct empowerment and support to remove intruders without the threat of himself being reprimanded or sued.[682]

Six years later, Brooke, now colonel of the 5th Infantry, was at Fort Howard near Green Bay, but discovered that frontiersmen were the same everywhere. He tried to remove or arrest intruders and whiskey sellers, but they always escaped conviction because most of the juries "have been participators" in the same lawlessness. The entire frontier culture was to blame, said Brooke, those "who feed and fatten on the vices or miseries of their soon deluded fellow beings."[683]

Officers were at an extreme disadvantage dealing with civilian authorities, especially when the federal government was often reluctant to support them. Suits against Colonels Twiggs and Kearny cost them much in time and money, and both men had to petition Congress for reimbursement. The Committee of Claims countered Judge James Doty's argument that the officers had no authorization to remove intruders, and concluded that they had acted properly and in accord with the spirit of the TIA. It finally reimbursed Twiggs for $726 and Kearny for $1,200. Over the years, the constant harassing lawsuits and lack of support gradually wore down the officers until

---

[681]   Executive Proceedings of Michigan Territory, January 1, 1826 to December 31, 1826, TPUS, V. 11, 1032.

[682]   Brooke to Jones, June 6, 1828, AGO, RG 94, M567, R0032.

[683]   Brooke to Jones, March 1, 1834, AGO, RG 94, M567, R0092.

some realized that it was easier to turn a blind eye to the lawbreak-ers.[684]

Also charged in the case with Kearny was Indian agent Jo-seph M. Street. Their reimbursement was only for half their losses, and Street protested. He had to raise money to meet bail, which was paid to the brother-in-law of the plaintiff, and then he had to beg his compensation from the money awarded to the plaintiff. "Why this should have been deemed necessary," Street told Secretary Cass, "when the money was for *my relief* from *him*, I am at a loss to imagine." He was "mortified to be sent to ask an indorsement of the Plaintiff to my draft for the money intended to relieve me from the effects of a Judgment obtained against me in the performance of the duties im-posed on me by my office." Street complained of the unfair treatment by Judge Doty, who refused to let him testify because he could not show that he had a direct order from the president to remove intrud-ers. He warned Cass that unless something was done to protect agents and officers "against the *cupidity of the Traders*, they will be reduced to the *alternative* of deciding between pecuniary ruin, on the one hand, and disobedience of orders on the other."[685]

At the same time, Twiggs, Kearny, and Street were defending themselves for doing their jobs, Capt. William R. Jouett, 1ˢᵗ Infantry, commanding at Fort Snelling, had confiscated a boatload of illegal liquor being taken up the Mississippi River by Joseph Renville of the American Fur Company. They sued him, he paid $642 to defend him-self, and he pled for reimbursement. "[I]t is a hard case for me to be harassed with vexatious suits for my official acts performed in obedi-ence to my orders, and have to advance my own money to defend the suits," while being penniless "until a bill for my relief can be passed through Congress."[686]

It was doubly hard when some congressmen received money from the fur companies to look the other way when they broke the law. The companies continued suing until the frustrated army gave up trying to enforce the TIA. Jouett's superior, Col. Zachary Taylor,

---

[684] Whittlesey to House of Representatives, April 9, 1832, ASPMA, V. 5, 7–10.

[685] Street to Cass, December 5, 1832, TPUS, V. 12, 551–52.

[686] Jouett to Jones, October 30, 1832, July 15, 1834, ASPMA, V. 5, 506 (quotations), 510, 511.

was also disgusted that influential companies sued officers, while being "harassed by sheriffs and dragged from place to place," hoping a penurious Congress would help them.[687]

The frontier was plagued with its nineteenth-century version of "ambulance-chasing" lawyers—but instead of waiting for the accidents to happen, they provoked them. Captain John Stuart, still recovering from his beating at Fort Smith, said that the post was too close to Arkansas Territory. The country was unhealthy, and the post abutted a lawless white population. Ubiquitous whiskey dealers were "influenced and controlled by a parcel of Crooking lawyers who are continually prowling about Military Posts...for the purpose of producing difficulties" among the civilians, officers, and soldiers. These lawyers cajoled the soldiers to shirk duty and insult their officers to provoke a harsh response, after which they could file charges. "Lawyers have been known to pay soldiers a considerable sum of money for cases of Assault and Battery against officers." The locals petitioned to keep the troops in Arkansas Territory claiming fear of the Indians, but, Stuart said, "they are in no danger of an invasion by the Indians, and their real motive is pecuniary interest alone." The people played this game as a "hobby"—they really wanted the army for the dollars it pumped into the economy. They demanded that the money "ought to be expended among the people of the Territory in place of among the *damned Indians*."[688]

High-ranking officers could be targets. General John E. Wool faced a court of inquiry because of charges by Alabama governor Clement C. Clay, which stated that Wool had usurped state powers by interfering with a citizen's property rights. Wool insisted his action was in accordance with the law. He had sent troops to the Cherokee lands in Alabama to keep whites from robbing them, to feed starving Indians who had been run off of their farms, to keep Georgia volunteers from molesting them, and to "permit no insults to be offered to them or any depredations committed on their property." When Wool learned that Nathaniel Steele had taken possession of a Cherokee ferry over the Coosa River, his investigation determined that the Indian and his heirs were the rightful owners. When he made Steele relin-

---

[687]   Taylor to Jones, July 15, 1834, ASPMA, V. 5, 510.
[688]   Stuart to Jones, September 19, 1833, TPUS, V. 21, 794–96.

quish the property, Governor Clay charged that Wool had illegally usurped the state's judicial powers. Wool argued that the treaty and the TIA authorized him to protect and defend the Indians' property rights. This time the Court agreed, stating that the laws did invest him with the "power of repossessing an Indian claimant of improvements wrongfully withheld by a white intruder."[689]

General Wool's frontier experience, like General Gaines's, was similarly enlightening. He came to protect settlers from Indians, but years of actual service on that frontier altered his perspective. The War Department did not understand the Indians, Wool said, "and no man can understand them until he goes among them." Wool found that they distrusted whites for the bad treatment they received and they were not willing to meekly submit and move west. "This is not fiction but truth." Wool, however, would do his best to see that they did move, because the alternative was worse. "They are the prey of the white man," on the verge of being "driven to a state of desperation," which would result in war.[690] Wool was unhappy with his duties. The only thing that made it tolerable, he said, was "the hope that I may stay cruelty and injustice and assist the wretched and deluded beings called Cherokees, who are only the prey of the most profligate and most vicious of the white men." The scenes throughout the countryside were "heart rending," and whites "like so many vultures, are watching, ready to pounce."[691]

Alexander Cummings had been tormented by civilians while at Fort Towson, but even as colonel of the 4th Infantry, he could not seem to shake the scourge. While on leave in Philadelphia in December 1841, he was arrested, with bail set at one thousand dollars, the result of a lawsuit for actions he allegedly took at Fort Brooke, Florida, in 1839. The plaintiff, James Lynch, said that he was the legitimate sutler at that post when Cummings and his soldiers "maliciously issued & enforced orders to destroy or injure the deponent's business." Cummings allegedly prevented Lynch's employees from

---

689   Wool to Byrd, July 22, 1836, AGO, RG 94, M567, R0154 ("permit no insults" quotation); Wool to Dunlap, August 12, 1836, AGO, RG 94, M567, R0154; ANC, V. 5, No. 14 (October 5, 1837), 222, 223 ("repossessing" quotation); ANC, V. 5, No. 16 (October 19, 1837), 244–47.
690   Wool to Harris, August 27, 1836, ASPMA, V. 7, 552.
691   Wool to Cass, September 10, 1836, AGO, RG 94, M567, R0134.

building a store to sell his merchandise, which was thus lost or damaged to the tune of $30,000. At the trial, Cummings said that General Taylor had initially banned Lynch from the post because an appointed sutler was already working there. After the company that owned the merchandise protested to Taylor, he allowed the goods to be unloaded and a store built. Cummings said he never disturbed Lynch or his business. The judge ultimately dismissed the case, saying that the only object Lynch had "was to erect a building for the purpose of selling whiskey." "Besides," he said, "he has sworn to the loss of $30,000, a sum that no man can make honestly in one year in the business he represents himself in." Cummings's nephew later told the colonel, "I sat opposite to Lynch at supper, but the rascal could not look me in the face."[692] Not all the lawsuits succeeded, but the army was significantly hampered by the constant harassment.

Occasionally the army sued civilians. Frontiersmen took it for granted that the forests belonged to them; they had historically denuded the forests to build farms and towns, or cut timber for direct sale, regardless of who owned the land. A major consumer of the timber was the U. S. Navy, and as the forests were depleted along the Atlantic coast, the large live oak stands in recently-acquired Florida Territory looked very promising. In the early 1820s, the navy sent timber contractors to the St. Johns River, while inspectors watched the area and navy brigs and cutters patrolled to restrict illegal activity. In 1833, a federal act authorized customs collectors to determine whether cut timber was taken from private or public lands. In January 1842, Hezekiah Thistle was appointed "Agent for preservation of Live Oak and other timber upon Public Land in East Florida," and hence the trouble began.[693]

The situation was exacerbated with the 1842 passage of the Armed Occupation Act. Authorities hoped flooding the area with white settlers would push out the Seminoles—unfortunately the solution was like trading a cold for malaria. The settlers moved in

---

692   Lynch deposition, December 1, 1841 ("maliciously issued" quotation), Cummings to Spenser, December 6, 1841, Cummings to Cummings, December 6, 1841, AGO, RG 94, M567, R0226.

693   Susan Parker, "Florida's live oaks were once a hot commodity," July 23, 2016, http://staugustine.com/news/local-news/2016-07-23/susan-parker-floridas-live-oaks-were-once-hot-commodity

less to start farms than to exploit the resources and run. Hezekiah Thistle, over-zealous in his crusade to protect the public land, confiscated timber, demanded proof of where the wood was cut, and filed lawsuits on uncooperative companies. Thistle had particular trouble with the firm of Ferris and Palmer after he seized their cut logs and offered them for sale. He called them trespassers and thieves and told Secretary of the Navy Able P. Upshur, that he was "determined to put a stop to such frauds upon Government, or I'll lose my life in the attempt."[694]

David L. Palmer and Darius Ferris told Upshur that they "always avoided depredating on public lands," that Thistle laid an injunction on all their timber—an action that was "extremely embarrassing"—and they wanted the persecution stopped. Former governor DuVal also chimed in, saying that Thistle's power had gone to his head, and "it is my opinion, he is not quite sane." Thistle had filled the St. Johns County court docket with ten lawsuits for illegal cutting, while DuVal argued that there were no more than ten acres of public land along the full 150 miles of the St. Johns River.[695]

Thistle countered that the land claims were phony; the so-called settlers either asserted ownership through unprovable old Spanish land grants or never registered their claims other than "bordering on some long pond, or cornering upon some cabbage tree." Thistle insisted that every foot of land that Palmer and Ferris cut belonged to the government. The company demanded Thistle be arrested for his "malicious and uncalled for interference," because he had declared that he would seize all timber "*whether it was cut on public land or not.*"[696]

On June 15, 1843, Palmer and Ferris exacted revenge. While Thistle was on business in Jacksonville, Ferris, assisted by Stephen Fernandez and one other, attacked and severely beat him. Witnesses said that the two men held Thistle while Ferris, "a very large athletic powerful man," pummeled him unmercifully. Fernandez allegedly

---

694   Thistle to Upshur, September 28, 1842, TPUS, V. 26, 550–51.
695   Palmer and Ferris to Upshur, November 1842, TPUS, V. 26, 573–74; DuVal to Upshur, December 10, 1842, TPUS, V. 26, 581–82.
696   Thistle to Upshur, January 30, 1843, TPUS, V. 26, 611–12; Palmer and Ferris to Upshur, February 25, 1843, TPUS, V. 26, 621.

wanted to be Port Collector for Jacksonville, and take Thistle's job, allowing his friends to cut all the timber they wanted. A sympathetic civilian insisted that the government was tyrannical and "must be met by the mob-spirit at every turn." There was nothing Thistle could do, because no redress would ever be obtained "for such an injury before the legal tribunal of this portion of the country."[697]

Thistle would not give in. He told the secretary that Ferris intended to kill him, but "I shall not quit my duty or perseverance on account of attacks made by these desperadoes." He said that when he recuperated he would return to the St. Johns River and continue confiscating illegally cut timber.[698]

In the meantime, U. S. Attorney General John Nelson ruled on the question of whether or not the settlers exploiting the Armed Occupation Act were authorized to cut timber for sale. He resolved that by taking up a quarter section the head of the family agreed to improve five acres, cultivate the land, and live there for five years. Not until he had resided there for the minimum time did he own the land. Therefore, "he has no right to cut or sell any timber, except for the purpose of clearing, cultivating, enclosing and occupying the land so settled." The law, Nelson declared, does not permit him "to pillage the public domain" only to abandon it and defeat the purpose of the enactment. This should have vindicated and satisfied Thistle, but apparently he believed the ruling still allowed settlers latitude to cut timber and sell it for private benefit.[699]

Far from being mollified, Thistle wanted an assistant to go after more violators. In August 1843, he listed his pending suits at St. Augustine, which included $500 against the owners of the brig *Nimrod*, for attempting to ship cut timber; $6,000 for the value of the timber; $100,000 against Palmer and Ferris for cutting live oak; $50,000 in damages against Parsons and Blanchard for cutting pine; and another $100,000 in damages against Palmer and Ferris for cutting timber on the Mosquito River.[700]

---

697   Bernard to Upshur, June 16, 1843, TPUS, V. 26, 663–64; Fraser to Upshur, June 23, 1843, TPUS, V. 26, 666–67.
698   Thistle to Upshur, June 16, 1843, TPUS, V. 26, 661–62.
699   Nelson to Henshaw, August 11, 1843, TPUS, V. 26, 715–16; Thistle to Henshaw, September 25, 1843, TPUS, V. 26, 742.
700   Thistle to Henshaw, August 28, 1843, TPUS, V. 26, 731.

Thistle continued his crusade until he was discharged in August 1845, with the government and the citizens likely relieved he was gone. As a private citizen, he morphed into one of the grasping souls he had once pursued. Thistle claimed the government owed him money for expenses but his claims were rejected. In 1856, he petitioned the Court of Claims for redress, stating that the law allowed him, as "informer, seizor and captor" of cut timber, to one-half the value of the confiscated property. The wood to be shipped on the *Nimrod* was valued at $12,997, so Thistle was owed $6,498. The court, however, followed the exact letter of the law, and said if the timber was shipped to a foreign country, the ship could be seized and forfeited to the U. S. and the captain would be fined $1,000. All penalties and forfeitures had to be sued for, recovered, and distributed, and only then would half be paid to the informer. The timber in question was not a fine, penalty, or forfeiture. "We are, therefore, of the opinion that the petitioner is not entitled to relief."[701]

Military officers and government agents felt unappreciated and resentful after years of similar experiences. They were sued by citizens and companies for removing intruders, confiscating illegally-obtained resources, or arresting whiskey sellers. While they tried to keep trespassers off public and Indian lands, they were themselves accused of depredating. They could not get a fair trial from local juries and the government was an indifferent ally. Officers had to defend themselves with their own money and hope Congress would reimburse them. Agents who sued private citizens were rarely supported and their own claims were rejected. Officers had to choose between financial ruin and disobedience of orders. In the years between the War of 1812 and the Mexican War, officers got a discomfiting lesson that the Indians were often less their enemy than the whites. When the Mexican War infused the army with hundreds of new officers appointed from civilian life—men the West Point officers increasingly despised—the thirty-year hiatus of the army trying to enforce the TIA and protect the Indians was over. It may have

---

[701] Hezekiah L. Thistle vs. the United States, July 25, 1856, *Reports from the Court of Claims submitted to the House of Representatives during the 1ˢᵗ Session of the 34th Congress, 1855–1856,* V. 1 (Washington: Cornelius Wendell, 1856), 1–6.

been easier to plead ignorance to lawlessness and look the other way, but relaxed enforcement only opened Pandora's box and enabled whites to run riot, eventually leading the army into more collisions with the Indians—something that it had tried to avoid for three decades. The upshot was just what Washington and Knox warned of half a century earlier—unregulated frontier whites caused war.

RETURN OF THE FILIBUSTERS: THE PATRIOT WAR

"Little better than a nation of pirates"

The word "filibuster" carried a far different meaning in the nineteenth century than it does today. Historically it was less a delaying tactic in the senate than a label for American adventurers who raised private military forces to invade foreign countries. Perhaps difficult to comprehend today, the filibusters were sometimes damned as pirates or mercenaries, but very often worshipped as home grown heroes in the Age of Romance and Manifest Destiny. Americans invaded bordering English, French, Spanish, and Mexican territories, and even lands in the Caribbean, Central and South America. The U. S. Neutrality Act of 1818 prohibited such private warfare, but never completely curtailed it. Americans who mistrusted a professional army, loved their citizen-soldiers, and took whatever they wanted, were malignancies on the body politic. As the West Point-dominated army became established in the 1820s, with a concurrent centralization of military control, filibusters had less opportunity to recruit, arm, and conduct extra-legal intrusions.[702]

If filibuster expeditions to foreign countries dwindled between 1815 and 1845, maybe the reasons were tougher laws and more army enforcement, but perhaps the filibusters simply performed a thinly-veiled metamorphosis. They need not invade foreign countries for land and riches while Indians were being expelled at home; they could steal what they wanted right here. Filibusters never disappeared—they became squatters and intruders.

The "foreign" aspect of filibustering spiked at times, such as in their most successful foray in American history, when three out of four Texan "rebels" in 1836 were filibusters who had crossed

---

[702]   Robert E. May, *Manifest Destiny's Underworld: Filibusters in Antebellum America* (Chapel Hill, NC: University of North Carolina Press, 2002), xi, xii; Watson, *Peacekeepers and Conquerors,* 37–38.

the border after October 1835, including frontiersmen such as Davy Crockett, to steal a huge territory from Mexico. A giant filibuster land theft was sugar coated as the Texas Revolution.[703]

The next significant attempt at theft of a foreign country occurred in 1837–1839, as filibusters, so-called "Patriots," invaded Canada. This attempt failed—the United States was much less inclined to attack Britain because it was better able to defend itself than Mexico. The episode was embarrassing, to say the least, and although it has been relegated to the dust-bin of American history, it thoroughly illuminates another attempt by greedy, lawless Americans to strip people of their land and property. By the late 1830s, Americans had removed most of the Indians from east of the Mississippi River and confiscated much of the vacated land. They had not yet begun the great migration/invasion of the trans-Mississippi West, but they did not stop looking for potential plunder closer to home.

Americans had long cast their covetous eyes on Canada. The 1814 Treaty of Ghent restored lands to the pre-War of 1812 owners, but solved nothing in northern Maine, which had been claimed and occupied by both England and America, and still contained many French settlers. There were constant petty arguments and thefts among them. Into the mix came the Baker, Bacon, and Harford families in the "lumber business," cutting timber in areas claimed by both nations, particularly along Maine's Aroostook River. They ignored cease-and-desist orders, and matters came to a head when Americans on John Baker's land erected an American flag to celebrate Independence Day, 1827. Baker and James Bacon, supported by the unruly crowd, declared independence from both nations. Americans raided British mail carriers and forbade them crossing their land. British and American subjects raided each other's farms and stole property and livestock. One settler filed a debt complaint against Baker, but when a Canadian constable arrived, the American settlers drove him out. A squad of British soldiers then arrested Baker. Special agent S. B. Barrell arrived to defuse the situation; he convinced them that negotiations were underway regarding the disputed territory, and the Americans in the area would have justice

---

[703]   May, *Manifest Destiny's Underworld*, 9.

and protection as long as "they would hereafter abstain from all acts of individual violence." Such a behavior modification would have been challenging for most frontiersmen, but the Maine border quieted down for a time.[704]

Tempers flared along most of the U. S.-Canadian border in 1837, when Britain rejected Canadian demands for political and economic reforms. Canadian rebels, calling themselves "Patriots" and wearing homespun as did the American revolutionaries, rioted and battled British troops, but being beaten in nearly every contest, many fled across the border into Vermont, New York, and Michigan. The Patriot leaders promised land and money if Americans helped them, and Americans needed little persuasion. In March, Colonel Hugh Brady, 2nd Infantry, in command at Detroit, heard rumors that Americans, who also styled themselves "Patriots," planned to invade Canada. Identifying themselves to the civilian border officers as hunters, they crossed the St. Clair River. Brady called them lawless men and believed they would be easily defeated. One author described them as thousands "of borderlands residents, many of them insecure, young laborers dependent on seasonal employment, [who] went off fighting for Canadian freedom."[705]

President Van Buren was distressed when so many Americans went off to fight. Reportedly three hundred headed to Montreal, while five hundred headed for Niagara. In December 1837, Americans and Patriots raised a rebel flag on Navy Island in the Niagara River, and set up a base from which to invade Canada. They hired the steamer *Caroline* from Buffalo to ferry supplies, guns, and recruits. Canadian authorities, assisted by the Royal Navy, crossed to the island in rowboats to capture the steamer, but it was not there. Making a fateful decision, they continued across to the American side and found the docked *Caroline*. They attacked, captured the vessel, sailed

---

[704] Wetmore to New Brunswick Court, October 13, 1827, Vaughn to Clay, February, 1828, Barrell to Clay, February 11, 1828, ASPFR, V. 6, 840–42, 846, 1017; Clay to Vaughn, November 17, 1827, Vaughn to Clay, November 21, 1827, NWR, December 15, 1827, V. 9, No. 16, 253–55.

[705] Kenneth R. Stevens, *Border Diplomacy: The Caroline and McLeod Affairs in Anglo-American-Canadian Relations, 1837–1842* (Tuscaloosa, AL: University of Alabama Press, 1989), 8–10; Brady to Jones, March 15, 1837, AGO, RG 94, M567, R0150; May, *Manifest Destiny's Underworld*, 10 (quotation).

Destruction of the Caroline, *George Tattersall.*
Public domain
When Canadians sank the steamer Caroline, which had been supplying American "Patriots" attacking Canada, it caused an international incident and nearly led to war.

it out into the river, set it ablaze, and let it go over the falls. One American was killed.[706]

Rumors flew. Newspapers reported an ever-increasing number of dead. It was as if the Northern border states sought to create their own "Gulf of Tonkin" incident to start a war. New York governor William L. Marcy said twelve were killed, the *Rochester Democrat* reported fifteen killed and seventeen wounded, the Buffalo *Commercial-Advertiser* said twenty-two died, the *Niles National Register* said thirty were dead, and by the time word reached New York City, allegedly forty unarmed Americans had been slaughtered in their sleep. Irate Americans sent hateful letters. One went to Lord Durham, the new governor-general of Canada: "Durham!! how do you like to have your Steam Boat Burnt." The British raiders "will git a Bowie knife in their damd Hart." If they really wanted to fight Americans they would get "a small tast of New Orleans there is a scrap brewing in Newyork with your damd steam ships next thing they will be burnt God Dam the Queen"[707]

It is not known what Durham thought of this nearly illiterate American's ravings, but his threats and reference to the Battle of New Orleans as a well-deserved whipping of the British by fighting frontiersmen, illustrated how much the puffery of that affair had permeated American consciousness. Britain allegedly made an un-

---

[706]   *Montreal Herald,* December 7, 1837, in NNR, December 16, 1837, V. 3, No. 16, 242; May, *Manifest Destiny's Underworld,* 10; Stevens, *Border Diplomacy,* 13–15.

[707]   Stevens, *Border Diplomacy,* 15, 16 (quotation); NNR, January 6, 1838, V. 3, No. 19, 289–90.

provoked attack, and Americans wanted revenge. Our sharp-shooting frontiersmen were always ready to drop that proverbial plow and pick up a gun. The Niagara natives were restless. A number of them sent a memorial to Congress and demanded war if the British did not immediately turn over to them the assassins who had attacked America. Aware of our "national cupidity" and our reputation "that we love money better than honor," the memorialists wanted no temporizing and refused to allow Britain to simply "pay for the blood of our citizens in gold." Without immediate justice, America would not "retain the respect of the people," and must therefore treat Britain "as an enemy."[708]

Unfortunately, the American way of war during this period was often analogous with the actions of mobs and bullies. It had been two hundred years since colonists had massacred five hundred Pequots, and such large-scale, bald aggressions had downsized into a *petite guerre* of skulking assassination and plunder. Yet, in the first flush of arousal, Americans formed up to attack Canada from several points. In January 1838, Colonel Brady said that many "deluded Americans" had enlisted heart and soul in the cause of the Patriots of Canada, and stole 450 guns from the county jail. At Fort Gratiot at the head of Lake Saint Clair, they stole two artillery pieces. At the mouth of the Detroit River they crossed over to Bois Blanc Island to attack Fort Malden in Upper Canada, but were repulsed. Having retreated to Michigan they were met by Governor Stevens T. Mason and a number of U. S. marshals, who confiscated weapons and made arrests. In Detroit, "after a trial of some hours," they were acquitted. Brady suspected they would "be annoyed by the rabble" until, he hoped, Canadian forces would drive the Americans out. If the Patriots were successful, Brady believed one-third of the Americans in the area would join and we would soon be at war. In his thirty-five years in the army, he had never more wanted regulars to aid civil authority, protect property, and quell the violent American borderers.[709]

---

[708]   Memorial of Citizens of Niagara County, February 19, 1838, ASPMA, V. 7, 972–73.

[709]   Brady to Scott, January 11, 1838, AGO, RG 94, M567, R0157.

Hugh Brady. *Library of Congress*
In command at Detroit, Colonel
Brady hoped the Canadians would
defeat the dangerous American militia forces gathering on the border.

Brady needed more men, but quickly realized he had made a mistake asking for Michigan militia. A number of them had stolen muskets from the Dearbornville arsenal to give them to the Patriots. Brady told Governor Mason he did not want any militia and would depend on the small number of soldiers trickling in from Buffalo and Chicago; to General Scott, Brady affirmed that any militia force on the border "would be dangerous to our peace."[710]

About one hundred infuriated Patriots in Cleveland, Ohio, went to Detroit to fight. A witness, who called them "all the thieves, black-legs, and scoundrels," was glad to see them go. In February, Lt. James T. Homans of the U. S. Navy, while on the road near Sandusky, Ohio, passed the party, now grown to nearly three hundred, intending to go Detroit and invade Canada. Eventually, 150 filibusters crossed the frozen Detroit River to take Fighting Island, but gunfire from the Canadian shore drove them off with five wounded. More Patriots went to Pelee Island in Lake Erie, to use it as a supply base to attack Fort Malden, but were themselves attacked by British and Canadian forces and lost fourteen killed, eighteen wounded, and eleven captured.[711]

Americans and Canadians raided a Vermont arsenal and crossed the border to establish the Independent Republic of Lower Canada. Approaching British soldiers scared them back into the U. S., where General Wool's regulars captured six hundred of them.

---

[710] Brady to Jones, February 15, 1838, AGO, RG 94, M567, R0157; Brady to Scott, March 14, 1838, AGO, RG 94, M567, R0157.

[711] Stevens, *Border Diplomacy*, 20 (quotation); Homans to Brady, February 5, 1838, AGO, RG 94, M567, R0157; May, *Manifest Destiny's Underworld*, 11; Edwin C. Guillet, *The Lives and Times of the Patriots: An Account of the Rebellion in Upper Canada, 1837-1838, and the Patriot Agitation in the United States, 1837-1842* (Toronto: Thomas Nelson & Sons, Limited, 1938), 101–02.

Because it would have been difficult to confine, feed, and prosecute them, Wool let them go. Several hundred volunteers prepared to assault Kingston, at the east end of Lake Ontario, but when they learned that armed Canadian militia were marching to oppose them, they retreated. In Buffalo, it was said that "patriotism has overrun this section of the state like a *wild fire*." Americans raided the arsenal and took one thousand small arms and many artillery pieces. The locals threatened anyone who did not share their "tornado of patriotism" and those who tried to keep their sanity "have been brow-beaten down by the others with the Shibboleth of TORY—TORY—TORY." The volunteers even boasted that they had killed 150 Canadians with their field pieces.[712]

President Van Buren issued a proclamation exhorting all citizens to peaceably return to their homes at the risk of arrest and punishment, but War Secretary Poinsett admitted to General Scott that the executive possessed no legal authority to employ the army to restrain citizens within U. S. jurisdiction who had not yet invaded anyone. He could only request that Scott "use your influence to prevent such excesses."[713]

Scott was temporarily a general without an army. He had just been vindicated by a court of inquiry concerning his conduct in the Florida War and was awaiting assignment. When Van Buren told him "Blood has been shed," and directed him to go to the Canadian frontier, Scott, with almost all of the army fighting the Seminoles, would have nothing to work with but his "rhetoric and diplomacy." He was told he could recruit locals, but he realized that would be akin to asking the fox to guard the henhouse, and his disparagement of citizen-soldiers is what got him in trouble in Florida. He went first to Buffalo and found the "whole town is in a blaze," but he was determined to cool them down. If not, the country would be "little better than a nation of pirates." Scott traveled wherever Patriots were rabble-rousing. He addressed crowds and emphasized their republican virtues, which included obedience to laws and due process. Likely assuming the general had large forces of regulars

---

[712]   Watson, *Peacekeepers and Conquerors*, 278; ANC, V. 6, No. 4 (January 25, 1838), 60–61. NNR, January 20, 1838, V. 3, No. 21, 321–22, 323 (quotations).
[713]   ANC, V. 6, No. 3 (January 18, 1838), 36–37.

backing him up, the crowds generally acceded to his pleas. The situation was helped by passage of an updated Neutrality Act in March 1838, which allowed the federal government more leeway to seize property and to fine and imprison its citizens if there was probable cause they were organizing a military expedition against a foreign country. The search and seizure aspect was decried by many would-be border terrorists—"pirates"—as Scott called them.[714]

When the first invasions did not succeed quite as the Patriots had hoped, they went "underground" and formed secret societies, such as the Canadian Refugee Relief Association, the Brother Hunters, and the rehashed Sons of Liberty. Collectively, they were often labeled "Hunters' Lodges." In March 1838, Lt. Col. Alex Cummings of the 2nd Infantry, very likely pleased he was no longer at Cantonment Towson, found himself at Sacket's Harbor, New York, where "persons of suspicious appearance have been lurking about the gun house & magazine at Madison Barracks," hoping to steal munitions for a planned attack on Canada. A few weeks later, Cummings learned "the notorious Bill Johnston" was in the area building two boats "for some desperate enterprise," possibly using the Patriot cause as a cover for evading the revenue laws or outright robbery.[715]

Cummings was correct. In May, a band of terrorists operating in the Thousand Islands area of the St. Lawrence River attacked the Canadian steam packet *Sir Robert Peel*. The gang of fifty men were dressed and painted as Indians, and the leader, Bill Johnston, also sported a false beard and wielded six pistols, a sword, and a rifle. Perhaps Johnston saw the historical connection with the Sons of Liberty dressed as Indians when they dumped British tea into Boston Harbor, but he evidently was more concerned with stealing a package containing $12,000 from the Bank of Upper Canada. After bullying and abusing the passengers, Johnston's men drove them ashore, towed the vessel into the lake, shouted, "Remember the *Caroline*," and burned it. Some passengers were missing, and those on shore believed they heard them crying for help from the sinking

[714]   Johnson, *Winfield Scott*, 129–32 (quotations); Stevens, *Border Diplomacy*, 28.

[715]   May, *Manifest Destiny's Underworld*, 11; Cummings to Jones, March 6, 1838, March 29, 1838, AGO, RG 94, M567, R0160.

ship.[716]

Sir George Arthur, the lieutenant governor of Upper Canada, issued a proclamation denouncing the deeds of the American "armed ruffians," and that the United States should "feel deeply the insult which this act of savage and cowardly violence…has inflicted upon their nation."[717] Shamelessly disregarding the fact that they were almost universally the aggressors, Americans sent up a howl of protest, claiming that hundreds of their compatriots were being held in Canadian prisons. Van Buren sent a veteran diplomat, Aaron Vail, to meet with Arthur. They inspected jails in several cities, but Vail found no large numbers of imprisoned Americans, beyond those who had been legitimately arrested and awaiting trial for crimes. Vail chose not to intervene on behalf of men who had violated the neutrality laws, and realized that the Canadians actually treated the prisoners better than Vail would have done; he privately told Arthur that the Patriots were the "scum" of the frontier.[718]

In June, about three hundred Patriot Hunters crossed the Niagara River to the Canadian shore, set up a camp, looted and destroyed property, but suffered four killed and thirty-one captured when Canadian militia and British regulars drove them back across the river. That same month, twenty-five Sons of Liberty, whom Colonel Brady called "desperadoes who call themselves Patriots," crossed the St. Clair River and plundered a store, escaped from the Canadian militia, and crossed back over only to have half of them captured by the collector of the Port of Detroit. Brady did not have enough men to patrol the river and guard the arsenal at Dearbornville, and said that more regulars "are absolutely required on this part of the frontier."[719]

Events seemed to have quieted down a bit on the Niagara frontier when a Major Webb, in command of the British Fort Erie, crossed over to Buffalo to transact some business. American "vagabonds" recognized him, and "feeling exceedingly patriotic assaulted

---

716 Stevens, *Border Diplomacy*, 37.

717 ANC, V. 6, No. 24 (June 14, 1838), 380.

718 Stevens, *Border Diplomacy*, 30–31.

719 Stevens, *Border Diplomacy*, 38; May, *Manifest Destiny's Underworld*, 13; Brady to Jones, June 29, 1838, AGO, RG 94, M567, R0158.

him very grossly, striking him and throwing eggs at him," while two town constables watched approvingly. In Detroit, three British officers of the Queen's Light Infantry also crossed over on business. They were accosted by a crowd shouting, "Tory, Tory," and "also by disgusting and abusive language, and were thrice pelted with stones, eggs, and mud." The officers retreated to the wharf, but found the ferry boat had just departed. They were cornered by a mob that tried to provoke them into drawing their swords, but had they done so, "there is not the slightest doubt they would all have been murdered." An ex-British officer who was present caustically labeled it typical conduct of the "free and enlightened citizens of the greatest republic in the world." An editorialist in a British journal said that the conduct of the Americans disgusted him: "The frontiers of the Union are peopled by as lawless and restless a race of miscreants as any in the world."[720]

"Do not let a white man murder what an Indian has spared!"

Realizing it could not rely on state militia to check the Patriots, Congress, in July 1838, reinstituted the 8th Infantry, which had been disbanded in the cost-cutting measures of 1821. A regiment that had not been needed for seventeen years was reinstituted, not to fight Indians, but to control white terrorists. Its colonel, William J. Worth, constantly moved his companies to hot spots along the northern frontier, occasionally accompanying Scott. Both men initially favored the Patriots, but like Gaines and Wool in the South, after dealing with frontier people personally, they quickly changed their minds. Worth, who first said the Patriots would "earn the proud title of liberators of Canada," soon lost all sympathy for them and sought to bring them to quick, stern justice.[721]

Army Commander General Alexander Macomb seemed oblivious to the depravity of the American borderers. From Sacket's Harbor he issued General Orders No. 1, excusing their activities

---

[720] ANC, V. 6, No. 26 (June 28, 1838), 405, 409, 414.

[721] Watson, *Peacekeepers and Conquerors,* 264–65; Francis R. Heitman, *Historical Register and Dictionary of the United States Army, Vol. 1* (Washington: GPO, 1903), 96–97.

with the astonishing statement that they were simply "not generally acquainted" with the law that forbade invading peaceful foreign countries. Macomb therefore circulated copies of the law, which made him "satisfied that the good citizens along the line, knowing the law, will, by their example and advice, endeavor to restrain all ill-advised and unlawful proceedings."[722]

Macomb's proclamation went unheeded, and Patriots, rebels, and filibusters continued to use the Canadian discontent as an excuse to cross the borders to rob, plunder, and kill. Major incursions occurred in November. One force of about four hundred rebels followed the Richelieu River, the old invasion route leading north from Lake Champlain toward Montreal, striking loyalist homes. Near La Prairie they attacked two farmers named Walker and Vitry who "were murdered in cold blood." British Hussars scattered the rebels. The village of Caughnawaga, upriver from Montreal, was the home of a band of Mohawks who had long ago come under French Catholic influence and relocated there to practice their faith. Patriots believed they would be easy prey and surrounded a church in which they worshipped. Colonial Americans in the previous century, afraid of Indians and slaves, had once passed laws requiring all free white men to carry weapons when attending public meetings and even while in church. The Patriots likely did not catch the irony of the situation when they surrounded a church filled with Indians, who promptly grabbed their weapons and rushed outside. One chief "raised the war-whoop, and seized the rebel next him and wrestled from him his musket." Others, with muskets, tomahawks, and pitchforks, "charged their foes, who scampered off as fast as they could, throwing down their arms as they fled." They caught about seventy rebels and marched them to Lachine where Canadian authorities jailed them.[723]

On November 11, about 400 Patriots crossed the St. Lawrence River from New York, in an attempt to take Prescott and Fort Wellington. They took the town, but most of their men were still on the American shore. When a U. S. marshal and regulars seized the

---

[722]   ANC, V. 7, No. 3 (July 19, 1838), 46.
[723]   NNR, November 17, 1838, V. 5, No. 12, 189–90; Cramer, *Armed America*, 32.

Battle of the Windmill. *Public domain*
In the 1838 American invasion of Canada, perhaps fifty "Patriots" were killed and one hundred captured in battle near Ogdensburg, New York.

supply vessels, about 150 Patriots were cut off. A sharp two-day fight occurred—the "Battle of the Windmill"—before hundreds of Canadian militia and British regulars forced their surrender. Estimates ran from 20 to 50 Patriots killed and 130 to 150 captured. One, John McDonnell, was found with papers on him that indicated he was "major general" of the Patriot army. While being hauled to jail, he was pelted with stones and mud. The *Montreal Herald* reported rumors that his rebels had planned "to sack and plunder Montreal, and that the Jews were all to be massacred." Patriot supporters insisted their men fought nobly and were beaten by overwhelming odds, with more than 2,000 engaged and 500 killed and wounded. Of those captured, it was said, "they are all, or nearly all, murdered." Actually, about 111 rebels in the mill surrendered and were marched away to Kingston for trial.[724]

One of the schooners that tried to ferry supplies to the Patriots was commanded by Bill Johnston, who had been at large in the Thousand Islands area, and had even made a proclamation admitting that "I, William Johnston…hold a commission in the Patriot service of Upper Canada," and "I commanded the expedition that captured and destroyed the steamer *Sir Robert Peel*." Johnston said he would continue to fight for Canada's independence, and with so many sympathizers, no one could catch him. Captain George McCall, 4th Infantry, said that Johnston "exercises an astonishing influence over all popular proceedings along this section of the frontier." Eventually, Johnston's piracy career ended when his vessel was captured by the marshal and American regulars. He went to trial in Watertown, New York, but one realistic local knew what would happen: "[T]hose men will escape punishment," he said, "for I understand that a majority of the jury are *patriots!* or sympathizers,

---

[724]   May, *Manifest Destiny's Underworld, 13*; NNR, November 17, 1838, V. 5, No. 12, 192, 200.

and will not convict." He never got to trial. The marshal, rightly concerned about the loyalty of the guards, discovered one morning in December that Johnston had somehow escaped jail during the night.[725]

One of the last of the larger, organized attempts to invade Canada occurred on December 3–4, 1838. Colonel Brady learned of the plan by more than three hundred of "these self-styled Patriots" to cross the Detroit River and attack Windsor. When Maj. Matthew M. Payne, 2nd Artillery, with the deputy marshal and twenty soldiers, discovered a cache of 162 guns, ammunition, and pikes hidden near the mouth of the Rouge River, Brady figured he had stopped the invasion. Nevertheless, the Patriots crossed the Detroit River at several points and converged on Windsor. When the British regulars counterattacked, the Patriots "broke & took to the woods," except for about forty who took canoes to Hog Island where fifteen were arrested by the marshal. Then, as was usually the case, they were released "for want of sufficient evidence to convict them." Brady believed that seventeen Patriots and four Loyalists were killed. He was disheartened by the Detroiters who abetted and cheered the attack and was certain that "the same spirit prevails extensively throughout the State." He felt helpless being subordinate to civil authorities, "a majority, of whom to say the least, are notoriously favorable to what is misnamed the Patriot cause!"[726]

British colonel John Prince was in command at Sandwich, just below Windsor. He awoke December 4 to the news that "brigands and pirates from Michigan" had begun an attack. He advanced with 130 Canadian militia, met 150 of them in an orchard outside of town and fired a volley into them, driving them back into the woods. Prince then learned another band was advancing toward Sandwich where his supplies and ammunition were left unguarded, and hurried to meet them. His presence deterred this force of Patriots, but meanwhile "upwards of 300 of the scoundrels" had entered Windsor and burned several houses, the militia barracks, and the steamboat *Thames*. Regulars with field guns from Fort Malden arrived, and

---

[725] ANC, V. 6, No. 26 (June 28, 1838), 414 ("I, William" quotation); McCall to Cummings, July 28, 1838, AGO, RG 94, M567, R0161; ANC, V. 7, No. 1, (July 5, 1838), 14 ("will escape" quotation); Stevens, *Border Diplomacy*, 43.
[726] Brady to Jones, December 6, 1838, AGO, RG 94, M567, R0159.

Prince advanced, but found "the brigands had evacuated the place" and were running north toward Lake Saint Clair, but not before they had committed mayhem. Prince said they "murdered in cold blood" Mr. Hume, assistant staff surgeon, who had tried to help the wounded. "Not content with firing several balls through him, the savages stabbed him in many places with their Bowie knives, and mangled his body with an axe. They also murdered a colored man who refused to join them. They burned the premises of Mr. Morin…and also two houses adjoining, and two of our men were burned to death within them." Prince estimated there were about 450 brigands all told, armed with muskets, bayonets, pistols, and "tremendous Bowie knives. A more murderous crew was never seen." Prince estimated that twenty-one Patriots were killed and twenty-six were captured.[727]

Characteristically, many Americans viewed events through a different lens. During the fighting in Windsor, the wharves in Detroit, said Prince, "were crowded with persons who rent the air with cheers in support of the brigands and pirates." The Detroit *Daily Advertiser*, while calling the affair a "mad-cap expedition," nevertheless called the destruction of the dwellings and steamboat a "successful conflagration." It was troubled that several of the Patriot bodies "were suffered to lie unburied and exposed…a prey to the dogs and hogs! This is brutality beyond precedent." It also accused Colonel Prince of shooting two Patriot prisoners "in cold blood."[728] Eyewitnesses both verified and denied the charges. A band of Indians helped drive the Patriots out of Windsor and took seven prisoners; the soldiers wanted to kill them, but they refused, saying, "*No, we are Christians! We will not murder them!*" Some soldiers insisted they die and Colonel Prince wavered, but several Canadian civilians stepped in and stated, "*For God's sake, do not let a white man murder what an Indian has spared!*" Prince spared them.[729]

The federal government was utterly embarrassed by the conduct of its citizens. The *Washington Globe* reported that "our misguided countrymen, who invaded Canada…have been cut up and destroyed. It appears that they were attacked by the very people

---

[727]   NNR, December 29, 1838, V. 5, No. 18, 281.

[728]   Ibid; Detroit *Daily Advertiser,* December 6, 1838, in NNR, December 22, 1838, V. 5, No. 17, 257.

[729]   NNR, September 21, 1839, V. 7, No. 4, 52.

who they were told claimed their sympathy and assistance, and who, on the contrary, regarded them as pirates and robbers." The *Globe* blamed propagandists who persuaded "young and inexperienced" Americans to engage in wicked deeds that would only bring opprobrium and dishonor to the country.[730]

Writing from Sacket's Harbor, Colonel Worth appealed to the British military for leniency for the "unfortunate dupes of designing demagogues" who were arrested in the invasions. Worth believed that "delusion and fraud" were practiced on unwitting Americans, who certainly would not have acted so rashly had they known better. President Van Buren condemned the invasions and called them "criminal assaults upon the peace and order of a neighboring country" by "misguided or deluded persons." He demanded Americans follow a strict neutrality and abhorred the "depredations by our citizens" as a violation of international law.[731]

The *Globe*, Worth, and Van Buren may have been deluding themselves—American aid to foreign rebels was not motivated by altruism as much as by avarice, and they were less unwitting dupes than willing disciples; Macomb was quite gullible to believe that simply reading them the law would make them change their behavior. By the end of 1838, most of the incursions reverted to characteristic small-scale raids of robbery and murder. For instance, Americans sought revenge against Canadian Edgeworth Usher, who allegedly was involved in capturing the *Caroline* and fought against the Patriots when they invaded Navy Island. Their true motive was revealed when a gang crossed from Buffalo to Chippewa, invaded the house of a Mr. Taylor, stole $500, and forced him to take them to Usher's. When he refused, they set his house on fire. Yielding, Taylor took them down the road where they stopped at the house of a man named Dobie, compelled Taylor to call him outside, and robbed him. Likewise, they forced Taylor to call Usher out. Seeing the armed men, Usher slammed the door, but someone shot through the window and killed him. With their prey dead and money in their

---

[730]   ANC, V 7, No. 23 (December 6, 1838), 367.
[731]   Worth to Commander of Her Majesty's military, November 23, 1838, in ANC, V. 7, No. 24 (December 13, 1838), 382; Van Buren to Congress, in ANC, V. 7, No. 24 (December 13, 1838), 369.

pockets, the gang returned to Buffalo.[732]

The good people of Oswego, New York, damned interfering civil authorities. When the tax collector and marshal were unable to stop a mob of three hundred from stealing guns and cannons, they called on Capt. Thomas P. Gwynne and his 8th Infantrymen for assistance. The mob only grew angrier and threatened to kill all of them. Gwynne held them back for forty-five minutes, but unwilling to shoot, he retreated to the barracks, "leaving the mob to triumph. The patriots then had their own sport," stealing a supply of gunpowder and firing the pieces until dark. To crown the episode, they returned the next night and "burned the collector and deputy marshal…in effigy."[733]

In January 1839, about twenty disguised Americans from Alburgh, Vermont, crossed the border to Caldwell Manor, Quebec, broke into the home of a man named Vosburgh, bound him and his son, and shot and stabbed them "in several places with bayonets and swords." They set fire to the house and barn, roasting a number of horses, cattle, and sheep, but ran away when a company of Canadian volunteers rushed to the scene. When the mob returned to Vermont, it burned down the house of a man named Mott, who did not support the Patriot cause. A few sympathetic Americans went to Caldwell Manor to help fight the fire at Vosburgh's. The *Montreal Gazette* wanted to acknowledge their "humanity and kindness," but they did not want to be identified, "fearful of the consequences, should the circumstances become known to their marauding and murdering neighbors." Some of the individuals involved in the attack were identified, and while Albany, New York's *Daily Advertiser* called for them to be delivered to Canada for justice, Vermont governor Silas H. Jennison declined, saying that the decision belonged to the federal government. While they argued over jurisdiction, the burnings and killings continued.[734]

James Grogan lived at Caldwell Manor and joined the Patriots in the mayhem. A New Yorker, Grogan fought in the War of

---

[732]   NNR, December 1, 1838, V. 5, No. 14, 218.

[733]   ANC, V. 8, No. 2 (January 10, 1839), 24.

[734]   NNR, February 16, 1839, V. 5, No. 25, 385; ANC, V. 8, No. 8 (February 21, 1839), 126 (quotations); ANC, V. 8, No. 9 (February 28, 1839), 143–44.

1812, but subsequently lived in Canada and was regarded as a notorious malefactor. When his neighbors ordered him to leave the province, he quickly went to Alburgh, leaving his wife and eleven children behind. When Canadian Loyalists came to the house one night they gave her the choice of joining her husband, or burning with her house. She "very prudently" joined him as her house and outbuildings were torched. The Loyalists also burned the homes of Patriot sympathizers Huxley, Clark, Johnson, and Manie. Grogan promptly took his gang into Canada and burned four farms. Canadian governor general Sir John Colborne demanded the culprits be extradited, but Van Buren declined. Canadians waited three years to get revenge, when soldiers crossed the border, kidnapped Grogan, and threw him in jail in Montreal. After vigorous protests, Grogan was released, very likely because both nations wished to ease diplomatic tensions.[735]

Outlaws used the Patriot cause as a cover for depredations. Benjamin Lett, considered a dangerous menace, had thieved with Bill Johnston, murdered a British officer, dynamited a monument to General Isaac Brock in Queenston, destroyed locks on the Welland Canal, and tried to burn British ships at Kingston. In February, Patriots set fire to the military barracks in Plattsburgh, New York, destroying two buildings and considerable army stores, along with a private residence.[736]

The cross-border raids were incessant. In July, Governor Colborne diplomatically requested that the U. S. "acquaint the American authorities of the lawless state of the frontier," because border inhabitants "are still exposed to the depredations of certain evil disposed persons from the United States."[737]

As the fighting from Vermont to Michigan degenerated into a series of cross-border robberies, burnings, and murders, the conflict flared up again in Maine along the Aroostook River, where

---

[735] NNR, January 12, 1839, V. 5, No. 20, 305 (quotation); Stevens, *Border Diplomacy*, 138–40.

[736] Stevens, *Border Diplomacy*, 57; ANC, V. 8, No, 11, (March 14, 1839), 175.

[737] Colborne to Officer Commanding at Plattsburgh, July 1, 1839, AGO, RG 94, M567, R0200.

Canadian and American squatters and timber-cutters continued to despoil the land. "Trespassers" on both sides were taken prisoner. In February 1839, Sheriff Hastings Strickland led a party to the contested area; Canadians hidden in the trees shot at them, but only hit Strickland's horse. The sheriff pursued, caught five, and hauled them to the American side. In March, British troops reached Madawaska, the American sector of Aroostook. With so many men shooting at each other among the trees it was too dangerous to steal the timber. Americans protested that they were attacked by "an armed mob of foreigners," kidnapped, and *ignominiously sent to a foreign dungeon.*[738]

Maine governor John Fairfield saw political opportunity in fanning the flames with a passionate speech to the Council, stating that no greater indignity could ever have been offered to any people, his state had been outraged, and all Americans were united in honor and patriotism. "How long are we thus to be trampled upon"—he asked—"our rights and claims derided; our power contemned, and the state degraded?" On February 19, Fairfield ordered out 10,343 militia. A resident of Bangor said that 1,700 Hall's Rifles arrived, with loads of blankets and supplies. Three hundred men of the city, including almost all of the fire department, organized into a battalion and demanded arms. Allegedly six hundred British troops had invaded near the mouth of the Aroostook. Militia built a breastwork twelve feet thick topped by field pieces. When they pulled out for the Aroostook, a witness said, "Our city has today presented the appearance of a sacked town."[739]

Before patriotism could begin another war, President Van Buren dispatched General Scott to defuse the situation. Scott persuaded Governor Fairfield, as well as New Brunswick governor John Harvey, to keep the peace pending an agreement made between the U. S. and Britain to remove their citizens from the contested area until a formal agreement could be reached. The boundary question was finally settled by the Webster-Ashburton Treaty of 1842.[740]

Cross-border raids continued for another year or more, but the Patriots' ardor was burning out. Still, in June 1842, G. A. Wether-

---

738 NNR, February 23, 1839, V. 5, No. 26, 402.
739 NNR, March 2, 1839, V. 6, No. 1, 2, 6.
740 Johnson, *Winfield Scott*, 134–35.

all wrote of his concerns to Colonel Brooke, now in command at Detroit. He warned of the "evil intentions of the Patriot banditti," who no longer organized in large forces, but continued to sneak across the border to engage in "burning and plundering a few farm houses." More troubling, he had contacts in Cleveland who had exposed a cache of arms and ammunition meant for a shady character they called "Captain Bill," whom Wetherall suggested might be the same Bill Johnston who had terrorized the border for years. He told Brooke that Brown's Hotel in Cleveland was a rendezvous place, as was the Eagle Hotel in Detroit, but he had no fear of the "villains" showing themselves in force because "fighting is not their policy or profession. They are midnight assassins, and must be dealt with accordingly."[741]

As the Patriot War faded away, large-scale filibustering activities also disappeared. The entire episode has been surprisingly underplayed and is comparatively unknown outside a small circle of history mavens. The Patriot War was more encompassing than is generally recognized, and comparisons with the concurrent Second Seminole War are noteworthy. About 10,200 regulars served in Florida from 1835 to 1842, although they were continuously cycled in and out, with never more than about 2,000 available for any one campaign—General Scott asserted that 3,000 "good troops (not volunteers)" would be needed to end the war.[742] Parts of three regular regiments, about 3,000 men, served in the Patriot War from 1838 to 1841. In Florida, about 30,000 civilian volunteers served. When the Aroostook incident was at its height, Congress appropriated $10 million and authorized Van Buren to call out 50,000 volunteers for Maine alone. Incredibly, perhaps 200,000 Patriots enrolled in the various Hunter's Lodges to attack Canada.[743] Exactly how many thousands of militia formed is unknown. The army did not want them, as they were too expensive, unruly, and anathema to army ethics and objectives.

Army regulars suffered much in Florida, losing 1,466 men— 328 killed in action and the remainder to disease. Regulars suffered

---

[741]   Wetherall to Brooke, June 27, 1842, AGO, RG 94, M567, R0246.
[742]   Mahon, *History of the Second Seminole War*, 161, 325.
[743]   Watson, *Peacekeepers and Conquerors*, 273, 281, 307.

no such losses in the Patriot War since they were not fighting, but attempting to prevent it. Civilian casualties make a better comparison. In Florida, only 55 civilians were killed in action. Along the northern border, about 97 were killed in battle, 88 were wounded, and about 250 were captured. Many were tried and about 10 were hanged, while more than 100 were transported to the prison colony in Van Diemen's Land.[744]

More civilians died in battle plundering Canadians than died plundering Seminoles. An example of how seriously the government took civilian insurgencies and acts of terrorism was illustrated in two nearly simultaneous events of the summer of 1794. American armies had been disastrously defeated by the confederated Indians in the Ohio Country in 1790 and 1791. Hoping never to be so embarrassed again, the federal government gave General Anthony Wayne command of the newly-created American Legion to defeat the Indians. In an army that only consisted of 5,400 men after the reorganization of 1792, Wayne controlled about 2,000 regulars, and with only about 900 engaged, he defeated the tribes at the Battle of Fallen Timbers in August 1794. That same summer, citizens in western Pennsylvania refused to pay the whiskey tax, attacked the collectors, and rebelled. The Federalist press decried the defiance of the destructive "ignorant herd," while James Madison labeled the rebels "universally...odious." President Washington called out volunteers, and 13,000 militia from four states assembled to crush the revolt. Washington's army nabbed only about 150 rebels in the dragnet, as the rest fled. A score were marched back to Philadelphia for trial, but only two were convicted, "an imbecile and a madman," and Washington pardoned them both.[745]

The 1794 federal response to American Indians (two thousand) versus American rebels (thirteen thousand) was revealing. The 1836 army consisted of 7,900 soldiers, and a reorganization in 1838

---

[744] Mahon, *History of the Second Seminole War*, 325; NNR, December 29, 1838, V. 5, No. 18, 279–81; Stevens, *Border Diplomacy*, 40.

[745] Heitman *Historical Register and Dictionary*, 562; Robert Wooster, *The American Military Frontiers: The United States Army in the West, 1783–1900* (Albuquerque, NM: University of New Mexico Press, 2009), 16–18; John Ferling, *Adams vs. Jefferson: The Tumultuous Election of 1800* (New York: Oxford University Press, 2004), 63–64.

increased it to 12,500.[746] The federal response to the seven-year Second Seminole War was to involve 2,000 regulars at most, but generally 1,000 to 1,500 soldiers served per year in Florida, while nearly 3,000 regulars served on the northern borders. The discrepancy in civilian participation was astounding. About 30,000 civilians signed up to fight Seminoles, but 200,000 civilians joined Patriot Hunter's Lodges to attack Canada, while another 50,000 volunteers were called up for the Aroostook "War." How many more thousands participated who had not joined any organizations is unknown. The war in Florida stemmed largely from frontiersmen's greed for land and loot; the war in Canada stemmed largely from frontiersmen's greed for land and loot. It was a familiar chorus; however, while they apparently believed it was more lucrative to pillage Canadians in the North, rather than hunting Seminoles for little remuneration in the South, they got their greedy fingers burned in both locations. It is worth noting that America often used more soldiers to fight its own citizens than it did the Indians. Many Americans continue to believe that their ploughman-hunter ancestors were the ones who kept America safe and out of war, yet they were most often the very ones who dragged us into war.

The army officers who dealt with the Patriots of the North made similar observations about their Southern cronies. Inspector General Wool said they were men unguided by "principle, honor or honesty"; Scott called them "mad wicked people"; Brady said they were "rabble," "marauders," and "desperadoes"; and Worth said they were "lawless and insane men." Officers at first believed that these frontier Patriots came from the lower classes and not from "respectable" citizens, but class standing and morality were not necessarily related. The disparities may have been a function of contrasting Whig and Jacksonian worldviews, but there was likely more to it.[747]

The persistence and tacit support of frontier terrorism over decades and across all geographic boundaries should have led perceptive observers to realize that this behavior—something very dark

---

[746]   Heitman *Historical Register and Dictionary,* 587, 589.
[747]   Watson, *Peacekeepers and Conquerors,* 267–69.

and troubling—was endemic in the American character. The refrain of "American exceptionalism" delivered from the mouths and keyboards of current pundits is a testament to our misunderstanding of history, as they paste smiley faces on iniquities unlearned, forgotten, or denied.

THE FRONTIERSMEN
APOTHEOSIS

"Something in the proximity of the woods"

J. Hector St. John de Crevecoeur was born in France in 1735, migrated to New France in 1755, and then to New York in 1764, where he was naturalized, married, had three children, and owned profitable farms in New York and New Jersey. Spending a few years in London during the American Revolution, he published *Letters from an American Farmer* in 1783, which became quite a literary success. Crevecoeur was fascinated with the beauty of the country, its plants, animals, and abundance. In an age of prose, his letters were said to "smell of the woods," as he romanced the beauties of nature and inspired poets. One historian said that Crevecoeur's book contained "a greater number of delightful pages" than almost any other eighteenth-century work.[748]

Delightful, perhaps, but Crevecoeur's insightful comments also contained many caustic criticisms of Americans. In his letter, "What is an American," he pulled no punches. Those who dwelt by the sea were bolder, more enterprising, and had more interests. Inland they degenerated. They were litigious, proud, obstinate, and freely placed censure and blame. Their Christian religion "curbs them not." The farther inland the less religion and the worse manners. The inhabitants near the "great woods" were the impure "offcast" pioneers who could not sustain themselves in civilization. They coveted large tracts of land, but their idleness, lack of economy, and debt "does not afford a very pleasing spectacle." In those districts, "contention, inactivity, and wretchedness must ensue." Their magistrates were no improvement; "they are often in a perfect state of war." He wrote that the "men appear to be no better than carnivorous animals of a superior rank," continuing that on the frontiers,

---

[748]   J. Hector St. John de Crevecoeur, *Letters from an American Farmer* (Mineola, NY: Dover Publications, Inc., 2005), iii, v, vi, xii, xiv.

"remote from the power of example and check of shame, many families exhibit the most hideous parts of our society." Those who sought to understand Americans, Crevecoeur said, and get a true idea of their "barbarous rudiments, must visit our extended line of frontiers where the last settlers dwell."[749]

Crevecoeur admitted he had no proof, but he believed the problem lay with the woods. "I must tell you, that there is something in the proximity of the woods, which is very singular." The men, animals, and plants that lived in the woods "are entirely different" from others. Somehow the wildness permeated the men. "This surrounding hostility immediately puts the gun into their hands." They begin to kill and it is goodbye to the plough. Eating wild meat makes them wild. They become "ferocious, gloomy, and unsociable," hate their neighbors and practice a lawless profligacy. "Indian natives are respectable, compared with this European medley. Their wives and children live in sloth and inactivity," and all are uneducated. "Thus our bad people are those who are half cultivators and half hunters," and they have contracted the vices of both the white and Indian worlds.[750]

Born in frontier Wisconsin in 1861, historian Frederick Jackson Turner became famous for his theories of how the New World wilderness shaped Americans into something unique—how there was "something in the woods." In an 1893 talk, "The Significance of the Frontier in American History," Turner claimed that the existence of "free" land and the advance of settlement explained American development. The process gave us our intellectual traits, coarseness, strength, inquisitiveness, invention, energy, individualism, and buoyancy. Being forged in the wilderness frontier furnace, we became exceptional; we became Americans.[751] This idea became perhaps the most cherished explanation of Americanism, and one of the most controversial. A strong counter argument was that pi-

---

[749]   Crevecoeur, *American Farmer*, 27–29.

[750]   Ibid, 31–33.

[751]   Frederick Jackson Turner, "The Significance of the Frontier in American History," *The Frontier in American History* (New York: Henry Holt and Co., 1920), 1–26.

oneers actually kept many of their European customs despite the challenges America threw at them. Tradition was important. Dissenting democracy, egalitarianism, individualism, and even religion did not spring up from the wilderness; they were carried there by the pioneers. God and the Devil shaped our character more than did the landscape.[752]

Still, Turner built his career expounding on how the frontier fashioned Americans: "American democracy was born of no theorist's dream; it was not carried in the *Susan Constant* to Virginia, nor in the *Mayflower* to Plymouth. It came out of the American forest, and it gained new strength each time it touched a new frontier."[753] Crevecoeur and Turner insisted the forest held some tangible essence—malevolent to the former and beneficial to the latter—but neither had proof. Turner biographer Allan G. Bogue said Turner's essays were mostly "undocumented assertion." "He did not present compelling evidence....In his mind the frontier was the dominant influence; he found it unnecessary to explain why he believed this to be true."[754]

Crevecoeur's harsher assessments are now nearly forgotten, and only the favorable passages are cited, very likely for the same reasons that Turner's theories were embraced—Americans could feel good about them. Myths, like prejudice, are tougher than facts. But just as times do not make the people—people make the times— so the "woods" did not change Americans into barbarians—they brought the barbarity with them. The rough frontier produced some iconic American heroes, but it never did create of the people a *tabula rasa*; those who peopled North America brought along their traditions, superstitions, fears, and hatreds, and never relinquished them. The American forests never contained a tincture of evil that somehow produced new monsters; the transplanted Puritans populated

---

[752]   T. Scott Miyakawa, *Protestants and Pioneers: Individualism and Conformity on the American Frontier* (Chicago, IL: University of Chicago Press, 1964), 238–239.
[753]   Turner, "The West and American Ideals," in *Frontier in American History*, 185.
[754]   Allan G. Bogue, *Frederick Jackson Turner: Strange Roads Going Down* (Norman, OK: University of Oklahoma Press, 1998), 245.

the wilderness with their own.[755]

The American exceptionalism myth matured in the years between Crevecoeur and Turner, but many of the people who lived during that century had a very different conception of just how exceptional those frontiersmen were. Military officers had a close-up look at their character and for the most part they detested what they saw. In 1840, Capt. James H. Prentiss believed that Arkansas settlers tried to provoke an Indian war so the government would reopen some forts and keep the army around. "They want money—that's all—I have often d___d the Indians, and now I include the frontier loafers with all my heart."[756] Fourth Infantry Lt. Henry Prince recorded a most withering and colorful denunciation. He was in Newnansville, Florida, on May 14, 1838, when he got orders sending his company to another post. He was ecstatic. "Farewell ye Crackers! & ye cracker girls & a farewell ye one-roomed log houses where lives, & sleeps, a generation. Farewell the dirty foot, slipshod, but never knew a stocking; the unwashed face; ropy hair; the swearing, lazy, idle slut! Ye slouched hats & grandsires coats, goodbye. Ye drinking, drawling, boasting, cowardly sliggards—Fare ye well!" Prince hoped he would never see Florida again. "Vile Country! I have risked my life three years for you! As the worst—most unwelcome—occurrence that could happen to your heartless population, I wish that your Indian

---

[755]   The discussion about the extent of frontier violence has been lengthy, but it appears that society, culture, and ethnicity have supplanted environmental explanations. The argument over whether the West or South was the more violent region seems to lie in favor of the South. Southerner Wilbur J. Cash believed Turner averted his eyes from the darker aspects of pioneer life, and asserted that the South was the more violent section. White "crackers" were extra lazy because they always held the blacks as sub-humans who would do all the hard work. Theirs was a "purely personal and puerile attitude which distinguishes the frontier outlook everywhere." (*The Mind of the South*, New York: Vintage Books, 1991, xviii, 42.) A few of the many studies on frontier violence include: John Hope Franklin, *The Militant South*; W. Eugene Hollon, *Frontier Violence: Another Look*; James M. Denham, *A Rogue's Paradise*; Richard M. Brown, *Strain of Violence and No Duty to Retreat*; Philip D. Jordan, *Frontier Law and Order*; Everett Dick, *The Dixie Frontier*; Edward L. Ayers, *Vengeance and Justice*; Grady McWhiney and Perry Jameson, *Attack and Die*; Richard Slotkin, *Regeneration Through Violence and Fatal Environment.*
[756]   Skelton, *An American Profession of Arms*, 298.

War may speedily terminate! And you left to work your bread out of the soils with neither Uncle Sam or the Indians in the way of your plundering hand!"[757]

A few officers crossed the line from loathing to suggesting murder. Captain Francis W. Brady, 2nd Infantry, got an unpleasant introduction to the white miners in Georgia in 1830. He said they were "the most abandoned part of the community," and their constant depredations on the Indians would lead to war. Brady's solution was to shoot them: "a few cartridges spent upon them, I think, would teach them to respect the laws and treaties of their country." That sentiment was shared. Another veteran gave the *Army and Navy Chronicle* his solution: "I would advise that an appropriation be made for hemp, to hang a squad of palefaces who infest the country much more to its detriment than a troop of red-skins." Then, referring to Andrew Jackson's hanging of the British "spies" in 1818, he concluded, "It would have good effect to *Ambristerize* a few of them."[758]

The military-civilian chasm, as the army vainly attempted to keep both whites and Indians from killing each other, was nearly unbridgeable in the years between the War of 1812 and the Mexican War. Some civilians exalted in the divide. The *St. Augustine News* declared, "The burning blood thrilling through our veins does not allow our hearts to throb with friendship," and those who sneered at "this unextinguishable fire of hate" were only "canting sentiment of a false philanthropy, overlooking the holier and more sacred rights due our own race." There would be no peace "without blood."[759] That sentiment was anathema to most Academy officers who had a much more compassionate attitude and who often held frontier whites in lower estimation than they did the Indians. The army's opinion was demonstrably evident.

Did others share the army's appraisal? Historian Ray Allen Billington, a devoted student of Turner, saw frontiersmen very dif-

---

[757] Frank Laumer, ed., *Amidst a Storm of Bullets: The Diary of Lt. Henry Prince in Florida 1836–1842* (Tampa, FL: University of Tampa Press, 1998), 118, 121–22.

[758] Watson, *Peacekeepers and Conquerors,* 107 ("a few cartridges" quotation); ANC, V. 11, No. 9 (August 27, 1840), 137 ("Ambristerize" quotation).

[759] ANC, V. 8, No. 20 (May 16, 1839), 315.

ferently, but through obvious filters of confirmation bias and motivated reasoning. Trying hard to prove that frontiersmen were the exceptional agents of American destiny, shaped by "something in the
woods," and bringing strength, freedom, and democracy, Billington
downplayed the evidence that contradicted his sanguine portrayal.
For instance, he cited portions of Crevecoeur that painted the yeoman farmer as happy, attuned with Nature, blessed with abundance,
and living the good life.[760] Crevecoeur might present such an impres-
sion—if one skipped all his criticisms.

Billington cited scores of European observers of Americans
in their native habitat, and although the accounts ran the gamut
from praise to denunciation, Billington dismissed the negatives, such
as the popular novels that showed cold-blooded frontiersmen killing
Indians like snakes. He denounced Europeans who depicted Yankees living in "a cultural backwash, peopled by tobacco-spitting,
dollar grabbing illiterates whose principle sport was gouging out
each other's eyes and biting off each other's noses." Billington called
the folks who derided the backwoods Americans nothing but To-
ries who were "unblushingly propagandists for aristocratic rule, and
were not above stooping to invention to accomplish their purpose."
They were anti-democratic "tall-tale tellers" who attempted "to convince readers that the West was a land of decadence where brutality
reigned."[761]

Those Europeans were not all liars. Elias Fordham, proud of
being truthful and even-tempered, decried the American sense of
liberty, saying that it was a license to do "anything and everything.
It has no limits but the weakness of man, no boundary but that of
his desires. To right oneself by violence, to oppose force to force, is
reckoned a virtue here." The frontiersmen he met had "lax morals;
few principles…[and] a careless haughtiness of manner." They had
a "fondness for ridicule," but offend them "and a knife or a dirk is

---

[760]   Ray Allen Billington, *Land of Savagery Land of Promise: The European Image
of the American Frontier in the Nineteenth Century* (New York: W. W. Norton & Co.,
1981), 19.

[761]   Ibid., 36–38, 73, 76. Eugene Hollon, a good Turnerian, also cited
traveler accounts, and like Billington, focused on the positive ones as the more
truthful. W. Eugene Hollon, *Frontier Violence: Another Look* (New York: Oxford University Press, 1974), 211–13.

drawn and aimed in an instant." Fordham knew a man who carried a knife with a ten-inch blade, who was fond of looking for strangers he considered cowards or scoundrels, and to intimidate them was "one of the greatest pleasures of his life." Said Fordham, "There is plenty of food for his spleen in this country." James Flint was also repelled by the bullying and boasting, by the "encomiums on American bravery and intelligence poured forth by men who are not remarkable for the latter quality, and who, by their ostentation, raise a doubt as to their possessing the former." But Flint probably spoke for many when he affirmed his genuineness. "There is no course of conduct that would belie my feelings more than attempting to misrepresent the character of the American people."[762]

Of course, there were plenty of Americans who claimed the visitors did misrepresent them. Adam Hodgson published a book of his observations which was discredited by *The North American Review* in 1824. Hodgson was tricked, it said. "A traveler should not believe all he hears, and be struck at the wonder at all he sees." A visitor could not comprehend the country's morals, manners, customs, laws, and government in a few months. Hodgson was without knowledge, a credulous trifler, and he believed the "idlest tales." His problem was his "propensity to think all people as honest and as well meaning as himself."[763]

Billington would have sustained the *Review*'s assessment, but might have missed the implication of American dishonesty. He steadfastly believed the Boone-Crockett-type characters were the real Americans who built a nation: "The squatters clearly deserved a hero's role...for theirs was the first genuine effort to conquer the wilderness." Billington did not like Europeans who cast Indians in heroic roles and accused them of re-writing history if they claimed, "Indians were innocent victims of white greed." To Billington, white men were the victims, but contrary depictions stigmatized them. "Thus did the image emerge of the American frontiersmen—and to a lesser degree of the American people as a whole—as heartless predators, stripping a defenseless minority of its birthright,

---

[762] Fordham, *Personal Narrative of Travels,* 221–23; Flint, *Letters from America,* 167–68, 291.
[763] *The North American Review,* V. 18, No 43 (April 1824), 233–34.

condemning them to reservations that were little better than prison camps, and dooming them to early extinction." He lamented that this image continued to haunt America.[764]

Billington's grief notwithstanding, the American myth transformed scorned intruders, speculators, and squatters into pleasant frontiersmen, pioneers, and settlers. Fortunately or unfortunately, the new image was far from accurate. Many of the disparaging European comments were spot on, and, in addition to painting Americans as predators, they also emerged as obnoxious, boastful, and vulgar.

"They possess an inordinate opinion of themselves"

Alexis de Tocqueville is one of the most often cited commentators on nineteenth-century America, but, like Crevecoeur, much of his negative observations are neglected. He said that Americans loved their politics, but it was all-consuming and even the most ignorant would grace you with their unwanted wisdom. "An American does not know how to converse but he argues; he does not speak but he holds forth." "If an American were to be reduced to minding his own business, he would be deprived of half of his existence." Americans, he said, were told that theirs is "the only religious, enlightened, and free nation" in the world. "They possess, therefore, an inordinate opinion of themselves and are not far from believing that they form a species apart from the rest of humanity." Americans "indulge in relentless pomposity," because being very small, they must exaggerate their greatness. Their writers and poets, along with their audience, wanting grandeur, succeed only in "a mutual exercise of corruption." Americans were very proud. "They look upon themselves with pleasure and readily assume that others are looking at them too."[765]

Visiting a public inn in Georgia, traveler Charles Latrobe remarked on the difficulty of getting the members of the proprietor's family "to the most common and ordinary interchange of civility

---

[764]   Billington, *Land of Savagery*, 148-9, 151, 153.
[765]   Tocqueville, *Democracy in America*, 284, 440, 565–66, 707.

or conversation." It seemed that civility was, to them, impertinence. "Monosyllables were the utmost that could be extracted." From what he saw in the slave states, Latrobe said, "the holders were to be pitied rather than the Negroes." During his travels he found aggravating "the custom of using inflated terms" in all portrayals, which were "calculated to mislead." Americans had "an utter absence of any thing like propriety and good taste." Latrobe visited Pottawatomies near Chicago, but after comparing them with the locals, he said that "the whites seemed to me more pagan than the red men."[766]

Englishman Elias Fordham actually settled on a 480-acre farm at Harmony, Indiana, in 1818, but soon found it was a mistake. He called it a "land of dirt, bad cooking, and discomfort of every kind." In the town tavern he found he had to keep clear of the men who "spit *everywhere*, and almost on *everything*," but, knowing he was a European, "they put me in a clean bed, [and] give me clean towels," which was more than they did for anyone else. Fordham did not share the Jeffersonian image of the sturdy yeoman farmer; he thought the hunters were more polite, virtuous, and hospitable. Farmers were rascals enough, but the worst were the boatmen and traders, with horse stealers and forgers among them. Where the houses in Ohio were dirty, those in Indiana and Illinois were "pigsties, in which men and women and children wallow in promiscuous filth."[767]

James Flint, who traveled through America from 1818 to 1820, found American literature to be poor, and the newspapers showed "that the *public* are not far advanced in taste." He traveled down the Ohio River, but could not wait to get away from the boatmen. "I have seen nothing in human form so profligate as they are. Accomplished in depravity, their habits and education seem to comprehend every vice. They make few pretensions to moral character." Flint considered the Ohio River route "the greatest thoroughfare of banditti in the Union." Thieves constantly stole boats and horses while newspapers ran ads for "runaway apprentices, slaves, and wives." The foul swearing disgusted him. "I have already heard more of it in America than twice the aggregate heard during the whole of

766   Latrobe, *Rambler in North America*, 14–15, 35, 64, 207.
767   Fordham, *Personal Narrative of Travels*, 204, 206, 216.

my former life."[768]

While swearing offended Flint, spitting drove Patrick Shirreff to distraction. Touring Illinois in 1835, Shirreff spent the night at an overcrowded inn where he had to share a pallet on the floor with five of the grimiest men he could imagine, with "fumes of whiskey and squirts of tobacco juice assailing me on every side, and I considered the partner of my bed more savage than the wolf of the forest." On the deck of a boat traveling upriver from Louisville, Kentucky, Shirreff stood too close to a "gentleman" chewing tobacco, who "sprinkled a mouthful of juice" on his coattails, whereupon he produced a filthy handkerchief and attempted to wipe it clean. Shirreff tried to appear unperturbed, but said, "There was nothing in America to which I was so long of getting reconciled, as the copious spitting," and the American preference for chewing tobacco he considered "an abomination."[769]

Tocqueville called the frontier a primitive place where "passions are more violent, religious morality has less authority, ideas are less formed." People had little control over each other and exhibited "disorderly habits."[770] One of those habits was unrestrained brawling. Americans loved to argue, and when their enlightened judgments failed to carry the day, they fought. Despite Billington's protests of European bias, travelers saw it firsthand. In Virginia in 1817, Elias P. Fordham noted how the locals constantly fought, even after dueling was banned. Instead of pistols, they "draw the dirks, which they usually wear, and stab one another upon very slight provocations." Fordham speculated why: "It seems there is something in the influence of the fervid sun, under which they live, or probably in their education." Pennsylvanians, Fordham said, were coarse in manners, obstinate in their rudeness, and careless of giving pain or offense, and when drunk, "they bite each other like dogs, or tear out each other's eyes."[771] James Flint saw fights "characterized by the most savage ferocity. Gouging, or putting out the antagonist's eyes,

---

[768]   James Flint, *Flint's Letters from America, 1818–1820* (Cleveland, OH: The Arthur H. Clark Company, 1904), 43, 113, 167.

[769]   Shirreff, *Tour Through North America*, 237, 275–76.

[770]   Tocqueville, *Democracy in America*, 360.

[771]   Fordham, *Personal Narrative of Travels*, 56, 64–65.

by thrusting the thumbs into the sockets, is part of the *modus operandi*." "Kicking and biting are also ordinary means used in combat; I have seen several fingers that had been deformed, also several noses and ears, which have been mutilated, by this canine mode of fighting." Patrick Shirreff said, "Gouging is performed by twisting the fingers into the hair of the victim, and with the thumb, forcing the eye out of its socket." He said that this savagery was long practiced in Kentucky and other western states, but he believed it was now "confined to the lowest blackguards."[772]

These allegations were pure falsehoods according to the *Niles Register*. While admitting that even some women "wear dirks by their sides," how could anyone imagine that it was a national characteristic? Rumors had it "that we killed a man daily, and devoured him, like cannibals, in a public square, out of the pure love of shedding human blood." It was said that ruffians fight, bite, and gouge out eyes. "It is true, several fatal contentions have recently happened," the *Register* explained, but that did not define the character of Americans. To the contrary, "the grand fact exists, that there is no people on the globe to be compared with us for…public virtue."[773]

Foreign travelers were not the only ones who made disparaging comments. Indian Affairs Commissioner Thomas McKenney and his servant trekked through Illinois in 1827, when they stopped in a settlement to purchase supplies. It was growing dark when they saw a dwelling with lights on, but as they neared, they were halted by a gaunt man with two threatening dogs. McKenney explained his business, and while talking he noticed a large woman inside, seated at a table with "some half dozen children, their hair standing, as if in fright." Their hands and heads were gyrating in spastic-like motions that raised McKenney's curiosity. Upon entering he saw that "they were all busy in warring with the mosquitoes." Familiar with backwoods travel, the commissioner was already equipped with thick clothing, gloves, and a veil worn over his face. The settler asked them to join them for supper, and McKenney, who was very fond of milk, wished "to taste it again." The woman placed a large wooden bowl on the table with a ladle half "buried in something, I knew not

---

[772]   Flint, *Letters from America*, 138; Shirreff, *Tour Through North America*, 236.

[773]   NWR, July 29, 1820, V. 18, No. 22, 386.

what." When the ladle was dipped and brought forth, the "thick, dark surface" was disturbed and he saw what appeared to be milk issuing from beneath. The constant mosquito-slapping continued, and McKenney saw "at every stroke, the crippled and wing-broken mosquitoes falling into the big bowl, and that was the beverage they were all eating with so much *gout*, was, sure enough milk, heavily sprinkled with crippled and dead mosquitoes." He abruptly excused himself on the grounds of haste, and asked if he could purchase some eggs instead—"my milk mania having been effectually cured."[774]

"Liberty here means...to cheat everybody"

Witnesses often mentioned frontier people's greed and dishonesty. Tocqueville observed: "I am not even aware of a country where the love of money has a larger place in men's hearts"; "stealing the public purse...[is] well understood by the first wretch who comes along"; the "desire for prosperity has become a restless and burning passion which increases each time it is satisfied"; it was the Indians' misfortune to come in contact with "the most avaricious people on the earth." Tocqueville believed commercial passions stirred Americans more than anything else. He called America "a nation of conquerors" whose people submit to a savage life in a quest "to acquire wealth, as the sole aim of their efforts." He engaged one man whose singular philosophy seemed to be, "I was poor and now, look, I am rich," and truth or falsity mattered not in the pursuit of wealth. As Americans opined, Tocqueville "marveled at the stupidity of human reason."[775]

Perceptive commentators had similar concerns two decades before Tocqueville. In 1816, the *Niles Register* affirmed that education was a pillar of freedom—"the only antidote that can be found against the meanness and selfishness of avarice and ambition." The "most disgraceful trait in our national character...is an inordinate love of gain." "It is too true—we see this foul spirit everywhere; inveterate, restless, resistless, and universal." Cupidity rose up from the lowest individual to the top, mingling in war and peace, filling public

---

[774] McKenney, *Memoirs*, 137–38.
[775] Tocqueville, *Democracy in America*, 64, 258, 330–31, 334, 387–88, 888.

office, "and there violently inflaming party opposition—carrying patriotism to the market and principle to the devil."[776]

Another visitor, identified only as "a British traveler," claimed that the people were immoral, dishonest, and whatever was expedient was lawful: "Ambition being the most prominent feature in the American character, in no respect qualified by any principle of morality, or regard for the law of nations." The traveler said Yankees were the most unscrupulous bargainers, but the *Register* saw this as a badge of honor. "When a Yankee commits a fraud, there is so much humor and ingenuity in it, that it passes into the collection of good stories." The tales spread, and this practice "keeps alive the reputation of the Yankee trick; and it is the celebrity, not the frequency, of their frauds that has given them character."[777] Apparently Yankee frauds were so good that it was rather humorous that credulous people would let themselves be conned.

Cheating appeared to be a national pastime, from the massive land fraud schemes to the one-on-one swindle. Charles Latrobe and a companion reached St. Marks, Florida, where a pin connecting the fore and rear wheels of their wagon had just "disjointed" and dumped them onto the road. The community, said Latrobe, "though now in the hands of the most speculative people on earth," was "garrisoned by nothing but cocks, hens, pigs and rats," and seemed to be decaying into the swamp. Nevertheless, he found a blacksmith, the "yellow Vulcan," he called him, who would repair the wagon. They waited a few hours until "Vulcan" finished "and made us pay bountifully for what he assured us was a brand new pin." They had not gotten far down the road when the wagon broke down again and they discovered "he had taken us in, by patching the old one." Near Chillicothe, Ohio, James Flint and others came to a sawmill at Paint Creek, where a woman asked how the travelers proposed to cross. She told them there was neither bridge nor boat, the water would be near chest-high, but she did happen to have some horses they could hire. They paid, but at the creek they realized they had been had. "Some of our party, (now increased to five)," said Flint, "indignant at the hoax, waded the stream. The water did not reach

---

[776]   NWR, September 28, 1816, V. 11, No. 5, 67.
[777]   NWR, August 31, 1816, V. 11, No. 1, 6.

to the knee."[778]

Swindling was simply Yankee cunning in the indigenous lexicon. William Faux said Americans viewed law as an imposition. "Liberty here means to do each as he pleases; to care for nothing and nobody, to cheat everybody." James Flint compared notes with another English traveler who had also met with "considerable losses by villainous insolvencies." He had been conned. Flint figured his companion was too good-natured and credulous, "and that he had fallen into the hands of several artful rogues; a class, it would seem, not wanting in America."[779]

The scamming, often blamed on the greedy Yankee, was ubiquitous. As Patrick Shirreff said, "New Englanders are not the only sharpers in America." There were "accomplished Yankees" everywhere. "Most of the people are poor, and grasp at wealth," while "successful fraud is seen as clear gain." A person might move to a new territory, but, "Every new settler is liable to be beset by all the knaves and cheats of the district on his first arrival." Shirreff was distressed that "the greedy and dishonest intercourse which takes place in many parts of North Americas must be repugnant to honorable feeling," but an appeal to honor was not likely to gather much of an audience.[780]

The malady of dishonesty stretched from coast to coast. In the Rocky Mountains, Isabella Bird stopped in a Front Range canyon on the road to Estes Park, where she boarded with the Chalmers family, who had come from Illinois and had taken up a "squatter's claim" to sell eggs and butter to passing emigrants. Mr. Chalmers never could get his sawmill to operate and his "house" had more holes than walls. Bird called them "queer"; Mr. Chalmers was an intolerant religious bigot who hated almost everyone, their son was a wild, yet melancholy youth, their daughter, "a sour, repellant-looking creature, with as much manners as a pig," and there were three other "un-childlike" children. Their actions and speech reminded her of "works of the flesh," if not of "the devil." Their suspicions,

---

[778]   Latrobe, *Rambler in North America,* 53–54; Flint, *Letters from America,* 118.

[779]   William Faux, *Memorable Days in America: Being a Journal of a Tour to the United States* (London, 1823, 194, in Billington, *Land of Savagery,* 268; Flint, *Letters from America,* 48–49.

[780]   Shirreff, *Tour Through North America,* 408–09.

dishonesty, and demeanor repulsed her, and she lamented: "This is hard greed, and the exclusive pursuit of gain, with the indifference to all which does not aid in its acquisition, are eating up family love and life throughout the West."[781]

Greed and dishonesty were not only the purview of the small-time con man. After Commissioner McKenney completed his treaty-making tour of the West in 1827, he came under fire for allegedly distributing anti-Jackson handbills. He weathered that crisis, but soon was involved in a scandal that implicated Tennessee governor Sam Houston and War Secretary John Eaton, both close friends of Jackson. Houston, seeking to get rich, wanted a government contract to feed the Indians being removed. He had to bid against others, but did not want to lowball to be selected. Houston offered McKenney kickbacks if he got him the contract and wanted to limit the time to submit bids so those west of the Mississippi River would not have time to counter his offer. When McKenney demurred, Houston went to the lowest bidder, Luther Blake, and said that if he withdrew, Houston would see that he "should make more out of this step, than he could realize if he should get the contract." Blake was infuriated that Houston got to see the bids and had attempted "to defraud...the government." Blake's bid was eight cents per ration, while Houston's was eighteen cents, and would have made him more than four million dollars. When Houston's scheme was exposed, he stormed into McKenney's office, "grating his teeth, saying, 'You shall suffer for it.'"[782]

Sure enough, within six months, McKenney was dismissed from office with a curt note from a war department clerk, who was also Secretary Eaton's brother-in-law. McKenney asked why, and was told that "General Jackson has long been satisfied that you are not in harmony with him in his views in regard to the Indians."[783] Meanwhile, Houston married a nineteen-year-old girl, separated from her eleven weeks later, and the ensuing scandal drove him from the governors' office. He moved to Indian Territory, took a Cher-

---

[781]   Isabella L. Bird, *A Lady's Life in the Rocky Mountains* (Norman, OK: University of Oklahoma Press, 1960), 39, 46–48.

[782]   McKenney, *Memoirs*, xiv, xv, 210–12, 213–14, 216, 222.

[783]   Remini, *Jackson & His Indian Wars*, 240.

okee wife, ran a trading post, and was so often inebriated that the Cherokees called him the "Big Drunk." Sometimes acting as Indian agent, he came to Washington, where Ohio congressman William Stanbery brought up Houston's fraudulent rations contract. In the spring of 1832, Houston severely beat Stanbery with a cane. He was arrested, but got off with a reprimand and a $500 fine. Jackson remitted the fine for "divers [sic] good and sufficient reasons," and Houston entered the white world again. He ditched his Cherokee trading post, and, enticed by possible riches through land speculation, headed to Texas to become another one of those legendary "frontier heroes."[784]

"No better place than a schoolroom to judge the character of a people"

The illiteracy of frontier Americans was quite evident to foreigners. Once again, Tocqueville provided many observations. The constant promotion of equality contaminated education, he said, for although primary schooling was readily available, "secondary is in the reach of no one." People were not necessarily stupid, but at the same time only a few were educated. There was no class in America, Tocqueville said, "which passes to its descendants the love of intellectual pleasures" or "holds the labors of the intellect in high esteem." They were free of the influence of "that natural aristocracy of knowledge and virtue." Encountering the works of the antebellum folklorist-writers, Tocqueville despaired, saying that there were "only a small number of noteworthy authors, no great historians, and not a single poet." Americans looked on real literature with disdain, and any "third-rank European town" published more literary works than "the twenty-four states of the Union put together." The dislike for the upper classes was also evident in government. Democratic instincts removed distinguished, qualified men from power. Intelligent, able men who could govern were seen by most as too reserved, mannered, and principled to do so, and thus removed themselves from consideration. Tocqueville: "I hold it proved that those

---

[784]   J. R. Edmonson, *The Alamo Story: From Early History to Current Conflicts* (Plano, TX: Republic of Texas Press, 2000), 169–70.

who consider universal suffrage as a guarantee of the excellence of the choice made are under a complete delusion."[785]

Americans reveled in their anti-intellectualism. Tocqueville said that education diminished the farther one traveled west from the seaboard. Trained teachers were few. One applicant for a job as local schoolmaster could barely read or add. "I never was much to school in my life," he said. "I cyphered as fur as division, an' it wa'nt long till I forgot it all. I don't pretend to much school larnin nohow." He got the job. It did not matter much, because few people saw the need for education. As one Illinois settler told a visitor: folks "don't calculate that books and the sciences will do as much for a man in these matters as a handy use of the rifle."[786]

Charles Latrobe thought education in America was done with "undue haste" and ended only in the accumulation of "superficial knowledge." He saw the time as one of decay in reasoning powers, an increase in fiction, and a dearth of classical works, demonstrating a "disposition to deteriorate." Elias Fordham was appalled at the lack of schooling, and claimed that the daughters of Indiana "are completely destitute of education." James Flint commented on American credulity, given their superstitions, belief in fortune telling, zodiacs, almanac predictions, and snake-oil salesmen, and concluded "the culture of the mind is much neglected." At an Ohio post office, the customers asked others for help in reading the addresses on packages and letters. A local newspaper bewailed the lack of schools and said that Ohioans grew to manhood "with scarcely any other intelligence than that derived from the feeble light of nature." Flint believed that most American defects could be traced to poor education, which in turn stemmed from a lack of culture. "The teacher is thus rendered anything but that object of reverence which becomes his office," and the student "is practically taught to look down on the learned man as an inferior and to despise the most useful attainments."[787]

---

[785]   Tocqueville, *Democracy in America*, 65, 231, 352.

[786]   John Regan, *The Emigrant's Guide to the Western States of America* (Edinburgh, 1852), 242 ("cyphered" quotation), and Eliza Farnham, *Life in Prairie Land* (New York, 1846), 330 ("rifle" quotation), in Billington, *Land of Savagery*, 181.

[787]   Latrobe, *Rambler in North America*, 81; Fordham, *Personal Narrative of Travels*, 168; Flint, *Letters from America*, 152–53, 170–71.

Americans distrusted "elites," and even fellow countrymen who received an advanced education at one of the country's own institutions were suspect, scorned, and even hated. Americans, according to Patrick Shirreff, believed the most "odious" scheme they faced was "an aristocracy of knowledge, education and refinement, which is inconsistent with the true democratic principle of absolute equality. They pledge themselves, therefore, to exert every effort, mental and physical, for the abolition of this flagrant injustice." But since it was impossible to make the ignorant equal to the intelligent, they engaged in what today is called "dumbing-down." "[I]t is their professed object to reduce the latter to the same mental condition with the former; to prohibit all supererogatory knowledge; to have a maximum of acquirement, beyond which it shall be punishable to go."[788]

Commissioner McKenney was even more pointed. He affirmed that a greater percentage of Cherokees could read either English or their own language "than can be found among the whites in any States of the Union." In fact, many Indians in the nineteenth century read and wrote in English, and they published 6,700 pieces of work between 1772 and 1924.[789]

Tocqueville asserted that a primary education was available to almost everyone, but the problem was that primary education was limited in time and short on facts. If American education was a sea, it might have stretched from coast to coast, but it was barely ankle-deep. Ruth M. Elson studied schoolbooks in the nineteenth century, and verified much of what contemporaneous observers recorded. After the Bible, school texts were the most read books, and they served to guard and promote traditional religious, social, and cultural mores. The purpose of schools was to instill character, morals, virtue, and patriotism, rather than intellectual development. In the 1770s, schools taught reading, writing, math, and religion. By 1825, grammar and geography were added. History was not a requirement until after the Civil War. Schools only became free gradually between 1827 and 1855, and in 1852, Massachusetts was the first

---

[788]   Shirreff, *Tour Through North America*, 292.
[789]   McKenney, *Memoirs*, 34; William Cronon, et al., eds., *Under an Open Sky: Rethinking America's Western Past* (New York: W. W. Norton & Co., 1992), 66.

state to make schooling compulsory. Amazingly, in 1800, the average *lifetime* length of school attendance was only four months, which by 1850 had increased to only twenty-two months. Schoolbooks emphasized memorization of values as much as facts. Country life was always depicted as better than city life and agriculture was the best occupation, while farmers were portrayed as the backbone of the country. The sense of a vengeful Calvinist God permeated the texts. As the Enlightenment faded and the Romantic Age developed, the texts reflected the emphasis on nationality over universality, shaped by rising racism, bigotry, and xenophobia. It became the burden of exceptional Americans to civilize and enlighten the world, and if it meant destroying people and nations to convert them, so be it. Primary readers taught boys that it was fun to beat a drum and march with a gun, and a glorious thing to die for one's country. The world of nineteenth-century schoolbooks, said Elson, "is essentially a world of fantasy—a fantasy made up by adults as a guide for their children, but inhabited by no one outside the pages of schoolbooks." It was a God-controlled world of heroes and villains where nothing could alter Americans' march toward material and moral perfection.[790]

Francis J. Grund, a German-born American journalist and teacher, observed that "there was probably no better place than a schoolroom to judge the character of a people...In so humble a place...may be read the commentaries on the past, and the history of the future development of a nation."[791] It was perhaps unfortunate that those schoolchildren and their descendants actually took those "lessons" to heart.

Observers of the time claimed that Americans had a mawkish, saccharine sense of patriotism, that when partnered with a boisterous attitude of superiority, bordered on the repellant. The schoolbooks fostered the love of God, state, and country, and patriotism was "the noblest of the social virtues." Even the elementary

---

[790]   Ruth Miller Elson, *Guardians of Tradition: American Schoolbooks of the Nineteenth Century* (Lincoln, NE: University of Nebraska Press, 1964), vii, 1–2, 5–6, 9, 25–26, 42, 65, 68, 327, 328, 337 (quotation).
[791]   Francis J. Grund, *The Americans in their Moral, Social, and Political Relations, V. 1* (London: Longman, 1837), 228.

readers extolled dead heroes and drilled into children's heads that, "It is pleasant and glorious to die for one's country."[792] Englishman Charles Latrobe perceived Americans were so sanguine over their institutions and way of life because they did not study European history, where they would find plenty of examples to "prove the probable mutability of their governments—because they are in their youth, and have, they believe, set out on a more excellent principle and under more favourable circumstances than any people since the world began." Latrobe wished Americans well, but said, "God forbid that we should ever be mad enough to fancy their systems are fit for our imitation." It bothered him that any doubts expressed by foreigners were all assumed "to originate in prejudice and jealousy," while their lack of understanding history and their haughty manner "would incline me to doubt their wisdom or ultimate success."[793]

Latrobe detected traits that are still with us. He doubted that the people's character, education, and habits could ever foster the growth of genius because of the American penchant for "false praise, false standards of excellence, and a compliance with the vitiated taste and models of the age." Everyone received applause and flattery, "and where this poison is administered to a young mind, removed from the opportunities of making comparison between his own works and those of real and mature excellence, its bad effect is commonly irretrievably destructive of future and justly merited distinction." It would be America's misfortune if she encouraged "her sons to look no further than themselves for their standard of excellence."[794]

Where most of the visitors commented on the bombastic patriotism of Westerners, Lt. Francis Hall, 14th Light Dragoons, saw those traits in aristocratic Tidewater denizens and was not impressed. "They seem, especially the plantation-bred Virginians, to have more pretension than good sense: the insubordination, in which they glory, both to parental and scholastic authority, produces, as might be expected, a petulance of manner, and frothiness of intellect," which lets them immodestly compare themselves to the old Romans. "Vir-

---

[792]   Elson, *Guardians of Tradition*, 282–83.
[793]   Latrobe, *Rambler in North America*, 68–69.
[794]   Ibid., 80.

ginians feel destined to govern," and pompously believed others awaited their wisdom, so "the land is literally over-run with orators of all sorts and sizes, almost as numerous and noisy as the frogs in the plague of Egypt." The "stump-orators" and "Slang-whangers" could be "found in every hole and corner of the favoured land."[795]

Americans have flattered themselves as being the best and the brightest. Tocqueville saw its inception. The greatest freedom of thought went with the most entrenched prejudices. "When an idea has seized the mind of the American people, be it correct or unreasonable, nothing is harder than to rid them of it." Americans refused to countenance any derogatory talk about themselves or their country. "There is nothing more irksome in the conduct of life than the irritable patriotism Americans have." Their narcissism was nauseating. "Americans seem irritated by the slightest criticism and appear greedy for praise...Doubting their own worth, they could be said to need a constant illustration of it before their eyes. Their vanity is not only greedy, it is also restless and jealous. It grants nothing while making endless demands." Tocqueville tried pampering his American confidants with sufficient praise about the greatness of their nation, but it was never enough. "A more intrusive and garrulous patriotism would be hard to imagine. It wearies even those who respect it."[796]

Living in the germinal America before independence, Crevecoeur reflected on man's heinous nature, indulging in crime, avarice, rapine, murder, prejudice, slavery, and tyranny, and believed our very essence was poisoned. "We certainly are not of the class of beings which we vainly think ourselves to be; man an animal of prey, seems to have rapine and the love of bloodshed implanted in his heart; nay, to hold it the most honourable occupation in society: we never speak of a hero of mathematics, a hero of knowledge, of humanity; no, this illustrious appellation is reserved for the most successful butchers of the world."[797]

It was American exceptionalism at its roots.

---

[795]   Francis Hall, *Travels in Canada and the United States in 1816 and 1817* (London: A. Stratham, 1818), 392–96.

[796]   Tocqueville, *Democracy in America*, 217, 277, 710.

[797]   Crevecoeur, *American Farmer*, 113.

GREGORY MICHNO

Civilizing the White Frontier

Between the War of 1812 and the Mexican War, as America strove for a historical identity, it also made the descent from Enlightenment to Romance, from universality to individualism, from environment to race, from reason to religion. The degeneration began during the American Revolution, which was not the same as the Revolutionary War. The Revolutionary War was the physical fight—the Revolution was the metamorphosis of thought that enabled it. As historian Robert Parkinson explained in *The Common Cause*, the "patriots" needed to propagate war stories that would cement the colonies. They purposely embraced derogatory stereotypes and prejudices of murderous, treacherous blacks, Indians, and foreigners to promote fear and hate, because fear and hate were primeval compulsions that aroused outrage, not the echoing of ephemeral concepts such as the inalienable rights of man. The high ideals of the Declaration of Independence were mere images for world approbation; the underlying racism, bigotry, and xenophobia were the necessary ingredients to win a war.[798]

With America born in such a primordial soup of prejudice, blacks, Indians, and aliens never had a chance, and with Britain out of the picture after 1815, Americans need not pretend any longer that human rights issues were essential. If the eighteenth century emphasized progress of the human race, the nineteenth century emphasized distinction of the races and inequalities. The "sciences" of craniology and phrenology were used to prove the superiority of the white Anglo-Saxon, a maverick, freedom-loving, heroic character who was just the one to spread the American way of life around the world. Proponents strove to prove their theories: *monogenists* stuck with the Bible and its single creation story and said blacks and Indians degenerated from the pure sons of Adam; *polygenists* abandoned scripture and argued that the decadent blacks and Indians had to have come from separate creations. It was not accidental that a nation that allowed slavery and eradicated Indians would provide fertile ground for such concepts. After 1815, presumptions of Anglo superiority helped plough a path through obstructing blacks and

---

[798]   Parkinson, *Common Cause*, 8, 10, 17, 21, 22.

Indians; in the 1820s, Jefferson wrote in Turnerian themes, and by 1830, with the Indian Removal Act, Indian policies based on Enlightenment ideals were almost wholly defunct.[799]

It may be that Indian removal was a watershed moment in the transformation from assimilation to segregation and ethnic cleansing. C. Vann Woodward found that "Jim Crow" laws, a formal expression of postbellum segregation codes, and comparable to the antebellum black codes, actually had origins in the years of Indian removal. A song and dance routine called "Jim Crow" was written in 1832, and the term had become an adjective by 1838.[800] Blacks had been enslaved and degraded since America's inception, and now Indians were no longer noble savages, but murderous "red-skins" on the verge of eradication.

By enforcing the TIA, the antebellum army attempted to brake the Indians' snowballing slide into oblivion. It was also charged with protecting Indians during the very complicated, nearly overwhelming process of removal. Because of compulsion, resistance, fraud, lawlessness, and violence, the army was much more involved in safeguarding the Indians during their journey west than they were in escorting white emigrants during the succeeding decades. Although by the time of the final Cherokee removals in the late 1830s, the army attitude had hardened and there was likely more coercion than protection, the army supervised a massive diaspora. Americans celebrate the westward movement of white pioneers in their iconic covered wagons traveling the Oregon Trail, but the heroism and sorrow of the Indian trek is often forgotten. The numbers tell part of the tale. An estimated 350,000 emigrants used the Oregon Trail in twenty-five years from 1841 to 1866. In an 1836 war department report, Secretary Cass calculated that about 32,000 Indians had already emigrated since 1830, and about 62,000 more were in the process. Richard M. Johnson, chair of the Committee on Military Affairs, estimated that about 250,000 Indians would

---

[799]   Gould, *Mismeasure of Man*, 63, 71, 74; *Horsman, Race and Manifest Destiny*, 18, 43, 56, 84, 114, 300.

[800]   C. Vann Woodward, *The Strange Career of Jim Crow* (New York: Oxford University Press, 2002), 7.

emigrate.[801] Add the tens of thousands of Indians who had already relocated since 1815, and it is evident that the Indian migration was fully as encompassing and extraordinary as the later white migration. And, the Indian exodus was fraught with more menace from thieving whites than the Oregon Trail emigrants were at risk from the Western tribes, yet the novels and films of white men attacking emigrating Indians are virtually nonexistent.

As America metastasized during these years, the army—at least the officer corps—was a comparative bastion of integrity, civility, discretion, and fairness. They were tasked with upholding treaties and laws and impartially protecting whites and Indians, but after a time spent in the wilderness, they understood who the transgressors usually were and that their job had changed: their main mission became *civilizing the white frontier.* That too became an impossible task. Stymied at every turn, attacked, hated, sued, and jailed, the army realized it was shackled with a losing proposition. Caught in a quandary, the easier solution was, if you couldn't beat them, join them. With Enlightenment hopes of assimilation and brotherhood seemingly shattered by racialism and removal policies, it was only a matter of time before the army, once a wall between egregious white behavior and the Indians, could no longer hold back the tide.

A major reason for the army's change in attitude may have been the lack of support on the home front. They were arrested, censured and sued for removing intruders or whiskey sellers. They were unable to get a fair trial from local juries, and even the government seemed loathe to support them. Officers had to defend themselves with their own money and hope for reimbursement, but an unsympathetic Congress was often in the pay of private companies that were hostile to the army. Caught between angry citizens and an often indifferent government, officers might have to choose between pecuniary ruin and disobedience of orders. Frontier officers realized that the Indians were very much less their enemy than the patriotic citizens they were supposed to defend, but they had to make a choice. The season of the army trying to enforce the TIA and pro-

---

[801]   Merrill J. Mattes, *The Great Platte River Road* (Lincoln, NE: Nebraska State Historical Society, 1969), 23; Cass to Johnson, February 19, 1836, Johnson to House of Representatives, March 3, 1836, ASPMA, V. 6, 149–54.

tect the Indians was over. It may have been easier and initially less costly for officers to avert their eyes when frontiersmen ran riot, but the slackening of army control was counterproductive. It may have made for fewer run-ins with the civilians, but it sanctioned more aggressive white behavior and increased fighting with the Indians of the plains, deserts, and mountains. So, the army only shifted adversaries; seeing the hopelessness of restraining the whites, it abdicated TIA enforcement and tacitly sanctioned white aggression.

Students of American history may be struck by the hiatus in Indian wars between the War of 1812 and the end of the Mexican War. With the exception of the Black Hawk and Seminole Wars, the notable lack of other Indian conflicts during the interregnum was much the result of the restraining influence of West Point officers. When the Mexican war infused the army with hundreds of new officers appointed from civilian life, the Academy-officered army was diluted by men possessing the frontier personalities they reviled. The frustrations with being bypassed for promotion by political favorites and armchair generals from civilian life, plus public animosity, non-support of the government, increasing racism and intolerance, the figurative transformation of Indians into a sub-human vanishing race, and the marketing of Anglo-Saxon superiority, led the army to rationalize its way into viewing the Indian, not the frontier white, as the real enemy. By the late 1820s the army was already feeling the full effects of the monster that had been created by the Revolutionary Generation. The Founders had made a pact with the Devil and the army had to pay the piper. It could not cope.

The attitude adjustment took time. Attacks by regulars against Indians increased after the Mexican War, but is was uneven across various frontiers. For instance, in California in May of 1850, Pomo Indians were accused of killing miners, but instead of investigating as the pre-war army might have done, Capt. Nathaniel Lyon and Lt. John W. Davidson attacked camps on Clear Lake and Russian River, killing more than 130 Pomos, with one of the scenes described by Lyon as "a perfect slaughter pen." In Nebraska in September, 1855, Col. William S. Harney attacked a Lakota village at Bluewater Creek. In command of the dragoons was Lt. Col. Philip St. George Cooke, who had once censured the unmanageable Illinois volunteers during the Black Hawk War, but now led regulars whose behavior was much like the volunteers.[802]

On the other hand, 1st Dragoon Col. Edwin V. Sumner retained his pre-war distrust of civilians who cried wolf. In 1837, Sumner had nearly gone to war with Missouri civilians who had wrongly accused and attacked Osages. Appointed military commander in New Mexico in 1851, he verbally battled with territorial governor James S. Calhoun and the civilians who constantly made false depredation accusations against the Utes and Jicarillas. Sumner challenged Calhoun to "state to me the scenes of desolation" Indians had caused, but Calhoun could not, and Sumner even threatened that if the "pernicious" whites continued to attack the Indians the army would punish them.[803]

Nevertheless, army officers became more reluctant to challenge civilian authority. The Civil War experience may have further damaged their discipline. After four long years of internecine warfare that included devastating battle casualties, vicious guerrilla fighting, draft riots, prison starvation, and murders of surrendered prisoners, the post-war army emerged toughened, cynical, and in no mood to suffer recalcitrant Indians. Battle-hardened, Generals William T. Sherman and Philip H. Sheridan approached Indian fighting with a very different attitude than did most antebellum officers. One statement attributed to Sheridan was emblematic: "The only good Indians I ever saw were dead." The army, now fully inculcated with the Darwin-Spencer concepts of survival of the fittest and the current racial and cultural stereotypes, made Indian-killing much less onerous.[804]

Drawing the army down a darker path during the post-Civil War "Gilded Age" was the incorporation and mechanization of America. Historian Alan Trachtenberg argued that this transformation begat increased xenophobia, racism, bigotry, social and cultural conflicts, and military aggression. Incorporation brought imposed solutions, not diplomacy or compromise. Land and natural resources were essential in this new regime, and no Indian obstruction would

---

[802]   Michno, *Encyclopedia of Indian Wars,* 6, 34–35.

[803]   Michno, *Depredation and Deceit,* 126, 133–35.

[804]   Paul Andrew Hutton, *Phil Sheridan and His Army* (Lincoln, NE: University of Nebraska Press, 1985), 100, 180.

be tolerated—the mechanization of violence would accelerate the drift. In 1849, Indian affairs were taken out of the hands of the War Department and placed with the Department of the Interior. After the Civil War, the military wanted to regain control, and General Sherman urged "the utter destruction and subjugation" of all who got in the way. Indians' free-roaming, pastoral way of life was no longer viewed in saccharine terms, but as the antithesis to productivity, property, and profit.[805]

Frontiersmen were not a bunch of little Crevecoeurs rambling through the woods, singing odes to daffodils, but the army's role in restraining them helped solidify the bucolic image of America. The antebellum army tried to keep the machine out of the garden, but failed; the postbellum army abandoned the moral high ground and helped pave the way for a callous, mechanized incorporation. The army discovered that frontiersmen couldn't shoot straight, figuratively and literally, but that only made them more dangerous. Early on, it saw that frontiersmen could act as terrorists, even in twenty-first century terms. First used to describe actions of the government of the French Revolution in the 1790s, the United Nations in 2005 defined terrorism as any action that "is intended to cause death or serious bodily harm to civilians and non-combatants, with the purpose of intimidating a population or compelling a Government or international organization to do or abstain from doing an act."[806]

As such, Americans attacking Mexico and Canada, or blacks and Indians, in contravention of the law, to intimidate, expel, or exterminate, fit the definition. Today we are concerned about foreign terrorists, but home-grown ones have operated for three hundred years. It is not new, but we have been loath to enunciate it, let alone acknowledge it as a seminal element of who we are. The government and the army never could successfully deal with the frontiersmen and realized that they were much more at risk from the civilians than vice versa. It was disconcerting to discover the killer was calling

---

[805]   Alan Trachtenberg, *The Incorporation of America: Culture and Society in the Gilded Age* (New York: Hill and Wang, 1982), ix, x, 30–31, 37.

[806]   "Annan lays out detailed five-point UN strategy to combat terrorism," *UN News Centre*, http://www.un.org/apps/news/story.asp?NewsID=13599#. WmjUR2wwtPY

from a phone inside your own house. Ultimately unable to cope with American terrorists, the government and army abdicated and joined in. Frontiersmen were not heroes to be exalted, but our chronic glorification of them may partially explain why we have fragmented into the destructive political, racial, ethnic, and religious divisions so palpable in the nation today. The *Little House on the Prairie* tale was a fantasy, a white dream of wholesomeness and exceptionalism that was pure myth. America never could build a wall long, strong, or tall enough to keep out terrorists, imported or home-grown. Observers mentioned something peculiar about Americans, speculating that their behavior was caused by something in the woods, something in the wilderness, something in the sun, or something in the soil. True, the soil was there, tractable and verdant, but nourishing to either good seed or bad. The environment cannot take the blame when so many Americans themselves were the bad seeds.

History as a Defense Mechanism

James Madison wrote that there was "a degree of depravity in mankind which requires a certain degree of circumspection and distrust," and although he likely used the word "mankind" as a collective allusion to the human race, there were plenty of homegrown references to reflect upon.[807] For more than two centuries Americans have been saturated with the idea that they are an upright, extraordinary people, but it stems from self-adulation, a narcissism deep within. The frontiersman we later fashioned as the consummate prototype and painted with a gilded veneer had a very different core. The frontiersmen-pioneers-settlers who were the foundation of American myth were often very unsavory. From the beginning, the U. S. government and military knew they were tasked with restraining an avaricious, belligerent people. They wanted land and took it. They attacked and killed Indians. They stole public lands or fraudulently secured title to them. They stole houses, property, timber, and slaves. They falsely accused Indians of depredations. Ostensibly individualists who wanted the government out of their lives, they begged for government assistance. They boasted of their heroism and prowess with guns, but were often poor marksmen who ran away from bat-

[807]   Madison, *Federalist Papers,* 275.

tles. They distrusted the army, but cried for its help whenever they got into a scrape. They sought to destroy the academy that supplied the army officers. They fought the army on the battlefield and in the courts. They rioted. They acted as terrorists. They could be hateful, racist, bigoted, and xenophobic. They were anti-intellectual. They were self-righteous. While very often the aggressors, they saw themselves as victims. Where the poet picked flowers and the historian picked fruit, the common man often peculated in offal.

Does it seem we have constructed too many straw men to cut off at the knees? Certainly there were other players who acted with such reckless licentiousness, but they were never placed in a Pantheon of illustrious dead to be eulogized in the public memory. Because frontiersmen have been sculpted into something they never were, and continue to be glorified as mythical heroes, demystification is absolutely necessary. The New Western historians of the latter twentieth century have debunked Turner, but if Turner was wrong and even irrelevant, his ideas are still strong. The public never lost its love for adventurous, romantic Western histories in novels or film, because myth remains stronger than academic opinion. Historians may be bored with the Western image, but cliché for scholars is still galvanizing for most Americans. The frontier myth remains.[808]

Why is it so difficult to debunk? What is the hold it has upon us? Perhaps because as a newborn nation in the 1780s, we had no history. As a young republic we struggled for an identity—we had no writers or poets, no "high claims upon which to build a national character."[809] With few traditions, and, with the possible exception of George Washington, no great generals, statesmen, artists, poets, or philosophers, no Lionheart, Nelson, or Wellington to carve from stone and place on a pedestal, we vainly searched for an icon. Our solution was perhaps the height of narcissism and conceit. We adopted the frontiersman, otherwise incarnated as Jefferson's yeoman farmer or Jackson's common man, and consecrated, venerated, and deified him. The frontiersman-commoner—so far from a god in the early to mid-nineteenth century—had to be re-crafted into some-

---

[808]   Cronon, et al., eds., *Under an Open Sky*, 4–5; Patricia Limerick et al., eds., *Trails: Toward a New Western History* (Lawrence, KS: University Press of Kansas, 1991), 69, 83.
[809]   NWR, September 28, 1816, V. 11, No. 5, 69.

thing much more appropriate. Our god had been created and molded into "us"—we became our god.

One might be reminded of Vespasian in 79 CE. As Sueto-
nius reported, the Roman Emperor was to have called out, "Vae,
puto deus fio." ("Dear me, I think I'm becoming a god"). People
need to love (and fear) their gods, so we had to redesign the reality
of a scheming semi-savage into the flattering image of an exceptional American. Since our behavior was inconsistent with that image, there was a serious problem of cognitive dissonance to alleviate.
People want to feel good about themselves and they expect that they
will practice good, moral, competent behavior. When their behavior
violates their self-expectations, dissonance is increased. The more
disparate the perceptions, the greater the need to correct them. A
remedy might be to change attitudes about poor past behavior and
admit error, or to artificially mitigate the reality of the poor behavior
by re-drawing the past into something it was not.[810] In other words,
align your ideas with your behavior or live with a perpetual brain
cramp. America chose to re-write its history.

The solution was a double-edged sword. Had we not done
so, the psychological discord would never have allowed us to reshape
the frontiersman into an idol that we could anthropomorphize as
ourselves. But because we chose that path, we walk on an eternal
ladder of dissonance. Any option we choose to rationalize our forefathers' behavior only resolves it halfway and opens the door to more
dissonance. We rationalize again to ease our minds, trying to find a
way to explain evil under an allegedly good God. The process, which
cannot be explained or justified by a belief in a virtuous God, leads
us to irrational beliefs. Opposition to reason leads to anti-intellectualism, which greases the slide into more irrationality. Often events do
not fall into the patterns we construct, and these perceptual failures,
with the right combinations and coincidences, can lead to superstition. We may see conspiracies and feel we are victims. Victims of
imagined conspiracies have more dissonance and seek further justifi-
cations to rectify them. It is a self-perpetuating machine of delusion

---

[810]   Leon Festinger, Henry W. Riecken, and Stanley Schacter, *When Prophesy Fails* (London: Pinter & Martin, 2005), viii, 3; Joel Cooper, *Cognitive Dissonance: Fifty Years of a Classic Theory* (London: Sage Publications Ltd., 2007), 2, 6–8, 96–97.

stoked by a centuries-long attempt to pretend we are something we are not. Comfort the mind and ease the slide into memory oblivion. Create a bogus narrative that facilitates a creation myth, a chosen people tale, a pioneer expansion celebration, a lost cause legend, or a Christian crusade. Fairy tales can be more soothing than reality. So, here is an alternative to Turner's rosy version of genesis: *American history is a defense mechanism to ease the cognitive dissonance caused by conscious misrepresentation of our frontier past in order to sustain our narcissism.*

There are no direct causes and effects and we search in vain for them. We love order, and try to find it where it is not. There is no direction to history, and it has no life, no mind, and no ability to form itself in cycles. There is nothing intrinsic about it that would lend itself to recurring patterns as we find in the seasons. History is not nature. Events simply flow from a continuous escalation of dissonance reduction. It is similar to a Hegelian pattern of thesis and antithesis trying to reach a synthesis—the ring on the merry-go-round that is forever just out of reach. An honest man can lose his ideals very gradually and unknowingly by rationalizing away inconsistencies. But self-justification is more dangerous than an explicit lie, because outwardly we may fool others, but inside, the soothed conscience simply allows one to increase the lie. One may end up committing horrendous actions that were initially inconceivable while standing on the first rung of that cognitive dissonance ladder.[811]

We have constructed an origin myth of self-glorification. In an individual, delusion of grandeur is the belief that one possesses superior qualities such as genius, fame, or omnipotence, and is most often a symptom of schizophrenia, but it can also be a symptom in psychotic or bipolar disorders. Grandiose delusions may have religious content, such as believing that one has received a special message from God. Sometimes this disorder is called "megalomania," but it is more accurately referred to as narcissistic personality disorder. In such disorders, patients have an exaggerated sense of their own worth and value.[812] Americans believed that it was their

---

[811] Carol Tavris, and Elliot Aronson, *Mistakes Were Made (but not by me): Why we Justify Foolish Beliefs, Bad Decisions, and Hurtful Acts* (Orlando, FL: Harcourt, Inc., 2007), 4–5, 10, 37.

[812] John M. Grohal, "Delusion of Grandeur," *PsychCentral,* https://psych-central.com/encyclopedia/delusion-of-grandeur/

manifest destiny to spread their brand of truth, justice, democracy, and Christianity to the world. From uncertainty, to proclivity, to conviction, to proselytization, to crusade, emboldened by their own propaganda, they set forth to remake the world in their image. But a nation constructed on a delusion of grandeur may be primed for a disastrous fall. Indoctrinating ourselves as the common-man Deity has not served us well. Americans outdid Vespasian: they not only molded themselves into icons, but trivialized and expanded the schema into a coast-to-coast "Gods 'R Us," serving only to further harm their image.

Old Frontiersmen Never Die

Try as historians may, they are unable to redefine the mythical hold a frontier-induced American exceptionalism has on our psyches. Turner has been debunked ad infinitum, but the frontiersman image he helped create will not go away. Part of the problem is that only handfuls of people read American history, while millions watch movies that paint a completely different picture. The acerbic American writer, Gore Vidal, who believed he was witnessing the end of American civilization, said that books were outmoded— movies and television had long eclipsed the press, and it was time to scrap the existing educational system and just show the students movies. Film would be the "great repository of historical consciousness in these United States of Amnesia. For many, Hollywood History is the only history."[813]

In 1893, Turner declared in his famous essay that the frontier was closed. The movie counterpart may have been in 1962, when the total number of Western movies and television series nosedived. *How the West Was Won*, said to be the last flicker of American innocence, was the closing paean to a genre that had passed its zenith. But also appearing that year were the elegiac Westerns *Lonely are the Brave*, *Ride the High Country*, and *The Man Who Shot Liberty Valence*, which all lionized men and times whose relevance had faded away— the latter film giving us the often quoted line: "This is the West, sir.

---

[813] Mark C. Carnes, ed., *Past Imperfect: History According to the Movies* (New York: Henry Holt and Company, 1996), 9.

When the legend becomes fact, print the legend."[814]

Film historian Michael Coyne wrote that the American "propensity for national narcissism" will not go away. A decade later, the 1972 film *The Life and Times of Judge Roy Bean* opened with the preface, "Maybe this isn't the way it was...it's the way it should have been." In the 1990s there was another resurgence of the Western, with films like *Dances with Wolves*, *Unforgiven*, and *Tombstone*, although under postmodernist terms with generic destabilization and questioning of traditional myths and master narratives.[815] While the Western can no longer take its old central themes for granted, it keeps regenerating like the unrelenting killers in contemporaneous, postmodern horror films.

While film reviewers, critics, and historians recorded the subordination of fact to legend and finally discovered there was no more "West" to win, and while it was long past time that we progressed to different themes, the public resisted, and Hollywood continued to give us what were essentially Westerns, replacing cowboys and Indians with cops and robbers, urban vigilantes, and even outer space heroes and villains. Where the baby boomers grew up on Hopalong Cassidy, the Lone Ranger, and Roy Rogers, the generation X'ers, sometimes called the "MTV generation," grew up with new heroes like Dirty Harry, Rambo, Luke Skywalker, Frodo Baggins, and Harry Potter. Only the names have changed. They continue to reinforce the dominant, polarized, cultural tendencies of managing conflict: deadly violence. Some observers of society still view it as Leo Marx did in the 1960's: Americans living a puerile fantasy, an adolescent culture perennially frozen in adolescent motives and angst.[816]

Some historians have argued that American audiences are not stupid—that they know the Western history they see on film is not a true record of their past, while others have disagreed, noting the difference between book readers and moviegoers is that moviegoers "basically think that whatever they see is true." The gullibility of the latter was highlighted in a film that satirized itself. In *Little Big*

---

[814]   Coyne, *Crowded Prairie*, 106–107, 115, 118–19.

[815]   Coyne, *Crowded Prairie*, 8; Janet Walker, ed. *Westerns: Films Through History* (New York: Routledge, 2001), 28.

[816]   Gregory Desilet, *Our Faith in Evil: Melodrama and the Effects of Entertainment Violence* (Jefferson, NC: McFarland & Co., Inc., 2006), 265, 275, 289–90.

Man (1970), snake-oil salesman Alardyce T. Merriwether told the young, naïve Jack Crabb that "two legged creatures will believe anything, and the more preposterous the better."[817]

Americans, nevertheless, remain mired in the exceptionalism fallacy: the notion that they are a people committed to freedom and justice, and have a God-given duty to disseminate their way of life to the world, even to the point of interference and intervention in foreign nations. The myth that subsumes us makes us emotionally susceptible to appeals of a sinister nature; "a perennial disposition that can be readily exploited for ideological purposes."[818] When American propaganda and myth are inseparable, benevolence shares the saddle with bellicosity.

Michael Kammen, in *Mystic Chords of Memory*, provided many cogent, sustaining insights: Americans have highly selective memories; invocations of the past can be used for innovation or resisting change; history is used for defining national or personal identity; the past can be used to serve partisan purposes; and memory is hard to separate from patriotism. Where ancient mythmaking centered on taking gods and goddesses and making them more human, American mythmaking was the reverse: we took ordinary men, some very unsavory, and made impossible idealized abstractions out of them. "We prefer plasticized apotheosis to historicized memory developed in judicious doses."[819]

Thus, entered the frontiersmen, followed by his black-sheep cousin, the cowboy.

Tim McCoy, an actor in many "B westerns" of the 1920s and 1930s, said shortly before his death in 1978 that he was disturbed at the recent movie trend where the heroes were out and the bad guys were in. "Why this is," he said, "I do not know...But I do mourn the passing of the hero, for we gave the young people

---

[817] Edward Buscombe and Roberta E. Pearson, eds., *Back in the Saddle Again: New Essays on the Western* (London: British Film Institute, 1998), 6; Carnes, ed., *Past Imperfect*, 23 ("see is true" quotation); Jacqueline Kilpatrick, *Celluloid Indians: Native Americans and Film* (Lincoln, NE: University of Nebraska Press, 1999), 87 ("two legged" quotation).

[818] Buscombe and Pearson, eds., *Back in the Saddle*, 61.

[819] Michael Kammen, *Mystic Chords of Memory: The Transformation of Tradition in American Culture* (New York: Vintage Books, 1993), 10, 12, 28.

someone to look up to, a figure to emulate, and, more often than is generally supposed, imposed upon ourselves an obligation to be true to that image. If people must live their lives cast in various parts, why should the prevailing roles not be dedicated to the highest standards and principles?" McCoy was consumed by the myth that the characters he played in the movies were the "good guys," a perception that does not stand up to analysis. Nostalgia and sentiment tell us less about reality than about our fantasies and anxieties.[820]

Of course we should scrupulously strive for lofty principles, but the invented Westerner McCoy portrayed did not exist—more historically accurate was the frontiersman who was paradoxically good, bad, and ugly. In a previous book, my argument was that Westerns of the latter twentieth century had succeeded in destroying the heroic images that McCoy lamented losing. My support of McCoy's paean to a past golden age was probably too tinged with nostalgia for a past that never was. As a baby boomer engrossed in the myth of Davy Crockett, I too, was part of the problem. As a historian, one might try to make amends. Where America finds itself today is partly because of how it has misrepresented its past. C. Vann Woodward warned of the perils of presentism, but said that since a historian lives in the present, he has obligations to the present as well as the past. The present begins the questioning. We cannot correct our errors without queries involved with the present. On the other hand, historian Patricia Limerick said a historian who believes that understanding the present will deepen our understanding of the past "will eventually have to eat crow."[821]

Back in the 1930s, de-bunkers tried tarnishing the celebrity image of the Daniel Boone and Davy Crockett characters. When Boone's role in the founding of Kentucky was minimized at a public commemoration, his devotees disrupted the ceremony as they walked off the stage in tears. The heroic Disney "Frontierland"

---

[820] Tim McCoy with Ronald McCoy, *Tim McCoy Remembers the West* (Lincoln, NE: University of Nebraska Press, 1988), 263–64.

[821] Gregory F. Michno and Susan J. Michno, *Circle the Wagons! Attacks on Wagon Trains in History and Hollywood Films* (Jefferson, NC: McFarland & Company, Inc., 2009), 196–200; C. Vann Woodward, *Thinking Back: The Perils of Writing History* (Baton Rouge, LA: Louisiana State University Press, 1986), 98; Patricia Limerick, *Something in the Soil: Legacies and Reckonings in the New West* (New York: W. W. Norton & Company, 2000), 155.

image ruled the 1950s and persisted into the 1980s. Scholars who discovered documents that suggested Crockett surrendered at the Alamo and was executed received hate mail and were labeled Communists. The Daughters of the Republic of Texas decided that John Wayne's version of events in the 1960 movie *The Alamo* was correct, while opposing views were dead wrong. As Michael Kammen concluded, myth beats fact, and mass culture and learned culture went on their separate paths.[822]

With their antediluvian belief in good and evil, Americans crave villains, but treasure their heroes. Many of the baby boomers, and perhaps some gen-X'ers and millennials, still venerate the frontiersmen-pioneers as the quintessential core of American exceptionalism, but as those generations fade away, perhaps a younger, more skeptical generation will correct that image and create a new myth. Still, historians have attempted that for half a century with only limited success. The moralistic maxim ascribed to Crockett, "Be always sure you're right, then go ahead," was also said to have been a major tenet of the John Wayne-type philosophy—and a paradigm of the ugly American.[823] We still love being descendants of the frontier gods we created. But legend is not fact. The idea that history is a separate force is a bedtime story—and it never ends—it is a timeless repetition of folly and correction.[824]

Return for a moment to 1836, after Davy Crockett had gone to Texas. A Democratic North Carolina newspaper, glad he was gone, called him "an illiterate buffoon and bully, with scarcely learning enough to write or spell his own name correctly." On March 3, the paper announced his death: "Davy Crockett's − last! − Rumor says Col. Davy Crockett, the congressional Whig buffoon, died soon after reaching Texas."[825]

Having anticipated and welcomed the incident that actually occurred three days later, the editorialist could not anticipate the consequences—apotheosis of a flawed archetype. We deified a bul-

---

[822]   Kammen, *Mystic Chords of Memory,* 489, 647.

[823]   "Be sure you're right, then go ahead," https://crockettlives.wordpress.com/2012/04/15/remembering-the-duke/ (accessed February 15, 2018).

[824]   Edward Luce, *The Retreat of Western Liberalism* (New York: Atlantic Monthly Press, 2017), 10–11.

[825]   North Carolina *Standard (Raleigh),* March 3, March 17, 1836.

lying buffoon and called him us—the personification of white trash hubris. Frontiersmen could be ignorant, avaricious, swindlers, terrorists, racists, bigots, and bullies who could neither shoot straight nor be straight shooters. But old frontiersmen never die—they don't even fade away. Today, modern Jacksonian populists wistfully seek a non-existent mythical past, offering a cure that is worse than the disease. They walk among us, still toting guns, still anti-intellectual, still in fear of those who dress or worship differently, and still assured of their righteousness—their legacy a haunting reminder of James Madison's warning: "Ignorance will be the dupe of cunning."[826] In the wake of the latest acts of gun violence, or racial, religious, and ethnic intolerance, Americans offer up their thoughts and prayers and repeat the chant, "We are better than this. This is not who we are."

Maybe it is.

---

[826]   Madison, *Federalist Papers,* 288.

BIBLIOGRAPHY

Frequently cited sources:

AGO: Letters Received by the Office of the Adjutant General, Main Series 1822–1860, National Archives and Records Administration, Record Group 94.

ANC: *Army and Navy Chronicle, and Scientific Repository*. 14 volumes. Benjamin Homans, William Q. Force, eds. Washington: T. Barnard, 1835–1842.

ASPC: American State Papers, Claims. 1 volume, 1789 – 1823.

ASPFR: American State Papers, Foreign Relations. 6 volumes, 1789 – 1828.

ASPIA: American State Papers, Indian Affairs. 2 volumes, 1789 – 1827.

ASPMA: American State Papers, Military Affairs. 7 volumes, 1789 – 1838.

ASPPL: American State Papers, Public Lands. 8 volumes, 1789 – 1837.

NNR: *Niles' National Register*. William O. Niles, Jeremiah Hughes, eds. Baltimore and Washington: 1837–1849. 22 volumes.

NWR: *Niles' Weekly Register*. Hezekiah Niles, ed. Baltimore, MD: 1811–1837. 52 volumes.

TPUS: Carter, Clarence Edwin, ed. *The Territorial Papers of the United States*. 28 volumes. Washington: GPO, 1934–1969.

USCSS: *United States Congressional Serial Set*, 23rd Congress, Senate Doc. 512, "Correspondence on the Subject of the Emigration of Indians," 1831–1833, 5 volumes.

Abel, Annie Heloise. "The History of Events Resulting in Indian Consolidation West of the Mississippi," *Annual Report of the American Historical Association for the Year 1906*, 2 vols. Washington, DC: American Historical Association, 1908.

The American Whig Review, aka *The American Review: A Whig Journal*. New York: Wiley and Putnam, 1844–1852.

"An Act to Regulate Trade and Intercourse with the Indian Tribes and to Preserve Peace on the Frontiers." http://avalon.law.yale.edu/18th_century/na030.asp

Annals of the Congress of the United States 1789–1824. Fourth Congress, 1st Session, Volume 5, December 7, 1795 to June 1, 1796. Washington D. C., Gales and Seaton, 1834–1856.

"Annan lays out detailed five-point UN strategy to combat terrorism." *UN News Centre.* http://www.un.org/apps/news/storyasp?News ID=13599#.WmjUR2wwtPY

Aron, Stephen. *How the West was Lost: The Transformation of Kentucky from Daniel Boone to Henry Clay.* Baltimore, MD: Johns Hopkins University Press, 1996.

Beecher, Lyman. *A Plea for the West.* Bedford, MS: Applewood Books, nd. First published Cincinnati, OH: Truman & Smith, 1835.

Bellesiles, Michael A. *Arming America: The Origins of a National Gun Culture.* New York, Vintage Books, 2000.

Berwanger, Eugene H. *The Frontier Against Slavery: Western Anti-Negro Prejudice and the Slavery Extension Controversy.* Urbana, IL: University of Illinois Press, 1967.

Billington, Ray Allen. *Land of Savagery Land of Promise: The European Image of the American Frontier in the Nineteenth Century.* New York: W. W. Norton & Co. 1981.

_____. *The Protestant Crusade 1800–1860: A Study of the Origins of American Nativism.* Rinehart & Company, Inc. 1952.

Bird, Isabella L. *A Lady's Life in the Rocky Mountains.* Introduction by Daniel J. Boorstin. Norman, OK: University of Oklahoma Press, 1960.

Black Hawk. *Life of Black Hawk.* Milo Milton Quaife, ed. New York: Dover Publications, Inc., 1994.

Bogue, Allan G. *Frederick Jackson Turner: Strange Roads Going Down.* Norman, OK: University of Oklahoma Press, 1998.

Bowes, John P. *Land too Good for Indians: Northern Indian Removal.* Norman, OK: University of Oklahoma Press, 2016.

Boylston, James R. and Allen J. Weiner. *David Crockett in Congress: The Rise and Fall of the Poor Man's Friend.* Houston, TX: Bright Sky Press, 2009.

Bryant, William Cullen. *The Prose Writings of William Cullen Bryant, V. 2.* Parke Godwin, ed. New York: D. Appleton & Company, 1889.

Buckley, Jay H. *William Clark Indian Diplomat.* Norman, OK: University of Oklahoma Press, 2008.

Buscombe, Edward and Roberta E. Pearson, eds. *Back in the Saddle Again: New Essays on the Western.* London: British Film Institute, 1998.

Carnes, Mark C., ed. *Past Imperfect: History According to the Movies.* New York: Henry Holt and Company, 1996.

Cash, W. J. *The Mind of the South*. New York: Vintage Books, 1991.

Coffman, Edward M. *The Old Army: A Portrait of the American Army in Peacetime, 1784–1898*. New York: Oxford University Press, 1986.

Congressional Globe, 25th Congress.

Cooke, Philip St. George. *Scenes and Adventures in the Army: Or, Romance of Military Life*. Santa Barbara, CA: The Narrative Press, 2004. Originally published Philadelphia, PA: Lindsay & Blackston, 1857.

Cooper, Thomas Cooper. *Two Essays: On the Foundation of Civil Government; On the Constitution of the United States*. New York: Da Capo Press, 1970. Originally published 1826.

Coyne, Michael. *The Crowded Prairie: American National Identity in the Hollywood Western*. New York: I. B. Taurus Publishers, 1997.

Cramer, Clayton E. *Armed America: The Remarkable Story of How and Why Guns Became as American as Apple Pie*. Nashville, TN: Nelson Current, 2006.

Crevecoeur, J. Hector St. John de. *Letters from an American Farmer*. Mineola, NY: Dover Publications, Inc., 2005. Originally published 1783.

Crockett, David. *The Autobiography of David Crockett*. Introduction by Hamlin Garland. New York: Charles Scribner's Sons, 1923.

Cronon, William, George Miles and Jay Gitlin, eds. *Under an Open Sky: Rethinking America's Western Past*. New York: W. W. Norton & Co., 1992.

Dauber, Michelle Landis. *The Sympathetic State: Disaster Relief and the Origins of the American Welfare State*. Chicago: University of Chicago Press, 2013.

Dauber, Michelle L. *The War of 1812, September 11th, and the Politics of Compensation*. V. 53, DePaul Law Revue, 2013: 289–354.

Denham, James M. *"A Rogue's Paradise" Crime and Punishment in Antebellum Florida, 1821–1861*. Tuscaloosa, AL: University of Alabama Press, 1997.

Desilet, Gregory. *Our Faith in Evil: Melodrama and the Effects of Entertainment Violence*. Jefferson, NC: McFarland & Co., Inc., 2006.

Dorson, Richard M. *American Folklore*. Chicago, IL: University of Chicago Press, 1959.

Dray, Philip. *At the Hands of Persons Unknown: The Lynching of Black America*. New York: The Modern Library, 2003.

Edmonson, J. R. *The Alamo Story: From Early History to Current Conflicts*. Plano, TX: Republic of Texas Press, 2000.

Ellisor, John T. *The Second Creek War: Interethnic Conflict and Collusion on a Collapsing Frontier*. Lincoln, NE: University of Nebraska Press, 2010.

Elson, Ruth Miller. *Guardians of Tradition: American Schoolbooks of the Nineteenth*

Century. Lincoln, NE: University of Nebraska Press, 1964.

Feldberg, Michael. *The Turbulent Era: Riot and Disorder in Jacksonian America*. New York: Oxford University Press, 1980.

Feldman, Jay. *When the Mississippi Ran Backwards: Empire, Intrigue, Murder, and the New Madrid Earthquakes*. New York: Free Press, 2005.

Ferling, John. *Adams vs. Jefferson: The Tumultuous Election of 1800*. New York: Oxford University Press, 2004.

Finley, James B. *Life Among the Indians; or, Personal Reminiscences and Historical Incidents Illustrative of Indian Life and Character*. Cincinnati, OH: Methodist Book Concern, 1860.

Flint, James. *Flint's Letters from America, 1818–1820*. Cleveland, OH: The Arthur H. Clark Company, 1904.

Fordham, Elias Pym. Frederic Austin Ogg, ed. *Personal Narrative of Travels in Virginia, Maryland, Pennsylvania, Ohio, Indians, Kentucky; and of a Residence in the Illinois Territory: 1817–1818*. Leopold Classical Library, nd. Originally published Cleveland, OH: Arthur H. Clark Co., 1906.

Foreman, Grant. *Indian Removal: The Emigration of the Five Civilized Tribes of Indians*. Norman, University of Oklahoma Press, 1953.

————. *Indians & Pioneers: The Story of the American Southwest Before 1830*. Norman, University of Oklahoma Press, 1936.

Franklin, Benjamin. *The Life and Writings of Benjamin Franklin*, vol. 2. Philadelphia: McCarty and Davis, 1834.

Frazer, Robert W. *Forts of the West: Military Forts and Presidios and Posts Commonly Called Forts West of the Mississippi River to 1898*. Norman, OK: University of Oklahoma Press, 1965.

Gilje, Paul A. *Rioting in America*. Bloomington, IN: Indiana University Press, 1996.

Glenn, Robert A. "The Osage War." *Missouri Historical Review*, V. 14, No. 2 (January 1920): 201–210.

Gould, Stephen Jay. *The Mismeasure of Man*. New York: W. W. Norton & Co., 1996.

Graves, Donald E. *Field of Glory: The Battle of Chrysler's Farm, 1813*. Toronto: Robin Brass Studio, 1999.

Grimsted, David, *American Mobbing, 1828–1861: Toward Civil War*. New York: Oxford University Press, 1998.

Grenier, John. *The First Way of War: American War Making on the Frontier, 1607–1814*. New York, Cambridge University Press, 2005.

Grohal, John M. "Delusion of Grandeur" *PsychCentral*. https://psychcentral.

com/encyclopedia/delusion-of-grandeur/

Grund, Francis J. *The Americans in their Moral, Social, and Political Relations*, V. 1. London: Longman, 1837.

Guillet, Edwin C. *The Lives and Times of the Patriots: An Account of the Rebellion in Upper Canada, 1837-1838, and the Patriot Agitation in the United States, 1837-1842.* Toronto: Thomas Nelson & Sons, Limited, 1938.

Hall, Francis. *Travels in Canada and the United States in 1816 and 1817.* London: A. Stratham, 1818.

Hamilton, Alexander, James Madison, and John Jay. *The Federalist Papers.* Mineola, NY: Dover Publications, Inc., 2014.

Harmon, George D. *Sixty Years of Indian Affairs: Political, Economic, and Diplomatic 1789–1850.* Chapel Hill, NC: University of North Carolina Press, 1941.

Heidler, David S. and Jeanne T. Heidler. *Indian Removal.* New York: W. W. Norton & Company, 2007.

Heitman, Francis R. *Historical Register and Dictionary of the United States Army*, Vol. 1. Washington: GPO, 1903.

Hitchcock, Ethan Allen. *Fifty Years in Camp and Field: The Diary of Major-General Ethan Allen Hitchcock, U. S. A.* Edited by W. A. Croffut. New York: G. P. Putnam's Sons, 1909.

Hofstadter, Richard. *Anti-Intellectualism in American Life.* New York: Vintage Books, 1962.

_____. *The Paranoid Style in American Politics and Other Essays.* New York, Vintage Books, 1967.

Hollon, W. Eugene. *Frontier Violence: Another Look.* New York: Oxford University Press, 1974.

Horsman, Reginald. *Race and Manifest Destiny: The Origins of American Racial Anglo-Saxonism.* Cambridge, MS: Harvard University Press, 1981.

Hutton, Paul Andrew. *Phil Sheridan and His Army.* Lincoln, NE: University of Nebraska Press, 1985.

Isenberg, Nancy. *White Trash: The 400-Year Untold History of Class in America.* New York: Viking, 2016.

Johnson, Timothy D. *Winfield Scott: The Quest for Military Glory.* Lawrence, KS: University Press of Kansas, 1998.

Jones, Landon Y. *Great Expectations: American and the Baby Boom Generation.* New York: Ballantine Books, 1980.

Jung, Patrick J. *The Black Hawk War of 1832.* Norman, University of Oklahoma

Press, 2007.

Kammen, Michael. *Mystic Chords of Memory: The Transformation of Tradition in American Culture*. New York: Vintage Books, 1993.

Kappler, Charles J., ed. *Indian Treaties 1778–1883*. Mattituck, NY: Amereon House, 1972.

Kelsey, Harry E., Jr. *Frontier Capitalist: The Life of John Evans*. Denver, CO: State Historical Society of Colorado, 1969.

Kilpatrick, Jacqueline. *Celluloid Indians: Native Americans and Film*. Lincoln, NE: University of Nebraska Press, 1999.

Knetsch, Joe, and Paul S. George. "A Problematical Law: The Armed Occupation Act of 1842 and Its Impact on Southeast Florida." *Tequesta* 1 (1993): 63-80.

Kohl, Lawrence F. *The Politics of Individualism: Parties and the American Character in the Jacksonian Era*. New York: Oxford University Press, 1989.

Kokomoor, Kevin D. "Indian Agent Gad Humphreys and the Politics of Slave Claims on the Florida Frontier, 1822-1830," Master of Arts Thesis, University of South Florida, 2008. http://scholarcommons.usf.edu/cgi/viewcontent.cgi?article=1341&context=etd

Latrobe, Charles Joseph. *The Rambler in North America 1832–1833*. London: R. B. Seeley & WE. Burnside, 1835.

Laumer, Frank, ed. *Amidst a Storm of Bullets: The Diary of Lt. Henry Prince in Florida 1836–1842*. Foreword by John K. Mahon. Tampa, FL: University of Tampa Press, 1998.

Limerick, Patricia. *Something in the Soil: Legacies and Reckonings in the New West*. New York: W. W. Norton & Company, 2000.

Limerick, Patricia, Clyde A. Milner II and Charles E. Rankin eds. *Trails: Toward a New Western History* Lawrence, KS: University Press of Kansas, 1991.

Lopez, Ian Haney. *Dog Whistle Politics: How Coded Racism Appeals Have Reinvented Racism & Wrecked the Middle Class*. New York: Oxford University Press, 2014.

Luce, Edward. *The Retreat of Western Liberalism*. New York: Atlantic Monthly Press, 2017.

Lusted, David. *The Western*. London: Pearson Education Limited, 2003.

Mahon, John K. *History of the Second Seminole War 1835–1842*. Gainesville, FL: University of Florida Press, 1967.

———. *The War of 1812*. New York: Da Capo Press, 1972.

Martin, James Kirby, and Mark Edward Lender. *"A Respectable Army": The Military*

Origins of the Republic 1763–1789. Chichester, UK: John Wiley & Sons, 2015.

Marx, Leo. *The Machine in the Garden: Technology and the Pastoral Ideal in America.* New York: Oxford University Press, 1964.

Mattes, Merrill J. *The Great Platte River Road*. Lincoln, NE: Nebraska State Historical Society, 1969.

May, Robert E. *Manifest Destiny's Underworld: Filibusters in Antebellum America.* Chapel Hill, NC: University of North Carolina Press, 2002.

McCoy, Tim with Ronald McCoy. *Tim McCoy Remembers the West.* Lincoln, NE: University of Nebraska Press, 1988.

McCullough, David. *The Pioneers: The Heroic Story of the Settlers Who Brought the American Ideal West.* New York: Simon & Schuster, 2019.

McKenney, Thomas L. *Memoirs, Official and Personal: Thomas L. McKenney.* Lincoln, NE: University of Nebraska Press, 1973.

Michno, Gregory F. *Dakota Dawn: The Decisive First Week of the Sioux Uprising, August 17–24, 1862.* New York: Savas Beatie LLC, 2011.

_____. *Depredation and Deceit: The Making of the Jicarilla and Ute Wars in New Mexico.* Norman, OK: University of Oklahoma Press, 2017.

_____. *Encyclopedia of Indian Wars: Western Battles and Skirmishes, 1850–1890.* Missoula, MT: Mountain Press Publishing Company, 2003.

_____. *The Three Battles of Sand Creek: In Blood, In Court, and as the End of History.* New York: Savas Beatie LLC, 2017.

Michno, Gregory F. and Susan J. Michno. *Circle the Wagons! Attacks on Wagon Trains in History and Hollywood Films.* Jefferson, NC: McFarland & Company, Inc., 2009.

_____. *Forgotten Fights: Little-Known Raids and Skirmishes on the Frontier, 1823 to 1890.* Missoula, MT: Mountain Press Publishing Company, 2008.

Michno, Gregory F. "Lynching and Christianity: A Three-Century American Witchhunt," TMs, 2014.

Military and Naval Magazine of the United States. Six vols. Benjamin Homans, ed. Washington, D. C.: Thompson and Homans, 1833–1836.

Missall, John and Mary Lou Missall. *The Seminole Wars: America's Longest Indian Conflict.* Gainesville, FL: University Press of Florida, 2004.

Miyakawa, T. Scott. *Protestants and Pioneers: Individualism and Conformity on the American Frontier.* Chicago, IL: University of Chicago Press, 1964.

Morris, John W., Charles R. Goins, and Edwin C. McReynolds. *Historical Atlas of Oklahoma.* Norman, OK: University of Oklahoma Press, 1965.

Nichols, Roger L. *General Henry Atkinson A Western Military Career*. Norman, OK: University of Oklahoma Press, 1965.

The North American Review. Boston: 1815–1940.

Novak, William J. *The People's Welfare: Law and Regulation in Nineteenth Century America*. Chapel Hill, NC: University of North Carolina Press, 1996.

Osborn, William M. *The Wild Frontier: Atrocities During the American-Indian War from Jamestown to Wounded Knee*. New York, Random House, 2000.

Parker, Susan. "Florida's live oaks were once a hot commodity." July 23, 2016. http://staugustine.com/news/local-news/2016-07-23/susan-parker-floridas-live-oaks-were-once-hot-commodity

Parkinson, Robert G. *The Common Cause: Creating Race and Nation in the American Revolution*. Chapel Hill, NC: University of North Carolina Press, 2016.

Prucha, Francis Paul. *American Indian Policy in the Formative Years: The Indian Trade and Intercourse Acts, 1790–1834*. Lincoln, NE: University of Nebraska Press, 1970.

_____. *Broadax & Bayonet: The Role of the United States Army in the Development of the Northwest, 1815–1860*. Lincoln, NE: University of Nebraska Press, 1995.

_____. *Sword of the Republic: The United States Army on the Frontier, 1783–1846*. Bloomington, IN; Indiana University Press, 1969.

Prucha, Francis Paul, ed., *Army Life on the Western Frontier: Selections from the Official Reports Made Between 1826 and 1845 by Colonel George Croghan*. Norman, OK: University of Oklahoma Press, 1958.

_____. *Documents of United States Indian Policy*. Lincoln, NE: University of Nebraska Press, 1990.

Remini, Robert V. *Andrew Jackson & His Indian Wars*. New York: Viking, 2001.

Reynolds, John. *My Own Times: Embracing also the History of My Life*. Belleville, IL: B. H. Perryman and H. L. Davison, 1855.

Rivers, Larry Eugene. *Slavery in Florida: Territorial Days to Emancipation*. Gainesville, FL: University Press of Florida, 2000.

Robbins, Roy M. *Our Landed Heritage: The Public Domain 1776–1936*. New York: Peter Smith, 1950.

Robertson, James O. *American Myth, American Reality*. New York: Hill & Wang, 1980.

Rosenberg, Bruce A. *Custer and the Epic of Defeat*. University Park, PA: Pennsylvania State University Press, 1974.

Sawicki, James A. *Cavalry Regiments of the US Army*. Dumfries, VA: Wyvern Publications, 1985.

Sheehan, Bernard. *Seeds of Extinction: Jeffersonian Philanthropy and the American Indian.* Chapel Hill, NC: University of North Carolina Press, 1973.

Shirreff, Patrick. *A Tour Through North America.* Edinburgh: Oliver and Boyd, 1835. Reprint: Carlisle, MS: Applewood Books, nd.

Shortt, Adam, and Arthur G. Doughty, eds. *Canadian Archives Documents Relating to the Constitutional History of Canada 1759–1791.* Ottawa: S. E. Dawson, 1907.

Silver, James W. *Edmund Pendleton Gaines: Frontier General.* Baton Rouge, LA: Louisiana State University Press, 1949.

Skelton, William B. *An American Profession of Arms: The Army Officer Corps, 1784–1861.* Lawrence, KS, University Press of Kansas, 1992.

Skogen, Larry C. *Indian Depredation Claims, 1796–1920.* Norman, OK: University of Oklahoma Press, 1996.

Slotkin, Richard. *The Fatal Environment: The Myth of the Frontier in the Age of Industrialization 1800–1890.* New York: HarperPerennial, 1994. Originally published by Athenaeum, 1985.

————. *Gunfighter Nation: The Myth of the Frontier in Twentieth-Century America.* New York: HarperPerennial, 1993. Originally published by Athenaeum, 1992.

Smith, Henry. "Indian Campaign of 1832." *Military and Naval Magazine of the United States,* V. 1, No. 6 (August 1833).

Smith, Henry Nash. *Virgin Land: The American West as Symbol and Myth.* Cambridge, MS: Harvard University Press, 1970.

Spencer, John W. *Reminiscences of Pioneer Life in the Mississippi Valley.* Davenport, IO: Griggs, Watson, & Day, 1872.

Statutes at Large of the United States of America. 18 volumes, 1789–1875.

————. 13th Congress, 3rd Session, V. 3.

————. 14th Congress, 2nd Session, V. 3.

————. 17th Congress, 1st Session, V. 3.

————. 17th Congress, 2nd Session, V. 3

————. 22nd Congress, 1st Session, V. 4.

————. 22nd Congress, 2nd Session, V. 4.

————. 24th Congress, 1st Session, V. 5.

————. 27th Congress, 2nd Session, V. 5.

Steckmesser, Kent Ladd. *The Western Hero in History and Legend.* Norman, OK: University of Oklahoma Press, 1965.

Stein, Mark. *American Panic: A History of Who Scares Us and Why.* New York:

Palgrave Macmillan, 2014.

Stephenson, George M. *A Political History of the Public Lands from 1840 to 1862, from Pre-emption to Homestead*. Boston, MS: Richard G. Badger, 1917.

Stevens, Kenneth R. *Border Diplomacy: The Caroline and McLeod Affairs in Anglo-American-Canadian Relations, 1837–1842*. Tuscaloosa, AL: University of Alabama Press, 1989.

Strickland, Rex W. "Establishment of 'Old' Miller County, Arkansas Territory." *Chronicles of Oklahoma*, V. 18, No. 2 (June 1940).

_____. "The Final Breakup of 'Old' Miller County." *Chronicles of Oklahoma*, V. 19, No. 1 (March 1941): 37–54.

_____. "Miller County, Arkansas Territory, the Frontier that Men Forgot." *Chronicles of Oklahoma*, V. 18, No. 1 (March 1940): 12–34.

Tavris, Carol and Elliot Aronson, *Mistakes Were Made (but not by me) Why we Justify Foolish Beliefs, Bad Decisions, and Hurtful Acts*. Orlando, FL: Harcourt, Inc., 2007.

Thistle, Hezekiah L. vs. the United States, July 25, 1856. *Reports from the Court of Claims submitted to the House of Representatives during the 1st Session of the 34th Congress, 1855–1856*, V. 1. Washington: Cornelius Wendell, 1856.

Tocqueville, Alexis de. *Democracy in America and Two Essays on America*. London: Penguin Books, 2003.

Trachtenberg, Alan. *The Incorporation of America: Culture and Society in the Gilded Age*. New York: Hill and Wang, 1982.

Turner, Frederick Jackson. "The Significance of the Frontier in American History." *The Frontier in American History*. New York: Henry Holt and Co., 1920.

Van Der Zee, Jacob. "The Opening of the Des Moines Valley to Settlement," *The Iowa Journal of History and Politics*, V. XIV, No. 4 (October 1916): 479–558.

Violette, Eugene M. *History of Adair County*. Kirksville, MO: Densville History Company, 1911.

Wakefield, John. *Wakefield's History of the Black Hawk War: A reprint of the first edition by John A. Wakefield, Esquire, from the press of Calvin Goudy, Jacksonville, Illinois, 1834*, Frank E. Stevens. Chicago, IL: The Caxton Club, 1908.

Waldrop, Christopher, ed., *Lynching in America: A History in Documents*. New York: New York University Press, 2006.

Walker, Janet, ed. *Westerns: Films Through History*. New York: Routledge, 2001.

Watson, Samuel J. *Jackson's Sword: The Army Officer Corps on the American Frontier,*

1810–1821. Lawrence, KS: University Press of Kansas, 2012.

_____. *Peacekeepers and Conquerors: The Army Officer Corps on the American Frontier, 1821–1846*. Lawrence, KS: University Press of Kansas, 2013.

Whisker, James B. *The Rise and Decline of the American Militia System*. Selinsgrove, PA: Susquehanna University Press, 1999.

White, Lonnie J. "Disturbances on the Arkansas-Texas Border, 1827–1831," *Arkansas Historical Quarterly*, V. 19 (Spring 1961): 95–110.

Whitney, Ellen M. ed., *The Black Hawk War, 1831–1832: V. 2, Letters and Papers, Part 1, April 30, 1831–June 23, 1832*. Springfield, IL: Illinois State Historical Library, 1973.

Williams, Jeffrey. *Religion and Violence in Early American Methodism: Taking the Kingdom by Force*. Bloomington, IN: Indiana University Press, 2010.

Winn, William W. *The Triumph of the Ecunnau-Nuxulgee: Land Speculators, George Troup, State Rights, and Removal of the Creek Indians from Georgia and Alabama, 1825–38*. Macon, GA: Mercer University Press, 2015.

Woodward, C. Vann. *The Strange Career of Jim Crow*. New York: Oxford University Press, 2002. Originally published 1955.

_____. *Thinking Back: The Perils of Writing History*. Baton Rouge, LA: Louisiana State University Press, 1986.

Wooster, Robert. *The American Military Frontiers: The United States Army in the West, 1783–1900*. Albuquerque, NM: University of New Mexico Press, 2009.

Young, Mary Elizabeth. *Redskins, Ruffleshirts, and Rednecks: Indian Allotments in Alabama and Mississippi, 1830–1860*. Norman, OK: University of Oklahoma Press, 1961.

INDEX

Atkinson, Henry, 91–92, 132–134, *135*, 154, 175, 251–252, 265
Augusta Mirror, 64
Austill, Jeremiah, 205, 206, 207, 209–210
Avant, James, 190

B

Bacon, James, 280
Bailey ("Major" in Georgia militia), 170
Bailey (contractor in Arkansas Territory), 78
Bailey, William, 233
Baird, Henry S., 268
Baker, John, 280
Balch, Alfred, 40
Ball, William, 51
Bancroft, Hubert Howe, 146
Barbour, James, 26, 28, 251, 253, 259, 260, 268
Barnard, Timothy, 197
Barnum, Ephraim K., 92–93
Barrell, S. B., 280
Barry, John W., 191
Bates, Frederick, 21, 23
Bates, Phineas, 260–261
Battle Creek, Missouri, 174
Battle of Fallen Timbers, 298
Battle of New Orleans, 126
Battle of Okeechobee, 156
Battle of the Windmill, *290*
Battle of the Withlacoochee, 149–150
Beall, Robert, 230
Bean (white who defrauded Cherokees of salt), 172–173
Beattie, William, 177
Beattie's Bluff, 218–219
Beecher, Lyman, 214–215, 217
Belding, L., 48, 51, 52–53, 54
Belknap, William G., 269
Bell, John R., 267–268
Bell, Richard H., 88

Bent, Charles, 267
Bent, Robert, 267
Bent, Silas, 267
Bent, William, 267
Benton, Thomas Hart, 82, 112, 114, 156
Beyond Good and Evil, 223
Big Black River, 218
Bigelow, George, 235
Bigelow, Jonas, 235
Big Neck (Chief), 173–175
Big Warrior (Creek chief), 184
Billington, Ray Allen, 305–306, 307
Bird, Isabella, 314–315
Bird, J., 92
Black Creek, Florida, 151
Blackfoot Indians, 169
Black Hawk, 107, *130*, 131–132, 133, 136
Black Hawk War, 76, 106, 131–137
Black River, 83
Blake, L., 50
Blake, Luther, 208, 315
Blake, Ruel, 219
Bleeding Kansas, 243
Blue, W., 56
Bluewater Creek, 325
Blunt, John, 175–177
Boggs, Lilburn W., 237, 239
Bogue, Allan G., 303
Bois Blanc Island, 283
Boone, Daniel, 138, 139–141, *141*, 335
Boone and Crockett Club, 145
Boone/Crockett mythology, 137–149
Boonesborough, Kentucky, 140
border, U. S./Canada, 280, 288–300
Borger, Frank, 207, 210
Boston Daily Advertiser, 215
Bothwell, Ebenezer, 196
Bowie, Jim, 221
Bowlegs (Chief), 64, 86

Fort Gibson, 186–187, 242, 245
Fort Gilmer, 92
Fort Gratiot, 245, 283
Fort Heileman, 154, 241
Fort Howard, 229, 231, 245, 268–269
Fort Jackson treaty, 193–194
Fort Jesup, 244, 250, 254
Fort Leavenworth, 91, 180, 238, 242
Fort Malden, 283, 284, 291
Fort Mitchell, 56, 203, 204, 206, 211, 212, 232
Fort Moniac, 92
Fort Reed, 189
Fort Sanford, 245
Fort Smith, 51
Fort Snelling, 245, 270
Fort St. Anthony, 88
Fort Taylor, 82
Fort Towson, 186, 187, 245
Fort Washita, 245
Fort Wellington, 289–290
Fort Winnebago, 93
Founding Fathers, views on Indians, 9
Fowler, John, 171, 254
Fowltown, Georgia, 194
Fox Indians, 88, 131–132, 134, 175, 245
Fox Lake, Wisconsin, 94
Franklin, Benjamin, 13, 95
fraudulent claims
    earthquake relief, 19–24
    Indian depredation, 9–17
    land claims, 24–31
    timber theft, 79–84
    whites stealing Indian land, 203
Freemasons, 259–260
French Mills, New York, 16–17
Fritz, Gideon, 27–28
frontier education, 316–319
frontiersman in popular culture, 333–337
frontiersman myth, 4
    negative aspects, 5–6
    reassessed, 301–308

G

Gadsden, James, 177
Gaines, Edmund P., *16*
    Black Hawk War, 131–132
    changing attitudes toward Indians, 86–87, 162–163, 227–228, 266
    and civilian contractors, 15–16
    on difficulties with militias, 125–126, 230
    First Seminole War, 194
    on illegal liquor trade, 188
    on need for security on western trails, 243, 244–245
    peacekeeping efforts, 256
    Texas Revolution, 154
Galt, Patrick H., 261
Gardiner, James B., 14
Garlinghouse, Joseph, 260–261
Garmigan (of Georgia militia), 186
Garner, James, 248
Gayle, John, 207, 208, 210, 212
Gentry, Richard, 156
Georgia/Florida borderlands, 63, 87
Georgia Journal, 64, 200
Gibson (Commissary General), 52, 54, 56–57, 74, 76–78
Gilje, Paul, 213
Gilmer, George P., 186
Girty, Simon, 203
Glasscock, Thomas, 195–196, 197, 198, 201
Glassell, James M., 233–234
Gnadenhutten, Ohio, 169, 193
government assistance, 95–109
government regulation, 115
government trading houses, 61
Graham, George, 29, 264
Gray, George, 247, 255, 257, 264
Grayson, Sampson, 57
Greene, Pardon C., 233–234
Greenville, Ohio, 76
Griffin, Jasper, 181
Grimsted, David, 217, 222–223

365

CPSIA information can be obtained
at www.ICGtesting.com
Printed in the USA
FSHW020008200320
68261FS